Lecture Notes in Computer Science

T0238011

Commenced Publication in 1973
Founding and Former Series Editors:
Gerhard Goos, Juris Hartmanis, and Jan van Leeuwen

Zoltán Horváth   Viktória Zsók
Andrew Butterfield (Eds.)

Implementation and Application of Functional Languages

18th International Symposium, IFL 2006
Budapest, Hungary, September 4-6, 2006
Revised Selected Papers

 Springer

Volume Editors

Zoltán Horváth
Viktória Zsók
Eötvös Loránd University
Faculty of Informatics
Department of Programming Languages and Compilers
1117 Budapest, Hungary
E-mail: {hz,zsv}@inf.elte.hu

Andrew Butterfield
University of Dublin
Department of Computer Science
O'Reilly Institute, Trinity College
Dublin, Ireland
E-mail: Andrew.Butterfield@cs.tcd.ie

Library of Congress Control Number: 2007932229

CR Subject Classification (1998): D.3, D.1.1, D.1, F.3

LNCS Sublibrary: SL 1 – Theoretical Computer Science and General Issues

ISSN   0302-9743
ISBN-10   3-540-74129-1 Springer Berlin Heidelberg New York
ISBN-13   978-3-540-74129-9 Springer Berlin Heidelberg New York

Springer is a part of Springer Science+Business Media

springer.com

© Springer-Verlag Berlin Heidelberg 2007
Printed in Germany

Typesetting: Camera-ready by author, data conversion by Scientific Publishing Services, Chennai, India
Printed on acid-free paper   SPIN: 12104406   06/3180   5 4 3 2 1 0

Preface

This volume presents the reviewed and revised selected papers of the 18th International Symposium on Implementation and Application of Functional Languages IFL 2006, held September 4–6, 2006, at Eötvös Loránd University, Budapest, Hungary.

The symposium was organized according to the traditions of the IFL workshop series. The aim of these workshops is to bring together researchers actively engaged in the implementation and application of functional and function-based programming languages. They provide an open forum for researchers who wish to present and discuss new ideas and concepts, work in progress, preliminary results, etc., related primarily but not exclusively to the implementation and application of functional languages. IFL became a symposium in 2006. A not necessarily exhaustive list of topics covered includes: language concepts, concurrent/parallel programming, type checking, concurrent/parallel program execution, compilation techniques, heap management, generic programming techniques, runtime profiling, (abstract) interpretation, performance measurements, automatic program generation, debugging and tracing, (abstract) machine architectures, verification, formal aspects, tools and programming techniques, array processing and demos of well working, useable tools and applications in functional languages.

IFL 2006 was held in the Faculty of Informatics, Eötvös Loránd University, Budapest, Hungary during the first week of September 2006. It attracted more than 60 participants presenting 40 contributions during the three days of the symposium.

All speakers attending the symposium were invited to submit a revised paper afterwards. The submitted papers were each carefully checked by readers selected from among the most qualified available and then revised once more by the lecturers. Each paper was reviewed by three or four referees and thoroughly discussed by four or five PC members. We are very grateful to the anonymous referees, all excellent researchers in functional programming, for the time and effort they devoted to reviewing the papers. Finally the PC decided to select 15 high-quality papers for publication in this volume.

We would like to acknowledge the work of all the members of the organizing committee and the student volunteers.

The web-page of the symposium can be found at
http://www.inf.elte.hu/rendezvenyek/ifl/.

March 2007

Zoltán Horváth
Viktória Zsók
Andrew Butterfield

Organization

IFL 2006 was organized by the Department of Programming Languages and Compilers, Faculty of Informatics, Eötvös Loránd University, Budapest, Hungary.

Executive Committee

Program Chair	Zoltán Horváth
	(Eötvös L. University, Hungary)
Organizing Chairs	Zoltán Horváth and Viktória Zsók
	(Eötvös L. University, Hungary)
Organizing Committee	Zoltán Csörnyei
	Gergely Dévai
	Péter Diviánszky
	Gáspár Erdélyi
	Hajnalka Hegedűs
	Zoltán Juhász
	Róbert Kitlei
	Anikó Királyné-Csizmazia
	Tamás Kozsik
	Ildikó László
	László Csaba Lőrincz
	László Lövei
	Mónika Mészáros
	Gabriella Nádas
	Adrienn Olajos
	Zoltán Porkoláb
	Beáta Reiz
	Csaba Seres
	Rozália Szabó-Nacsa
	Máté Tejfel
	(Eötvös L. University, Hungary)
Organizing Partner	Judit Juhász (Managing Director, Pannonia Tourist Service)

Program Committee

Matthias Blume	Toyota Technological Institute, Chicago, USA
Zoran Budimac	University of Novi Sad, Serbia
Andrew Butterfield	Trinity College Dublin, Ireland
Ralf Hinze	University of Bonn, Germany
Zoltán Horváth	Eötvös Loránd University, Budapest, Hungary, Chair
Tamás Kozsik	Eötvös Loránd University, Budapest, Hungary
Hans-Wolfgang Loidl	Ludwig-Maximilians-University Munich, Germany
Rita Loogen	Philipps-University Marburg, Germany
Frédéric Loulergue	University of Orleans, France
Simon Marlow	Microsoft Research, Cambridge, UK
Marco T. Morazán	Seton Hall University, New Jersey, USA
Yolanda Ortega-Mallén	University Complutense of Madrid, Spain
Rinus Plasmeijer	Radboud University Nijmegen, The Netherlands
Jaroslav Porubän	Technical University of Kosice, Slovakia
Anna Soós	Babeş-Bolyai University, Cluj-Napoca, Romania
Doaitse Swierstra	Utrecht University, The Netherlands
Peter Thiemann	University of Freiburg, Germany
Germán Vidal	Technical University of Valencia, Spain

Sponsoring Institutions

The symposium was supported by Nokia Hungary, Siemens PSE Hungary and by the Faculty of Informatics, Eötvös Loránd University, Budapest, Hungary.

Table of Contents

On Optimising Shape-Generic Array Programs Using Symbolic Structural Information

Kai Trojahner[1], Clemens Grelck[2], and Sven-Bodo Scholz[2]

[1] University of Lübeck
Institute of Software Technology and Programming Languages
trojahner@isp.uni-luebeck.de
[2] University of Hertfordshire
Department of Computer Science
{c.grelck,s.scholz}@herts.ac.uk

Abstract. Shape-generic programming and high run time performance do match if generic source code is systematically specialised into non-generic executable code. However, as soon as we drop the assumption of whole-world knowledge or refrain from specialisation for other reasons, compiled generic code is substantially less efficient. Limited effectiveness of code optimisation techniques due to the inherent lack of knowledge about the structural properties of arrays can be identified as the single most important source of inefficiency.

However, in many cases partial structural information or structural relationships between arrays would actually suffice for optimisation. We propose symbolic array attributes as a uniform scheme to infer and to represent partial and relational structural information in shape-generic array code. By reusing the regular language to express structural properties in intermediate code, existing optimisations benefit from symbolic array attributes with little or no alteration. In fact, program optimisation and identification of structural properties cross-fertilise each other. We outline our approach in the context of the functional array language SAC and demonstrate its effectiveness by a small case study.

1 Introduction

Shape-generic array programming means writing functions, modules and entire programs in a style that completely or at least partially abstracts from the structural properties of the arrays involved. For example, a shape-generic matrix multiplication function is one that is applicable to pairs of matrices of any size, as long as the extent of the second axis of the first matrix equals the extent of the first axis of the second matrix. In fact, shape-generic array programming even goes one step further and allows functions to abstract not only from the extents of arrays along given axes, but even from the number of axes (or dimensionality or rank). For example, the element-wise multiplication of two arrays can be specified exactly once and applied to pairs of vectors, matrices, tensors and even higher-dimensional arrays.

Z. Horváth, V. Zsók, and A. Butterfield (Eds.): IFL 2006, LNCS 4449, pp. 1–18, 2007.

The functional array programming language SaC [1,2] supports shape-generic array programming. Multi-dimensional arrays are characterised by their *rank*, an integer denoting the number of axes of an array, and their *shape*, a vector containing the extent along each axis. By step-wise abstraction from rank and shape, the type system of SaC distinguishes between three classes of array types, named *shape classes*:

1. Array of Known Shape (AKS),
2. Array of Known Dimensionality (AKD) and
3. Array of Unknown Dimensionality (AUD).

An AKS type, for example `int[10,10]`, describes the set of all arrays of some base type and a certain shape (including fixed rank). An AKD type, for example `int[.,.]`, defines the number of axes, but leaves the extent along each axis open. Finally, an AUD type like `int[*]` encompasses all arrays of a given base type regardless of their structure. Together, the array types form a natural hierarchy that induces a subtype relationship, e.g. $\texttt{int[10,10]} \prec \texttt{int[.,.]} \prec \texttt{int[*]}$.

When it comes to compiling shape-generic programs into executable code, it turns out that the run time performance of compiled AUD code is significantly inferior to compiled AKD code, which in turn is significantly inferior to compiled AKS (i.e. non-generic) code (cf. Section 5). This observation can be attributed to essentially two independent sources of inefficiency: Firstly, generic code requires the shape vector to be maintained in the heap at run time rather than being a set of compile time constants. The lack of a static rank knowledge also entails that no suitable nesting of loops can be generated to traverse an array. Instead, we must rely on a relatively inefficient loop structure. Secondly, and more gravely, many optimisation techniques are less effective if they lack structural information on the arrays involved. This holds for standard code transformations like constant folding, common subexpression elimination and loop unrolling just as for array-specific optimisations [3,4,5] or optimisations in the memory management subsystem [6].

Our recent work focussed on careful identification of where and how far to specialise [7]. Still, specialisation is not always the solution since sufficient structural information may lack at compile time or the number of specialisations may grow beyond feasability. Fortunately, many code optimisation techniques can benefit from more modest gains in structural knowledge than those resulting from specialisation. For example, it may be useful to know the extent of an AKD array along certain but not all axes. Or, we may exploit that an AUD array has at least two inner axes of which we may even figure out the extent. Or, we may improve programs utilising the knowledge that certain arrays have the same shape or the same dimensionality as others.

This work aims at making such fine-grained structural information below the level of shape classes available to optimisations by compile time inference. We introduce *symbolic array attributes* as uniform representations of the ranks and shapes of all arrays involved in an intermediate code representation. More precisely, we associate each definition of an array with new symbolic identifiers for its rank and its shape. Like an array identifier is bound to an expression defining that array, the associated rank and shape identifiers are bound to expressions that extract the definition of the array's rank and shape from its original definition. Any array-valued expression effectively is replaced by a triple of expressions. The first one is the original expression defining both structure and element values of the array. The second expression defines the shape, but abstracts from element values. The third expression defines the rank, but abstracts from concrete extents along the array's axes. Whereas the original code describes the relationships between arrays on the level of rank, shape and element values all at the same time, the augmented code explicates these relationships at each level individually.

Since all three elements of the expression triples are regular expressions of the language, they are automatically subject to a plethora of optimisations like constant folding, constant/variable propagation or common subexpression elimination to name just a few. This has a dual effect: The optimisations benefit from symbolic structural information while at the same time the structural information is improved by the optimisations.

It is characteristic for our approach to represent and exploit structural and relational properties of arrays in a purely compiler directed way. In particular, the source language remains entirely unaffected. An alternative approach would be to refine the type system towards using a variant of dependent types [8]. In contrast to our work, that would require a substantial extension to SAC as a programming language having a major impact on the style of programming.

The remainder of this paper is organised as follows: Section 2 defines a core language that we use to illustrate our ideas. We formally define how we introduce symbolic array attributes in Section 3 and how we use them for optimisation in Section 4. In Section 5 we illustrate our approach by a small case study. We discuss some related work in Section 6 and conclude in Section 7.

2 Introducing SaC$_{mini}$

Many features of SAC are irrelevant for the context of this paper. Therefore, we define a core language called SAC$_{mini}$, which exposes the relevant features in a condensed and simplified form. As defined in Fig. 1, a SAC$_{mini}$ program is a sequence of potentially mutually recursive function definitions. Each function definition consists of a return type, a function name, a typed parameter list in parentheses and a code block. A code block is a sequence of variable-expression bindings terminated by a goal-expression, that follows the key word **return**. Alternatively, we may have a conditional where each branch either leads to a further conditional or terminates with a goal-expression. This SAC-style notation merely is a syntactic variation of a nesting of let-expressions and conditional expressions in other functional languages.

Any expression (and hence any variable) denotes an array, which is characterised by a *rank scalar*, a *shape vector* and a *data vector*. While the latter acts as a store for element values, all structural information is encoded in the rank scalar and the shape vector. The rank scalar describes the rank or dimensionality

$$
\begin{array}{lcl}
Program & \Rightarrow & \lceil FunDef \rceil^* \\[4pt]
FunDef & \Rightarrow & Type\ Id\ (\ \lceil\ Param\ \lceil\ ,\ Param\ \rceil^*\ \rceil\ )\ \ Block \\[4pt]
Param & \Rightarrow & Type\ Id \\[4pt]
Block & \Rightarrow & \{\ \lceil Id\ =\ Expr\ ;\ \rceil^*\ Return\ \} \\
 & \mid & \{\ \lceil Id\ =\ Expr\ ;\ \rceil^*\ Cond\ \} \\[4pt]
Return & \Rightarrow & \textbf{return}\ (\ Id\ )\ \ ; \\[4pt]
Cond & \Rightarrow & \textbf{if}\ (\ Id\ )\ Block\ \textbf{else}\ Block \\[4pt]
Expr & \Rightarrow & Const\ \mid\ Id\ \mid\ FunAp\ \mid\ Vector\ \mid\ With \\[4pt]
FunAp & \Rightarrow & Fun\ (\ \lceil\ Id\ \lceil\ ,\ Id\ \rceil^*\ \rceil\ ) \\[4pt]
Vector & \Rightarrow & [\ \lceil\ Id\ \lceil\ ,\ Id\ \rceil^*\ \rceil\ ] \\[4pt]
With & \Rightarrow & \textbf{with}\ \lceil Generator\ Block \rceil^*\ \textbf{genarray}\ (\ Id\ ,\ Id\ ) \\[4pt]
Generator & \Rightarrow & (\ \lceil Id\ \texttt{<=}\ \rceil\ Id\ \texttt{<}\ Id\ ) \\[4pt]
Type & \Rightarrow & AKS\text{-}Type\ \mid\ AKD\text{-}Type\ \mid\ AUD\text{-}Type \\[4pt]
AKS\text{-}Type & \Rightarrow & BaseType\ [\ \lceil\ IntConst\ \lceil\ ,\ IntConst\ \rceil^*\ \rceil\ ] \\[4pt]
AKD\text{-}Type & \Rightarrow & BaseType\ [\ .\ \lceil\ ,\ .\ \rceil^*\ ] \\[4pt]
AUD\text{-}Type & \Rightarrow & BaseType\ [\ \texttt{*}\ ]
\end{array}
$$

Fig. 1. Syntax of SAC_{mini}

of the array; the shape vector describes an array's extent along each dimension. Consequently, the rank scalar denotes the length of the shape vector. In this model, scalars are rank zero arrays with an empty shape vector and a data vector consisting of a single element. Arrays can be nested as long as the whole array remains representable by rank, shape and data vector, i.e., all elements of an array must have the same element type and shape.

In addition to the usual scalar constants and identifiers, expressions may be applications of defined or of built-in functions. Built-in functions include the usual arithmetic, logic and relational operators on scalars. Whenever appropriate, we use infix notation for applications to improve readability. Array-specific built-in operations are limited to the following:

- $\texttt{dim}(A)$ yields the rank scalar of array A.
- $\texttt{shape}(A)$ yields the shape vector of array A.
- $\texttt{sel}(iv,A)$ yields the element of A at the index specified by the integer vector iv.
- $\texttt{modarray}(A,iv,v)$ yields a new array that is equivalent to A except for the element at index position iv, which is set to the scalar value v.
- $\texttt{reshape}(shp,A)$ returns a new array whose data vector is given by the one of A but whose shape vector equals shp.

In applications of both $\texttt{sel}$ and $\texttt{modarray}$ the length of the index vector must coincide with the rank of the array; in applications of $\texttt{reshape}$ the product of the elements of the desired shape vector must match that of the elements of the existing shape vector.

Unlike SAC, SAC$_{mini}$ only supports non-nested expressions, i.e., arguments to a function application for example may only be identifiers, but not expressions again. This restriction simplifies the definition of compilation schemes; it can easily be achieved in a preprocessing step (from full SAC) by recursively extracting nested expressions and binding them to new identifiers. Nevertheless, we allow ourselves to use nested expressions wherever appropriate to improve the readability of code examples.

SAC$_{mini}$ also features a simplified version of SAC's versatile array comprehension construct called WITH-loop. A WITH-loop of the form

$$\text{with } \ldots \text{ genarray}(shp, def)$$

defines an array whose shape is given by appending the integer vector shp with the shape of the *default value* def. Each element of a WITH-loop-defined array is either set to the default value or computed according to the specification given in one of the *parts*. Each part consists of a *generator*, which defines a set of index positions, and an associated expression block, which determines the values of array elements at index positions covered by the generator.

A generator ($lb <= iv < ub$) defines a rectangular index range delimited by a lower bound vector lb and an upper bound vector ub. A missing lower bound specification defaults to a zero vector with the length of ub. The index variable iv is introduced in the generator, and its scope is limited to the associated expression; it represents the current index position. Multiple parts allow us to define different array elements according to different specifications. In order to ensure deterministic results, the index sets defined by the various generators of an individual WITH-loop must be pairwise disjoint.

SAC$_{mini}$ and likewise SAC only have a very small set of built-in functions on arrays. A comprehensive set of compound operations on arrays is provided as a

```
bool select( int idx, bool[.] array)
{
  res = sel( [idx], array);
  return( res);
}

bool[*] select( int[.] idx, bool[*] array)
{
  shp = drop( select( 0, shape( idx)), shape( array));

  res = with (iv < shp) {
          elem = sel( idx ++ iv, array);
          return( elem);
        } genarray( shp, 0);
  return( res);
}
```

Fig. 2. Generalised selection functions

standard library, where they are defined by means of WITH-loops. Even many existing primitive functions are not intended for the general use, but rather serve as implementation vehicles for more general standard library functions. As an example, take the definition of a general selection facility in Fig. 2. The first instance of select takes a single integer and a vector.[1] In this case, the type information is sufficient to directly apply the built-in primitive sel without risking a run time error. The second instance of select implements the general case of selection: If the length of the selection vector is less than the dimensionality of the array to be selected from, selection yields an entire subarray. We achieve this by first dropping as many elements from the shape vector of the array as given by the length of the selection vector before we create an array of that shape. In the most relevant special case, the length of the selection vector actually coincides with the dimensionality of the array such that the application of drop yields the empty vector. Hence, the subsequent WITH-loop creates an array with an empty shape vector, which effectively is a scalar. Both auxiliary functions drop and vector concatenation (++) can be found in Fig. 3. For a more detailed explanation of the various SAC language features see [2]; a formal semantics may be found in [7].

```
int[.] drop( int v, int[.] a)
{
  dl = shape(a)[0] - v;
  ds = [dl];

  res = with ([i] < ds) {
          drel = a[i + v];
          return( drel);
        } genarray( ds, 0);
  return( res);
}

int[.] (++) (int[.] a, int[.] b)
{
  sa = shape(a);
  sb = shape(b);

  res = with ([i] < sa) {
          ael = a[i];
          return( ael);
        }
        ( sa <= [i] < sa + sb) {
          bel = b[i - sa[0]];
          return( bel);
        } genarray( sa + sb, 0);
  return( res);
}
```

Fig. 3. Auxiliary functions needed for the generalised selection

---

[1] We use the base type bool here as an example only.

3 Symbolic Array Attributes

In non-generic array code (shape class AKS) any structural relationship between arrays is properly expressed by their types. In non-specialised generic code, however, this property is immediately lost. For example, an application of the built-in function `modarray`

$$v = \mathtt{modarray(a,iv,0)};$$

is known to yield an array v with a shape identical to that of the first argument a. Hence, the type inference system assigns v the type of a. Supposed a has a non-generic AKS type, this accurately reflects the structural relationship between a and v. However, if a has a generic AKD type say `int[.]`, then v is also assigned the type `int[.]`. This still reflects that a and v do have the same rank, but the fact that both actually have the same shape is not expressed. In the AUD case, we do not even know the equality of rank. This lack of information severely limits our opportunities for code optimisation.

Symbolic array attributes are meant to fill this gap and provide a systematic means to express partial structural information both with respect to individual arrays as well as structural relationships between different arrays. We augment any variable-expression binding in a function body with two (flattened) expressions: one to denote the array's rank (enclosed in round brackets) and one to denote the array's shape (enclosed in square brackets):

$$(v_d)\,[v_s]\ \ v\ =\ expr\,;$$

Only scalar constants, constant arrays and identifiers may occur in attribute positions. More complex sub-expressions are lifted into additional variable-expression bindings. Thus, despite appearing on the left-hand side of the assignment operator, symbolic array attributes are no less proper expressions than those on the right-hand side. Depending on the shape class of an array, the contents of v_d and v_s may vary, as outlined in the table below.

Shape class	v_d	v_s	Example
AKS	$Const$	$Array\ const$	$(0)\,\mathtt{[[]]}$
			$(2)\,\mathtt{[[10,10]]}$
AKD	$Const$	Id	$(2)\,\mathtt{[s]}$
AUD	Id	Id	$(d)\,\mathtt{[s]}$

Although rank and shape of an array may not be known until run time, we can consult their symbolic compile time representations using the attribute access functions $\mathcal{D}$ and $\mathcal{S}$. If the identifier a has been attributed with the pair $(d)\,[s]$, then $\mathcal{D}(a)$ gives d and $\mathcal{S}(a)$ yields s. The knowledge about the shape-preserving properties of `modarray`, can now be encoded by assigning the result v exactly those attributes of the modified array a:

$$(\mathcal{D}(a))\,[\mathcal{S}(a)]\ \ v\ =\ \mathtt{modarray}(a\,,iv\,,val\,);$$

In Fig. 4 we show the transformation scheme $\mathcal{SAA}$ that introduces symbolic array attributes and, thus, makes array ranks and shapes explicit in terms of SAC$_{\mathsf{mini}}$ expressions. Rules of the form

$$\mathcal{C}\,[\![\,expr\,]\!] = expr\prime$$

$$\mathcal{SAA}[\![\, type \ fun\,(params\,) \ \{ \ body \ \} \ ]\!]$$
$$= type \ fun\,(\mathcal{R}[\![\, params \,]\!]) \ \{ \ \mathcal{MIR}[\![\, params \,]\!]; \ \mathcal{SAA}[\![\, body \,]\!] \ \}$$

$$\mathcal{SAA}[\![\, \texttt{if} \ (c) \ then \ \texttt{else} \ else \ ]\!] = \texttt{if} \ (c) \ \mathcal{SAA}[\![\, then \,]\!] \ \texttt{else} \ \mathcal{SAA}[\![\, else \,]\!]$$

$$\mathcal{SAA}[\![\, \texttt{return}(a); \,]\!] = \texttt{return}(a);$$

$$\mathcal{SAA}[\![\, v \ = \ c; \ R \,]\!] = (0)\,[[]] \ v \ = \ c; \ \mathcal{SAA}[\![\, R \,]\!]$$

$$\mathcal{SAA}[\![\, v \ = \ \texttt{sclprf}\,(args\,); \ R \,]\!] = (0)\,[[]] \ v \ = \ \texttt{sclprf}\,(args\,); \ \mathcal{SAA}[\![\, R \,]\!]$$

$$\mathcal{SAA}[\![\, v \ = \ a; \ R \,]\!] = (\mathcal{D}(a))\,[\mathcal{S}(a)] \ v \ = \ a; \ \mathcal{SAA}[\![\, R \,]\!]$$

$$\mathcal{SAA}[\![\, v \ = \ \texttt{shape}(a); \ R \,]\!] = \begin{cases} (1)\,[[1]] & v_s \ = \ [\mathcal{D}(a)]; \\ (1)\,[v_s] & v \ = \ \texttt{shape}(a); \\ \mathcal{SAA}[\![\, R \,]\!] \end{cases}$$

$$\mathcal{SAA}[\![\, v \ = \ \texttt{reshape}(s\,,a); \ R \,]\!] = \begin{cases} (0)\,[[]] & v_d \ = \ \mathcal{S}(s)\,[0]; \\ (v_d)\,[s] & v \ = \ \texttt{reshape}(s\,,a); \\ \mathcal{SAA}[\![\, R \,]\!] \end{cases}$$

$$\mathcal{SAA}[\![\, v \ = \ \texttt{modarray}(a\,,iv\,,v); \ R \,]\!]$$
$$= (\mathcal{D}(a))\,[\mathcal{S}(a)] \ v \ = \ \texttt{modarray}(a\,,iv\,,v); \ \mathcal{SAA}[\![\, R \,]\!]$$

$$\mathcal{SAA}[\![\, v \ = \ []; \ R \,]\!] = (1)\,[[0]] \ \texttt{v} \ = \ []; \ \mathcal{SAA}[\![\, R \,]\!]$$

$$\mathcal{SAA}[\![\, v \ = \ [a_0,\ldots,a_{n-1}]; \ R \,]\!] = \begin{cases} (0)\,[[]] & v_d \ \ = \ 1 \ + \ \mathcal{D}(a_0); \\ (1)\,[[1]] & v_{s_s} \ = \ [v_d]; \\ (1)\,[v_{s_s}] & v_s \ \ = \ [n] \ \texttt{++} \ \mathcal{S}(a_0); \\ (v_d)\,[v_s] & v \ \ \ = \ [a_0,\ldots,a_{n-1}]; \\ \mathcal{SAA}[\![\, R \,]\!] \end{cases}$$

$$\mathcal{SAA}[\![\, v \ = \ fun\,(args\,); \ R \,]\!] = \mathcal{R}[\![\, v \,]\!] = \ fun\,(args\,); \mathcal{MIR}[\![\, \mathcal{T}[\![\, fun \,]\!]\, v \,]\!]; \mathcal{SAA}[\![\, R \,]\!]$$

$$\mathcal{SAA}[\![\, v \ = \ \texttt{with} \ parts \ \texttt{genarray}(s\,,d); \ R \,]\!]$$
$$= \begin{cases} (0)\,[[]] & v_d \ = \ \mathcal{S}(s)\,[0]; \\ (v_d)\,[s] & v \ = \ \texttt{with} \ \mathcal{SAA}[\![\, parts \,]\!] \ \texttt{genarray}(s\,,d); \\ \mathcal{SAA}[\![\, R \,]\!] \end{cases} \quad \text{if } \mathrm{D(d)} \equiv 0$$

$$= \begin{cases} (0)\,[[]] & s_{s_0} \ = \ \mathcal{S}(s)\,[0]; \\ (0)\,[[]] & v_d \ \ = \ s_{s_0} \ + \ \mathcal{D}(d); \\ (1)\,[[1]] & v_{s_s} \ = \ [v_d]; \\ (1)\,[v_{s_s}] & v_s \ \ = \ s \ \texttt{++} \ \mathcal{S}(d); \\ (v_d)\,[v_s] & v \ \ \ = \ \texttt{with} \ \mathcal{SAA}[\![\, parts \,]\!] \ \texttt{genarray}(s\,,d); \\ \mathcal{SAA}[\![\, R \,]\!] \end{cases} \quad \text{otherwise}$$

$$\mathcal{SAA}[\![\, (\ lb \ \texttt{<=} \ iv \ \texttt{<} \ ub) \ block \ R \,]\!]$$
$$= (\ lb \ \texttt{<=} \ \mathcal{SAA}'[\![\, iv \,]\!][\![\, ub \,]\!] \ \texttt{<} \ ub) \ \mathcal{SAA}[\![\, block \,]\!] \ \mathcal{SAA}[\![\, R \,]\!]$$

$$\mathcal{SAA}'[\![\, iv \,]\!][\![\, ub \,]\!] = (1)\,[\mathcal{S}(ub)] \ iv$$

$$\mathcal{SAA}'[\![\, [i_1,...,i_d] \,]\!][\![\, ub \,]\!] = [(0)\,[[]] \ i_1,..., \ (0)\,[[]] \ i_d]$$

Fig. 4. Transformation scheme for inserting symbolic array attributes

denote the context-free replacement of a program fragment *expr* by a another program fragment *expr*. The scheme $\mathcal{SAA}$ does not only express the relationships between the arguments and the shapes of the results of the SAC_{mini} built-in functions, but also ensures proper attribute annotation at function boundaries.

Identifiers bound to constants or applications of scalar-valued functions (including dim) are assigned the attribute pair (0) [[]]. Identifiers bound to the values of other identifiers (i.e. a = b;) share the same pair of attributes. By definition, the result of function shape(a) is a vector of length equal to the rank of a. This correspondence is expressed in the symbolic array attribute (1) [[$\mathcal{D}(a)$]], which is converted into flat code to adhere to our grammar. Vice versa, the rank of the result of reshape(s,a) is determined by the length of vector s, which is accessed by selecting the first element from the shape of s.

The vector construct [$a_0, \ldots, a_{n-1}$] yields an array whose rank is given by increasing the rank of a_0 by one. The shape vector is obtained by concatenating [n] and the shape vector of $a_0{}^2$ using the function (++) depicted in Fig. 3.

The WITH-loop with ... genarray(shp,def) generalises array construction. The rank of its result can be computed by adding the rank of the default value def^2 to the length of vector shp. Similar to vector construction, computing the shape vector requires to concatenate shp and the shape vector of def. The index vector is also annotated with symbolic array attributes by the auxiliary scheme $\mathcal{SAA}'$ before the main scheme is recursively applied to the parts. Here, we exploit the restriction that index vector and boundary vectors must coincide in length.

As explained so far, $\mathcal{SAA}$ inserts symbolic array attributes that describe an array's rank and shape in terms of existing arrays within the scope of the function body. For obvious reasons this approach can neither be carried over to function parameters nor to arrays defined by function applications. In both cases, we fall back to introducing applications of the built-in functions dim and shape. This is formalised by the auxiliary scheme $\mathcal{MIR}$ shown in Fig. 5. Scheme $\mathcal{R}$ only serves to provide fresh identifiers and thus avoid naming conflicts. The relationship between rank, shape and value of a function parameter or an application result is established by the additional application of an internal pseudo function saabind:

$$(d)[s]\ v' = \texttt{saabind}(d,s,v);$$

The assignment associates the identifier v' with the rank d and the shape s. However, it makes no statement about the array attributes of v which may not be present at all. Thus, the above line is substantially different from

$$(d)[s]\ v' = v;$$

which states that v' and v are identical and thus have the same attributes.

---

2 By definition all elements of a vector must have the same shape. Likewise, all elements of an array created using a genarray-WITH-loop must match the default element in shape. If the compiler does not manage to guarantee this property by static analysis, the code generator inserts a run time check into compiled code. Thus, we may safely adopt one representative here, which is either the first element of a non-empty vector or the default element of a WITH-loop.

$$\mathcal{MIR}[\![\, t\, [s_1,\dots,s_d]\ a\,]\!] = \begin{cases} (0)\,[[]] & a_d = d\,; \\ (1)\,[[d]] & a_s = [s_1,\dots,s_d]\,; \\ (d)\,[[s_1,\dots,s_d]]\ a & = \mathtt{saabind}(a_d,a_s,\mathcal{R}[\![\, a\,]\!])\,; \end{cases}$$

$$\mathcal{MIR}[\![\, t\, [\bullet_1,\dots,\bullet_d]\ a\,]\!] = \begin{cases} (0)\,[[]] & a_d = d\,; \\ (1)\,[[d]] & a_s = \mathtt{shape}(\mathcal{R}[\![\, a\,]\!])\,; \\ (0)\,[[]] & a_{s_1} = a_s[0]\,; \\ \dots \\ (0)\,[[]] & a_{s_d} = a_s[d-1]\,; \\ (1)\,[[d]] & a_s{}' = [a_{s_1},\dots,a_{s_d}]\,; \\ (d)\,[a_s]\ a & = \mathtt{saabind}(a_d,a_s{}',\mathcal{R}[\![\, a\,]\!])\,; \end{cases}$$

$$\mathcal{MIR}[\![\, t\, [*]\ a\,]\!] = \begin{cases} (0)\,[[]] & a_d = \mathtt{dim}(\mathcal{R}[\![\, a\,]\!])\,; \\ (1)\,[[1]] & a_{s_s} = [a_d]\,; \\ (1)\,[a_{s_s}] & a_s = \mathtt{shape}(\mathcal{R}[\![\, a\,]\!])\,; \\ (a_d)\,[a_s]\ a & = \mathtt{saabind}(a_d,a_s,\mathcal{R}[\![\, a\,]\!])\,; \end{cases}$$

Fig. 5. Compilation scheme for representing array attributes at function boundaries

Depending on the shape class of the argument, different code patterns are used. For AKS arrays, both attributes are simple constants. This also holds for the rank attribute of AKD arrays. Their shape, however, must be determined dynamically. The elements of the shape vector are selected one by one and reassembled to form a new vector. Doing so we introduce mirrors for the whole shape vector and for all the elements which can be obtained by selecting from the new shape vector. In the AUD case, the pattern essentially applies `dim` and `shape`. The additional code line serves to encode the correspondence between the length of the shape vector and the rank of the array. The auxiliary scheme $\mathcal{T}$ used in the rule function application yields the base type of the function value.

4   Effects of Symbolic Array Attributes

Symbolic array attributes provide uniform access to the ranks and shapes of arrays even if these properties are unknown until run time. In conjunction, they reflect all static relationships between rank scalars, shape vectors and array values within one function. A compiler may now exploit this information as a foundation for program optimisation. In particular, symbolic array attributes allow the compiler to statically eliminate data dependencies resulting from accessing array rank and shape properties.

Fig. 6 shows the basic partial evaluation steps that exploit symbolic array attributes. All applications of $\mathtt{dim}(a)$ and $\mathtt{shape}(a)$ are replaced by the corresponding attribute values $\mathcal{D}(a)$ and $\mathcal{S}(a)$, respectively. Even applications of $\mathtt{saabind}(d,s,a)$ can actually be eliminated if there are symbolic array attributes for a identical to $(d)\,[s]$, which may well happen as a result of function inlining. Although these transformations seem simple, they are in fact crucial

$$\mathcal{SVO}[\![\,\mathtt{dim(a)}\,]\!] = \mathcal{D}(a) \qquad\qquad \text{if } \mathcal{D}(a) \text{ defined}$$

$$\mathcal{SVO}[\![\,\mathtt{shape(a)}\,]\!] = \mathcal{S}(a) \qquad\qquad \text{if } \mathcal{S}(a) \text{ defined}$$

$$\mathcal{SVO}[\![\,\mathtt{saabind}(a_d, a_s, a)\,]\!] = a \qquad \text{if } \mathcal{D}(a) \equiv a_d \wedge \mathcal{S}(a) \equiv a_s$$

Fig. 6. Optimisation schemes for `dim`, `shape`, and `saabind`

for triggering a plethora of further optimisations that may even not be aware of symbolic array attributes.

By means of symbolic array attributes the available information on partial structural information of individual arrays as well as the structural relationships between different arrays are explicitly modeled in terms of regular SAC_{mini} expressions. As such they are subject to standard optimisations like constant folding, constant/variable propagation or common subexpression elimination to name just a few. Relationships between arrays like shape equality are expressed in the most natural way: by having all queries for the shape of one or another array be replaced by the same (symbolic) identifier. High-level optimisations like WITH-loop-folding [3] or WITH-loop-fusion [5] and memory management techniques like update-in-place or memory reuse [6] benefit from this information with little or no alteration. Likewise, *shape cliques* [9] can be identified without further analysis: all arrays belonging to the same shape clique have the same symbolic shape identifier.

Symbolic array attributes make exactly those rank and shape computations explicit in intermediate code that otherwise would be created by the code generator at a much later stage of the compilation process. If not a single optimisation applies, we end up with the same code generated in the end as without symbolic array attributes. However, our experience shows that typically our optimisations are quite effective, and, hence, rank and shape computation are partially performed at compile time and shared among different arrays in many cases.

5 Case Study

In this section, we demonstrate how symbolic array attributes influence the compilation process. Instead of quantifying performance using a broad range of benchmarks, our case study aims at illustrating in detail how program optimisation is affected and why symbolic array attributes allow us to generate more efficient code. For this purpose, we choose a small but very important example: element-wise mapping of a function to an array in a shape-generic way. In the absence of higher-order functions in SAC_{mini} (and in SAC), we need a concrete definition for each scalar operator. This functional pattern appears in abundance in generic SAC applications.

Fig. 7 shows the standard library implementation of extending the scalar boolean negation operator to boolean arrays of any shape. Essentially, the function (!) defines the result array to have the same shape as the argument array

```
bool[*] (!) ( int[*] a)
{
  s = shape(a);
  res = with (iv < s) {
          ael = a[iv];
          return( !ael);
        } genarray( s, false);
  return( res);
}
```

Fig. 7. Case study: element-wise mapping of a function to a generic array

```
bool[*] (!) ( int[*] a')
{
  (0) [[]]    ad  = dim(a');
  (1) [[1]]   ass = [ad];
  (1) [ass]   as  = shape(a');
  (ad)[as]    a   = saabind(ad,as,a');
  (1) [[1]]   shs = [ad];
  (1) [shs]   s   = shape(a);
  (0) [[]]    rd  = shs[0];
  (rd)[s]     res = with ((1)[shs] iv < s) {
                        (0)  [[]]   d   = shape(iv)[0];
                        (0)  [[]]   ss  = shape(s)[0];
                        (0)  [[]]   dl  = ss - d;
                        (1)  [[1]]  ds  = [dl];
                        (0)  [[]]   dd  = shape(ds)[0];
                        (dd) [ds]   shp = with ([(0)[[]]j] < ds) {
                                              (0)[[]] drel=s[j+d];
                                              return(drel);
                                          } genarray(ds,0);
                        (0)  [[]]   aed = shape(shp)[0];
                        (aed)[shp]  ael = with ((1)[dub] jv < shp) {
                                              (0)[[]] elem=sel(iv++jv,a);
                                              return(elem);
                                          } genarray(shp,0);
                        return( !ael);
                    } genarray( s, false);
            return( res);
}
```

Fig. 8. The example with inlined functions and symbolic shape attributes

with all elements being set to the negated values of the corresponding elements of the argument array. As the function signature deliberately leaves the structure of argument arrays unrestricted, selection into the argument array refers to the second instance of **select** from Fig. 2. Hence, it also relies on the auxiliary functions **drop** and (**++**) shown in Fig. 3.

Fig. 8 shows the intermediate code after inlining the functions **select** and **drop**. Due to the limited space we refrain from inlining the application of **++** as well. Without symbolic shape attributes no further optimisation would be possible. It is needless to say that this code shows a very poor run time performance. There is one WITH-loop alone for computing the shape shp of the selected element which is a relict from the drop function. Although it is bound to always yield the same result, the WITH-loop is evaluated for each element of the new array res. It cannot be lifted out of the outer WITH-loop because it depends on the index vector iv via ds, dl and d. Even worse, as the selected element is a scalar, shp must always be the empty vector []. Hence, the following WITH-loop will only produce a single element by selecting into the array a at position iv++[] = iv.

However, annotating the code with symbolic array attributes, as described in Section 3, drives the optimisation process way beyond. The key to eliminating overhead in the outer WITH-loop lies in the highlighted code section in Fig. 8. By identifying that iv and s have in fact the same shape, it becomes apparent that the shape of the selected element is [], i.e., the element turns out to be scalar. The symbolic shape attributes allow us to partially evaluate both shape(iv) and shape(s) to shs, such that both d and s become shs[0], which is further resolved to ad. Exploiting the algebraic property that $x - x = 0$ makes dl become zero and thus ds turns into the constant vector [0]. Hence, standard optimisations transform the four highlighted lines of code in Fig. 8 into

```
(0) [[]]   d  = ad;
(0) [[]]   ss = ad;
(0) [[]]   dl = 0;
(1) [[1]]  ds = [0];
```

The optimisation process continues in a similar fashion. With ds = [0], the inner WITH-loop that computes shp, the shape of the element selected from a, is known to merely yield the empty vector []. As a consequence, the symbolic array attributes of ael have been refined to constants, namely (0)[[]]. Furthermore, with shp = [], the WITH-loop performing the selection itself can be unrolled, yielding ael = sel(iv++[], a), which in turn is simplified to ael = sel(iv, a).

Finally, by eliminating common subexpressions and dead code, we obtain the code shown in Fig. 9. The result looks strikingly similar to the original program in Fig. 7. However, instead of being forced to use the expensive generic selection function from Fig. 2, we now employ the built-in function sel. Moreover, the symbolic array attributes clearly reflect the shape equality between argument and result. This property is exploited by the compiler to generate code that tries to immediately reuse the memory that holds a for storing res [6].

In order to quantify the effect of the transformations enabled by symbolic array attributes in our case study, we have created a synthetic micro benchmark: We run 100 negations of an array of 2000 × 2000 elements[3] on a 3 GHz Intel Xeon processor. Fig. 10 shows program run times and memory consumption of the micro benchmark for compiled AKS, AKD and AUD code. Symbolic array

---

[3] SAC stores boolean values as integers rather than bits. Hence, we need approximately 16MB of memory to store one array.

```
bool[*] (!) ( int[*] a')
{
  (0) [[]]   ad  = dim(a');
  (1) [[1]]  ass = [ad];
  (1) [ass]  as  = shape(a');
  (ad)[as]   a   = saabind(ad,as,a');
  (ad)[as]   res = with ((1)[ass] iv < as) {
                     (0)[[]] ael = sel( iv, a);
                     return( !ael);
                   } genarray( as, false);
             return( res);
}
```

Fig. 9. The fully optimised example

attributes have no impact on the compilation of non-generic code. The AUD variant profits the most from the extended optimisation capabilities: execution time is reduced by 95% from 149.5s to 7.1s. This is not surprising given how much overhead has been eliminated from the intermediate program. The remaining slowdown with respect to the AKS program is explained by the lower efficiency of the AUD array traversal code. In both the AUD and the AKD case, symbolic array attributes enable memory reuse, thereby reducing space requirements to the AKS level. The AKD program especially benefits from this: its run time is reduced by 28%, approaching the AKS run time.

In generic array programming, small functions like the negation on arrays serve as building blocks for more complex operations. Fig. 11 illustrates this concept by means of a shape-generic implementation of element-wise logical implication. The function is composed of negation and disjunction, where the implementation of the latter follows the familiar pattern. Since our type system cannot express the shape conformability restriction on the argument arrays, we use an application of `reshape` instead. The run time figures show that symbolic array attributes have a drastic effect beyond the improvements we observed in the compilation of the individual components. Since the applications of **shape**

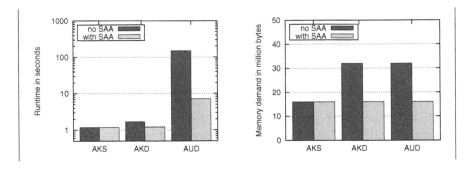

Fig. 10. Run time and memory impact of symbolic array attributes

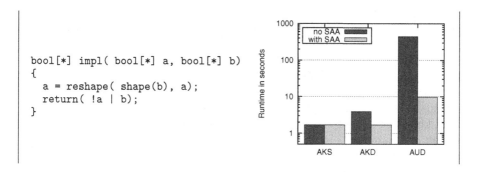

```
bool[*] impl( bool[*] a, bool[*] b)
{
   a = reshape( shape(b), a);
   return( !a | b);
}
```

Fig. 11. Run time performance of logical implication on arrays

used in the constituent functions have been removed, WITH-loop-folding is able to merge the two consecutive WITH-loops performing negation and disjunction. Hence, the AKD execution time is reduced by 56% from 3.9s to 1.7s, once more reaching the performance level of the AKS variant. The AUD run time drops by almost 98% from 442.5s to 9.8s, making the once prohibitively expensive shape-generic program useful in practice.

6   Related Work

An example for the importance of structural information for array processing is Jay's FISH [10]. In FISH, each function f is accompanied by a shape function #f that maps the shape of the argument to the shape of the result. Shape inference proceeds by complete static evaluation of these shape functions and rejects all programs for which it fails. As a consequence, FISH does not support non-uniform functions like take and drop for which the result shape depends on argument values rather than only shapes.

SAC is less restrictive than FISH and properly supports non-uniform operations. However, efficiency of compiled code nevertheless depends on the accuracy of the available shape information [11]. To improve structural information we previously focused on a combination of partial evaluation and selective function specialisation [7]. Bernecky recently introduced the concept of *shape cliques*, sets of arrays of provably equal shape [9], and investigated their impact on a selected optimisation: index vector elimination. Symbolic array attributes generalise the concept of shape cliques by representing partial and relational structural information explicitly in the code. In particular, symbolic array attributes allow us to identify shape cliques, but go beyond this specific application.

Runtime performance is not a key issue in untyped, interpreted array languages like MATLAB, APL or J. However, as soon as attempts are indeed made to accelerate program execution, structural array properties gain interest. For example, the FALCON MATLAB compiler [12] by de Rose and Padua infers either precise shapes or rather fuzzy approximations like notMatrix and notScalar. Recently, Joisha and Banerjee [13] presented an approach for inferring symbolic array shapes that is based on modeling the shape semantics of the built-ins in an algebraic system and evaluation of the resulting expressions using term rewriting. Another approach taken by McGosh [14] is to use propositional logic to represent the constraints on the variables. The shape constraints of each statement are expressed as sequences of clauses, before a whole-procedure solution for all shapes is computed by finding *n-cliques* in the constraint graph. In the domain of APL Bernecky proposed array predicates [15] as a framework to represent knowledge about arrays that exceeds structural information, e.g., a vector may be attributed as *sorted* if it is the result of a sort operation. In a setting dominated by powerful built-in operations such predicates can be maintained and exploited at a later stage, e.g. to avoid (re-)sorting of an already sorted array.

All the approaches mentioned so far share with ours the aim to identify information that is hidden in the code. An alternative class of approaches enable the user to express constraints on arrays by more expressive type systems. Dependent types [8] naturally lend themselves for this purpose as they allow the use of (dynamic) terms to index within families of types. Unfortunately, the problem of type equality is generally undecidable as it boils down to deciding whether two index terms denote the same value. For example, Augustsson's CAYENNE [16] is a fully dependently typed language. Its type system is undecidable and it lacks phase distinction. Both problems can be overcome by restricting the type language. For example, EPIGRAM [17,18] (Altenkirch, McBride, McKinna) rules out general recursion in type-forming expressions to retain decidability. Other, light-weight approaches such as Xi and Pfenning's DML [19], Xi's *applied type system* [20], and Zenger's *indexed types* [21] allow term-indexing into type families only for certain *index sorts*. The type-checking problem can then be reduced to constraint solving on these sorts, which is decidable.

Our work is in part inspired by the above mentioned dependently typed programming systems. Symbolic array attributes may be regarded as index-terms into the type family of multi-dimensional arrays of a given base type with SAC itself being used as the term language. However, our approach does not aim at providing stronger typing facilities, but at obtaining a uniform representation of the knowledge already present in a program. In consequence, there is no obligation of keeping type equality decidable. There is also a relation to work which aims at optimising dependently typed programs. Xi and Pfenning report successful array bounds check elimination [22], Xi even outlined a scheme for dead code removal through dependent types in DML [23]. McKinna and Brady describe optimisations in the compilation of EPIGRAM to remove compile time only values from terms as well as array bounds checks [24].

7   Conclusion and Future Work

We have proposed a novel approach to represent incomplete structural information on shape-generic arrays inferred by the compiler. The appealing characteristic of our symbolic array attributes is that they map information from the domain of shapely types into the domain of the expression language where a plethora of optimisation techniques wait to be reused to improve the compile time knowledge on structural properties of shape-generic arrays. As a consequence, we observe a cross-fertilisation between code optimisation and gathering of additional structural information. Our case study demonstrates how our technique may substantially improve the run time behaviour of shape-generic code without the need for specialisation into non-generic code. Although we have illustrated the concept of symbolic array attributes in the context of SAC, the ideas can be carried over to other settings with support for generic array programming rather straightforwardly.

A limitation of our approach so far is the fact that our analysis is mostly intra-functional. Function inlining and function specialisation with respect to symbolic array attributes are two ways to infer structural properties across function boundaries. However, both are somewhat orthogonal to our approach. Instead, we intend to embed our current work in a more general framework that actually extends the shape-generic type system by a variant of dependent types adapted to the special needs of shape-generic programming. This step would allow us to express structural relationships between function parameters and function results in a systematic way. Symbolic array attributes would then serve as an implementation vehicle for type inference and as an interface between the type system and the optimisation framework.

References

1. Scholz, S.B.: Single Assignment C — Efficient Support for High-Level Array Operations in a Functional Setting. Journal of Functional Programming 13(6), 1005–1059 (2003)
2. Grelck, C., Scholz, S.B.: SAC — A Functional Array Language for Efficient Multi-threaded Execution. International Journal of Parallel Programming 34(4), 383–427 (2006)
3. Scholz, S.B.: With-loop-folding in SAC — Condensing Consecutive Array Operations. In: Clack, C., Hammond, K., Davie, T. (eds.) IFL 1997. LNCS, vol. 1467, pp. 72–92. Springer, Heidelberg (1998)
4. Grelck, C., Scholz, S.B., Trojahner, K.: With-Loop Scalarization: Merging Nested Array Operations. In: Trinder, P., Michaelson, G.J., Peña, R. (eds.) IFL 2003. LNCS, vol. 3145, pp. 118–134. Springer, Heidelberg (2004)
5. Grelck, C., Hinckfuß, K., Scholz, S.B.: With-Loop Fusion for Data Locality and Parallelism. In: Butterfield, A., Grelck, C., Huch, F. (eds.) IFL 2005. LNCS, vol. 4015, pp. 178–195. Springer, Heidelberg (2006)
6. Grelck, C., Trojahner, K.: Implicit Memory Management for SAC. In: Grelck, C., Huch, F. (eds.) Hardware Specification, Verification and Synthesis: Mathematical Aspects. LNCS, vol. 408, Springer, Heidelberg (1990)
7. Grelck, C., Scholz, S.B., Shafarenko, A.: A Binding-Scope Analysis for Generic Programs on Arrays. In: Butterfield, A. (ed.) IFL 2005. LNCS, vol. 4015, pp. 212–230. Springer, Heidelberg (2006)
8. Martin-Löf, P.: Intuitionistic Type Theory. Biblio-Napoli (1984)

9. Bernecky, R.: Shape Cliques. In: Horváth, Z., Zsók, V., eds.: Proceedings of the 18th International Symposium on Implementation of Functional Languages, IFL 2006, Budapest, Hungary, September 4-6, 2006, Eötvös Loránd University 1–12 (2006)

10. Jay, C., Steckler, P.: The Functional Imperative: Shape! In: Hankin, C. (ed.) ESOP 1998 and ETAPS 1998. LNCS, vol. 1381, pp. 139–153. Springer, Heidelberg (1998)

11. Kreye, D.: A Compilation Scheme for a Hierarchy of Array Types. In: Arts, T., Mohnen, M. (eds.) IFL 2001. LNCS, vol. 2312, pp. 24–26. Springer, Heidelberg (2002)

12. de Rose, L., Padua, D.: Techniques for the translation of matlab programs into fortran 90. ACM Transactions on Programming Languages and Systems 21(2), 286–323 (1999)

13. Joisha, P., Banerjee, P.: An algebraic array shape inference system for matlab. ACM Transactions on Programming Languages and Systems 28(5), 848–907 (2006)

14. McCosh, C.: Type-based specialization in a telescoping compiler for matlab. Master Thesis TR03-412, Rice University, Houston, Texas, USA (2003)

15. Bernecky, R.: Reducing Computational Complexity with Array Predicates. In: Picchi, S., Micocci, M. (eds.) Proceedings of the International Conference on Array Processing Languages (APL'98), Rome, Italy, pp. 46–54. ACM Press, New York (1998)

16. Augustsson, L.: Cayenne – a language with dependent types. In: International Conference on Functional Programming. pp. 239–250 (1998)

17. McBride, C., McKinna, J.: The view from the left. Journal of Functional Programming 14(1), 69–111 (2004)

18. Altenkirch, T., McBride, C., McKinna, J.: Why dependent types matter. Manuscript, available online (2005)

19. Xi, H., Pfenning, F.: Dependent Types in Practical Programming. In: Aiken, A. (ed.) Proceedings of the 26th ACM SIGPLAN-SIGACT Symposium on Principles of Programming Languages (POPL'99), pp. 214–227. San Antonio, Texas, USA, ACM Press, New York (1999)

20. Xi, H.: Applied Type System (extended abstract). In: Berardi, S., Coppo, M., Damiani, F. (eds.) TYPES 2003. LNCS, vol. 3085, pp. 394–408. Springer, Heidelberg (2004)

21. Zenger, C.: Indexed types. Theorectical Computer Science 187(1-2), 147–165 (1997)

22. Xi, H., Pfenning, F.: Eliminating array bound checking through dependent types. In: Proceedings of ACM SIGPLAN Conference on Programming Language Design and Implementation, Montreal, pp. 249–257 (1998)

23. Xi, H.: Dead code elimination through dependent types. In: Gupta, G. (ed.) PADL 1999. LNCS, vol. 1551, pp. 228–242. Springer, Heidelberg (1999)

24. McKinna, J., Brady, E.: Phase distinctions in the compilation of epigram. Draft, available online (2005)

Index Vector Elimination
— Making Index Vectors Affordable

Robert Bernecky[1], Stephan Herhut[2], Sven-Bodo Scholz[2], Kai Trojahner[3],
Clemens Grelck[2], and Alex Shafarenko[2]

[1] University of Toronto, Canada
bernecky@acm.org
[2] University of Hertfordshire, UK
{s.a.herhut,s.scholz,c.grelck,a.shafarenko}@herts.ac.uk
[3] University of Lübeck, Germany
trojahner@isp.uni-luebeck.de

Abstract. Compiling indexing operations on n-dimensional arrays into
efficiently executable code is a challenging task. This paper focuses on
the reduction of offset computations as they typically occur when transforming index vectors into offsets for linearized representations of n-
dimensional arrays. We present a high-level optimization to that effect
which is generally applicable, even in the presence of statically unknown
rank (n). Our experiments show run-time improvements between a factor
of 2 and 16 on a set of real-world benchmarks.

1 Introduction

Languages that permit us to express algorithms in a terse, consistent manner
enhance our thought processes, providing us with what Ken Iverson called "tools
of thought" [1]. Data-parallel array languages, such as SAC, APL, and J, fall into
this class of programming languages. They offer the programmer such benefits
as shape-invariant programming, terse expression, and simpler control flow.

Some of these benefits arise from the use of *index sets* to specify data-parallel
indexing operations on multi-dimensional arrays [2,3,4]. Index sets may be
thought of as arrays of *index vectors*, in which each index vector specifies a
single element or an entire sub-array to be selected from an array. For example,
the index vector [3,4] in SAC could be used to select the element in row three
and column four of a rank-2 matrix, or to select the matrix of shape [7,6] at
hyperplane three and plane four from a tensor of shape [9,8,7,6].

As powerful as index vectors are on the level of algorithmic specifications, they
open a Pandora's Box of troubles when it comes to generating highly efficient
executable code from them. If index vectors actually appear in code generated
by an array-language compiler, run-time performance can be severely degraded.
One source of performance degradation is memory management overhead arising
from dynamic allocation and deallocation of all arrays, including index vectors.
To avoid superfluous memory allocations and, even more importantly, to avoid
superfluous array copying, reference counting is used as predominant garbage

Z. Horváth, V. Zsók, and A. Butterfield (Eds.): IFL 2006, LNCS 4449, pp. 19–36, 2007.

collection technique. Although quite some research went into optimizing this technique, such as the work described in [5,6,7], the dynamic creation of index vectors within the innermost loops often cannot be avoided.

Another major source of performance degradation due to index vectors appears whenever the n-dimensional arrays they select from are internally represented in a linearized fashion. This requires all index vectors within selections to be translated into offsets within the linearizations of the arrays they select from. Although this may seem an inexpensive operation – $n - 1$ additions and $n - 1$ multiplications per selection into an n-dimensional array – it turns out that indexing operations are usually heavily used within inner loops and, therefore, have a significant impact on the overall run-time.

In a setting with fixed array dimensionality (rank) or shape, the runtime impact can be alleviated by scalarizing indexing operations and consecutively applying standard optimization techniques. However, in generic array programming languages such as SAC, where the programmer is not bound to predefine the dimensionality of an array, scalarizing indexing operations often is not possible. In this paper, we describe INDEX-VECTOR-ELIMINATION (IVE), an optimization technique that independently of the static shape-knowledge is able to eliminate redundant offset computations.

The paper is organized as follows: the next section gives a brief introduction of a stripped-down version of SAC which serves as our model language. Section 3 presents an example which demonstrates the potential for code improvements due to array indexing within a typical loop kernel, and identifies the improvements that our optimization targets. A formalization of INDEX-VECTOR-ELIMINATION, presented in Section 4, provides the required transformation schemes for our model language SAC_λ. Section 5 presents some performance figures for a set of real-world benchmarks. We discuss related work in Section 6 and draw some conclusions in Section 7.

2 SAC_λ

We now describe a stripped-down version of SAC, comprising only the bare essentials of the language: its syntax has been modified to a λ-calculus style, in order to ease comprehension by a functional-programming audience.

Figure 1 shows the syntax of SAC_λ. A program consists of a set of mutually recursive function definitions and a designated main expression. Essentially, expressions are either constants, variables or function applications. Since SAC does not, at present, support higher-order functions nor nameless functions, all abstractions (function definitions) are explicitly user-defined. Function applications are written in C-style, *i.e.*, with parentheses around arguments, rather than around entire applications of functions. Constants are either scalars or vectors of expressions enclosed by square brackets. The reader may note here, that our formal description of SAC_λ distinguishes between *LetExpr*, *Expr*, and *Val* where one would usually expect just *Expr*. This measure eases the formal specification of code transformations in later sections. Since a transformation of the general

$$Program \quad\Rightarrow \lceil FunId = \lambda Id\lceil\ , Id\ \rceil^*\ . LetExpr\ ;\ \rceil^*$$
$$\mathbf{main} = LetExpr\ ;$$

$$LetExpr \quad\Rightarrow Val$$
$$|\quad \mathbf{let}\ Id = Expr\ \mathbf{in}\ LetExpr$$

$$Expr \quad\Rightarrow Val$$
$$|\quad FunId\ (\ Val\ \lceil\ , Val\ \rceil^*\ )$$
$$|\quad Prf\ (\ Val\ \lceil\ , Val\ \rceil^*\ )$$
$$|\quad \mathbf{if}\ Val\ \mathbf{then}\ LetExpr\ \mathbf{else}\ LetExpr$$
$$|\quad \mathbf{with}(\ Val <= Id < Val\ )\ : LetExpr$$
$$\mathbf{genarray}(\ Val\ , Val\ )$$

$$Val \quad\Rightarrow Const$$
$$|\quad [\ \lceil Val\ \lceil\ , Val\ \rceil^*\ \rceil\ ]$$
$$|\quad Id$$

$$Prf \quad\Rightarrow \mathbf{shape}\ |\ \mathbf{dim}\ |\ \mathbf{sel}\ |\ *\ |\ ...$$

Fig. 1. The syntax of SAC$_\lambda$

case into this restricted form is rather straight-forward, we take the liberty to ignore some of these restrictions in our examples whenever this improves their readability.

SAC$_\lambda$ provides a few built-in array operators, referred to as primitive functions (Prf). Among these are **shape** and **dim** for computing an array's shape and dimensionality (rank), respectively. A selection operation, **sel**, is also provided; it takes two arguments: an index vector, specifying the element to be selected, and an array from which to select. These basic array operations are complemented by element-wise extensions of arithmetic and relational operations, such as *multiply* (*) and *greater-than-or-equal* (>=), respectively. For improved readability, we use the latter in infix notation throughout our examples.

On top of this language kernel, SAC provides the WITH-loop, a language construct for defining array operations in a generic way. In the interest of simplified exposition, we consider only a restricted form of the WITH-loop; fully-fledged WITH-loops are described in [3].

As can be seen from Figure 1, WITH-loops in SAC$_\lambda$ take the general form:

$$\mathbf{with}\ (\ lower\ \mathbf{<=}\ iv\ \mathbf{<}\ upper)\ : expr$$
$$\mathbf{genarray}(\ shape,\ default)$$

where iv is an identifier, *lower*, *upper*, and *shape* denote expressions that should evaluate to vectors of identical length, and *expr* and *default* denote arbitrary expressions that must evaluate to arrays of identical shape. Such a WITH-loop defines an array of shape *shape*, whose elements are either computed from the expression *expr* or from the default expression *default*. Which of these two values is chosen for an individual element depends on the element's location, *i.e.,* it depends on its index position. If the index is within the range specified by the lower bound *lower* and the upper bound *upper*, *expr* is chosen, otherwise *default* is taken. As a simple example, consider this WITH-loop, which computes the vector [0, 2, 2, 2, 0]:

```
with ([1] <= iv < [4]) : 2
genarray( [5], 0)
```

Note that the use of vectors for the shape of the result and the bounds of the index space (also referred to as the "generator" ') allows WITH-loops to denote arrays of arbitrary rank. Furthermore, the "generator expression" *expr* may refer to the index position through the "generator variable" *iv*. For example, the WITH-loop

```
with ([1,1] <= iv < [3,4]) : sel([0], iv) + sel([1], iv)
genarray( [3,5], 0)
```

yields the matrix $\begin{pmatrix} 0\,0\,0\,0\,0 \\ 0\,2\,3\,4\,0 \\ 0\,3\,4\,5\,0 \end{pmatrix}$.

We can formalize the semantics of SAC_λ by a standard big-step operational semantics for λ-calculus-based applicative languages as defined in several textbooks, *e.g.*, [8]. The core relations, *i.e.*, those for conditionals, abstractions, and function applications can be used in their standard form. Hence, only those relations pertaining to the array specific features of SAC_λ are shown in Figure 2.

As a unified representation for n-dimensional arrays we use pairs of vectors $<[\,shp_1, \ldots, shp_n], [\,data_1, \ldots, data_m]\,>$ where the vector $[\,shp_1, \ldots, shp_n]$ denotes the shape of the array, *i.e.*, its extent with respect to the n individual axes, and the vector $[\,data_1, \ldots, data_m]$ contains all elements of the array in a linearized form. Since the number of elements within an array equals the product of the number of elements per individual axis, we have $m = \prod_{i=1}^{n} shp_i$. The linearization we choose is row-major, *i.e.*, elements that correspond to variations in the rightmost index only are consecutive in the vector of elements.

The first two evaluation rules of Figure 2 show how scalars as well as vectors are transformed into the internal representation. The rule VECT requires that all elements need to be of the same shape, thereby ensuring shape consistency in the overall result.

The next three rules formalize the semantics of the main primitive operations on arrays: `dim`, `shape`, and `sel`. There are two aspects of the SEL rule to be observed: Firstly, we require the selection index to be of the same length as the shape of the array to be selected from. This ensures scalar values as results. If a more versatile selection is required, *i.e.*, a selection that may return entire subarrays, this can be achieved by embedding the selection operation into a WITH-loop. Secondly, the selection requires a transformation of the index vector into a scalar offset l into the linearized form of the array. The sum of products used here reflects the row-major linearization we have chosen.

$$\text{CONST} : \frac{}{n \rightarrow\; <\; [],\; [n]\; >}$$

$$\text{VECT}\;\; :\;\; \frac{\forall i \in \{1,\ldots,n\} : e_i \rightarrow\; <\; [\,s_1,\,\ldots,\,s_m\,],\; [\,d_1^i,\,\ldots,\,d_p^i\,]\; >}{[\,e_1,\,\ldots,\,e_n\,] \rightarrow\; <\; [\,n,\;\; s_1,\,\ldots,\,s_m\,],\; [\;\; d_1^1,\,\ldots,\,d_p^1,\,\ldots,\,d_1^n,\,\ldots,\,d_p^n\,]\; >}$$

$$\text{DIM}\;\;\; :\;\; \frac{e \rightarrow\; <\; [\,s_1,\,\ldots,\,s_n\,],\; [\,d_1,\,\ldots,\,d_m\,]\; >}{\texttt{dim(}\;e) \rightarrow\; <\; [],\; [n]\; >}$$

$$\text{SHAPE}\; :\;\; \frac{e \rightarrow\; <\; [\,s_1,\,\ldots,\,s_n\,],\; [\,d_1,\,\ldots,\,d_m\,]\; >}{\texttt{shape(}\;e) \rightarrow\; <\; [\,n\,],\; [\,s_1,\,\ldots,\,s_n\,]\; >}$$

$$\text{SEL}\;\;\;\; :\;\; \frac{iv \rightarrow\; <\; [\,n\,],\; [\,i_1,\,\ldots,\,i_n\,]\; > \qquad e \rightarrow\; <\; [\,s_1,\,\ldots,\,s_n\,],\; [\,d_1,\,\ldots,\,d_m\,]\; >}{\texttt{sel(}\;iv,\;e) \rightarrow\; <\; [],\; [\,d_{l+1}\,]\; >}$$

$$\text{where } l = \sum_{j=1}^{n} \left(i_j * \prod_{k=j+1}^{n} s_k \right)$$

$$\Longleftrightarrow\; \forall k \in \{1,\ldots,n\} : 0 \leq i_k < s_k$$

$$*\;\;\;\;\; :\;\; \frac{e_1 \rightarrow\; <\; [\,s_1,\,\ldots,\,s_n\,],\; [\,d_1^1,\,\ldots,\,d_m^1\,]\; > \qquad e_2 \rightarrow\; <\; [\,s_1,\,\ldots,\,s_n\,],\; [\,d_1^2,\,\ldots,\,d_m^2\,]\; >}{\texttt{*(}\;e_1,\;e_2) \rightarrow\; <\; [\,s_1,\,\ldots,\,s_n\,],\; [\,d_1^1 * d_1^2,\,\ldots,\,d_m^1 * d_m^2\,]\; >}$$

$$\text{WITH}\;\;\; :$$
$$e_l \rightarrow\; <\; [\,n\,],\; [\,l_1,\,\ldots,\,l_n\,]\; >$$
$$e_u \rightarrow\; <\; [\,n\,],\; [\,u_1,\,\ldots,\,u_n\,]\; >$$
$$e_{shp} \rightarrow\; <\; [\,n\,],\; [\,shp_1,\,\ldots,\,shp_n\,]\; >$$
$$e_{def} \rightarrow\; <\; [],\; [\,d\,]\; >$$
$$\forall i_1 \in \{l_1,\ldots,u_1 - 1\} \;\ldots\; \forall i_n \in \{l_n,\ldots,u_n - 1\} :$$
$$(\lambda\, Id.e_b\,[\; i_1,\;\ldots,\;i_n\,]) \rightarrow\; <\; [],\; d^{[i_1,\ldots,i_n]}\; >$$
$$\texttt{with(}\; e_l\; \texttt{<=}\; Id\; \texttt{<}\; e_u\;)\; :\; e_b\; \texttt{genarray(}\; e_{shp},\; e_{def}\texttt{)}$$
$$\rightarrow\; <\; [\,shp_1,\,\ldots,\,shp_n\,],\; [\; d^{[0,\ldots,0]},\,\ldots,\; d^{[shp_1 - 1,\ldots,shp_n - 1]}\,]\; >$$
$$\text{where } d^{[x_1,\ldots,x_n]} = d$$
$$\text{iff } \exists j \in \{1,\ldots,n\} : x_j \in \{0,\ldots,l_j - 1\} \cup \{u_j,\ldots,shp_j - 1\}$$

Fig. 2. An operational semantics for SAC_λ

Element-wise extensions of standard operations such as the arithmetic and relational operations are demonstrated by the example of the rule for multiplication ($*$).

The last rule gives the formal semantics of the WITH-loop in SAC_λ. The first three conditions require the lower bound, the upper bound and the shape expression to evaluate to vectors of identical length. The next two conditions relate to the default expression e_{def} and the generator expression e_b, respectively. They ensure that both the default expression and generator expression evaluate to scalar values. Since the generator expression may refer to the index variable, this is formalized by transforming the generator expression into an anonymous function and by evaluating a pseudo-application of this function to all indices specified in the generator. The lower part of the WITH-loop-rule shows how the values from the individual generator expression evaluations and the value of the default expression are combined into the overall result. The result shape vector, which stems from the shape expression, comprises a concatenation of the data vectors from the individual generator expression evaluations. Since the generator does not necessarily cover the entire index space, the default expression values need to be inserted whenever at least one element of the index vector $[i_1, \ldots, i_n]$ is outside the generator range, i.e., $\exists j \in \{1, ..., n\} : x_j \in \{0, ..., l_j - 1\} \cup \{u_j, ..., shp_j - 1\}$. Formally, this is achieved by the "where clause" of the rule WITH.

3   A Motivating Example

Let us consider the following definition of an n-dimensional array R:

```
...let
    R = A + shift( cv, A + B)
in ...
```

where A, B, and cv are variables that are defined by some surrounding context indicated by the three dots. We assume here that A and B denote n-dimensional arrays of identical shape and that cv is an identifier that denotes an n-element vector. Let us, furthermore, assume that + is a user-defined function that extends scalar addition to n-dimensional arrays in an element-wise fashion, and that shift implements an n-dimensional shift operation. Inlining the definitions of these functions results in a nesting of WITH-loop-defined let expressions of the form:

```
...let
    R = let
           C = with( 0*shape( A) <= iv < shape( A)) :
                  sel( iv, A) + sel( iv, B)
               genarray( shape( A), 0)
       in let
             D = with( cv <= iv < shape( C)) :
                    sel( iv-cv, C)
                 genarray( shape( C), 0)
           in with( 0*shape( A) <= iv < shape( A)) :
                  sel( iv, A) + sel( iv, D)
              genarray( shape( A), 0)
    in ...
```

Optimizations such as WITH-LOOP-FOLDING[3] transform this expression into an expression that contains a single WITH-loop:

```
...let
    R = with( cv <= iv < shape( A)) :
           sel( iv, A) + sel( iv-cv, A) + sel( iv-cv, B)
        genarray( shape( A), 0)
    in ...
```

A translation of such an expression into C-code leads to a loop nesting where the innermost loop contains the computation of sel(iv, A) + sel(iv-cv, A) + sel(iv-cv, B) as well as an assignment of the resulting value into the array R at the index position iv. As we can see from the semantics definition in Section 2, these operations require the indices iv and iv - cv to be translated into suitable offsets. Using vect2offset(*iv, shp*) as a short-cut notation for this conversion of indices into offsets, we obtain code within the innermost loop that is similar to:

```
A_off0 = vect2offset ( iv, shape(A));
for( k = 0; k < shape(iv)[0]; k++) {
   jv[k] = iv[k] - cv[k];
}
A_off1 = vect2offset ( jv, shape(A));
B_off0 = vect2offset ( jv, shape(B));
R[R_off0] = A[A_off0] + A[A_off1] + B[B_off0];
```

where the write-back offset R_off0 is defined by the surrounding loop constructs. The n-element vector jv serves as a compiler-introduced variable that holds the result of the element-wise vector-subtraction iv-cv computed by the for-loop in lines 2-4. A closer look at the example reveals that all arrays involved have the same shape: we demanded A and B to have the same shape, which guarantees the element-wise addition to be well-defined. Similarly, the result needs to be of the same shape as well, since the shift operation's result matches the shape of its array argument.

With this knowledge of matching shapes, we can deduce that vect2offset(jv, shape(A)) and vect2offset(jv, shape(B)) in fact compute the same offset allowing us to reuse A_off1 within the selection into B. Following the same line of reasoning for R and A, we can reuse R_off0 for A_off0. These modifications lead to an improved loop body of the form:

```
for( k = 0; k < shape(iv)[0]; k++) {
   jv[k] = iv[k] - cv[k];
}
A_off1 = vect2offset ( jv, shape(A));
R[R_off0] = A[R_off0] + A[A_off1] + B[A_off1];
```

In order to improve this code further, we need to exploit the relation between iv and jv and the consequent relation between R_off0 and A_off1. This, in turn, requires us to have a closer look at the definition of vect2offset. From the semantics definition in Section 2 we obtain that an index vector $[i_1, ..., i_n]$ into an array of shape $[s_1, ..., s_n]$ corresponds to to the offset $\sum_{j=1}^{n} (i_j * \prod_{k=j+1}^{n} s_k)$. From linear algebra, we know that

Lemma 1. *For all vectors $iv, cv, shp \in \mathbb{Z}^n$ we have* vect2offset(*iv + cv, shp*) = vect2offset(*iv, shp*) + vect2offset(*cv, shp*).

Proof. By definition of vect2offset *we have:*

$$\text{vect2offset(iv + cv, shp)}$$
$$= \sum_{i=1}^{n} ((\text{iv}_i + \text{cv}_i) * \prod_{j=i+1}^{n} \text{shp}_j)$$
$$= \sum_{i=1}^{n} (\text{iv}_i * \prod_{j=i+1}^{n} \text{shp}_j) + \sum_{i=1}^{n} (\text{cv}_i * \prod_{j=i+1}^{n} \text{shp}_j)$$
$$= \text{vect2offset(iv, shp) + vect2offset(cv, shp)}$$

This linearity in the first argument of `vect2offset` lets us lift the loop-invariant part of the index computation from the loop body by pre-computing an offset:

$$\text{coffset = vect2offset(cv, shape(A))}$$

and by defining `A_off1` as:

$$\text{vect2offset(jv, shape(A)) + coffset}$$

Subsequently, we can reuse the offset `R_off0` within the computation of `A_off1`, which yields a loop body of the form:

```
A_off1 = R_off0 + coffset;
R[R_off0] = A[R_off0] + A[A_off1] + B[A_off1];
```

Assuming `A` to be an n-dimensional array, our optimizations have reduced the number of arithmetic operations within the loop body from $7 * n - 4$ to 3, *i.e.*, we eliminate 70% of the arithmetic operations when `A` is a rank-2 matrix, and 84% when `A` is of rank 3. Furthermore, since all `vect2offset` operations have been eliminated, neither `iv` nor `jv` need to be allocated or freed within the loop body anymore.

4   Index Vector Elimination

From our example, we can see that the intended optimizations cannot be done on the level of SAC_λ itself. Instead, we need to apply them to a level that is closer to the generated C code. The way we achieve this is to make the transformation of index vectors into offsets explicit and to separate it from the selection into the linearized array representation.

4.1   Splitting the Selection Operation

The basic idea is to introduce two new primitive operations: `vect2offset` and `idxsel`, which represent the offset computation and the selection within the linearized representation, respectively. A formal definition of their semantics is given in Figure 3. The VECT2OFFSET rule is almost identical to the SEL rule. The only difference is that instead of returning an element from the array, only the scalar offsel l is returned. This allows the IDXSEL rule to simply expect a scalar as index argument for a selection in the linearized representation of the array. Together, these two operations can be used to replace applications of the operation `sel`. The code transformation to that effect is shown in Figure 4. It shows the essential rule of a transformation scheme SPLIT which recursively traverses SAC_λ programs and replaces every occurrence of an application `sel( `iv`, A)` by an expression of the form `idxsel( vect2offset( `iv`, A), A)`. However, the nesting restrictions on SAC_λ require a slightly more complex pattern to look for and a nesting of let expressions as replacement. Note here, that all inserted

$$iv \rightarrow < [\, n], [\, i_1, \ldots, i_n] >$$
$$\text{VECT2OFFSET} : \quad \frac{e \rightarrow < [\, s_1, \ldots, s_n], [\, d_1, \ldots, d_m] >}{\text{vect2offset}(\ iv,\ e) \rightarrow < [], [\, l] >}$$
$$\text{where } l = \sum_{j=1}^{n} (i_j * \prod_{k=j+1}^{n} s_k)$$
$$\iff \forall k \in \{1, \ldots, n\} : 0 \le i_k < s_k$$

$$idx \rightarrow < [], \ l >$$
$$\text{IDXSEL} \quad : \quad \frac{e \rightarrow < [\, s_1, \ldots, s_n], [\, d_1, \ldots, d_m] >}{\text{idxsel}(\ idx,\ e) \rightarrow < [], [\, d_{l+1}] >}$$
$$\iff 0 \le l < m$$

Fig. 3. Operational semantics for **vect2offset** and **idxsel**

$$
\text{SPLIT} \left[\!\!\left[\begin{array}{l} \texttt{let} \\ \quad Id = Expr \\ \texttt{in } Expr_b \end{array} \right]\!\!\right] \rightsquigarrow
\begin{cases}
\begin{array}{ll}
\texttt{let} & \text{if } Expr \equiv \texttt{sel}(\ iv,\ A) \\
\quad idx = \texttt{vect2offset}(\ iv, A) & \\
\texttt{in let} & \\
\quad\quad Id = \texttt{idxsel}(\ idx, A) & \\
\quad\quad \texttt{in SPLIT}[\![Expr_b]\!] & \\
\texttt{let} & \\
\quad Id = \texttt{SPLIT}[\![Expr]\!] & \text{otherwise.} \\
\texttt{in SPLIT}[\![Expr_b]\!] &
\end{array}
\end{cases}
$$

Fig. 4. Inserting explicit index computations

identifiers idx need to be unique, *i.e.*, they must not be used anywhere else in the given program. Those rules of the SPLIT scheme that match the remaining constructs of SAC_λ are not shown as they only propagate the scheme into all existing sub-expressions.

The soundness of this transformation follows directly from the semantics of sel, vect2offset, and idxsel:

Theorem 1. SPLIT *is sound wrt. the semantics of* SAC_λ

Proof. From the semantics definitions in Figure 2 and Figure 3 we can see that it suffices to show that

$$iv \rightarrow < [\, n], [\, i_1, \ldots, i_n] >$$
$$\frac{e \rightarrow < [\, s_1, \ldots, s_n], [\, d_1, \ldots, d_m] >}{\text{idxsel}(\ \text{vect2offset}(\ iv,\ e),\ e) \rightarrow < [], [\, d_{l+1}] >}$$
$$\text{where } l = \sum_{j=1}^{n} (i_j * \prod_{k=j+1}^{n} s_k)$$
$$\iff \forall k \in \{1, \ldots, n\} : 0 \le i_k < s_k$$

We have

$$e \to < [\, s_1, \, \ldots, \, s_n], \, [\, d_1, \, \ldots, \, d_m] >$$
$$iv \to < [\, n], \, [\, i_1, \, \ldots, \, i_n] > \qquad \text{[VECT2OFFSET]}$$
$$\texttt{vect2offset}(\, iv, \, e) \to < [], \, [\, l\,] >$$

$$e \to < [\, s_1, \, \ldots, \, s_n], \, [\, d_1, \, \ldots, \, d_m] > \qquad \text{[IDXSEL]}$$
$$\texttt{idxsel}(\, \texttt{vect2offset}(\, iv, \, e), \, e) \to < [], \, [\, d_{l+1}] >$$
$$where \; l = \sum_{j=1}^{n} (i_j * \prod_{k=j+1}^{n} s_k)$$
$$\Longleftrightarrow \; \forall k \in \{1, \ldots, n\} : 0 \leq i_k < s_k \quad \wedge \quad 0 \leq l < m$$

All that remains to show is that the condition $0 \leq l < m$ is redundant. $0 \leq l$ follows directly from the definition of l and the requirement that $0 \leq i_k < s_k$ for all k. From the latter we can furthermore deduce that $l = \sum_{j=1}^{n} (i_j * \prod_{k=j+1}^{n} s_k) \leq$

$$\sum_{j=1}^{n} ((s_j - 1) * \prod_{k=j+1}^{n} s_k) = \sum_{j=1}^{n} (\prod_{k=j}^{n} s_k - \prod_{k=j+1}^{n} s_k) = \prod_{k=1}^{n} s_k - \prod_{k=n+1}^{n} s_k < \prod_{k=1}^{n} s_k = m.$$
$$q.e.d.$$

Once all offset computations are explicit, the three optimizations explained informally in the previous section can now be formalized.

4.2 Reusing Offset Computations

In order to reuse offset computations, we must identify expressions of the form $\texttt{vect2offset}(iv, \, A)$ and $\texttt{vect2offset}(iv, \, B)$ where the shapes of A and B are statically known to match. There are several ways to determine this equality. Once the shapes of A and B are statically known [9], equality can be statically decided. Even without the presence of static shape knowledge, shape equality often can be statically decided using inference techniques such as *Shape Clique Inference*, outlined in [10], or *Symbolic Array Attributes*, outlined in [11]. For our purposes here, we assume this information to be available.

Figure 5 shows the key rule of a transformation scheme REUSE that identifies such situations and replaces the second application of $\texttt{vect2offset}$ by the offset computed from the first one. The REUSE scheme maps SAC_λ programs and an environment S of identifier triples to a potentially modified program. Triples (iv, A, idx) each represent an existing definition of an offset idx by an application of $\texttt{vect2offset}$ to an index vector iv and an array A. The scheme starts out with an empty environment and traverses into all subexpressions. Whenever an application $\texttt{vect2offset}(iv, \, A)$ is found, the environment is searched for an entry (iv, B, idx) with $\texttt{shape}(B) = \texttt{shape}(A)$. If found, the application of $\texttt{vect2offset}$ is replaced by the variable idx, otherwise a new triple is appended to the end of S, denoted by $+\!\!+$ as symbol for concatenation. Note that our syntactic restrictions ensure that we always find identifiers in argument position.

$$\text{REUSE} \left[\!\!\left[\begin{array}{l} \texttt{let} \\ \quad Id = Expr, \ S \\ \texttt{in } Expr_b \end{array} \right]\!\!\right]$$

$$\rightsquigarrow \begin{cases} \begin{array}{ll} \texttt{let} & \text{if } Expr \equiv \texttt{vect2offset(} iv, \ A) \\ \quad Id = idx & \text{and } \exists < iv, \ B, \ idx> \ \in S \\ \texttt{in REUSE}[\![Expr_b, \ S]\!] & \text{with } shape(\ A) = shape(\ B) \\[1.5em] \texttt{let} & \text{if } Expr \equiv \texttt{vect2offset(} iv, \ A) \\ \quad Id = Expr & \text{and } \not\exists < iv, \ B, \ idx> \ \in S \\ \texttt{in REUSE}[\![Expr_b, \ S +\!\!+ < \ iv, \ A, \ Id >]\!] & \text{with } shape(\ A) = shape(\ B) \\[1.5em] \texttt{let} & \\ \quad Id = \texttt{REUSE}[\![Expr, \ S]\!] & \text{otherwise.} \\ \texttt{in REUSE}[\![Expr_b, \ S]\!] & \end{array} \end{cases}$$

Fig. 5. Reusing index computations

The soundness of this transformation follows almost directly from the shape equality predicate:

Theorem 2. REUSE *is sound wrt. the semantics of* SAC_λ.

Proof. Given a subexpression $\texttt{vect2offset(} iv, \ A)$. *From the definitions in Figure 5 we know that* $< iv, \ B, \ idx> \ \in S$, *iff we already encountered a subexpression of the form* idx = $\texttt{vect2offset(} iv, \ B)$ *while traversing the program. Given that* $\texttt{vect2offset(} iv, \ A) \rightarrow < [], \ [\ l \ ] >$ *and the shape equivalence of A and B, we can conclude that* $\texttt{vect2offset(} iv, \ B) \rightarrow < [], \ [\ l \ ] >$. *As all identifiers and* idx *in particular are unique, i.e. there is only a single assignment, it follows that* $idx \rightarrow < [], \ [\ l \ ] >$. $\hfill q.e.d.$

4.3 Reusing WITH-loop Offsets

The REUSE scheme introduced in the previous subsection only detects previous applications of `vect2offset` as potential reuse candidates. From our example in Section 3, we have seen that we often can reuse the offset for storing individual WITH-loop-computed elements into the overall WITH-loop-result. Due to the data-parallel nature of WITH-loops, this "assignment" and thus the required offset is not explicit in SAC_λ. We formalize this optimization on a higher level than the generated C-code by taking a similar approach as with the initial splitting of the `sel` operation. We transform our WITH-loops into a slightly lower-level variant `idxwith` that makes the "write-back-offset" explicit. Its syntax differs from that of standard WITH-loops only by an additional identifier within the generator. This second generator variable introduces a name for the write-back-offset which in the body of the WITH-loop can be referred to. The formal semantics of `idxwith` are given in Figure 6. As we can see from the semantics it is almost identical to that of the standard WITH-loop. In fact, the only difference is that

$$e_l \rightarrow < [\, n\,], [\, l_1, \ldots, l_n\,] >$$
$$e_u \rightarrow < [\, n\,], [\, u_1, \ldots, u_n\,] >$$
$$e_{shp} \rightarrow < [\, n\,], [\, shp_1, \ldots, shp_n\,] >$$
$$e_{def} \rightarrow < [\,], [\, d\,] >$$
$$\forall i_1 \in \{l_1, ..., u_1 - 1\} ... \forall i_n \in \{l_n, ..., u_n - 1\} :$$

IDXWITH :
$$(\lambda\, Id\,.(\lambda\, Idx\,.\, e_b\, p)\, [\; i_1,\; \ldots,\; i_n\,]) \rightarrow < [\,], \; d^{[i_1, \ldots, i_n]} >$$
$$\texttt{idxwith}(\; e_l \;\texttt{<=}\; Id, Idx \;\texttt{<}\; e_u) \;:\; e_b \;\texttt{genarray}(\; e_{shp},\; e_{def})$$
$$\rightarrow < [\, shp_1, \ldots, shp_n\,], [\; d^{[0, \ldots, 0]},\; \ldots,\; d^{[shp_1 - 1, \ldots, shp_n - 1]}\,] >$$
$$\text{where } d^{[x_1, \ldots, x_n]} = d$$
$$\text{iff } \exists j \in \{1, ..., n\} : x_j \in \{0, ..., l_j - 1\} \cup \{u_j, ..., shp_j - 1\}$$
$$\text{and } p = \sum_{j=1}^{n} (i_j * \prod_{k=j+1}^{n} shp_k)$$

Fig. 6. Further extended operational semantics for SAC_λ

$$
\text{REUSE}
\begin{bmatrix}
\begin{bmatrix}
\texttt{let} \\
\quad Id = \texttt{with}(\; lb \;\texttt{<=}\; iv < ub) : Expr_{body} \\
\qquad\qquad \texttt{genarray}(\; shp,\; def) \\
\texttt{in } Expr
\end{bmatrix}, S
\end{bmatrix}
$$

$$
\rightsquigarrow
\begin{array}{l}
\texttt{let} \\
\quad Id = \texttt{idxwith}(\; lb \;\texttt{<=}\; iv,\; wlidx < ub) : \\
\qquad\qquad \text{REUSE}[\![Expr_{body},\; S \texttt{++} < iv, Id, wlidx >]\!] \\
\qquad \texttt{genarray}(\; shp,\; def) \\
\quad \texttt{in REUSE}[\![Expr,\; S]\!]
\end{array}
$$

Fig. 7. Reusing WITH-loop offsets

the body expression e_b now is extended by two variable definitions rather than one: Id for the actual index vector and Idx for the corresponding write-back-offset.

Before we can try to use this new offset, we need to transform all WITH-loops accordingly. This is achieved by slightly extending the REUSE scheme from the previous section. The additional rule presented in Figure 7 replaces all standard WITH-loops by the new `idxwith`-version. Again, all introduced identifiers $wlidx$ need to be unique.

Whenever a WITH-loop is transformed, a new triplet is added to the environment containing the name of the index variable iv, the name of the array to be computed Id, and the write-back-offset $wlidx$ introduced by the `idxwith`-version of the WITH-loop. This information can then be used for the substitution of redundant `vect2offset` computations as described in the previous subsection.

Theorem 3. *The extended* REUSE *is sound wrt. the semantics of* SAC_λ.

Proof. Analog to Theorem 2.   *q.e.d.*

4.4   Splitting Offset Computations

In our motivating example, we have seen that splitting an offset computation whose index vector stems from a sum/difference of vectors into a sum/difference of offset computations often triggers further reuse or other optimizations such as LOOP-INVARIANT-REMOVAL [12]. With the offset computations being made explicit by the SPLIT scheme, we can now define another scheme SOC which detects such situations and transforms the offset computation accordingly. Similar to the REUSE scheme, the SOC scheme takes an additional parameter which carries quadruples consisting of 3 identifiers and one arithmetic operation; it collects these quadruples $(Id, LinOp, jv, kv)$, which represent an application of either + or - (denoted by $LinOp$) to two arrays jv and kv whose result is kept in a variable Id, while traversing through the program. Whenever the traversal finds an application of vect2offset to an identifier that is the first component of any of the quadruples seen so far, the code transformation is triggered. Figure 8 shows the main rule of the SOC scheme. Due to our restricted syntax both situations of interest are captured in the context of a let expression. If an addition or a subtraction is encountered, a new quadruple is inserted into the environment. Applications of vect2offset are only transformed if the index argument is known to be a sum/difference of vectors, i.e., if a quadruple with the index variable as first component is contained in the environment. Note here, that the scheme is applied recursively to the result of the transformation. This ensures that arbitrary nestings of index operations will be properly split. In all other cases, the transformation is applied to the subexpressions only.

$$
\mathrm{SOC}\left[\!\!\left[\begin{array}{l}\texttt{let}\\ \quad Id = Expr,\ E\\ \texttt{in}\ Expr_b\end{array}\right]\!\!\right]
$$

$$
\leadsto \left\{
\begin{array}{ll}
\begin{array}{l}\texttt{let}\\ \quad Id = Expr\\ \texttt{in}\ \mathrm{SOC}[\![Expr_b,\ E\ \cup\ <\ Id,\ LinOp,\ jv,\ kv\ >]\!]\end{array} & \begin{array}{l}\text{if } Expr \equiv\\ \quad LinOp(\ jv,\ kv),\end{array}\\[3em]
\mathrm{SOC}\left[\!\!\left[\begin{array}{l}\texttt{let}\\ \quad jv_{off} = \texttt{vect2offset}(\ jv,\ A)\\ \texttt{in let}\\ \qquad kv_{off} = \texttt{vect2offset}(\ kv,\ A),\ E\\ \quad\texttt{in let}\\ \qquad\quad Id = LinOp(\ jv_{off},\ kv_{off})\\ \qquad\texttt{in}\ Expr_b\end{array}\right]\!\!\right] & \begin{array}{l}\text{if } Expr \equiv\\ \quad \texttt{vect2offset}(\ iv,\ A)\\ \text{and}\\ \quad <\ iv,\ LinOp,\ jv,\ kv>\ \in E\end{array}\\[5em]
\begin{array}{l}\texttt{let}\\ \quad Id = Expr\\ \texttt{in}\ \mathrm{SOC}[\![Expr_b,\ E]\!]\end{array} & \text{otherwise.}
\end{array}
\right.
$$

Fig. 8. Splitting of vect2offset operations on linear combinations

Theorem 4. SOC *is sound wrt. the semantics of* SAC_λ.

Proof. The theorem follows immediately from Lemma 1.   *q.e.d.*

Although the transformation is correct wrt. the semantics of SAC_λ its application bears several problems.

Firstly, the semantics does not make any assumptions about the representation of the indices. However, Lemma 1 only holds for index vectors from $\mathbb{Z}^n$ not for finite subsets of $\mathbb{Z}^n$ such as n-element `integer`-vectors. Here, we may have to deal with overflow problems: while an expression `vect2offset( iv-cv, A)` may be within the limits of a given `integer` format, `vect2offset( iv, A)` or `vect2offset( cv, A)` may not. As a consequence, a transformed program may yield a runtime error although the untransformed one does not. The only way to avoid this problem is to restrict the transformation to those cases where we can statically prove that the offset computations are within the limits of the chosen index representation. It turns out that this is the frequent case as the indices are usually composed from a WITH-loop-generated index and a constant offset vector. For both of these, a static guarantee can be computed if the shape of the array to be selected from is statically known.

The second difficulty with this transformation stems from the fact that the transformation by itself leads to a code degradation if we are dealing with vectors of length ≥ 2: We replace a vector addition of an n-element vector (n operations) and an offset computation ($2*n-2$ operations) by one scalar operation and two offset computations ($4*n-4$ operations). Only the fact that this transformation often triggers other optimizations such as the REUSE scheme of the IVE or LOOP-INVARIANT-REMOVAL has a positive runtime effect. As a consequence, a conservative implementation needs to apply a reverse transformation if such sums of offset computations remain after an application of the aforementioned optimizations.

These considerations lead to the following order of transformations during IN-DEX-VECTOR-ELIMINATION: First, we apply the SPLIT-scheme in order to make the offsets explicit, followed by the SOC-scheme which may generate further offset computations. Then, we apply REUSE and LOOP-INVARIANT-REMOVAL in order to get rid of as many offset computations as possible. Finally, we revert those transformations of the SOC-scheme whose components have neither been eliminated nor have been moved by LOOP-INVARIANT-REMOVAL.

5   Performance

In our motivation example, we were able to save at least 70% of the arithmetic instructions within the inner loop by applying INDEX-VECTOR-ELIMINATION provided we were dealing with at least rank 2 arrays. Of course, this represents a best-case scenario, as we were able to remove all index computations. To get an idea of the impact of INDEX-VECTOR-ELIMINATION on real-world applications, we measured the performance gains archived by applying INDEX-VECTOR-ELIMINA-TION to two sets of benchmarks: The first set is taken from a SAC benchmark

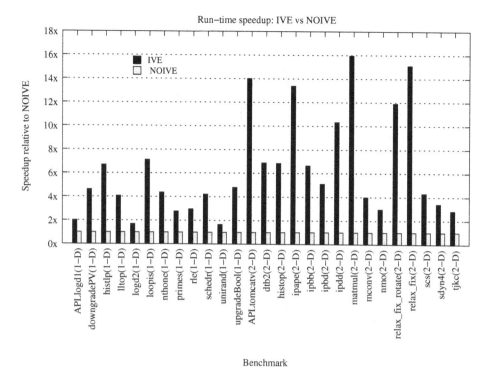

Fig. 9. Performance with and without IVE

suite that has previously been used for comparisons with FORTRAN, whereas the remainder are APL-derived, APEX-generated SAC programs. Our benchmark suite represents a mix of array ranks. However, all our benchmarks are either dominated by rank-1 or by rank-2 arrays.

5.1 Experimental Framework

We used an AMD-based platform (Opteron 165 (1.8GHz)) equipped with 4GB of RAM, operating SuSE Linux 10.1 64-bit. For compiling the SAC source code we used the current version of the `sac2c` compiler (rev 15076) with the GNU `gcc` compiler version 4.1.0 as the back-end compiler. We enabled the default set of optimizations, which include standard optimizations, such as COMMON-SUB-EXPRESSION-ELIMINATION, LOOP-INVARIANT-REMOVAL and LOOP-UNROLLING, as well as SAC-specific optimizations like WITH-LOOP FOLDING, WITH-LOOP SCALARIZATION and WITH-LOOP FUSION (for details on the default optimizations of SAC see [3]). The resulting C code was compiled using the `-O3` option of `gcc`.

To enable measurement of the impact of INDEX-VECTOR-ELIMINATION on the run time of each benchmark, we created one executable with INDEX-VECTOR-ELIMINATION enabled and one with that optimization disabled. We measured execution time using **user time** from the Linux `/usr/bin/time` function.

5.2 Analysis

Our results are presented in Figure 9. For each benchmark there are two bars: a black one representing the runtime with IVE enabled and a light gray one denoting the runtime with IVE disabled. Since the IVE-enabled times were always faster, we use the non-IVE times as a reference time, displaying speedups against that time rather than absolute runtimes. Higher black bars indicate higher runtime performance.

We sorted the benchmarks according to their dominant array rank: rank-1 examples are on the left; rank-2 ones are on the right. We can see that the rank-1 examples gain by a factor of 2 to 4 times. Since we know that rank-1 arrays cannot profit from any reuse or splitting of offset computations, this effect can be attributed to the avoidance of dynamic allocation of 1-element vectors. The stark variation in the effect derives from the differences in memory access/computation ratios found in the various benchmarks.

For the rank-2 examples, the gains vary even more. Here, our reuse optimizations and the offset computation splittings contribute as well, producing speedups between about 3 and 16 times. The gain in speedup *vs.* the rank-1 examples thus varies between a factor of 1.5 and 4, showing that our theoretical example falls nicely into that range.

6   Related Work

INDEX-VECTOR-ELIMINATION addresses a rather specific setting: the translation of n-dimensional selections specified as shape vectors into scalar offsets into linearized representations of n-dimensional arrays. This setting prevails in array languages such as APL, NIAL, and J. However, most of these languages have traditionally been interpreted, rather than compiled, because it was thought, for many years, that language semantics precluded effective application of optimizations such as INDEX-VECTOR-ELIMINATION. Of the several APL compiler projects that have been conducted, including [13,14,15,16,17,18], most do not achieve a very high-level of optimization. The APEX [18] compiler is the only project we are aware of that aims at utmost run-time efficiency. That run-time efficiency was enabled, in some degree, by the advent of Static Single Assignment, and the SISAL project. The former was a key factor in improving data flow analysis; the latter pushed the state of the art with respect to vector-oriented optimizations. Both of these ultimately had an impact on run-time code efficiency.

Although the SISAL compiler achieved very good run-time performance [19], a counterpart to INDEX-VECTOR-ELIMINATION was not required, as SISAL represents n-dimensional arrays as nestings of vectors. However, that run-time representation is less favorable for higher-dimensional problems, as described in [18,20]. These observations led to a proposal for *true n-dimensional arrays* in SISAL [21]. Although several implementation issues and optimizations on these linearized representations are described in [20,22] none of them pertains to IVE.

The APEX project recently switched from generating SISAL code to generating SAC code, to avoid fundamental algebraic limitations of nested vectors as a method of representing arrays. and in order to be able to make use of optimizations such as INDEX-VECTOR-ELIMINATION. In fact, run-time deficiencies of APEX-generated SAC-code partially triggered this research.

One key element of INDEX-VECTOR-ELIMINATION is the existence and use of a shape predicate as explained in Section 4. It can be derived from such techniques as *Shape Clique Analysis* [10] or *Symbolic Array Attributes* [11].

7   Conclusions

This paper presents INDEX-VECTOR-ELIMINATION, an optimization for avoiding run-time overhead arising from index vectors and their conversions into scalar offsets for linearized array representations. We describe three program traversals which, when orchestrated properly, for most examples, eliminate all index vectors within the innermost loop and reuse, to a large extent, offset computations. We formally describe the transformations, prove their soundness, and discuss their effectiveness in terms of arithmetic operations involved.

Although the run-time overhead may seem negligible, it turns out that nearly all array-dominated applications can benefit significantly from IVE. Our measurements for a set of benchmark kernels on a variety of array ranks show that speedups of 2 to 16 can be expected depending on the predominant array rank and the nature of the application.

Acknowledgments

We thank the anonymous referees for their valuable feedback and the European Union IST-FET research project Æther for funding this work. For more information on Æther, see www.aether-ist.org.

References

1. Iverson, K.E.: Notation as a tool of thought. Communications of the ACM vol. 23(8) (1979)
2. International Standards Organization: International Standard for Programming Language APL. ISO N8485 edn (1984)
3. Scholz, S.B.: Single Assignment C — efficient support for high-level array operations in a functional setting. Journal of Functional Programming 13(6), 1005–1059 (2003)
4. Hui, R.K., Iverson, K.E.: J Dictionary (1998)
5. Cann, D.: Compilation Techniques for High Performance Applicative Computation. Technical Report CS-89-108, Lawrence Livermore National Laboratory, LLNL, Livermore California (1989)
6. Cann, D., Evripidou, P.: Advanced Array Optimizations for High Performance Functional Languages. IEEE Transactions on Parallel and Distributed Systems 6(3), 229–239 (1995)

7. Grelck, C., Trojahner, K.: Implicit Memory Management for SaC. In: Grelck, C., Huch, F., Michaelson, G.J., Trinder, P. (eds.) IFL 2004. LNCS, vol. 3474, pp. 335–348. Springer, Heidelberg (2005)

8. Pierce, B.: Types and Programming Languages. MIT Press, Cambridge, ISBN 0-262-16209-1 (2002)

9. Grelck, C., Scholz, S.B., Shafarenko, A.: A Binding-Scope Analysis for Generic Programs on Arrays. In: Butterfield, A., Grelck, C., Huch, F. (eds.) IFL 2005. LNCS, vol. 4015, Springer, Heidelberg (2006)

10. Bernecky, R.: Shape Cliques. In: Horváth, Z., Zsók, V., eds.: Proceedings of the 18th International Symposium on Implementation of Functional Languages (IFL'06), Eötvös Loránd University (2006)

11. Trojahner, K., Grelck, C., Scholz, S.B.: On Optimising Shape-Generic Array Language Programs using Symbolic Structural Information. In: Horváth, Z., Zsók, V. (eds.) Proceedings of the 18th International Symposium on Implementation of Functional Languages (IFL'06). Revised Selected Papers, LNCS, vol. 4449, Springer, Heidelberg (2006)

12. Morel, E., Renvoise, C.: Global optimization by suppression of partial redundancies. Commun. ACM 22(2), 96–103 (1979)

13. Bernecky, R., Brenner, C., Jaffe, S.B., Moeckel, G.P.: ACORN: APL to C on real numbers. ACM SIGAPL Quote Quad 20(4), 40–49 (1990)

14. Weigang, J.: An Introduction to STSC's apl compiler. APL89 Conference Proceedings, ACM SIGAPL Quota Quad 15, 231–238 (1989)

15. Ching, W.M.: An APL/370 compiler and some performance comparisons with APL interpreter and FORTRAN. ACM SIGAPL Quote Quad 16(4), 143–147 (1986)

16. Wiedmann, C.: Field results with the APL compiler. ACM SIGAPL Quote Quad 16(4), 187–196 (1986)

17. Budd, T.A.: An APL compiler for the UNIX timesharing system. ACM SIGAPL Quote Quad 13(3) (1983)

18. Bernecky, R.: APEX: The APL parallel executor. Master's thesis, University of Toronto (1997)

19. Cann, D.: The Optimizing SISAL Compiler: Version 12.0. Lawrence Livermore National Laboratory, LLNL, Livermore California. Part of the SISAL distribution (1993)

20. Oldehoeft, R.: Implementing Arrays in SISAL 2.0. In: Proceedings of the Second SISAL Users' Conference. pp. 209–222 (1992)

21. Böhm, A., Cann, D., Oldehoeft, R., Feo, J.: SISAL Reference Manual Language Version 2.0. CS 91-118, Colorado State University, Fort Collins, Colorado (1991)

22. Fitzgerald, S., Oldehoeft, R.: Update-in-place Analysis for True Multidimensional Arrays. In: Böhm, A., Feo, J., eds.: High Performance Functional Computing. pp. 105–118 (1995)

Functional–Based Synthesis
of a Systolic Array for GCD Computation

Laura Ruff[1] and Tudor Jebelean[2]

[1] Babeş-Bolyai University Cluj
laura@cs.ubbcluj.ro
[2] RISC-Linz
tjebelea@risc.uni-linz.ac.at

Abstract. We synthesise a systolic pass-through array for the computation of the greatest common divisor (GCD) of multiple precision integers. The synthesis method uses the conceptual similarity between the inductive structure of a systolic array (a head processor followed by an identical tail array) and the inductive decomposition of the argument by a functional program. By formal analysis, we identify the structure of the functions which can be realized by pass-through arrays. Then, by equational rewriting, we transform the expression of the list function which must be realized into an expression having the required structure. The resulting expression reveals the scalar function which must be implemented by each individual processor.

1 Introduction

Systolic parallelisation of GCD computation was quite challenging, because the traditional *Euclidean algorithm* is not appropriate for systolic computations, since it works in most–significant–digits–first (MSF) manner. The first systolic device was developed in [1] using an improvement of the least–significant–digits–first (LSF) *binary GCD algorithm* of [8], namely the *plus–minus algorithm*. A slight improvement of the latter is presented in [5] together with its systolic implementation in a parallel–serial fashion (input parallel, output serial). It turns out that a serial version (pass-through auto-configurable array with pre-processed input) is much simpler to realize in hardware [6]. The array synthesised in this paper is an extension of the latter, as it additionally detects termination.

The literature on [semi]automatic synthesis of systolic arrays is abundant. However, most of these methods (see a short survey in [7] or in [9]) follow an *iterative view* of systolic arrays (and computations): the arrays (and the computations) are represented as [multidimensional] matrices of a certain size (many methods only work for a fixed size). This leads to complex operations over the multidimensional index space, and to many repetitions in the synthesis process.

In this paper we use a *functional view* (or inductive view): an infinite systolic array is composed of a *head processor* and an identical *tail array*. Similarly, functional programs for list operations are usually described in terms of the

Z. Horváth, V. Zsók, and A. Butterfield (Eds.): IFL 2006, LNCS 4449, pp. 37–54, 2007.
© Springer-Verlag Berlin Heidelberg 2007

head and the tail of the argument. By exploiting this similarity, we demonstrate on the GCD algorithm that the synthesis problem can be solved by [essentially] rewriting of the functional programs. This approach has been pioneered in our previous paper [7], where we presented the synthesis of *online systolic arrays* for the multiplication of polynomials and integers.

The concrete synthesis process is based on a formal study of the structure of the functions which can be realized by systolic arrays. *A scalar* function – that is, a function which takes a fixed set of scalars and produces a fixed set of scalars – can be realized by an individual processor without internal state. We are interested in synthesising *list functions* – that is, functions which take a list of scalars and produce a list of scalars (in fact, each element of these lists may be a fixed set of scalars). For instance, by pipelining a list through an individual processing element (PE), one realizes a list function, which we call the *transitive extension* of the scalar function realized by the respective processor. Of course, not all list functions can be realized in such a way. More complex functions can be realized by using a feed back of the output into the input (this leads to a processor with internal state). Moreover, the internal state can store a fixed set of previous inputs, and furthermore one can construct an array of such processors in which the communication is unidirectional. The list function realized by any of such devices satisfies certain equations which involve the scalar function of the individual processors and certain "standard" list functions (like *head* and *tail*).

We express the algorithm for GCD computation as a recursive list function, and then we transform the respective expression by systematic rules until it fits to the equations found above. This transformation process also reveals the scalar functions which describe the behaviour of the individual processors in the array.

The method works completely automatically and it is implemented in the *Theorema* system (www.theorema.org) [2], basically as a set of rewrite rules, together with a simulator which allows the visualisation of concrete computations. The *Theorema* system is a mathematical assistant developed at RISC–Linz under the supervision of B. Buchberger, and combines facilities for proving, solving, and computing for the purpose of exploring mathematical theories and algorithms.

2 Formal Background

In order to make the paper [as much as possible] self–contained, we repeat here the description of the main concepts from [7], however with some significant additions: definition of regular and of transitive functions and some of their basic properties.

2.1 Scalars and Lists

Both the systolic arrays and the functional programs which we consider in this paper act upon lists (finite or infinite) of fixed-size objects.

A fixed-size object is an object of a *scalar type*: a scalar type is an elementary type or a fixed-size tuple of scalar types. An elementary type (such as a finite set of symbols or a fixed-precision number type) can have only a finite number of instantiations. A fixed-size object will be called a *scalar*.

A *list type* over a certain scalar type characterises all the tuples (finite and infinite) of objects of that scalar type. A *list* is an object of a certain list type.

The length of a list X is denoted by $\|X\|$ and it is ∞ if the list is infinite.

We will denote by a^n the list of n elements all equal to a and by a^∞ the infinite constant list with elements a.

For any list $X = \langle x_0, x_1, \ldots, x_n, \ldots \rangle$, we denote by $H[X] = x_0$ the *head* of it, and by $T[X] = \langle x_1, \ldots, x_n, \ldots \rangle$ the *tail* of it. The kth tail of X: $T_k[X] = \langle x_k, x_{k+1}, \ldots, x_n, \ldots \rangle$ is obtained by iterating T k times and removes the first k elements of X. By convention, $T_0[X] = X$, and note that $T_1 = T$. The kth head of X is $H_k[X] = H[T_k[X]]$ and gives the $(k+1)^{\text{th}}$ element of X (thus $H_0 = H$).

The *prefix* of order n of a list is $P_n[X] = \langle x_0, \ldots, x_{n-1} \rangle$, that is, it selects the first n elements of the list.

The *concatenation* of two lists is denoted by "$\smile$":

$$\langle a_0, a_1, \ldots, a_k \rangle \smile X = \langle a_0, a_1, \ldots, a_k, x_0, x_1, \ldots \rangle.$$

The first operand must be finite, but the second may also be infinite. We also use "$\smile$" for *prepending* a scalar to a (finite or infinite) list: $a \smile X = \langle a \rangle \smile X$.

Since in practice one actually uses only finite lists, we consider here only lists having a finite number of "interesting" values. Namely, we use (as in the theory of cellular automata) a special *quiescent symbol* "$" (which belongs to all scalar types) in order to encode the "blank" values. Thus, an infinite list will start to have only blank values after a certain finite number of elements. Furthermore we will not allow "$" to be interspersed among other elements, however we allow a list to start with a certain number of blanks.

2.2 Functions

Functions from scalar types to scalar types will be called *scalar functions*. Informally, scalar functions can be computed in constant time.

Functions from list types to list types will be called *list functions*. We will consider *only list functions acting upon infinite lists and producing infinite lists*.

We assume that our scalar functions produce blanks when applied to blanks, and our list functions are producing lists of blanks when applied to lists of blanks.

Since we have in mind concrete computations over lists, it is reasonable to consider those list functions F whose values can be computed in an incremental fashion: the values of any finite prefix of $F[X]$ can always be computed from some finite prefix of X:

Definition. A function F on infinite lists is called *regular* iff, for any natural n, there exists a natural m, such that for any list X of length $n + m$, and for any infinite lists Y, Y':

$$P_n[F[X \smile Y]] = P_n[F[X \smile Y']] \ .$$

The minimal m as above is called the *regularity index* of F, denoted $r_F[n]$.

A function whose regularity index is constant is called *look–ahead* function. The constant $r_F[n] = k$ is called the *look–ahead* index. We also use the term *k–look–ahead* function for a look–ahead function whose look–ahead index is k.

A 0–look–ahead function is called *online* function. That is, the nth value of an online function depends only on the first n elements of the input.

Hereafter we will consider only list functions which are regular and look–ahead.

Note that for an online function, the regularity condition for $n = 0$ is:

$$H[F[x \smile X]] = H[F[x \smile X']],$$

thus one may define the function $F_H[x] = H[F[x \smile \$^\infty]]$. F_H is called the scalar projection of the online function F, and obviously:

$$F_H[x] = H[F[x \smile X]] \quad \text{and} \quad F[x \smile X] = F_H[x] \smile T[F[x \smile X]].$$

However, one must take care that only online functions have a scalar projection.

A special rôle will be played by list functions which commute with T:

$$F[T[X]] = T[F[X]], \quad \text{or simply} \quad FT = TF.$$

We will call these functions *transitive*.

For online transitive functions we have: $F[x \smile X] = F_H[x] \smile F[X]$, thus the function F is "constructed" by its scalar projection F_H. In other words, if one has a scalar function f, one can construct its *transitive extension* $\mathbf{f}$ by

$$\mathbf{f}[x \smile X] = f[x] \smile \mathbf{f}[X].$$

From this follows:

Property 1. An online function is transitive if and only if it is the transitive extension of its scalar projection.

2.3 Functional Programs

A program describing a scalar function f is an expression involving elementary scalar functions (considered as "known"): $f[x] = E$. (Note that we use square brackets for function application, but we will sometimes omit them when the context is sufficiently clear.) A program describing a list function F must indicate how to compute the result, by starting from the tail and the head of the argument: $F[x \smile X] = \mathcal{E}[x, X]$, where $\mathcal{E}$ is a mixed (scalar–list) expression involving already known functions, but also F. The simplest definitions have the shape: $F[x \smile X] = E[x] \smile \mathcal{E}[X]$, where E is a scalar–and $\mathcal{E}$ is a list–expression.

Note that the syntactic restriction to one argument (and one value) is not essential. Indeed, a multiple scalar can be assigned a new scalar type, and a multiple list can be seen as single list by transposition:

$$\langle x \smile X, \; y \smile Y, \ldots \rangle^T = \langle x, y, \ldots \rangle^T \smile \langle X, Y, \ldots \rangle^T.$$

Therefore functions with mixed-type (scalar and list) argument and/or mixed-type value reduce to functions taking one scalar and one list and producing one scalar and one list. The most general case is:

$$F[x, y \smile Y] = \langle E[x, y], \mathcal{E}'[x, y, Y] \rangle \ .$$

For the sake of presentation, in the sequel we will use sometimes functions having multiple arguments, however these are understood to be of the form exhibited above. That is, if several scalars occur as arguments, the function is assumed to have only one scalar argument, which is the transposed of the tuple of those scalars. Similarly, if several lists occur as arguments, the function is assumed to have only one list argument, which is the transposed of the tuple of those list arguments.

Unfolding: A very important transformation of expressions describing list functions is unfolding. This consists in isolating the scalar expression which represents the first element of the list computed by the list function, by transformations of the expression of the function. The transformations use certain straightforward unfolding rules (presented in more detail in [7]), as well as the functional definitions of the functions which occur in the expressions. The examples presented in the rest of this paper illustrate this transformation, and also give a hint that it is relatively easy to implement as a set of equational rewrite rules.

Unfolding provides a systematic method for the detection of online transitive functions: if we manage to transform the expression of $F[x \smile X]$ into the expression $E[x] \smile \mathcal{E}[x, X]$, then the function is online and $E[x]$ is its scalar projection. Moreover, the function is transitive if and only if $F[X] = \mathcal{E}[x, X]$.

3 GCD Computation

Let $a = a_0 + 2 * a_1 + 2^2 * a_2 + \dots$ and $b = b_0 + 2 * b_1 + 2^2 * b_2 + \dots$ be two integers expressed in radix two. We use the lists of digits as representations of the numbers, and we assume that the least significant digits are at the beginning. The lists may be considered infinite, since padding zeroes at the end of the finite representation does not change the value of the number. In fact, the GCD algorithm below may produce intermediate negative values, and it is designed for numbers in *complement representation*. The representation of a negative number will be padded with ones.

The *PlusMinus* algorithm for GCD computation (from [5], which improves [1], which is based on [8]) proceeds in three steps:

First step: We remove the common least significant null digits of a and b and obtain a_s and b_s, that is, we divide both a and b by the same power of 2, say 2^k. The GCD of these numbers, $GCD' = GCD(a_s, b_s)$ is called the "pseudo-GCD" of a and b, and obviously $GCD = 2^k * GCD'$, and GCD' is not divisible by 2.

Our systolic device will perform this operation, and then compute the pseudo-GCD, but will not handle the computation of k, neither the multiplication by 2^k. In a practical situation, it is reasonable to assume that the systolic array is under the control of some main device (either a usual computer or some other complex hardware), which supplies the input operands and collects the result. We assume that the final multiplication (in fact a shift) by 2^k is performed by this main device, and also one sees that it is straightforward to add to the systolic array a counter which identifies the value of k and sends it to the main device.

Second step: We interchange a_s and b_s if necessary, such that the least significant digit of a_s is 1. This is an invariant throughout the rest of the algorithm, which simplifies the operations.

Third step: We calculate now the pseudo GCD of a and b (the a and b from the following algorithm are actually the a_s and b_s obtained in the previous steps).

$$GCD[a, b] = a, \text{ if } b = 0 \tag{1}$$

$$= GCD\left[a, \frac{b}{2}\right], \text{ if } b_0 = 0 \tag{2}$$

$$= GCD\left[b, \frac{a+b}{4}\right], \text{ if } (b_0 = 1) \wedge (a_1 \neq b_1) \tag{3}$$

$$= GCD\left[b, \frac{a-b}{4}\right], \text{ if } (b_0 = 1) \wedge (a_1 = b_1) \tag{4}$$

The last three transformations are correct because the pseudo GCD is not divisible by 2. Note also that these transformations preserve the invariant $(a_0 = 1)$, thus a cannot become 0 (therefore $GCD[0, b] = b$ is not necessary).

Termination follows from the decrease of maximum of the significant lengths of a and b. Indeed, by adding or subtracting the arguments in the respective cases, the last two bits of the numbers always become zero. Since the sum or the difference will be at most one bit longer, after two shifts it will become one bit shorter. (The full details of the analysis are presented in [4].)

Note that the usage of complement arithmetic is essential for the correct implementation of this algorithm. Indeed, since only the least significant digits of a and b are inspected, it is not known which is greater, thus at a certain moment one or both of the arguments may be negative.

4   Systolic Processors

We use the term "systolic processor" for designating just a fixed size[1] processor, with or without internal memory. In this section we study the behaviour of several types of such processors, namely we investigate the properties of the functions which are realized by them.

4.1   Systolic Processor Without Internal State

This is the simplest building block of a systolic array. The processor depicted in Fig. 1 receives as input the list $X = \langle x_0, x_1, x_2, \ldots \rangle$ and computes the output

---

[1] As opposed to an *arbitrary size* systolic array.

list $Y = \langle y_1, y_2 \ldots \rangle$. The transition function, that is the computation performed by the processor at each time step is f, such that $y_{t+1} = f[x_t]$, for $t = 0, 1, 2, \ldots$. If the processor computes $Y = F[X]$, then its functioning is characterised by:

$$F[x \,\overset{\cdot}{\smile}\, X] = f[x] \,\overset{\cdot}{\smile}\, F[X] \; . \tag{5}$$

From the discussion in the previous section, it follows that the class of functions which can be realized by a systolic stateless processor is exactly the class of online transitive functions.

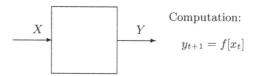

Computation:

$$y_{t+1} = f[x_t]$$

Fig. 1. Systolic processor without internal state

Problem: Find f, when F is given.
Method: Unfold F and if the result is an equation of the form (5), then f is found by projection.

Example 1. *Polynomial addition.*
Let A, B be the list of the coefficients of two univariate polynomials (least degree first, padded with $ at the end). We want to compute $F[A, B] = A + B$.

We unfold F:

$$F[A, B] = (a_0 \,\overset{\cdot}{\smile}\, A_1) + (b_0 \,\overset{\cdot}{\smile}\, B_1) = (a_0 \,\overset{\cdot\cdot}{+}\, b_0) \,\overset{\cdot}{\smile}\, F[A_1, B_1] \; . \tag{6}$$

Equation (6) is of the form (5), thus we conclude that the transition function should be $f[a, b] = a \,\overset{\cdot\cdot}{+}\, b$. (Where $ \,\overset{\cdot\cdot}{+}\, x = x \,\overset{\cdot\cdot}{+}\, \$ = x$).

4.2   Systolic Processor with Internal State

The architecture of a systolic processor with internal state, depicted in Fig. 2 has as additional element the internal state register r. The list of values of the internal state register is denoted by R.

The output list Y computed by the processor is characterised by the equation:

$$F[r, x \,\overset{\cdot}{\smile}\, X] = f_y[r, x] \,\overset{\cdot}{\smile}\, F[f_r[r, x], X] \; . \tag{7}$$

We denote by $G[R, X]$ the function computed by the array, that includes all the values of the internal state:

$$G[r \,\overset{\cdot}{\smile}\, R, x \,\overset{\cdot}{\smile}\, X] = \langle f_y[r, x], f_r[r, x] \rangle \,\overset{\cdot}{\smile}\, G[R, X] \; . \tag{8}$$

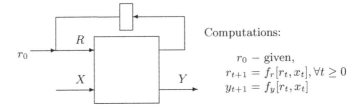

Fig. 2. Systolic processor with internal state register

One notes that G is the transitive extension of $g[r, x] = \langle f_y[r, x], f_r[r, x] \rangle$.
Such a PE is similar to one without internal state, but having input $\langle R, X \rangle$.

Problem: Find $F[r, X]$, r_0, f_y and f_r, when $F'[X]$ is given, such that (7) holds
and $F'[X] = F[r_0, X]$.

Method: We first unfold $F'[X]$:
$F'[x \smile X] = f'[x] \smile \mathcal{F}'[x, F'[X]]$. From $\mathcal{F}'$ we guess F and r_0, then we unfold F.

Example 2. *Integer addition.*
*Let A, B be the list of digits of two arbitrary large integers (least significant digits
first) in some radix β. We want to compute the function $F'[A, B] = A + B$.*

$$F'[A, B] = (a_0 \stackrel{..}{+} b_0)_{mod\beta} \smile (\underbrace{\lfloor \frac{a_0 \stackrel{..}{+} b_0}{\beta} \rfloor \stackrel{.}{+} A_1 + B_1)}_{F} \ .$$

The result of unfolding suggests for F the form $F[c, A, B] = c \stackrel{.}{+} (A + B)$.

$$F[c, A, B] = (a_0 \stackrel{..}{+} b_0 \stackrel{..}{+} c)_{mod\beta} \smile (\lfloor \frac{a_0 \stackrel{..}{+} b_0 \stackrel{..}{+} c}{\beta} \rfloor \stackrel{.}{+} A_1 + B_1) \ .$$

From here we have

$$f_y[c, a, b] = (a \stackrel{..}{+} b \stackrel{..}{+} c)_{mod\beta}$$
$$f_c[c, a, b] = \lfloor \frac{a \stackrel{..}{+} b \stackrel{..}{+} c}{\beta} \rfloor$$

The initial value $c_0 = 0$ is obtained from $F[c_0, A, B] = F'[A, B]$.

4.3   Systolic Processor with Delay

For a positive constant k, let us consider functions $F[X]$ having the property:

$$F[X] \ = \ G[X, T[X], T[T[X]], \ldots, T_k[X]] \ . \tag{9}$$

for some online transitive function G. We show now that such a function can be
computed by a so called systolic processor with k-delay.

Since G can be computed by a single processor, we only need to use k input channels for the shifted elements of the same input X.

One can in fact avoid the multiplication of the input by introducing k transition registers, denoted by $dx|1|, dx|2|, \ldots, dx|k|$, which perform the computation shown on Fig. 3. This solution will result in a delay of the result with k steps.

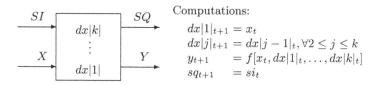

Computations:
$$dx|1|_{t+1} = x_t$$
$$dx|j|_{t+1} = dx|j-1|_t, \forall 2 \leq j \leq k$$
$$y_{t+1} = f[x_t, dx|1|_t, \ldots, dx|k|_t]$$
$$sq_{t+1} = si_t$$

Fig. 3. Systolic processor with k-delay

We denote the initial values of the transition registers $dx|1|, dx|2|, \ldots, dx|k|$ with $x_{-1} = T_{-1}[X], x_{-2} = T_{-2}[X], \ldots, x_{-k} = T_{-k}[X]$ respectively. These are blank values, which do not contribute to the computation of the result.

Register $dx|k|$ realizes the list X_{-k}, $dx|k-1|$ the list $X_{-(k-1)}$ and so on..., finally $dx|1|$ realizes the list X_{-1}, while the input x generates the list X. However such a processor can output the first result only beginning with the $k+1^{th}$ time step. If we consider the generated list expressions after k steps, then register $dx|k|$ can be associated with the list $T_k[X_{-k}] = X$, register $dx|k-1|$ with the list $T_k[X_{-(k-1)}] = T[X] \ldots$, register $dx|1|$ with the list $T_k[X_{-1}] = T_{k-1}[X]$ and the input x with the list $T_k[X]$.

The processor has an output y at each time step, but in case of this processor-type the first "interesting" output appears only at the $k+1^{th}$ time step. If the constant k is known, one can obtain the result by simply dropping the first k elements of Y (that is one considers only $T_k[Y]$), but a more general solution is to introduce a control signal S that indicates the appearance of the real results.

The elements of the control signal SI are output unchanged at the next time step (SQ) as shown on Fig. 3. The the first $k-1$ elements of the SI input representing the control signal are 0, while the other elements starting with the kth one are 1, thus an output y at time step t is considered to be a valid output if the corresponding sq_t is 1.

Problem: Find the scalar projection of G, when $F[X] = G[X, T[X], \ldots T_k[X]]$ is given.

Method: Unfold F and verify that the result has property (9).

Introduce the transition registers $dx|1|, \ldots, dx|k|$ and add the control signal SI, then project the occurrence of $T_k[X]$ into register x, and all occurrences of $T_i[X]$ $(0 \leq i \leq k-1)$ into the corresponding transition register $dx|k-i|$ to find f.

Note that some of the arguments $X, T[X], \ldots, T_{k-1}[X]$ could also be missing. In this case we only need the transition registers from the one corresponding to $T_{k-1}[X]$ to the register associated with $T_{min}[X]$.

In the case when $F[X] = G[T_k[X]]$ no transition register is needed, but the control signal still can be used to indicate the appearance of the first result.

Example 3. *The shift operation.*
Let $X = \langle A, B \rangle$ be the input consisting of two lists, and let $Y = \langle A, T_2[B] \rangle$ be the desired output.

By using the selector functions $F_A[X] = A$ and $F_B[X] = B$, the result is expressed as $Y = \langle F_A[X], F_B[T_2[X]] \rangle$. Since both F_A and F_B have property (5), it results that $F[X, T_2[X]] = \langle F_A[X], F_B[T_2[X]] \rangle$ has property (9).

Because in this example $k = 2$, we introduce two transition registers $dx|1|$ and $dx|2|$ (each of them has a component for A and B, thus we also can talk about four registers denoted by $da|1|$, $db|1|$, $da|2|$ and $db|2|$. Similarly we can see the input channels a and b, being the two components of the input x).

By projecting X into $dx|2|$ and $T_2[X]$ into the input channel x we get the computations performed by the processor: $y = \langle F_A[dx|2|], F_B[x] \rangle$. In other terms: $y = \langle da|2|, b \rangle$. The list corresponding to the control signal is $SI = \langle 0, 0, 1, 1, 1, \ldots \rangle$.

4.4   Auto-Configurable Systolic Processor (with Delay)

Let us suppose that $F[X]$ depends on a fixed length (say k) prefix of X. That is, $F[X] = G[\langle H[X], H_1[X], \ldots, H_{k-1}[X] \rangle, T_k[X]]$, where G has the property

$$G[a, x \smile X] = g[a, x] \smile G[a, X]. \tag{10}$$

Note that in the case of a mixed type function $G[a, X]$, this property can be rewritten (by considering the scalar a as a parameter) as:

$$G_a[x \smile X] = g_a[x] \smile G_a[X],$$

which is of the form of (5) – thus G_a is the transitive extension of g_a.

We used the notation $a = \langle H[X], H_1[X], \ldots, H_{k-1}[X] \rangle$, in order to write the property (10) in the form of (5), however this means that the processor "knows" the $H[X], H_1[X], \ldots H_{k-1}[X]$ scalar values, or at least these values are preloaded in some local registers of the processor. Alternatively, we can use k static registers (denoted by $x|0|$, $x|1|$, $\ldots x|k-1|$, as shown on Fig. 4) that will store the first k values of the input, then beginning with the $k+1^{th}$ time step the "interesting" results start to appear on the output.

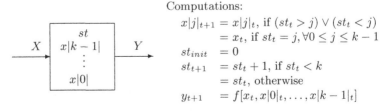

Computations:
$$x|j|_{t+1} = x|j|_t, \text{ if } (st_t > j) \vee (st_t < j)$$
$$= x_t, \text{ if } st_t = j, \forall 0 \le j \le k-1$$
$$st_{init} = 0$$
$$st_{t+1} = st_t + 1, \text{ if } st_t < k$$
$$= st_t, \text{ otherwise}$$
$$y_{t+1} = f[x_t, x|0|_t, \ldots, x|k-1|_t]$$

Fig. 4. Systolic processor that computes $F[x_0, x_1, \ldots, x_{k-1}, T_k[X]]$

A static register $x|j|$ stores the input x at time step $t = j$, then it keeps its value unchanged. As the PE is not aware of the time, a state register st is introduced, initialized with 0, then incremented at each time step up to the value of k.

An *auto-configurable processor* constitutes a particular case of such processors: If in the expression of the function $G[\langle x_0, x_1, \ldots, x_{k-1}\rangle, T_k[X]]$ the scalars x_0, x_1, ..., x_{k-1} do not contribute directly to the computation of the result, they are only used to verify whether a condition holds or not, then the functioning of the processor can be optimized by introducing a state register s. Rather then verifying the condition at each time step, the state register s will be set at the kth time step according to the condition that depends on $x_0, x_1, \ldots, x_{k-1}$. Afterwards, beginning with time step $k + 1$ (when the first interesting result should be computed), the result will depend on the value of the state register s which does not change anymore. (Thus the respective PE is "configured" to perform a certain operation.)

Note that in this case we actually do not need the values $x_0, x_1, \ldots, x_{k-1}$ after the kth time step, so it is useless to store them. In this case we can use transition registers instead of static registers, and the state register st is not needed. $k - 1$ transition registers are sufficient, then in the kth time step $H_{k-1}[X] = x_{k-1}$ is input to the processor, while x_0, x_1, ..., x_{k-2} are stored in the transition registers $dx|k - 2|$, $dx|k - 3|$, ..., $dx|1|$, respectively. At this time step the state register s can be set according to the first k values of X, then beginning with the $k + 1^{th}$ step the results can be computed in function of the state register's value.

Except for the state register, the processor is functioning just like a processor with $k - 1$-delay, that is, it also can compute a function of the form $F[x_0, \ldots, x_{k-1}, X, T[X], \ldots, T_{k-1}[X]]$ (with the restriction that in the case of the first $k - 1$ elements of the result – $H_j[F], 0 \leq j \leq k - 1$ – the jth result depends only on the first j elements of the input, that is on $x_0, \ldots x_j$, the state register is not involved). Thus we can call it auto-configurable systolic processor with $k - 1$ delay. Moreover an auto-configurable processor, that sets its state register according to the first k values of the input can be combined wit a processor with m-delay. The number of transition registers used should be $max(k - 1, m)$.

The question is how does the processor know when the state register s should be set. This problem can be solved by using the same control signal SI as in the case of a PE with delay. The list of input signals SI will have $k - 2$ leading 0 elements, then starting with position $k - 1$ the value of the elements will be 1 and the first 1 value will indicate the moment when s has to be set. The state register s is initialized with a blank value, denoted by $\$$.

The computations performed by such a processor are shown on Fig. 5.

Problem:
Find $f = \langle g_y, g_{cond}\rangle$, when $F[X] = G[x_0, \ldots, x_{k-1}, (X, T[X], \ldots,)T_k[X]]$ is given, such that for G the property (5) (respectively property (9)) holds.

Method: Unfold F and verify that the appropriate property holds.

Introduce the $k - 1$ transition registers.

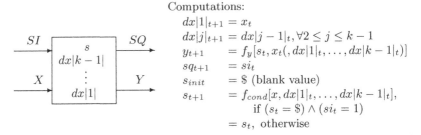

Computations:

$$dx|1|_{t+1} = x_t$$
$$dx|j|_{t+1} = dx|j-1|_t, \forall 2 \leq j \leq k-1$$
$$y_{t+1} = f_y[s_t, x_t(, dx|1|_t, \ldots, dx|k-1|_t)]$$
$$sq_{t+1} = si_t$$
$$s_{init} = \$ \text{ (blank value)}$$
$$s_{t+1} = f_{cond}[x, dx|1|_t, \ldots, dx|k-1|_t],$$
$$\quad \text{if } (s_t = \$) \wedge (si_t = 1)$$
$$= s_t, \text{ otherwise}$$

Fig. 5. Auto-configurable systolic processor (with $k-1$-delay)

g_{cond} is a function that associates to "if" statements integer values from $\{1, 2, \ldots m\}$, where m is the number of different cases that depend on $x_0, x_1, \ldots, x_{k-1}$ in the definition of F.

Obtain g_y by projection. Each "if $cond_i(x_0, x_1, \ldots, x_{k-1})$" statement is projected to a corresponding "if $s = i$" statement. (The other projection rules are similar to the rules for processors with delay.)

Neither of the following two examples is a typical one, but we will use them in building up the systolic array for GCD computation. A more complex example for such a processor is presented in Sect. 6.

Example 4. *Conditional exchange.*
Let $X = \langle A, B \rangle$ be the input consisting of two lists. The input should be transformed into $\langle B, A \rangle$ only if a_0 equals a certain constant α.

Using $F_A[X] = A$ and $F_B[X] = B$ we can write:

$$F[H[X], X] = \langle F_B[X], F_A[X] \rangle, \text{ if } F_A[H[X]] = \alpha$$
$$= X, \qquad\qquad\qquad \text{if } F_A[H[X]] \neq \alpha$$

Both F_A and F_B have property (5), so one can easily verify that $F_{H[X]}$ also satisfies property (5). Because $k = 1$ no transition register is needed, but because F depends on X, the first output will already appear at the first time step, at the same moment when the state register s is set.

The function F involves two "if"-statements. The first one will be projected to $s = 1$ and the second one to $s = 2$. The computations performed by the processor are described on Fig. 6. For the list of results we use the notation $Y = \langle Y_A, Y_B \rangle$. The list corresponding to the control signal is $SI = \langle 1, 1, \ldots \rangle$

Example 5. *Deleting the least significant zeroes.*
Let $A = \langle a_0, a_1, \ldots \rangle$ be the list representation of a binary integer. We want to cut off the least significant zeroes of A, which means we want to compute $Y = F[A] = T_k[A]$ such that $H_k[A] = 1$ and $H_j[A] = 0, \forall 0 \leq j \leq k-1$.

The first remark is that here only the kth tail of the input appears in the computation of the result, which means that we do not need any transition register.

Computations:

$$y_{t+1} = \langle b_t, a_t \rangle, \text{ if } (s_t = 1) \vee ((s_t = \$) \wedge (a_t = exch))$$
$$= \langle a_t, b_t \rangle, \text{ if } (s_t = 2) \vee ((s_t = \$) \wedge (a_t \neq exch))$$
$$sq_{t+1} = si_t$$
$$s_{init} = \$$$
$$s_{t+1} = 1 \qquad \text{if } (s_t = \$) \wedge (si_t = 1) \wedge (a_t = exch)$$
$$= 2 \qquad \text{if } (s_t = \$) \wedge (si_t = 1) \wedge (a_t \neq exch)$$
$$= s_t, \qquad \text{otherwise}$$

SI, *SQ*, *A*, *s*, *YA*, *B*, *YB*

Fig. 6. Auto-configurable systolic processor for the input-exchange problem

The second remark is that here k is not known in advance, but it can be computed in function of the input, which induces a slight modification in the computation of the control signal that indicates the appearance of the first result, respectively in the computation of the state register s: both of them will be computed in function of the input A rather then using the input SI. The output SQ is computed in the following way:

$$sq_{t+1} = 0 \text{ , if } (s_t = \$) \wedge (x_t = 0)$$
$$= 1 \text{ , if } (s_t \neq \$) \vee (x_t = 1)$$

The computations for s are:

$$s_{t+1} = 1, \text{ if } (s_t = \$) \wedge (x_t = 1)$$
$$= s_t, \text{ if } (s_t \neq \$) \vee (x_t = 0)$$

The first 1 value of SQ indicates the beginning of the output.

$T_k[A]$ is projected to the input register a, thus the computation of the result (we denote the output register associated to it with y) is very simple: $y_{t+1} = a_t$.

5   Unidirectional Pass–Through Array

An unidirectional array consists of processing elements (PEs) that modify the input and send the result to the next PEs in serial manner.

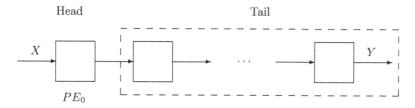

Head   Tail

X $\cdots$ Y

PE_0

Fig. 7. Unidirectional Pass-Through array

Figure 7 presents the functional view of such an array: we can say that it is composed of a head processor (PE_0), while the rest of PEs form the tail array (the part of the array marked with dashed line), the functioning of which is similar to the whole array.

The list X is the global input to the array (its elements are fed into the array through PE_0 at each time step). If the array computes the function $F[X]$ and the head processor PE_0 outputs the modified list $G[X]$ that satisfies property (5), then the tail array will compute $F[G[X]]$.

The recursive equation characterizing the functioning of the array has the form

$$F[X] = F[G[X]] \ , \tag{11}$$

where G is an online transitive function.

Problem: Find the scalar projection of G when a recursive description of the form (11) of F is given.

Method: Determine $G[X]$ from the recursive description of F. The problem reduces to the design of a single systolic processor computing G.

The condition for termination has to be analyzed separately. Note that (11) does not tell anything about the termination of the problem. We either know the number of iterations (and from here we can conclude the number of PEs), or a special termination condition is given (which also depends on the input), then the transition function should also verify this condition.

6   Unidirectional Systolic Array for GCD Computation

In Sect. 3 we described an algorithm for GCD computation. Hereafter we describe the design of the corresponding unidirectional systolic array.

Let $A = \langle a_0, a_1, \ldots \rangle$ and $B = \langle b_0, b_1, \ldots \rangle$ be the list representation of the two inputs a and b.

Step 1 can be performed by a single processor (see example 5).

Step 2 can also be performed by a single processor (see example 4).

Step 3 The expression (2) contains $b/2$, which means a shift to the right of the digits of b, that is $T[B]$ in the list representation. Similarly, the equivalent of $b/4$ is $T_2[B]$.

Therefore we can rewrite (1)-(4) as:

$$
\begin{aligned}
GCD[A, B] &= A, & &\text{if } B = 0 \\
&= GCD[A, T[B]], & &\text{if } H[B] = 0 \\
&= GCD[B, T_2[A + B]], & &\text{if } (H[B] = 1) \wedge (H_1[A] \neq H_1[B]) \\
&= GCD[B, T_2[A - B]], & &\text{if } (H[B] = 1) \wedge (H_1[A] = H_1[B])
\end{aligned}
$$

The function GCD appears three times on the RHS of the definition. Thus the computation of the GCD function can be also written as:

$$
\begin{aligned}
GCD[\langle A, B \rangle] &= A, & &\text{if } B = 0 \\
&= GCD[\langle A, T[B] \rangle, & &\text{if } H[B] = 0, \\
&\quad \langle B, T_2[A + B] \rangle, & &\text{if } (H[B] = 1) \wedge (H_1[A] \neq H_1[B]), \\
&\quad \langle B, T_2[A - B] \rangle, & &\text{if } (H[B] = 1) \wedge (H_1[A] = H_1[B])] \ ,
\end{aligned}
$$

which is of the form (11) (except for the first equation, which is the stop condition and will be discussed later).

We know that if $a_0 = b_0 = 1$, then $T_2[A - B] = T_2[A] - T_2[B]$, when $a_1 = b_1$ and $T_2[A + B] = 1 \overset{.}{+} T_2[A] + T_2[B]$, when $a_1 \neq b_1$. If we use the notation $X = \langle A, B \rangle$ and F_A and F_B are the already used functions that return the A respectively B component of the input, the function K computed by a PE is:

$$
\begin{aligned}
K[H[X], H_1[X], X, T[X], T_2[X]] &= \\
&= \quad \langle F_A[X], F_B[T[X]] \rangle \qquad \text{if } F_B[H[X]] = 0 \qquad (12) \\
&= \langle F_B[X], 1 \overset{.}{+} F_A[T_2[X]] + F_B[T_2[X]] \rangle \quad \text{if } (F_B[H[X]] = 1) \wedge \\
&\qquad\qquad\qquad \wedge (F_A[H_1[X]] \neq F_B[H_1[X]]) \quad (13) \\
&= \quad \langle F_B[X], F_A[T_2[X]] - F_B[T_2[X]] \rangle \quad \text{if } (F_B[H[X]] = 1) \wedge \\
&\qquad\qquad\qquad \wedge (F_A[H_1[X]] = F_B[H_1[X]]) \quad (14)
\end{aligned}
$$

Equation (12) satisfies property (5), while (13) and (14) satisfy property (7). The latter two equations induce the introduction of an internal state register, denoted by r. It will store the carry from the addition (respectively subtraction) operation (for details see example 2). The carry is initialized with 1 respectively 0 when s is set, depending whether addition or subtraction has to be performed.

On the other hand we can conclude from the form of the definition of the K function (equations (12)-(14)) that the function can be computed by an auto-configurable processor with 2-delay. Two transition variables are introduced to delay the input. Because in the "if" statements appear only the first two elements of the input, the state register will be set at the time step when the second input is fed into the PE. The list of control signals will be $SI = \langle 0, 1, 1, 1, \ldots \rangle$.

Note that here we are not interested in indicating the appearance of the first result ($k = 2$ is known), but it is very important that the list of control signals SQ that leaves the processor PE_0 is an adequate sequence of control signals which are input to the next PE. This means that the control signals associated to the first element of the result should be 0, the other values 1. To obtain such a list of output signals one needs to delay the control signal, too by $k = 2$ elements (two transition registers for the control signal have to be included, as shown on Fig. 8, in the same way as the inputs are delayed).

Stop condition: The condition $B = 0$ as it is can only be verified if we provide some information about the length of the inputs. If the processor knows the beginning of the input (from the control signal) and another signal indicates the end of the input, then the processor can decide when the input is null (note that in our case this can only be the input B).

The indication of the size of the input is achieved by associating an additional tag-bit to each binary digit of the input. The value of the tag-bit is 0 for each significant digit of the binary number and 1 beginning with the sign bit of the number.

Now the input lists A and B both have two components $xx = \langle tx, x \rangle$, where tx is the tag-bit (indicating the end of the input) and x is the digit. Let Tag, and Dig be the selector functions for the tag-bits respectively the digits.

Because A and B are binary numbers, in the expression $(A+B)/4$ ($T_2[A+B]$ in list notation) $A+B$ can have at most one more digit than the longest of A and B. This means that $(A+B)/4$ is at least one digit shorter than the longest argument. This insures the termination of the algorithm [4].

The list of tag-bits that indicate the longest argument is given by $Tag[A] \wedge Tag[B]$ (where $\wedge$ is the bitwise "and" operation). Therefore the tag-list corresponding to a number that is "one digit shorter" than the longest argument is: $T[Tag[A] \wedge Tag[B]] = T[Tag[A]] \wedge T[Tag[B]]$.

The computation of the GCD can now be rewritten in the following way:

$$
\begin{aligned}
GCD[\langle A, B \rangle] = A, && \text{if } (H[Dig[B]] = 0)\wedge \\
&& (H_1[Tag[B]] = 1) \\
= GCD[\langle A, T[B] \rangle], && \text{if } (H[Dig[B]] = 0)\wedge \\
&& (H_1[Tag[B]] = 0), \\
\langle B, \langle T[Tag[A]] \wedge T[Tag[B]], && \\
1 \overset{\cdot}{+} T_2[Dig[A]] + T_2[Dig[B]] \rangle\rangle, \text{if } && (H[Dig[B]] = 1)\wedge \\
&& (H_1[Dig[A]] \neq H_1[Dig[B]]), \\
\langle B, \langle T[Tag[A]] \wedge T[Tag[B]], && \\
T_2[Dig[A]] - T_2[Dig[B]] \rangle\rangle, && \text{if } (H[Dig[B]] = 1)\wedge \\
&& (H_1[Dig[A]] = H_1[Dig[B]])]
\end{aligned}
$$

The final expression for K can be automatically projected into the scalar space (using the rules described in Sect. 4.4) in order to obtain the description of a PE.

Figure 8 presents the structure of a PE for the 3rd step of the GCD computation. $dxx|j|$ (where x stands for either a or b and j is 1 or 2) denotes the transition register with two components: $\langle dtx|j|, dx|j| \rangle$, where the first component is the correspondent of the tag-bit and the second one corresponds to the digit. We use the notation xxi for the two components of the input $\langle tai, ai \rangle$ or $\langle tbi, bi \rangle$. Note that both functions, Dig and Tag commute with T and H.

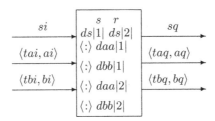

Fig. 8. PE for the problem of GCD computation

The computations of the PE are (with x standing for both a and b for brevity):

$$
\langle aq_{t+1}, bq_{t+1} \rangle = \langle \$, \$ \rangle \text{ if } s_t = \$ \tag{15}
$$
$$
= \langle da|2|_t, \$ \rangle \text{ if } s_t = 1 \tag{16}
$$

$$= \langle da|2|_t, db|1|_t \rangle \text{ if } s_t = 2 \tag{17}$$

$$= \langle db|2|_t, low[ai_t \overset{..}{+} bi_t \overset{..}{+} r_t] \rangle \text{ if } s_t = 3 \tag{18}$$

$$= \langle db|2|_t, low[ai_t \overset{..}{-} bi_t \overset{..}{-} r_t] \rangle \text{ if } s_t = 4 \tag{19}$$

$$\langle taq_{t+1}, tbq_{t+1} \rangle = \langle \$, \$ \rangle \text{ if } s_t = \$ \tag{20}$$

$$= \langle dta|2|_t, \$ \rangle \text{ if } s_t = 1 \tag{21}$$

$$= \langle dta|2|_t, dtb|1|_t \rangle \text{ if } s_t = 2 \tag{22}$$

$$= \langle dtb|2|_t, dta|1|_t \wedge dtb|1|_t \rangle \text{ if } (s_t = 3) \vee (s_t = 4) \tag{23}$$

$$r_{init} = \$ \tag{24}$$

$$r_{t+1} = 1 \text{ if } (s_t = \$) \wedge (si_t = 1) \wedge (db|1|_t = 1) \wedge (bi_t \neq ai_t) \tag{25}$$

$$= high[ai_t \overset{..}{+} bi_t \overset{..}{+} r_t] \text{ if } s_t = 3 \tag{26}$$

$$= 0 \text{ if } (s_t = \$) \wedge (si_t = 1) \wedge (db|1|_t = 1) \wedge (bi_t = ai_t) \tag{27}$$

$$= high[ai_t \overset{..}{-} bi_t \overset{..}{-} r_t] \text{ if } s_t = 4 \tag{28}$$

$$= r_t \text{ otherwise} \tag{29}$$

$$dxx|1|_{t+1} = xxi_t \tag{30}$$

$$dxx|2|_{t+1} = dxx|1|_t \tag{31}$$

$$sq_{t+1} = ds|2|_t \tag{32}$$

$$ds|2|_{t+1} = ds|1|_t \tag{33}$$

$$ds|1|_{t+1} = si_t \tag{34}$$

$$s_{init} = \$ \tag{35}$$

$$s_{t+1} = 1 \text{ if } (s_t = \$) \wedge (si_t = 1) \wedge (db|1|_t = 0) \wedge (tbi_t = 1) \tag{36}$$

$$= 2 \text{ if } (s_t = \$) \wedge (si_t = 1) \wedge (db|1|_t = 0) \wedge (tbi_t = 0) \tag{37}$$

$$= 3 \text{ if } (s_t = \$) \wedge (si_t = 1) \wedge (db|1|_t = 1) \wedge (bi_t \neq ai_t) \tag{38}$$

$$= 4 \text{ if } (s_t = \$) \wedge (si_t = 1) \wedge (db|1|_t = 1) \wedge (bi_t = ai_t) \tag{39}$$

$$= s_t, \text{ otherwise} \tag{40}$$

The result is given by the PE whose the state register s is set to 1.

Note: The stop condition only detects the termination of the transformations of the argument: from this point on, all the remaining PE's must leave the arguments unchanged. Effective termination of the algorithm on a concrete systolic array is a closely related, but different issue. Since a concrete systolic array has a finite number of PE's, the result (i. e. pseudo GCD) will be generated at the right-hand-side of the array only if the number of PE's exceeds the number of steps which are necessary for the particular arguments of the respective computation. In practice, this problem can be tackled in various ways, which are in fact the same for all the arrays of this type. One solution is to handle arguments of a maximum known size by an array having a number of processors superior to the upper bound of the number of steps. Another solution is to pick-up the output even if the computation is not finished, and then to re-enter it into the re-initialized array. The latter allows to handle arguments of arbitrary size, even though the array is fixed, which is an interesting feature specific to pass-through arrays.

7 Conclusions

By exploiting the similarity between the inductive structure of a systolic array and the inductive decomposition of the argument by a functional program, we developed an elegant and efficient method for the automatic synthesis of a quite non-trivial array for the computation of the integer GCD of binary numbers.

The *case study* presented here paves the way for further theoretical investigation into the applications and theoretical development related to this similarity.

Acknowledgements. The *Theorema* system is supported by FWF (Austrian National Science Foundation) – SFB project F1302. The research presented here is also part of the project *e-Austria Timisoara*, which is supported by BMBWK (Austrian Ministry of Education, Science, and Culture), BMWA (Austrian Ministry of Economy and Work). The first author was partially supported by a CEEPUS scholarship.

References

1. Brent, R.P., Kung, H.T.: A systolic algorithm for integer GCD computation. 7th Symp. on Computer Arithmetic, pp. 118–125. IEEE Computer Society Press, Los Alamitos (1985)
2. Buchberger, B., et al.: Theorema: Towards Computer-Aided Mathematical Theory Exploration, Journal of Applied Logic 4(4), 470-504 (2006)
3. Jebelean, T.: A Generalization of the Binary GCD Algorithm. In: ISSAC'93, pp. 111–116. ACM Press, New York (1993)
4. Jebelean, T.: Systolic Multiprecision Arithmetic (PhD Thesis). Technical Report 94-37, RISC-Linz (April 1994)
5. Jebelean, T.: Designing Systolic Arrays for Integer GCD Computation. In: ASAP 94, pp. 295–301. IEEE Computer Society Press, Los Alamitos (1994)
6. Jebelean, T.: Auto-Configurable Array for GCD Computation. In: Glesner, M., Luk, W. (eds.) FPL 1997. LNCS, vol. 1304, pp. 457–461. Springer, Heidelberg (1997)
7. Jebelean, T., Szakács, L.: Functional-Based Synthesis of Systolic Online Multipliers. In: SYNASC-05, pp. 267–275. IEEE Computer Society Press, Los Alamitos (2005)
8. Stein, J.: Computational problems associated with Racah algebra. J. Comp. Phys. 1, 397-405 (1967)
9. Szakács, L.: Automatic Design of Systolic Arrays: A Short Survey. RISC Technical report 02-27, University of Linz, Austria (December 2002)

Comparing Alternative Evaluation Strategies for Stream-Based Parallel Functional Languages*

Mercedes Hidalgo-Herrero, Yolanda Ortega-Mallén, and Fernando Rubio

Universidad Complutense de Madrid, Spain
mhidalgo@edu.ucm.es, yolanda@sip.ucm.es, fernando@sip.ucm.es

Abstract. In parallel functional languages, like Eden, lazy and strict evaluation are commonly mixed. Thus, the parallel performance of these languages depends on the strategy used to fix the degrees of laziness/strictness. By using an implementation of Eden's operational semantics, we analyze the influence of alternative evaluation models on Eden skeletons performance. In particular, we assess the performance of different implementations of a skeleton that uses stream-based communications.

Keywords: Parallel functional programming, skeletons, semantics.

1 Introduction

Declarative programming languages in general, and functional languages in particular, have shown excellent possibilities for their parallelization. The parallel functional language Eden [2,12] keeps its high-level nature inherited from the non-strict functional language Haskell [13], which Eden extends with a set of *coordination* features to control the parallel evaluation of processes.

Haskell uses normal order evaluation with share of reductions to avoid repeating computations. However, if expressions are evaluated only under demand then the exploitation of parallelism is highly restricted. Therefore, Eden overrides the pure lazy approach by combining non-strict functional application with eager process creation and eager communication, so that there is always demand for the evaluation of the output of an Eden process. This produces *speculative* computations that calculate results that may finally not be used. Moreover, the degree of speculation for an Eden program is variable, depending on the number of processors, the speed of basic operations, and so on.

The *explicit definition of processes* is done in Eden by using abstract schemes for describing the behavior of processes (*process abstractions*) and *process instantiations* that provide process abstractions with input parameters for the dynamic creation of *child processes* together with the unidirectional channels necessary to communicate with the corresponding *parent process*. Once a process is running, only fully evaluated data objects are communicated. The only exceptions are lists, which are transmitted in a *stream*-like fashion, i.e. element by element. Each list element is first evaluated to full normal form and then transmitted.

---

* Work supported by projects TIC2003-07848-C02-01, TIC2003-01000, TIN2006-15660-C02-01, PAC06-0008.

Z. Horváth, V. Zsók, and A. Butterfield (Eds.): IFL 2006, LNCS 4449, pp. 55–72, 2007.

Table 1. Evaluation alternatives

	Evaluation before copy (EC)	Process abstraction evaluation (PAE)	Instantiation copy (IC)
1	yes	parent	yes
2	yes	parent	no
3	yes	child	yes
4	yes	child	no
5	no	child	yes
6	no	child	no
7	no	parent	yes
8	no	parent	no

A crucial decision is how to distribute the computation between a process and its offspring. If the parent completes as much work as possible before delegating to its children —for instance by bounding to a *weak head normal form* (whnf) every dependent variable of the process body (or abstraction) before creating a process— then this may lead to a poor parallelization. On the contrary, if each child evaluates the process abstraction as well as its application to the input parameters then repeated computations can be produced when certain subexpressions are evaluated independently by several children of the same parent. Although this can be avoided by the programmer by forcing the evaluation in the parent of these common subexpressions, this requires more programming work and it is error-prone. Currently, the latter option has been adopted for Eden and its actual implementation. Nevertheless, we are interested in studying other possibilities; specifically the combinations that are gathered in Table 1, where EC (*evaluation before copy*) stands for the option of evaluating every needed binding before being copied to the initial heap of a newly created process (or the receiver process in the case of a communication); IC (*instantiation copy*) represents the copy of bindings from one process to another corresponding to pending process instantiations; and PAE (*process abstraction evaluation*) indicates the alternatives for the evaluation of a process abstraction in the case of an instantiation: either by the parent process, or by the child.

We investigate these alternative semantics for Eden, in particular how the behaviour of parallel skeletons in Eden can be affected. To this end, we have defined a formal semantics for each variation (see [5] and [12] for details), and we have implemented (in Haskell) an interpreter capable of dealing with all of them and of providing several measures (parallelism, communications, etc.) useful for the analysis. By doing so, we can compare the advantages and disadvantages of each strategy from a semantical and an efficiency point of view.

This paper is a continuation of the work presented in [6] and devoted to the analysis of different variations to override laziness in order to introduce parallelism. The analysis in that first work is quite limited because streams were not considered, thus greatly reducing the choice of skeletons that we could use for our examples. Let us remark that dealing with streams is a key issue in Eden. Without streams, processes would communicate in a monolitic way: they would only receive a single data at the beginning, and produce a single data at the end of its computation. Thus, processes could not compute and communicate in interleaving. This fact reduces the versatility of the language. In fact, streams are needed for most of the skeletons and programs written in Eden. In the present work we have extended our interpreter with streams for communication, so that we are able to analyze more interesting examples. For instance, we have implemented parallel versions of the map&reduce skeleton, and we can analyze the advantages of each of these implementations.

Organization of the paper. We start by describing the calculus that assembles the essentials of Eden and that is used to write the examples shown in the present work. Next, in Section 3 we explain how to define and implement in Eden some simple parallel skeletons. Section 4 describes the environment that we have developed for obtaining profiling information. In Section 5 these profiling tools are used with a parallel version for calculating the sum of Euler numbers by using the *map&reduce* skeleton. We end the paper by presenting our conclusions and by outlining our future work in this topic.

2 Eden's Essentials

Figure 1 shows the (abstract) syntax of an untyped λ-calculus extended with natural numbers, arithmetic operators, recursive lets, conditional expressions, process instantiation, and a simple mechanism for defining lists and dealing with them. This simple calculus captures the essential features of Eden: a non-strict high level language extended with a coordination level represented by processes. Besides, it proves to be sufficient for our purposes.

$$
\begin{array}{lll}
E ::= & n & \text{number} \\
 \mid & E_1 \ op \ E_2 & \text{arithmetic} \\
 \mid & x & \text{identifier} \\
 \mid & \backslash x.E & \lambda\text{-abstraction} \\
 \mid & E_1 E_2 & \text{application} \\
 \mid & E_1 \# E_2 & \text{process instantiation} \\
 \mid & \texttt{let} \ \{x_i = E_i\}_{i=1}^n \ \texttt{in} \ E & \text{local declaration} \\
 \mid & \texttt{if0} \ E_1 \ E_2 \ E_3 & \text{conditional} \\
 \mid & /\backslash[x_1 : x_2].E_1 \| E_2 & \Lambda\text{-abstraction} \\
 \mid & L & \text{list} \\
L ::= & [E_1 : E_2] & \text{non empty list} \\
 \mid & \texttt{Nil} & \text{empty list} \\
op ::= & + \mid - \mid * \mid / &
\end{array}
$$

Fig. 1. Eden core syntax

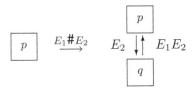

Fig. 2. Process creation in Eden

In the syntax description $n \in \mathcal{N}$ denotes natural numbers, $x \in Var$ denotes identifiers, $E \in Exp$ represents expressions, $L \in List$ represents lists, and $op \in OP$ corresponds to the arithmetic operations over natural numbers, i.e. addition, substraction, multiplication and division. The expression $\texttt{let } \{x_i = E_i\}_{i=1}^n \texttt{ in } E$ is an abbreviation of $\texttt{let } x_1 = E_1, \ldots, x_n = E_n \texttt{ in } E$.

The calculus identifies process abstractions with one-argument functions, so that processes are created with a unique input channel and a unique output channel. When evaluating an expression $E_1 \# E_2$ inside a process p, a new child process q is created. The parent process, p, sends through the input channel for q the value of E_2 to q which evaluates E_1 E_2 and returns the result (to its parent) via its output channel. This behaviour is illustrated by the diagram in Figure 2. The key difference between application and instantiation is the former non-strictness versus the latter eagerness.

A conditional expression $\texttt{if0 } E_1 \ E_2 \ E_3$ evaluates to E_2 when the expression E_1 evaluates to 0, and it evaluates to E_3 otherwise.

The $/\backslash$-construction is a combination of lambda-abstraction and pattern matching for lists; thus, the expression $((/\backslash[x_1 : x_2].E_1 \| E_2) \ L)$ evaluates to E_1 if the list L is empty, and evaluates to E_2 otherwise. In the latter the pattern $[x_1 : x_2]$ is matched against the list L.

We use two simple examples to illustrate the behaviour of our calculus. In the first example we compute in parallel $x^2 + y^2$, being x and y the input parameters of our main function f:

```
sqr = \x. x * x
f = \x. \y. let a = sqr # x
                b = sqr # y
            in a + b
```

During the evaluation of f applied to any two numerical values two new processes are created: One to compute x^2 and the other to compute y^2. Both processes are created by the unique parent process, that is also responsible for adding the results obtained from both children.

We can easily generate more complex process topologies. For instance, given a list of numbers we can define a function computing the square of each of the numbers:

```
sqrs = /\[x:xs].Nil [] [sqr x : sqrs xs]
```

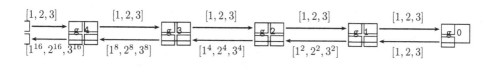

Fig. 3. Processes hierarchy for `g 4 [1,2,3]`

Then, given a natural number n and a list of numbers xs we can use the following program to compute $x_i^{2^n}$ for each $x_i \in xs$:

```
g = \n. \xs. if0 n
             xs
             let n' = n sub 1
                 xs' = (g n') # xs
             in sqrs xs'
```

Notice that we do not create a new process to compute $x_i^{2^0}$. However, in order to compute $x_i^{2^{n+1}}$, a new process is created to recursively compute $x_i^{2^n}$ and the parent process computes the squares of the values received. In practice, this definition creates a pipeline-like topology. For instance, for computing (`g 4 [1:[2:[3:Nil]]]`) four new processes are created following the scheme shown in Figure 3. It is important to remark that in Eden lists are transmitted in a stream-like fashion. Thus, a process receiving as input a list of elements can start working on its first task without needing to receive the rest of inputs. Analogously, in case a list is to be sent as output, its elements are sent as soon as they are available. So, in our example all the processes shown in Figure 3 can be working simultaneously on different data.

In the second example we have used an instantiation of the form (`g n'`) # `xs` so that the process abstraction is not just a variable, but the application of a function to a parameter. Thus, depending on the model of evaluation used (see Table 1), the responsible for evaluating such application can be either the parent or the child process.

The following example illustrates how options in Table 1 lead to different evaluations. We have chosen a short although intricate example, so that many differences can be appreciated:

```
main =  let idId = id id
            id = \x. x
            qidId = \z. idId
            p1 = id # id
            p2 = idId # id
            p3 = p2 # id
            p4 = qidId # id
        in p2
```

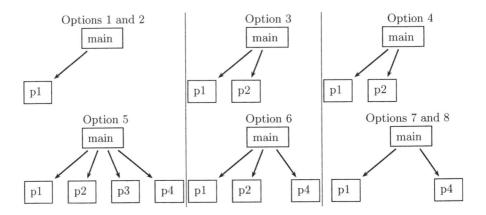

Fig. 4. Different topologies depending on semantic options

This expression contains four instantiations, but depending on the semantic option they give rise to new processes or not in the first step of the evaluation (the corresponding process topologies/trees are shown in Figure 4):

p1: The process is created regardless of the semantic option.

p2: This process is created only if the children evaluate process abstractions (PAE = child), i.e. options 3, 4, 5, and 6.

p3: This instantiation depends on the evaluation of p2, which in turn is a process creation. Consequently, it is created if the abstraction is evaluated by the child (PAE = child) and variables bound to process creations are copied (IC = yes). Moreover, since it depends on unevaluated free variables, the process creation is subject to their evaluation when EC = yes. Consequently, this process only appears in the sixth semantics.

p4: The abstraction of this expression is already evaluated, but it contains a free variable that has not been evaluated yet. The creation of the process will take place only if unevaluated bindings are allowed to be copied, that is, options 5, 6, 7, and 8.

Notice that in this example all variables correspond semantically to the identity function.

3   Defining Skeletons

Eden has proven to be highly suitable for a programming methodology based on *algorithmic skeletons* (see [9,11]), with the double advantage that skeletons can be implemented and used within the same language. Thus, the programmer can either directly use the skeletons previously provided, or modify them to suit his needs; or even create new skeletons, thus extending the collection. Actually,

Eden's library provides a rich set of skeletons covering many common parallel patterns such as *parallel map*, *parallel divide-and-conquer*, *parallel search*, and others, as well as typical process topologies like pipelines, grids, rings, and so on. The interested reader can find in [9,14,11,12] Eden's definition of these and other skeletons, together with their corresponding cost models, examples of application, and runtime results.

The concrete implementations of the skeletons have a heavy influence on its effectiveness. Thus, the majority of skeleton-oriented approaches use low-level languages for the implementation of their skeletons; aiming to produce correct and highly efficient implementations, but reduces the flexibility and versatility of the approach, as the set of skeletons is usually fixed. In contrast, Eden offers the possibility of implementing and using skeletons for parallel programming, by implementing them as polymorphic higher-order functions. Let us remark that process abstractions in Eden are not just annotations, but first class values which can be manipulated by the programmer (i.e. passed as parameters, stored in data structures, and so on). This facilitates the definition of skeletons as higher order functions. The Eden programmer can choose the process topology and the task granularity, but cannot decide on matters like the placement of processes in processors. Thus, the efficiency of Eden's skeletons depends on the implementation of Eden, and it is influenced by the semantics of the language. Hence, a detailed analysis of different semantics options can help to improve the efficiency of Eden's skeletons.

The most classical and simple skeleton is `map`. Given a list of inputs `xs`, and a function `f` to be applied to each of them, a different process can be used to compute the application of the function to each element of the list:

```
parMap = \f.(/\[y:ys].Nil [] [(f # y):((parMap f) ys)])
```

Notice that each new process receives its input data through an input channel. Then, it applies function *f* to the received data, and finally it returns the result of the computation through an output channel. Let us remark that, in case a list is to be sent through a channel, its elements will be sent one by one in a stream-like fashion.

It is not necessary to explicitly use constructions for synchronizing the processes. The main process initially sends a task to each of the *worker* processes of the `parMap`. Afterwards, as soon as any of the workers finishes its assignment, the result is automatically sent to the main process. The computation finishes when the main process has received all the results needed.

Different variations of this skeleton can be considered. For instance, input data could be passed as a parameter to the process. Notice that when the parent pass data to the child through a channel, the responsible for evaluating such data is always the parent. However, if data are not passed through a channel, but they are passed as a parameter, in many situations the child will be responsible for its computation. That is, the process has to extract every input value. As each child computes its own inputs, it can be considered as a self-service variation of the basic parMap:

```
parMapSS = (\f.(/\[y:ys].Nil []
                    (Let f' = (\x (\dummy  (f x)))
                     in [((f' y) # 0):((parMapSS f) ys)]))))
```

`parMap` and `parMapSS` are essential primitive skeletons used to create a set of independent processes, but they can be improved easily by reducing the number of processes to be created. In a `mapFarm` the number of processes to be created is fixed (for instance, it can be the number of processors). The implementation first distributes evenly the tasks among the processes, then `parMap` is applied, and finally the results are collected. Notice that, due to the lazy evaluation, these three tasks are not done sequentially, but in interleaving. As soon as any of the workers has computed one of the elements of its output list, it sends this sub-result to the main process, and it goes on computing the next element. Notice that communications are asynchronous, so that it is not necessary to wait for acknowledgments from the main process. When the main process has received all the needed results, it finishes the computation.

The Eden source code of this skeleton is shown below, where the number of processors, as well as the distribution and collection functions, are parameters of the skeleton:

```
mapFarm = \np.\unshuffle.\shuffle.\f.\xs.
          shuffle (parMap (map f) (unshuffle np xs))
```

Different strategies to split the work into the different processes can be used provided that, for every list `xs`, `(shuffle (unshuffle np xs)) == xs`. In fact, we have already predefined several pairs of functions, so that the programmer can choose the best strategy for each case. For instance, we can distribute the tasks in a round-robin fashion.

3.1 Map&Reduce

Next we present how to define the map&reduce skeleton we will use in section 5 to implement our running example. The sequential specification of this classical scheme is a combination of a map and a fold function:

```
mr :: (a->b) -> (b->b->b) -> b -> [a] -> b
mr = \f.\g.\e.\tasks.foldl g e (map f tasks)
```

where function `b` is expected to be commutative and associative.

Different parallel implementations of the map&reduce skeleton can be easily implemented. For instance, following the ideas presented before for the parallel map, we can implement a farm-like version:

```
mrFarm = \np.\unshuffle.\f.\g.\e.\tasks.
             let taskss   = unshuffle np tasks
                 workingF = mr f g e tasks
                 results  = parMap (workingF f g e) taskss
             in foldl g e results
```

Let us remark that an **unshuffle** function is used to distribute the tasks among processes, but it is unnecessary to merge them afterwards with a **shuffle** function. The reason is that we assume that the function **g** is associative and commutative. Thus, the order in which the results are combined does not matter.

As we have commented in the case of the **map** skeleton, sometimes we can use a better implementation if the list of tasks can be easily created by the workers. In case the time needed to communicate the list of tasks is greater than the time needed to compute it, a self-service version is better. In that case, each of the children can select its own tasks:

```
mrSS = \np.\unshuffle.\f.\g.\e.\tasks.
          let taskss   = unshuffle np tasks
              workingF = mr f g e tasks
              results  = parMapSS (workingF f g e) taskss
          in foldl g e results
```

Obviously, the previous skeletons can be simplified by providing a predefined unshuffle function, and by assuming that the number of processes to be created is equal to the number of available processors (noPe):

```
mrFarm' = \f.\g.\e.\tasks.
             mrFarm noPe myUnshuffle f g e tasks
mrSS' = \f.\g.\e.\tasks.
             mrSS noPe myUnshuffle f g e tasks
```

4   Environment

In order to implement an interpreter for Eden core, we have completely based its development on the operational semantics presented in [5]. Therefore, its correctness is guaranteed. The development of interpreters based on formal semantics is common in the literature (see e.g. [3,1]). Our interpreter is written in Haskell, so the flexibility of the implementation is increased. Therefore, it can be easily modified to obtain different versions. Particularly, all the semantic alternatives shown in Table 1 have been programmed. That is, eight different implementations for Eden core are provided. Besides, all the versions of the semantics are implemented using the same basic machinery, that is, there is only one interpreter that offers eight different modes. Thus, the code is reused for implementing all the strategies. Moreover, it is ensured that the variations among the various implementations are just those originated by the different semantics. That is, the efficiency of the implementations cannot interfere the performance measures of the various modes.

This environment is more than a simple interpreter to execute our programs under diverse semantics. In addition to obtaining the final result of the execution, other useful pieces of information are also provided. First, the user can ask the interpreter to produce as output an html file showing the evolution of the state of the processes step by step. By doing so, we can use this output as a pedagogical tool to show what is the actual behaviour of a semantics.

Second, our environment incorporates a set of profiling tools to help to analyse the performance of the executions. In this sense, the output is similar to other profilers such as GranSim [10], Paradise [4], or GranSP [8]. Although our results are not so realistic because our environment is not implemented by modifying the runtime system of the corresponding compiler, we have more flexibility. In fact, the main advantage of our environment compared to Paradise is that we can analyze the performance of the same program using different semantic alternatives.

As it can be expected, our tools can be used independently of the concrete semantics mode used in each execution. The interpreter output data allows us to obtain simple information as:

- Total number of overall steps needed to finish the execution (i.e. time needed to execute it assuming infinite processors).
- Total number of basic steps needed to finish the execution (i.e. time needed to execute it with a unique processor).
- Total number of messages sent during the execution.
- Maximal parallelism degree during the execution.
- Average parallelism degree during the execution.
- Amount of extra work done by the parallel execution compared to the work done in the sequential version.

Apart form the information about the overall system, the same data is returned for each concrete process. That is, the tools can show us the number of steps or the number of communications separately performed by each process. Moreover, our environment allows us to generate more complex profiling information. Particularly, several graphical outputs can be produced. The most useful graphics we can currently generate are the following:

Overall parallelism. It shows the evolution in time of the number of active threads of the system. An example of such graphics can be seen in Figure 5.

Parallelism per process. It shows the evolution in time of the number of active threads inside each process. An example of such graphics can be seen in Figure 6.

5   Application Example: Sum of Euler Numbers

In this section we consider a very simple example implemented by using the parallel map&reduce skeleton explained in Section 3.1. The aim of the example is twofold: (1) to illustrate what kind of profiling information can be obtained by using our system; and (2) to analyze the differences between alternative implementations of the same skeleton when considering the semantics options discussed in the introduction.

The Euler number of a given value x is the number of integers smaller than x that are relatively prime to x. We are interested in computing the sum of

Table 2. Measures for `SumEuler` 8 with `noPe` = 2 and using Farm

	Run Time	Work	Maximum Parallelism	Average Parallelism	Number of Processes	Number of Comms
1(2)	1213	2828	7	2.331	3	12
3(4)	1217	2841	7	2.334	3	12
5(6)	1217	2841	7	2.334	3	12
7(8)	1213	2828	7	2.331	3	12

Table 3. Measures for `SumEuler` 8 with `noPe` = 2 and using Self-service

	Run Time	Work	Maximum Parallelism	Average Parallelism	Number of Processes	Number of Comms
1(2)	1538	2836	8	1.8439	3	4
3(4)	1538	2836	8	1.8439	3	4
5(6)	1546	2851	8	1.8441	3	4
7(8)	1545	2849	8	1.8440	3	4

the Euler numbers of the first n numbers. This problem has been proposed in
[15] to compare the way in which different parallel languages based on Haskell
are used, and we think it can also be useful to compare the semantic options
of our language, as well as to compare alternative implementations of the basic
skeletons.

The sequential version of the program (written in Haskell) is as follows:

```
euler x = length (filter (relprime x) [1..(x-1)])
relprime x y = gcd x y == 1
sumEuler n = sum (map euler [n,n-1..1])
```

5.1   Farm vs. Self-service

The program fits perfectly the map&reduce scheme, since the `euler` function
is mapped while `sum` folds the set of results into a single one. Moreover, it is
relatively simple to compute the list of tasks that each worker should receive.
Thus, it can be interesting to analyze the advantages/disadvantages of using a
self-service implementation compared to using a farm-like version of the skeleton.

The implementation in core Eden is trivial:

```
euler = \x. let numbers = numsLessThanTo n 1
            in length (filter (relPrime x) numbers)
sumEuler = \n. let numbers = numsLessThanTo n 1
               in mrSS' euler add 0 numbers
```

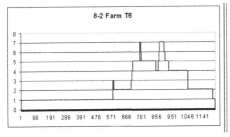 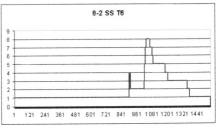

Fig. 5. Total number of active threads for `SumEuler` 8 with `noPe` = 2 using the farm (left) and self-service (right) implementations with option 6

Obviously, in case we want to use the farm implementation of the skeleton we only need to replace `mrSS'` with `mrFarm'`.

In the rest of this section we analyze the performance differences obtained with this example when considering the semantic options shown in Table 1. Let us remark that in this example it is irrelevant how we treat the copy of instantiations (column IC in Table 1), because none of the processes to be created depends on a not yet evaluated instantiation. Therefore, options 1 and 2 are equivalent, as well as 3 with 4, 5 with 6, and, finally, 7 with 8.

The measures for farm and self-service computations are gathered in Tables 2 and 3. It is clear that the farm computations end up sooner than those corresponding to self-service. Besides, the amount of work is also less in the farm case. Then, it could seem that the self-service version is less efficient. However, we have to consider another parameter: communication. The communication ratios satisfy the following formula:

$$comm_{Farm} = comm_{SS} + [number\ of\ tasks]$$

If communications in the system were expensive, then either both versions would result equally efficient or the farm algorithm would be less efficient.

Graphics in Figure 5 show the total activity using a concrete evaluation alternative (number 6 in Table 1) both with the farm and the self-service implementations. Analogously, the activity for each process created during the computations is represented in the graphics gathered in Figure 6. Due to lack of space, we do not include the graphics obtained with the rest of evaluation options. The interested reader can find them in [7]. Next we study four issues: amount of duplication of work, execution time, parallelism degree, and load balance.

Work Duplication. In the skeletons that we are considering, it is more relevant to study work duplication in the case of self-service. Since when a process is going to be created there are parameters that have to be evaluated, work duplication may occur in option 6.

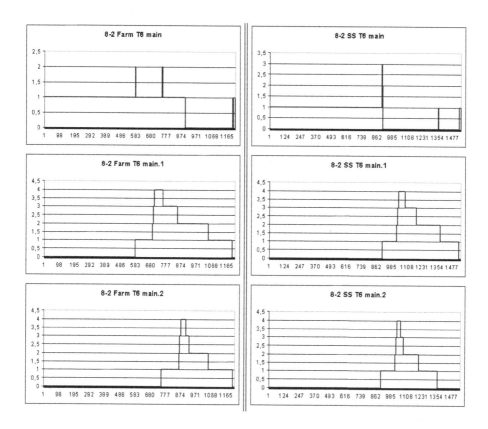

Fig. 6. Processes activity for `SumEuler` 8 with `noPe = 2` using the farm (left) and self-service (right) implementations with option 6

Options 2 and 4 stipulate that free variables must be evaluated before being copied. Then, the instantiation parameters must be evaluated by the parent process. Consequently, work duplication does not take place.

In the case of option 8 the parent must evaluate the abstraction of the instantiation, and by doing so it evaluates the parameters as well. Therefore, work duplication increases and processes are created sooner than in the previous cases.

Finally, in option 6 bindings can be copied unevaluated and the process abstraction is evaluated by the children. Thus, child processes are created even earlier.

This fact becomes clear when an enlargement is applied to the graphics (see Figure 7). The reason is that the amount of computation of these parameters is small with respect to the evaluation of the output of the processes (greatest common divisor, sums, and so on).

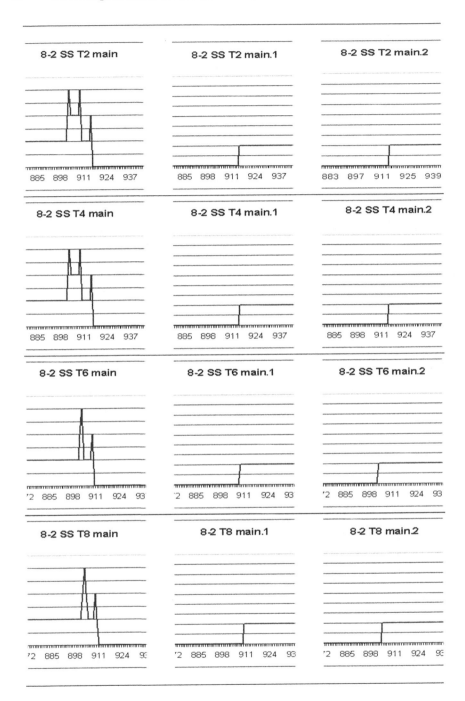

Fig. 7. Zoom of processes activity for self-service and for semantic options T2,T4,T6 and T8, with 2 processors

Parallelism Degree. We observe that the maximal degree of thread parallelism in the main process is greater in the self-service version (3 threads). In options 2, 4, and 8, the reason for this is that there are two potential processes waiting for the evaluation of their parameters —the whole list of tasks— in order to be created. Then, the evaluation of all the unevaluated free variables is demanded, and this evaluation is carried out by the parent. However, in option 6, the increase is due to the creation of the first child when the main process is demanding the addends.

In contrast, the processes in the farm only wait for the first value of their list of tasks. Therefore, the evaluation demand for their creation is small in comparison to the self-service algorithm. Consequently, the amount of activity in the main process is reduced, although the time to produce it is enlarged.

In both cases, farm and self-service, the maximal parallelism degree of the system is registered when at least one child is computing its output. This proves that the system profits from this instantiations. Besides, this parallelism entails activity of the parent process. Therefore, without the creation of the children the runtime would increase considerably.

With respect to the average parallelism, in the farm algorithm it is higher. This result is due to the reduction in the runtime, keeping a similar amount of work in both, the farm and the self-service schemes.

Load Balance. In the graphics we observe that in the self-service version the period of inactivity of the main process is greater than in the farm. The reason for this behaviour is that the main process is waiting for the children to finish their tasks, and this waiting period begins just after the creation of the children. Then it is easy to deduce that the farm algorithm produces a better load balance between the parent and the children. This reduction of process parallelism in the self-service produces the runtime increase mentioned above.

The difference in load balance is due to the way information is passed to the children. In the farm, the parent/main process sends the elements of the list of tasks one by one to the children, so that the latter are working while the former is preparing the next value.

By contrast, in the self-service version the list is a parameter, not a value to be communicated. Then, in options 2 and 8 the list is evaluated by the parent. Besides, in option 4 the list is also evaluated by the parent because bindings must be evaluated before being copied. Only in option 6 the evaluation of the list is carried out by the children, so that the parent can be considered overloaded at the beginning and remains almost idle the rest of the time.

Let us now analyze in more detail the semantic option influence in load balance. We have already recalled that in options 2 and 8 the parent must evaluate the process abstractions of its children. Consequently, the graphics for the farm scheme show differences in the parent activity periods, for instance when process main.1 is created. These periods are larger in options 2 and 8 than the corresponding lapses for options 4 and 6. A similar behaviour is observed when the self-service skeleton is used.

Table 4. Measures for the short example in Section 2

	Run Time	Work	Maximum Parallelism	Average Parallelism	Number of Processes	Number of Comms
1(2)	7	**17**	4	2.429	5	8
3(4)	8	20	6	2.5	5	8
5	8	28	**11**	**3.5**	6	**10**
6	8	21	7	2.625	5	8
7(8)	7	20	6	2.857	5	8

Summarizing Results. We have observed that the main differences do not arise by the chosen semantic option, instead they are due to the version of the skeleton. When communications in the system are expensive or difficult, the self-service algorithm is more suitable. Otherwise, the farm structure reduces considerably the runtime and the computing activity.

Although the impact on the performance of the version of the skeleton is greater than the impact of the semantic option, the latter is relevant too. Moreover, the improvements due to the chosen semantics do not require programming effort: The semantic options are already available.

Regarding the analysis of the best semantic option, we have already stated that the decision about copying instantiations is irrelevant in the present case, although there are some differences between the other semantic choices. Option 1 produces the fastest computations, although, as we have analyzed above, it entails work duplication and reduces the load balance between the parent and the children.

In order to analyze an example where the decision about copying instantiations is important, we will consider again the example presented in Section 2. The measures obtained in that case are summarized in Table 4. Observing the rows corresponding to options 5 and 6, it is clear that copying process instantiations influences on the number of processes in the system and the total amount of work: One extra process is created in the case of option 5, and work duplication is increased (28 vs 21 work units). In case the number or processors is limited, the runtime would increase considerably. Besides, any benefit associated to option 5 is insignificant if communications are expensive.

6   Conclusions and Future Work

Analyzing the influence of different lazy/strict semantic alternatives on the efficiency of parallel functional languages is an important topic. Throughout this paper, we have presented an integrated framework to deal with such analyses. By using our tools, we have studied how diverse semantic options may influence the performance of programs written in Eden. Moreover, we have also used our tools to compare the efficiency of different implementations of a skeleton. As it can be

Table 5. Measures using the divide&conquer skeleton

	Run Time	Work	Maximum Parallelism	Average Parallelism	Number of Processes
1(2)	452	1715	**14**	3.79	7
3(4)	**410**	1719	11	**4.19**	7
5(6)	446	1838	10	4.12	7
7(8)	459	1836	8	4	7

expected, the influence of the concrete implementation of the skeleton is greater than the influence of the evaluation strategy. However, choosing the appropriate semantics option can also improve the performance without programming effort.

Our framework is made up of two parts: an interpreter easily adaptable to cover diverse semantic options (indeed eight different semantics are currently supported), and a set of profiling tools that return data about the programs executed with the interpreter.

In order to test the usefulness of our framework, we have analysed the well-known parallel map&reduce skeleton. This case study has helped us to show the influence of the semantic options on several aspects of the parallel execution. In particular, changes in the amount of duplicated work, in the execution time, in the parallelism degree, and in the load balance.

Our first line of future work is to extend our profiling tools to obtain information about the amount of speculative work. Because of Eden's override of laziness, we are interested in measuring how much unnecessary calculation is done. Nevertheless, our future work will mainly focus on analysing a wider set of skeletons, and also a wider set of programs implemented by using those skeletons. For instance, we have already tested the divide&conquer skeleton (Table 5 summarizes the measures obtained using it to compute the factorial of a given number), and we are currently working on more complex topologies. So, after a more detailed study, we will be able to arrive at a decision about which semantic options should be used to improve Eden's performance. Besides, we will be able to detect (and correct) inefficiencies in the current implementation of Eden's skeletons library.

Since our main aim is to improve the efficiency of Eden's implementation, first we have to decide which semantic option is better on average from an efficiency point of view; not only the efficiency in time determines the decision, but also other aspects such as the amount of communications. Second, the Eden abstract machine should be adapted to fulfill the characteristics of such semantic option. Finally, the corresponding adjustment should be carried out on the compiler.

Acknowledgments

The authors would like to thank the anonymous referees for their valuable comments on a draft version of the paper.

References

1. Baker-Finch, C., King, D.J., Hall, J., Trinder, P.W.: An operational semantics for parallel call-by-need. Technical Report 99/1, Faculty of Mathematics and Computing, The Open University (1999)
2. Breitinger, S., Loogen, R., Ortega -Mallén, Y., Peña, R.: Eden: Language definition and operational semantics. Technical Report 96/10, Reihe Informatik, FB Mathematik, Philipps-Universität Marburg, Germany, http://www.mathematik.uni-marburg.de/~eden/, (1996)
3. Broy, M., Hinkel, U., Nipkow, T., Prehofer, C., Schieder, B.: Interpreter verification for a functional language. In: Thiagarajan, P.S. (ed.) Foundations of Software Technology and Theoretical Computer Science. LNCS, vol. 880, pp. 77–88. Springer, Heidelberg (1994)
4. Hernández, F., Peña, R., Rubio, F.: From GranSim to Paradise. Trends in Functional Programming (Selected papers of the First Scottish Functional Programming Workshop) 1, 11–19 (2000)
5. Hidalgo-Herrero, M., Ortega-Mallén, Y.: An operational semantics for the parallel language Eden. Parallel Processing Letters (World Scientific Publishing Company) 12(2), 211–228 (2002)
6. Hidalgo-Herrero, M., Ortega-Mallén, Y., Rubio, F.: Analyzing the influence of mixed evaluation on the performance of Eden skeletons. Parallel Computing 32(7-8), 523–538 (2006)
7. Hidalgo-Herrero, M., Ortega-Mallén, Y., Rubio, F.: An integrated framework for comparing alternative semantics for parallel functional languages. In: Draft Proceedings of the 20th International Workshop on Implementation of Functional Languages, IFL'06 (2006)
8. King, D.J., Hall, J., Trinder, P.W.: A Strategic Profiler for Glasgow Parallel Haskell. In: Hammond, K., Davie, T., Clack, C. (eds.) IFL 1998. LNCS, vol. 1595, pp. 465–474. Springer, Heidelberg (1999)
9. Klusik, U., Loogen, R., Priebe, S., Rubio, F.: Implementation skeletons in Eden: Low-effort parallel programming. In: Mohnen, M., Koopman, P. (eds.) IFL 2000. LNCS, vol. 2011, pp. 71–88. Springer, Heidelberg (2001)
10. Loidl, H.W.: GranSim user's guide. GRASP/AQUA Proyect, Glasgow University (1996)
11. Loogen, R., Ortega-Mallén, Y., Peña, R., Priebe, S., Rubio, F.: Patterns and Skeletons for Parallel and Distributed Computing. In: Rabhi, F.A., Gorlatch, S. (eds.) Parallelism Abstractions in Eden, ch. 4, pp. 95–128. Springer, Heidelberg (2002)
12. Loogen, R., Ortega-Mallén, Y., Peña, R.: Parallel functional programming in Eden. Journal of Functional Programming 15(3), 431–475 (2005)
13. Peyton Jones, S.L. (ed.): Haskell 98 language and libraries: the Revised Report. Cambridge University Press, Cambridge (2003)
14. Rubio, F.: Programación funcional paralela eficiente en Eden. PhD thesis, Dept. Sistemas Informáticos y Programación, Universidad Complutense de Madrid (2001)
15. Trinder, P.W., Loidl, H.W., Pointon, R.F.: Parallel and Distributed Haskells. Journal of Functional Programming 12(4+5), 469–510 (2003)

Parallel Coordination Made Explicit in a Functional Setting

Jost Berthold and Rita Loogen

Philipps-Universität Marburg, Fachbereich Mathematik und Informatik
Hans Meerwein Straße, D-35032 Marburg, Germany
{berthold,loogen}@informatik.uni-marburg.de

Abstract. We present a low-level coordination language for Haskell which can be used as an implementation language for parallel Haskell extensions. It has been developed in the context of the latest Eden implementation (based on the Glasgow-Haskell-Compiler, GHC, version 6) and it is thus referred to as the "EDen Implementation language", EDI. EDI provides a small set of directly implemented primitive operations for basic thread control, system information, and communication. We explore the expressiveness and performance of both Eden and its low-level implementation language EDI in comparison. It turns out that hardly any differences in performance can be observed. The main advantage of EDI in comparison to Eden is more accurate control of parallel execution. Our long-term goals are maintenance and structured implementation of Eden and a solid low-level implementation language, which can be used for other parallel Haskells as well.

1 Introduction

The area of parallel functional programming exhibits a variety of approaches, the common bases of which are referential transparency of functional programs and the ability to independently evaluate subexpressions. While some approaches pursue the target of (semi-)automatic parallelisation for special data structures (i.e. *data parallelism*), other dialects are more explicit in parallel coordination and allow what we call *general-purpose parallelism*, able to capture task-oriented parallelism. It is generally accepted [2,17] that functional languages allow a clean distinction between a computation (or "base") language and independent coordination constructs for parallelism control.

The parallel functional language Eden [7] adds constructs for the dynamic creation of processes and communication channels to the non-strict functional computation language Haskell. The Eden programming model is semi-explicit general-purpose parallelism: Parallel processes are programmer-controlled, while communication is system-controlled. Eden has been implemented by layers on top of the Glasgow Haskell compiler (GHC) [14]. The central part is the Eden module, which implements the Eden constructs in Haskell using a few primitive operations provided by the parallel extension of the GHC runtime environment (RTE).

Z. Horváth, V. Zsók, and A. Butterfield (Eds.): IFL 2006, LNCS 4449, pp. 73–90, 2007.

Any explicit parallel runtime support must express *operational* properties of the execution entities and will – in the end – rely on an imperative-style description. Parallelism support in its basic form must be considered as imperative and thus encapsulated in monads. Yet programmers might wish for a higher level of abstraction in their parallel programs and, for instance, use algorithmic skeletons [13] (higher-order functions for common parallel patterns), because they are not interested in gory details of implementation. Some parallel languages and libraries offer a fixed set of predefined skeletons and special, highly optimised implementations. On the other hand, with a more explicit general-purpose parallel language, a programmer can express *new* skeletons specific to the application.

Whether to hide or show the imperative basics is a question of language design. Eden tries to achieve a compromise between extremes in these matters: it exposes the execution unit of parallel processes to the programmer, but sticks to a functional model for their use. Eden processes differ from functions by additional strictness and remote evaluation. Further Eden language features allow for reactive systems and arbitrary programmer-controlled communication, which is (necessarily) opposed to referential transparency.

In this paper, the Eden implementation primitives will be considered as a language of their own, the *EDen Implementation language*, EDI for short. In contrast to Eden, EDI uses explicit communication and the IO monad to encapsulate side-effects. We compare expressiveness and performance of Eden and EDI. While the differences in performance can be neglected, the programming styles are substantially different. EDI allows an accurate control of parallelism, useful for system programming, whereas the higher abstraction of Eden is favourable for application programming, but often obscures what exactly is happening during parallel execution. The primary goal of this work is a structured Eden implementation, using a low-level implementation language which can be used for other parallel Haskells as well.

The paper is organised as follows: Section 2 describes Eden and its implementation. The primitive operations used in Eden's implementation constitute the Eden implementation language EDI. Section 3 discusses skeleton programming in Eden and EDI. Selected Eden skeletons have been re-programmed in EDI. Moreover, pitfalls of EDI programming are discussed. The paper ends with a discussion of related work in Section 4 and conclusions in Section 5.

2 Eden Language and Implementation

2.1 Eden Language Constructs

The parallel Haskell extension Eden [7] is an explicit general-purpose language for parallel programming, which gives programmers control over parallel processes. Eden allows to define *process abstractions* by a constructing function process and to explicitly *instantiate* (i.e. run) them on remote processors using the operator (#). Processes are distinguished from functions by their operational property of remote execution.

```
process :: (Trans a, Trans b) => (a -> b) -> Process a b
( # )    :: (Trans a, Trans b) => Process a b -> a -> b
```

For a given function f, evaluation of the expression (process f) # arg leads to the creation of a new (remote) process which evaluates the application of function f to argument arg. The argument is evaluated locally and sent to the new process.

Processes are encapsulated units of computation which communicate their inputs and results via *channels*. All values are reduced to normal form prior to sending, which implies additional strictness for processes. If input or output of a process is a tuple, each component will be evaluated and communicated by an own concurrent thread. Lists will be communicated element by element, values of other types will be communicated in single messages.

Communication between processes is automatically managed by the system and hidden from the programmer, but additional language constructs allow to explicitly create and access communication channels and to create arbitrary process networks. In the next subsection, we are showing how this feature is used to handle the hidden communication explicitly in the lower levels of the Eden system.

The task of parallel programming is simplified by a library of predefined skeletons [6]. Skeletons are higher-order functions defining parallel interaction patterns shared in many parallel applications. The programmer may use such known schemes from the library to achieve an instant parallelisation of a program.

2.2 Layers of the Eden Implementation

The implementation of Eden extends the runtime environment (RTE) of the Glasgow-Haskell-Compiler (GHC) [14] by a small set of primitive operations for process creation and communication between processes. These primitives merely provide very simple basic actions for process creation, data transmission between the machines' heaps, and system information. More complex operations are encoded in a functional module, called the *Eden module*. This module relies on the side-effecting primitive operations to encode Eden's process creation and communication semantics. The code on module level abstracts from many administrative issues, profiting from Haskell's support in genericity and code reuse. Moreover, it will protect the basic primitives from being

	Eden Program		
Sequential Haskell Libraries	Skeleton Library		
	Eden Module		
	Primitive Ops		
Sequential RTE	**Parallel RTE**		

Fig. 1. Layered Eden implementation

misused. This leads to an organisation of the Eden system in layers (see Fig. 1): program level – skeleton library – Eden module – primitive operations – parallel runtime environment. This will greatly improve the maintainability of the highly complex system.

The basic layer implementing the primitive operations is the GHC runtime environment, extended for parallel execution on clusters using MPI [9] or PVM [12] as a middleware. The runtime system manages communication channels and thread termination; this will not be discussed further in this paper.

Primitive Operations. The current implementation of Eden is based on six primitives for system information, communication, and thread creation. The lowest level of the Eden module (shown in Fig. 2) consists of embedding the primitives in the IO monad to encapsulate the side-effects, and adds Haskell data types for communication mode and channels.

```
noPe      :: IO Int                          number of processor elements
selfPe    :: IO Int                          ID of own processor element
createC   :: IO ( ChanName' a, a )           channel name creation
connectToPort :: ChanName' a -> IO ()        channel installation
sendData  :: Mode -> a -> IO ()              send data on implicitly given channel
fork      :: IO () -> IO ()                  new thread in same process

data ChanName' = Chan Int# Int# Int#         a single channel: IDs from RTE
data Mode = Stream | Data                    data modes: Stream or Single data
       | Connect | Instantiate Int           special modes: Connection, Instantiation
```

Fig. 2. Primitive operations to implement Eden

The first two primitives provide system information like the total number of processor elements (`noPe`) or the number of the processor element running a thread (`selfPe`).

For communication between processes, `createC` creates a new channel on the receiver side. It returns a channel name, containing three RTE-internal IDs: (PE, processID, portID) and (a handle for) the channel contents. Primitives `connectToPort` and `sendData` are executed on the sender side to connect a thread to a channel and to asynchronously send data. The send modes specify how the receiver sends data: either as an element of a stream (mode `Stream`), or in a single message (mode `Data`), or (optionally) just opening the connection (mode `Connect`). The purpose of the `Connect` mode is to provide information about future communication between processes to the runtime system. If every communication starts by a `Connect` message, the runtime system on the receiver side can terminate threads on the sender side evaluating unnecessary data.

For thread management, there is only the primitive `fork`, which creates a new thread (in the same process). Spawning a new process is implemented as sending data with the send mode `Instantiate`. The `Int` argument allows to explicitly place the new process on a certain processor. If it is zero, the RTE automatically places new processes in round-robin manner.

Eden Module: Overloaded Communication. The primitives for communication are used inside the Eden Module to implement Eden's specific data

```
newtype ChanName a = Comm (a -> IO())

class NFData a => Trans a where
   -- overloading for channel creation:
   createComm :: IO (ChanName a, a)
   createComm = do (c,v) <- createC
                   return (Comm (sendVia c), v)
   -- overloading for streams:
   write      :: a -> IO()
   write x = rnf x 'seq' sendData Data x

sendVia ch d = do connectToPort ch
                  write d
```

Fig. 3. Type class `Trans` of transmissible data

```
-- list instance (stream communication)
instance Trans a => Trans [a]
 where write  l@[]  = sendData Data l
       write (x:xs) = do (rnf x 'seq' sendData Stream x)
                         write xs

-- tuple instances (concurrency by component)
instance (Trans a, Trans b) => Trans (a,b)
  where createComm = do (c1,v1) <-createC
                        (c2,v2) <-createC
                        return (Comm (send2Via c1 c2), (v1,v2))

send2Via :: ChanName' a -> ChanName' b -> (a,b) -> IO ()
send2Via c1 c2 (v1,v2) = do fork (sendVia c1 v1)
                            sendVia c2 v2
```

Fig. 4. Eden Module: Overloading for communication

transmission semantics. The module defines type class `Trans` of transmissible data, which contains overloaded functions, namely `createComm` to create a high-level channel (type `ChanName`), and `write` to send data over channels.

As shown in Fig.3, the high-level channel `ChanName` is a *data communicator*, a function which performs the required send operation. It is composed by supplying the created primitive channel as a first argument to the auxiliary function `sendVia`. The latter, evaluated on sender side, first connects to the channel, and then calls function `write` to evaluate its second argument to normal form[1] and send it to the receiver in `Data` mode.

The two functions in `Trans` are overloaded as follows: `write` is overloaded for streams, which are communicated elementwise, and `createComm` is overloaded for tuples, which are evaluated concurrently by one thread for each component. Fig. 4 shows the instance declarations for lists and pairs. `write` communicates lists elementwise in `Stream` mode, and `createComm` for pairs creates two primitive channels, using the auxiliary function `sendVia` for `forking` threads.

Eden Module: Process Abstraction and Instantiation. The Eden constructs `process` and (`#`) render installation of communication channels between parent and child process, as well as communication, completely implicit, whereas the module internally uses *explicit* communication channels provided by `Trans` and the primitive operations.

Fig. 5 shows the definition of process abstractions and instantiations in the Eden module. Process abstractions embed a function `f_remote` that is executed by a newly created remote process. This function takes a communicator `sendResult` to return the results of the process to the parent process, and a primitive channel `inCC` to send a communicator function (of type `ChanName a`) for its input channels to the parent process. The remote process first creates input channels, i.e. the corresponding communicator functions and the handle to access the received input. It connects to the channel `inCC` and sends the input communicator with mode `Data` on it. Afterwards, the process will evaluate the expression (`f input`) and send the result to the parent process, using the communicator function `sendResult`.

The instantiation operator (`#`) relies on the function `instantiateAt`, which defines the parent side actions for the instantiation of a new child process. The embedded function `f_remote` is applied to a previously created result communicator and a primitive channel for receiving the input, and the resulting IO action is sent to the designated processor *unevaluated*. A new thread is forked to send the input to the new process. As its name suggests, `instantiateAt` may place the new process on the PE specified by the parameter `pe`; or else uses the automatic round-robin placement if the parameter is 0.

Additionally the Eden module provides a variant `createProcess` of the instantiation, which differs in the type of the result value, *lifted* to immediately deliver a value in weak head normal form (whnf). This is e.g. necessary to create a series of processes without waiting for process results (see the `parMap` skeleton explained in the next section).

Eden coordination constructs have a purely functional interface, as opposed to the primitive operations encapsulated in the IO monad. Instantiation and process behaviour are described as a sequence of IO actions based on the primitives but, finally, the functional type of the instantiation operator (`#`) will be obtained by `unsafePerformIO`, the back door out of the IO monad.

---

[1] The NFData class provides an evaluation strategy [15] `rnf` to force normal-form evaluation of any data type.

```
data Process a b = Proc (ChanName b -> ChanName' (ChanName a) -> IO())

process :: (Trans a, Trans b) => (a -> b) -> Process a b
process f = Proc f_remote
   where f_remote (Comm sendResult) inCC
           = do (sendInput, input) <- createComm -- input communicator
                connectToPort inCC              -- sent back...
                sendData Data sendInput         --     ...to parent
                sendResult (f input)            -- sending result

( # ) :: (Trans a, Trans b) => Process a b -> a -> b
p # x = unsafePerformIO (instantiateAt 0 p x)

instantiateAt :: (Trans a, Trans b) =>
               Int -> Process a b -> a -> IO b
instantiateAt pe (Proc f_remote) procInput
     = do (sendResult,  r )     <- createComm -- result communicator
          (inCC, Comm sendInput) <- createC   -- input comm. (reply)
          sendData (Instantiate pe)        -- spawn process
                  (f_remote sendResult inCC)
          fork (sendInput procInput)       -- send input concurrently
          return r                         -- return placeholder

-- variant of ( # ) which immediately delivers a whnf
data Lift a = Lift a
deLift (Lift x) = x

createProcess :: (Trans a, Trans b) => Process a b -> a -> Lift b
createProcess p i
     = unsafePerformIO (instantiateAt 0 p i >>= \x ->
                        return (Lift x))
```

Fig. 5. Eden Module: Process abstraction and instantiation

3   Imperative Coordination in a Declarative Setting

Eden provides a purely declarative interface, but aims to give the programmer *explicit* control of parallelism in the program. Eden programs can be read twofold, from a computational and from a coordinational perspective:

– Instantiation of a previously defined process abstraction denotationally differs from function application by the additional strictness due to Eden's eager communication policy, but yields the same result as application of a strict function.

- Process abstraction and instantiation will hide any process communication, but expose the degree of parallelism of an algorithm directly by the number of instantiations.

However, the additional strictness introduced by eager communication is a crucial point for tuning parallel programs. On the one hand, it is required to start subcomputations at an early stage and in parallel. On the other hand, adding too much artificial strictness to a program can easily lead to deadlock situations. A complex Eden program normally uses a suitable skeleton library, optimised for the common case and circumventing common pitfalls of parallelism. Eden can also describe new specialised *skeletons*, and programming these is a different matter. Efficiently programming skeletons in Eden requires intimate knowledge of Eden specifics and a clear concept of the evaluation order in a demand-driven evaluation. Concentrating on the coordination view of Eden, programming skeletons can profit from a more *explicit* approach, as offered by Eden's implementation language EDI. EDI can be considered – necessarily at a lower level – as a fully-fledged alternative Eden-type language, which renders communication and side-effects explicit and will force to use the IO monad for parallel execution.

3.1   Low-Level Parallel Programming in EDI

Evaluation and Communication Decoupled.   In contrast to Eden's communication semantics, EDI communication is completely independent of the underlying computation. If a communicated value is not needed by the sender for a local computation, it will be left unevaluated by sending. This, of course, is not intended for parallel processes supposed to compute subresults. Programs in EDI therefore use evaluation strategies [15] to explicitly initiate the computation of a value to be sent. Although EDI does *not* encode coordination by strategies, using the class `NFData` and its normal form evaluation strategy `rnf` is a necessary part of EDI programming. We present and evaluate some parallel skeletons programmed in EDI and compare them with Eden skeletons.

Parallel Map.   The higher-order function `map` applies a given function to all elements of a list. In a straightforward parallelisation, a process is created for each element of the resulting list. This can be expressed easily in Eden using process abstraction and instantiation, or programmed explicitly in EDI.

```
-- Eden's parallel map
parMap :: (Trans a, Trans b) => (a -> b) -> [a] -> [b]
parMap f xs = map deLift ([ createProcess (process f) x | x <- xs ]
                         'using' whnfspine)

-- auxiliary function for demand control
whnfspine :: Strategy [a]
whnfspine [] = ()
whnfspine (x:xs) = x 'seq' whnfspine xs
```

The Eden version shown here uses the instantiation operator `createProcess`, which encodes all necessary communication and concurrency. Additional demand by 'using' whnfspine is necessary to force the immediate creation of all processes. Please note the use of createProcess instead of (#), which is necessary because the strategy whnfspine would otherwise wait for the whnf of each process' result prior to forcing the creation of the next process.

```
-- monadic Edi parmap using primitive operations only:
parMapIO :: NFData b => (a -> b) -> [a] -> IO [b]
parMapIO f xs = do cs <- createCs (length xs)
                   sequence_ [ sendData (Instantiate 0) (doF ch x)
                             | (x,ch) <- zip xs (fst cs) ]
                   return (snd cs)
       where doF c x = do connectToPort c
                          let fx = f x
                          (rnf fx 'seq' sendData Data fx)

createCs :: NFData a => Int -> IO ([ChanName' a],[a])
createCs n = do cList <- sequence (replicate n createC)
                let lists@(cs, vs) = unzip cList
                (rnf cs 'seq' return lists)
```

The EDI version is explicitly monadic (but might, of course, escape from the IO monad by unsafePerformIO at top level). Prior to spawning the child processes, the caller creates a set of channels (by a simple abstraction createCs over the single channel creation createC). Each remote computation (defined by function doF) will receive one of these channels for sending back the result. The second parameter of doF is the *input*, potentially unevaluated. Whilst the Eden process instantiation spawns an own concurrent thread in the calling machine to send this input in normal form, the EDI version acts as a *demand-driven* parallel map (parmap_dm), useful to avoid bottlenecks in the caller. The latter can, of course, be modelled in Eden as well, by adding a dummy argument to the function applied to the list elements:

```
parmap_dm:: (Trans a, Trans b) => (a -> b) -> [a] -> IO [b]
parmap_dm f xs = map deLift
                   ([ createProcess (process (\() -> f x)) () | x <- xs ]
                    'using' whnfspine)
```

An advantage of the EDI code is that the Lift - deLift trick as well as the explicit demand control using the strategy whnfspine is no longer necessary to create a series of processes.

Figure 6 shows runtime and speedup measurements for a small test program with the two demand-driven parMap versions, also including the previous Eden implementation (based on GHC 5) for comparisons. The program computes the sum of Euler Totients, $\sum_1^n \varphi(k)$ for $n = 25000$. Of course, the test program does not spawn an own process for every number $\varphi(k)$ to be computed – the task granularity would be much too fine. Numbers are distributed evenly among few processes, one on each available processor. And since the values are summed up afterwards (map is followed by a parallel fold), each process(or) computes the partial sum in parallel as well.

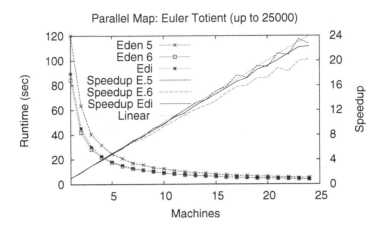

Fig. 6. Parallel `map/fold` example, Eden 5, Eden 6 and EDI

The *sequential* base performance of the previous Eden 5 system apparently is much worse (44% longer runtime); therefore speedup degrades slightly for the new implementation. The negligible difference between Eden 6 and EDI shows that the overhead for the module code is minor, and only the way input data is transmitted is relevant, depending on the concrete application.

Nondeterminism, Concurrency and Parallelism. In the previous example, tasks have been distributed statically, in advance. When subtasks are of highly irregular complexity, or when the number of subtasks may vary depending on the input, *dynamic* load balancing is one of the most desired properties of a parallel `map` skeleton. The purely functional coordination constructs of Eden are not sufficient to describe dynamic task distribution; therefore Eden offers a nondeterministic additional construct `merge` for merging a list of streams into a single stream. Data is added to the output stream as soon as it is available in any of the input streams, in nondeterministic order. As shown in Fig. 7, this can be used for a *workpool* scheme, i.e. a `map` skeleton in master/worker scheme, where a worker process gets a new task every time it returns a result. A prefetch parameter determines the number of initial tasks assigned to a worker. It should be used to avoid workers running out of work.

In this simple version, the computation results are returned unsorted, in the order in which they have been sent back by the workers. In order to indicate which worker has completed a task, every worker tags its results with its id, a number between 1 and `np`. All result streams `fromWorkers` are merged nondeterministically in the master process. The worker numbers are then separated from the proper results, and serve as requests for new work. The auxiliary function `distribute` takes as arguments the list of requests and the available tasks, and distributes the tasks to `np` sublists, as indicated by the requests list. The number of initial requests is determined by skeleton parameter `prefetch`. A crucial

```
edenWP :: (Trans t, Trans r) =>
     Int -> Int -> (t -> r) -> [t] -> [r]
edenWP np prefetch f tasks = results
  where fromWorkers = map deLift
                      (zipWith createProcess workerProcs toWorkers)
                                  'using' whnfspine
        workerProcs = [process (zip [n,n..] . map f) | n<-[1..np]]
        toWorkers         = distribute tasks requests
        (newReqs, results) = (unzip . merge) fromWorkers
        requests          = initialReqs ++ newReqs
        initialReqs       = concat (replicate prefetch [1..np])
        distribute :: [t] -> [Int] -> [[t]]
        distribute tasks reqs = [taskList reqs tasks n | n<-[1..np]]
        where taskList (r:rs) (t:ts) pe
                    | pe == r    = t:(taskList rs ts pe)
                    | otherwise  =    taskList rs ts pe
              taskList _     _        _ = []
```

Fig. 7. Eden workpool skeleton using `merge`

```
ediWP :: (NFData t, NFData r) =>
     Int -> Int -> (t -> r) -> [t] -> IO [r]
ediWP np prefetch f tasks = do
          (wInCCs, wInCs) <- createCs np
          (wOutCs, wOuts) <- createCs np
          sequence_ [ sendData (Instantiate 0) (worker f wOutC wInCC)
                       | (wOutC,wInCC) <- zip wOutCs wInCCs ]
          taskChan <- newChan
          fork (writeList2Chan taskChan
                   ((map Just tasks) ++ (replicate np Nothing)))
          sequence_ [ fork (inputSender prefetch inC taskChan answers)
                       | (inC,answers) <- zip wInCs wOuts ]
          return (concat wOuts)
```

Fig. 8. EDI workpool skeleton, using concurrent `inputSender` threads

property of the function `distribute` is that it must be "incremental", i.e. can deliver partial result lists without the need to evaluate requests not yet available.

A recent extension to this skeleton may even be nested and applied to computations where the results computed by workers may lead to new additional tasks [11].

```
worker :: (NFData t, NFData r) =>
          (t -> r) -> ChanName' [r] -> ChanName'(ChanName'[t]) -> IO ()
worker f outC inCC
      = do (inC, inTasks) <- createC -- create channel for input
           connectToPort inCC        -- send channel to parent
           sendData Data inC
           connectToPort outC        -- send result stream
           sendStream ((map f) inTasks)
    where sendStream :: NFData r => [r] -> IO ()
          sendStream    []  = sendData Data []
          sendStream (x:xs) = do (rnf x `seq` sendData Stream x)
                                 sendStream xs


inputSender :: (NFData t) =>
              Int -> ChanName' [t] -> Chan (Maybe t) -> [r] -> IO ()
inputSender prefetch inC concHsC answers
      = do connectToPort inC
           react ( replicate prefetch dummy  ++ answers)
    where dummy = undefined
          react :: [r] -> IO ()
          react [] = return ()
          react (_:as) = do
                  task <- readChan concHsC -- get a task
                  case task of
                    (Just t) -> do (rnf t `seq` sendData Stream t )
                                   react as
                  Nothing  -> sendData Data [] -- and done.
```

Fig. 9. worker process and inputSender thread for EDI workpool

However, the workpool skeleton can also be implemented without the need for Eden's merge construct, nor the sophisticated distribute. Instead, we can use a nondeterministic construct of Concurrent Haskell: a channel which is read by concurrent sender threads inside the master. A channel (data type Chan) in Concurrent Haskell models a potentially infinite stream of data which may be consumed concurrently by different threads. Due to nondeterministic scheduling, channel operations are in the IO monad, like the EDI coordination constructs. Figure 8 shows a workpool skeleton which returns its result in the IO monad.

The master needs channels not only to receive the results, but also to initiate input communication with the workers, thus two sets of np channels are created. A set of worker processes is instantiated with these channels as parameters. As shown in Fig.9, each worker creates a channel to receive input, sends it to the parent, and then connects to the given output channel to send the results as a stream.

```
ring :: (Trans a, Trans b,
         Trans r) =>
        Int ->
        (Int -> i -> [a]) ->
        ([b] -> o) ->
        ((a,[r]) -> (b,[r]))
        -> i -> o
```

```
ring size makeInput processOutput ringWorker input = ...
```

Fig. 10. A ring skeleton in Eden, type and communication structure

We use a `Maybe` type in order to indicate termination. The `taskChan` is created and (concurrently) filled with the tagged task list (`map Just tasks`), followed by np termination signals (`Nothing`). The task channel is concurrently read by several input senders, one for every worker process, which will be forked next. Every input sender consumes the answers of one worker and emits one new task per answer, after an initial `prefetch` phase. The master process collects the answers using `concat`, the Haskell prelude function to concatenate a list of lists. A slight variant of this would be to sort the answers list in the order indicated by tags which are added to tasks to memorise their initial order.

It should be noted that the EDI version of the workpool looks slightly more specialised and seems to use more concurrent threads than the – considerably shorter – Eden version. Since EDI uses explicit communication, the separate threads to supply the input become obvious. The Eden version works in quite the same way, but the concurrent threads are created implicitly by the process instantiation operation `createProcess`. Apart from one separate thread filling the channel with available tasks, both versions have exactly the same degree of concurrency; it is not surprising that both workpool implementations are similar in runtime and speedup.

Once the master process uses concurrent threads and the IO monad, it may easily be extended in different ways. One very useful extension would be to include a state in the master process, e.g. a "current optimal" solution for a branch-and-bound algorithm, or a dynamically increasing task pool, or using a stack instead of a FIFO queue for task management. Depending on the particular requirements for the master state, its implementation in a purely functional style may become quite cumbersome (see [8] for a case study). The explicitness of parallelism, communication and concurrency inflates the EDI code, but is advantageous when implementing specialised versions of skeletons.

A Ring Skeleton. The examples given up to now are showing, more or less, how Eden and EDI are interchangeable and comparable in performance. There are however situations where Eden's implicit concurrency and eagerness can lead to unwanted behaviour, and the source code usually does not clearly indicate the errors.

A ring of interconnected processes can be defined using Eden channels [1]. Fig. 10 shows the type signature of a highly parameterised ring skeleton, and

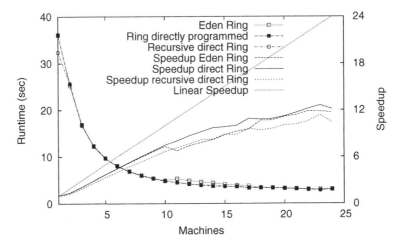

Fig. 11. Ring example: Warshall's algorithm (500 node graph), Eden vs. directly programmed, specialised ring

depicts its process and communication structure. Parameters are the ring size, a function `makeInput` preparing the initial input to all ring processes, a similar function (`processOutput`) to construct the final output, and the functionality of the ring processes. All ring processes are identical and receive two inputs, one (of type `a`) from the caller and one (of type `[r]`, a stream) from their predecessor in the ring.

This skeleton may also be specified at a lower level in EDI, with the advantage that the communication, explicit anyway, may be optimised for the special application, e.g. when input is statically determined, or when the ring output is not relevant.

As in the previous examples, there are no big runtime differences in the general case. Fig. 11 shows measurements for an example program, Warshall's algorithm to compute the complex hull of a directed graph.

This skeleton description is coherent at first sight, but some questions may arise when using it. The given type restricts the ring communication to a stream. This is a sensible restriction since, with a non-stream type, the ring necessarily degenerates to a pipeline, or simply deadlocks. Likewise, Eden constructs can express the case where the initial input (of type `a`) to the ring processes is static and thus embeddable into the process abstraction, as shown for `parMap`.

A more subtle detail can lead to problems when the general ring skeleton is used in a special context: If the initial ring process input (or output) happens to be a tuple, the programmer might expect that each component will be evaluated concurrently, as usual in Eden. However, the ring implementation adds an additional parameter to the input: Channels to the ring neighbours must be exchanged prior to computation. The ring process abstraction internally is of type `Process (a,ChanName [r]) (b,ChanName [r])` and, thus, does *not* use concurrency for components of their external input and output – the ring will immediately deadlock if the components of type a expose non-local data dependencies. A different Eden implementation of the ring, specialised to avoid this problem, is possible, but the difficulty is to find out the reason for the deadlock. Neither the calling program, nor the skeleton source code will clearly indicate the problem; it will remain hidden in the overloaded communication inside the Eden module.

Downside of Explicitness. As we have shown previously, the explicitness of EDI can help to optimise skeletons for particular cases and save time in spotting errors due to Eden's complex implicit communication semantics. On the other hand, programming in EDI considerably inflates the code and may have other pitfalls. Evaluation control prior to communication is the most important of these, since the implemented sendData primitive does not imply any prior evaluation. As EDI is purely monadic and deliberately simple, the programmer has to specify *every* single action.

Another possible source of errors is the all-purpose character of sendData, which uses the same primitive for data transmission, communication management, and process instantiation, distinguished only by the different send modes. Sending data by the wrong mode may lead to, e.g., a bogus process without any effect, as shown here:

```
badIdea_no1 :: Int -> a -> IO ()
badIdea_no1 pe data = sendData (Instantiate pe) data
```

If the data sent is, say, a number, its remote evaluation will have no effect at all, although its type is perfectly correct, due to the liberal typing of the primitive. In the example above, an auxiliary function for instantiation should force that the data sent is an action of type IO().

```
spawnProcessAt :: Int -> IO () -> IO ()
spawnProcessAt pe action = sendData (Instantiate pe) action
```

Moreover, for data communication, threads are supposed to connect to a channel prior to communication and might cause obscure runtime errors if the wrong connections are created. Although the simple channels of EDI are strongly typed, this two-step communication allows to create erroneous communication sequences not discovered at compile time. The following (perfectly well-typed) function expects a *wrong* channel type and then does not connect prior to sending in one case, or alternatively uses the wrong send mode.

```
badIdea_no2 :: ChanName' Double -> [Double]   -- types do not match
                       -> IO ()
badIdea_no2 c (n:ns)= do sendData Stream n    -- not yet connected
                         badIdea_no2 c ns
badIdea_no2 c    [] = do connectToPort c
                         sendData Stream []   -- wrong send mode
```

When evaluating this function, a run-time error will occur because the receiver's heap becomes corrupted.

As above, combining connection and send operation by a type-enforcing auxiliary function can detect the error. The applied evaluation strategy can as well be included in such a combined function.

```
sendEvalDataOver :: Strategy a -> ChanName' a -> a -> IO()
sendEvalDataOver eval ch d = do connectToPort c
                                (eval d 'seq'
                                    sendData Data d)
```

The only disadvantage here is that a separate function for sending lists is needed, since the send mode becomes hard-coded.

In order to streamline the interface between Haskell and the runtime system, the primitive sendData has been given the liberal type Mode -> a -> IO (), which is why erroneous usage of the primitive will not be detected at compile time. Hence, the solution to these problems consists in typed auxiliary functions which will restrict the argument types in such a way that the primitives will be used as intended. Obviously, it is necessary to superimpose a layer of type-checking auxiliary functions over the primitive operations to improve error detection during type checking in EDI.

4   Related Work

EDI considered as a language provides extensions to existing concepts of Concurrent Haskell [5], as implemented in GHC. Thread concurrency is *extended* by process parallelism, communication in EDI is handled using channel communication instead of the shared synchronised heap cells (MVars) of Concurrent Haskell. As we have already underlined by one of our examples, both approaches can be sensibly combined. Latest efforts in Haskell implementations aim to extend Concurrent Haskell's thread concurrency to OS level for multiprocessor support in the threaded GHC runtime system [3]. Combining this future multicore support with the distributed-memory-parallelism provided by EDI is one of our long-term goals.

In the field of parallel functional languages, many language concepts follow more implicit approaches than Eden and, necessarily, its implementation language. Although intended as a low-level implementation language, EDI can be used as a language for distributed programming with explicit asynchronous communication.

Glasgow Distributed Haskell (GdH) [10] is the closest relative to EDI in this respect and provides comparable language features, especially location-awareness and dynamically spawning remote IO actions. However, GdH has been designed with the explicit aim to extend the virtual shared memory model of Glasgow Parallel Haskell (GpH) [16] by features of explicit concurrency (Concurrent Haskell [5]). Our implementation primarily aimed at a simple implementation concept for Eden and thus does not include the shared-memory-related concepts of GdH. Indeed, we think that GdH can be implemented with minimal extensions to our implementation.

Port-based distributed Haskell (PdH) [4] is an extension of Haskell for distributed programming. PdH offers a dynamic, server-oriented port-based communication for first-order values between different Haskell programs. In contrast to our implementation, its primary aim is to obtain open distributed systems, interconnecting different applications – integrating a network library and a stock Haskell compiler.

5 Conclusions and Future Work

We have presented a new implementation for the parallel functional language Eden, based on a lean low-level interface (EDI) to a sophisticated parallel Haskell runtime environment. Although essentially following previous concepts, the new implementation makes the side-effecting primitive operations explicit and allows to express parallel coordination in an imperative manner, while the computation language remains purely functional.

While EDI provides a low-level flexible and powerful approach to controlling coordination in a functional setting, Eden abstracts from many details, thereby simplifying the development of parallel programs, but partly losing coordination control. Runtime comparisons show that programs written in Eden and EDI will show the same performance as long as their behaviour is equivalent. This is because Eden is implemented on top of EDI. From the programmer's point of view, the Eden level of abstraction would be an asset if everything worked out fine. On the other hand, getting things right is much more difficult in Eden than on the EDI level of abstraction.

We have briefly mentioned the spectrum of parallel functional languages expressible by EDI and using our framework. Our Eden implementation based on EDI can be used to easily obtain prototype implementations for other parallel extensions of Haskell, mainly extensions at higher abstraction levels.

One of our research goals is to keep alive and advance a general-purpose parallel Haskell. The comparison of Eden and EDI undertaken in this paper is a step towards redesigning Eden and will need further investigation. Several other areas lend themselves to further research. Combining the concepts we developed for the runtime with state-of-the-art hardware techniques, such as multicore support, or modern wide-area network infrastructure (Grid Technology), is the most important goal. Likewise, by applying these concepts to a different computation language, the influences of the host language will emerge, and parallelism extensions can be cleanly separated from their sequential base or concrete application.

References

1. Berthold, J., Loogen, R.: The Impact of Dynamic Channels on Functional Topology Skeletons. In: Tiskin, A., Loulergue, F., (eds.), HLPP 2005: 3rd International Workshop on High-level Parallel Programming and Applications, Coventry, UK (2005)
2. Hammond, K., Michaelson, G. (eds.): Research Directions in Parallel Functional Programming. Springer, Heidelberg (1999)

3. Harris, T., Marlow, S., Jones, S.P.: Haskell on a Shared-Memory Multiprocessor. In: Haskell '05: Proceedings of the 2005 ACM SIGPLAN workshop on Haskell, ACM Press, New York (September 2005)
4. Huch, F., Stolz, V.: Implementation of Port-based Distributed Haskell. In: Mohnen, M., Koopman, P. W. M., (eds.), IFL'01: Implementation of Functional Languages, 13th International Workshop, Draft Proceedings, Stockholm, Sweden (2001)
5. Jones, S.P., Gordon, A., Finne, S.: Concurrent Haskell. In: POPL '96: Proceedings of the 23rd ACM SIGPLAN-SIGACT symposium on Principles of programming languages, ACM Press, New York (1996)
6. Loogen, R., Ortega-Mallén, Y., Peña, R., Priebe, S., Rubio, F.: Parallelism Abstractions in Eden. In: Rabhi, F.A., Gorlatch, S. (eds.) Patterns and Skeletons for Parallel and Distributed Computing, ch. 4, Springer, Heidelberg (2003)
7. Loogen, R., Ortega-Mallén, Y., Peña-Marí, R.: Parallel Functional Programming in Eden. Journal of Functional Programming 15(3), 431–475 (2005)
8. Martínez, R., Pena, R.: Building an Interface Between Eden and Maple: A Way of Parallelizing Computer Algebra Algorithms. In: IFL'03: Implementation of Functional Languages, 15th International Workshop, Edinburgh, UK, Selected Papers, LNCS vol. 3145, Springer, Heidelberg (2003)
9. MPI-2: Extensions to the Message-Passing Interface. Technical report, University of Tennessee, Knoxville (July 1997)
10. Pointon, R., Trinder, P., Loidl, H.-W.: The design and implementation of Glasgow Distributed Haskell. In: IFL'00: Implementation of Functional Languages, 12th International Workshop, Aachen, Germany, Selected Papers, LNCS vol. 2011, Springer, Heidelberg (2000)
11. Priebe, S.: Dynamic Task Generation and Transformation within a Nestable Workpool Skeleton. In: Nagel, W.E., Walter, W.V., Lehner, W. (eds.) Euro-Par 2006. LNCS, vol. 4128, Springer, Heidelberg (2006)
12. PVM: Parallel Virtual Machine. Web page. *http://www.epm.ornl.gov/pvm/*
13. Rabhi, F.A., Gorlatch, S. (eds.): Patterns and Skeletons for Parallel and Distributed Computing. Springer, Heidelberg (2003)
14. The GHC Developer Team. The Glasgow Haskell Compiler. Website *http://www.haskell.org/ghc.*
15. Trinder, P., Hammond, K., Loidl, H.-W., Peyton Jones, S.: Algorithm + Strategy = Parallelism. Journal of Functional Programming 8(1), 23–60 (1998)
16. Trinder, P., Hammond, K., Mattson, Jr., J., Partridge, A., Peyton Jones, S.: GUM: a Portable Parallel Implementation of Haskell. In: PLDI'96: Proceedings of the ACM SIGPLAN'96 Conference on Programming Language Design and Implementation, ACM Press, New York (1996)
17. Trinder, P.W., Loidl, H.W., Pointon, R.F.: Parallel and distributed Haskells. Journal of Functional Programming 12(4, 5), 469–510 (2002)

Low-Level Programming in Hume:
An Exploration of the HW-Hume Level

Kevin Hammond[1], Gudmund Grov[2], Greg Michaelson[2], and Andrew Ireland[2]

[1] School of Computer Science,
University of St Andrews, St Andrews, Scotland
Tel.: +44-1334-463241
kh@dcs.st-and.ac.uk
[2] Dept. of Mathematics and Computer Science,
Heriot-Watt University, Edinburgh, Scotland
Tel.: +44-131-451-3422
{gudmund,air,greg}@macs.hw.ac.uk

Abstract. This paper describes the HW-Hume level of the novel Hume language. HW-Hume is the simplest subset of Hume that we have identified. It provides strong formal properties but posseses limited abstraction capabilities. In this paper, we introduce HW-Hume, show some simple example programs, describe an efficient software implementation, and demonstrate how important properties can be exposed as part of an integrated formally-based verification approach.

1 Introduction

The novel Hume language embeds a strict, purely functional *expression layer*, that describes computations, within a *process layer*, that describes a system of asynchronous communicating processes. By varying the structure of the Hume expression layer, a number of distinct Hume levels can be identified, where each level fully contains the level below, but increases the difficulty of providing accurate cost information and other properties. *Full-Hume*, or *Hume*, is a Turing-Complete language based on concurrent finite state automata whose transitions are controlled by pattern matching over rich types to initiate actions described by general recursive expressions. *PR-Hume*, restricts repetition to primitive recursion, enabling decidable termination. *Template-Hume* only permits repetition through pre-defined higher-order operators. *FSM-Hume* is a finite-state language with fixed size types and first order functions. Finally, *HW-Hume*, aimed at hardware realisation, is a relatively impoverished language for manipulating tuples and vectors of bits, with exact time and space use prediction.

We have previously introduced the Hume language [22], defining the different levels of Hume, as outlined above, and shown how translations may be made between levels [21]. We have also demonstrated that it is possible to construct bounded space cost models for FSM-Hume [23], and for time and space up to PR-Hume [34,35]. We are in the process of constructing automatic analyses to provide bounds on amortised time and space cost information on levels up to PR-Hume. This paper considers HW-Hume in considerably more depth than in the general papers mentioned above [21,22]. Section 2 introduces HW-Hume and provides some simple examples; Section 3 discusses formal verification of safety, liveness and real-time properties using model-checking; Section 4

Z. Horváth, V. Zsók, and A. Butterfield (Eds.): IFL 2006, LNCS 4449, pp. 91–107, 2007.

describes a software implementation of HW-Hume and provides some performance results; Section 5 discusses possible hardware implementations; Section 6 describes related work; and finally, Section 7 concludes.

2   HW-Hume

HW-Hume programs (Figure 1) are built from a series of *box* declarations linked using static *wires*. Multiple identical instances of a box may be defined using a *template* for subsequent *instantiation*. A single HW-Hume box comprises a set of pattern-directed rules, rewriting a set of inputs to a set of outputs, plus appropriate type information for each input/output. The most primitive type of value is a bit, which may be grouped into fixed-size vectors or tuples in either a pattern or an expression. Patterns and expressions may be formed from bit literals, variables, the wildcard pattern _, vector or tuple structures, or (at the top level) the asynchronous * construct, which ignores its input and produces no output. τ defines the valid HW-Hume types: bit types, **word** 1; the unit type, (); tuple types $\tau_1 \times \ldots \times \tau_n$; bounded vector types, **vector** n **of** τ, where n is the bound; and named types, *typeid*.

2.1   Boxes and Coordination

HW-Hume *boxes* are abstractions of processes that correspond to (usually finite) state machines. The left-hand-side (pattern part) of each rule defines the situations in which that rule may be *active*, i.e. could be executed. The right-hand-side of each rule is an expression specifying the results of the box when the rule is activated and matches the corresponding pattern. A box may become active when any of its rules are active, i.e.

program ::=	$decl_1$; ... ; $decl_n$;	$n \geq 1$
decl ::=	*box* | *wire* | *type* | *template* | *instantiation*	
box ::=	**box** boxid *ins outs* (**match** | **fair**) *matches*	
ins/outs ::=	($ioid_1 :: \tau_1$, ... , $ioid_n :: \tau_n$)	$n \geq 0$
τ ::=	**word** 1 | () | $(\tau_1 , \ldots , \tau_m)$ | **vector** n **of** τ | typeid	$m \geq 2, n \geq 1$
matches ::=	$match_1$ | ... | $match_n$	$n \geq 1$
match ::=	(pat_1 , ... , pat_n) $\rightarrow$ *expr*	$n \geq 0$
expr/pat ::=	0 | 1 | varid | _ | * | () | ($expr_1/pat_1$, ... , $expr_n/pat_n$)	$n \geq 2$
	| **vector** $expr_1/pat_1$ ... $expr_n/pat_n$	$n \geq 1$
wire ::=	**wire** $link_1$ **to** $link_2$ [**initially** *expr*]	
link ::=	boxid . ioid | deviceid	
type ::=	**type** typeid = τ	
template ::=	**template** templateid *ins outs* (**match** | **fair**) *matches*	
instantiation ::=	**instantiate** templateid **as** boxid [* nat]	

Fig. 1. HW-Hume Syntax

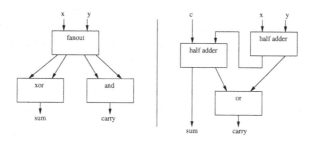

Fig. 2. a) Half-adder b) Full-adder

they may match the inputs that have been provided. In this case, the box runs to completion, producing any required outputs. For example, we can define boxes to implement *xor*, *and*, and a two-in to four-out *fanout* as:

```
box xor          box and          box fanout
in (a,b::Bit)    in (a,b::Bit)    in (x,y::Bit)
out (x::Bit)     out (x::Bit)     out (x1,y1,x2,y2::Bit)
match            match            match
   (1,1) -> 0       (1,1) -> 1       (x,y) -> (x,y,x,y);
|  (0,0) -> 0    |  (_,_) -> 0;
|  (_,_) -> 1;
```

For each box, we first specify the names and types of the inputs and outputs – here all single bits. Note that boxes may use the same names: these are always qualified externally by the box name. We then specify the pattern-matching rules that take the given inputs and produce the correct output. The final rule in the first two cases uses "anonymous" variable patterns, defined using _. HW-Hume boxes are connected into a static process network using wires to connect one specific output to one specific input. For example, Figure 2 shows: (a) a *half adder* built from a fanout box, an and box and an xor box; (b) a *full adder* built from two half adders and an or, where the half adder is either built from simpler components as in (a) or defined in its own right from a truth table:

```
box or           box half-adder
in (a,b::Bit)    in (x,y::Bit)
out (x::Bit)     out(s,c::Bit)
match            match
   (0,0) -> 0       (0,0) -> (0,0)
|  (_,_) -> 1;   |  (0,1) -> (1,0)
                 |  (1,0) -> (1,0)
                 |  (1,1) -> (0,1);
```

In either case, the boxes are then wired into a static process network using the obvious wiring declarations. The use of a static process network allows strong program properties to be obtained, as discussed in Section 3.

Asynchronous Language Constructs. Unlike the widely-used synchronous languages for real-time systems, such as Lustre [10], Signal [17] or Esterel [8], HW-Hume is an asynchronous language, allowing the expression of hardware/software systems that are not explicitly clocked, and where individual boxes may produce outputs without synchronising on their inputs. The two main mechanisms for asynchronicity in Hume are to allow some or all inputs/outputs to be *ignored*, using ∗, and to allow *fair matching* on rules, where on each box cycle the first rule considered is that after the one that succeeded on the previous cycle. The ∗-pattern indicates that the corresponding input position should be ignored, i.e. the match always succeeds without demanding any input. ∗ can also be used in a top-level expression position. For example, a multiplexer can be described by the rules below, where the fourth rule will discard the selector if no other input is available.

```
type Bit = word 1;
type Byte = vector 8 of Bit;
type Selector  = (Bit,Bit);

box multiplexer
in (b1, b2, b3 :: Byte, sel :: Selector)    out  (b :: Byte)
fair
     (b,   *,   *,         (0,0)) -> b
  |  (*,   b,   *,         (0,1)) -> b
  |  (*,   *,   b,         (1,0)) -> b
  |  (*,   *,   *,         _    ) -> *;
```

Note that, in this example, although there is no explicit input clock signal, the selector input acts as a trigger, effectively requiring synchronisation between the selector and the corresponding input. A more asynchronous version can be produced, if required, by simply eliminating the selector input.

```
box multiplexer2
in (b1, b2, b3 :: Byte)   out  (b :: Byte)
fair
     (b,   *,   *) -> b
  |  (*,   b,   *) -> b
  |  (*,   *,   b) -> b;
```

Now each input is immediately mapped to the output without waiting for some selector to be present. Outputs are chosen from the three possibilities fairly [5,22]. Multiplexing is an example of an operation that cannot easily be expressed in a single-layer purely functional notation, since it is non-deterministic at the box level. Despite this local idea of non-determinacy (an essential part of the problem specification), it is important to realise that *the system as a whole* is still deterministic in that it will respond identically to the same inputs received at the same relative times [22].

2.2 A Simple Traffic Lights Example in HW-Hume

As a more detailed example, we consider a set of traffic lights, as used in the UK, which displays a sequence of red (stop), red and amber (prepare to go), green (go) and amber (prepare to stop) lights[1]. We might encode these state changes as:

---

[1] A variant of this example has also been used in [21] to illustrate inter-level transformations.

light(s)	state	meaning	red	amber	green
red	0	stop	1	0	0
red/amber	1	prepare to go	1	1	0
green	2	go	0	0	1
amber	3	prepare to stop	0	1	0

where a 1 indicates that the corresponding light is on and a 0 that it is off. In HW-Hume, we could model a traffic light as a box which changes state when it receives a signal. We encode the state as a two-bit binary number, and the light settings as a tuple of bits. So that we can reuse the lights definition later, we will use a template definition:

```
template trafficlights
in  (signal::Bit, state::(Bit,Bit))
out (state'::(Bit,Bit),lights::(Bit,Bit,Bit))
match
  (1,(0,0)) -> ((0,1),(1,1,0))
| (1,(0,1)) -> ((1,0),(0,0,1))
| (1,(1,0)) -> ((1,1),(0,1,0))
| (1,(1,1)) -> ((0,0),(1,0,0));

instantiate trafficlights as lights;

wire change              to  lights.signal;
wire lights.state        to  lights.state';
wire lights.lights       to  display;
```

where change and display are unspecified external connections. On each box cycle, if the signal on change is 1 then, for the current state, a new setting on lights is sent to display and a new state is produced on state'. Unlike the earlier, *combinational* examples we have seen, this is an example of *sequential logic*: it is necessary to record the state value as feedback between box iterations.

3   Verifying HW-Hume Programs

Because of the cost and difficulty involved in applying bug fixes, low-level system designs often possess strong correctness criteria. This is especially true for hardware, where there is a long tradition of using automated verification and formal methods to enhance confidence in the correctness of such systems. In particular *model checking* [12] has been successfully applied to many hardware systems. In this approach, a property is specified in a temporal logic, and its correctness against a given model (program) is verified algorithmically by exploring the complete state space of the model.

We exploit TLA+ [29] which combines TLA (Temporal Logic of Actions [28]) with a variant of ZF set-theory and which allows both system (model) and properties to be specified in the same logic. The validity of a program property can therefore be expressed by logical implication: *Program* ⇒ *Property*. This validity can then be checked by the TLC model checker [29] for TLA⁺. TLA(⁺) also have a proof system, meaning we can give deductive proofs of properties, which will be required in the higher levels of Hume. It has a similar layering to Hume, and this together with both the algorithmic and deductive proofs support, made TLA fit really well into our work. In HW-Hume, individual box definitions are fairly simple, and the most interesting properties (and errors!) consequently arise when combining two or more boxes. We therefore illustrate our approach using a slightly extended version of the traffic light example, where two instances of the `trafficlights` template are connected to model a complete road junction under the control of the `controller` box below.

```
instantiate trafficlights as lights * 2;

box controller
in  (state :: (Bit,Bit,Bit))
out (state' :: (Bit,Bit,Bit), lights1,lights2 :: Bit)
match
  (0,0,0) -> ((0,0,1),1,*)   -- lights1: Red -> Red-amber
| (0,0,1) -> ((0,1,0),1,*)   -- lights1: Red-amber -> Green
| (0,1,0) -> ((0,1,1),1,*)   -- lights1: Green -> Amber
| (0,1,1) -> ((1,0,0),1,*)   -- lights1: Amber -> Red
| (1,0,0) -> ((1,0,1),*,1)   -- lights2: Red -> Red-amber
| (1,0,1) -> ((1,1,0),*,1)   -- lights2: Red-amber -> Green
| (1,1,0) -> ((1,1,1),*,1)   -- lights2: Green -> Amber
| (1,1,1) -> ((0,0,0),*,1);  -- lights2: Amber -> Red
```

In the remainder of this section we will discuss both safety and liveness properties of this program. We also show how time analysis of the expression layer can be combined with TLA⁺ to verify bounded real-time properties of the coordination layer.

3.1 Safety Properties

A *safety property* specifies that certain undesired behaviour never occurs [4]. The safety-part of a specification therefore specifies what a good behaviour is, but does not require that something actually happens. We formalise the safety part of the traffic light example as follows. Let *Prog* denote the safety part of our program. The state space consists of $\bar{\imath}$, all the internal variables used in any box, and $\overline{w}$, all the wires used in the program. These are given an initial value by *Init*. For each box, we define actions $\mathcal{N}_{l1}$, $\mathcal{N}_{l2}$ and $\mathcal{N}_{ctl}$ which update the state space. Since TLA⁺ is a logic rather than a programming language, these actions are defined as predicates on a before-step and an after-step, where all variables in the after-step are primed. For example, if $l1$ can be executed then $\mathcal{N}_{l1}$ will match the (unprimed) input wires (unfairly). If it succeeds, then the (primed) input wires are set to empty since there are no * in the pattern, and the primed outputs are updated with the result of the computation. A *next-action* $\mathcal{N}$ updates the complete state space, and is defined in terms of the execution of all the boxes in the program ($\mathcal{N}_{l1} \wedge \mathcal{N}_{l2} \wedge \mathcal{N}_{ctl}$). It must have the form $[\mathcal{N}]_{(\bar{i},\overline{w})}$, which abbreviates $\mathcal{N} \vee (\bar{i},\overline{w})' = (\bar{i},\overline{w})$. This is an important feature since it allows "internal actions" that do not alter the state space. Since we are working in a temporal logic, this next-action is required to hold throughout execution. We therefore prefix the action with the temporal *always* operator ($\square$) to give $\square[\mathcal{N}]_{(\bar{i},\overline{w})}$. In the traffic lights program, only state transitions are specified: at any given time/state we do not know which lights are on and which are off. Since we are interested in the current colour of the lights, we introduce two auxiliary variables, tl_1 and tl_2, to expose this information in the model. These variables emulate the actual lights, allowing us to formalise the required safety properties much more naturally. We assume that the lights are initially red. The action $\mathcal{N}_{tl_1,tl_2}$ updates these variables if (and only if) the corresponding light changes colour. *Prog2* extends *Prog* with these definitions. Note that these auxiliary definition do not change the behaviour of *Prog*:

$$Prog2 \triangleq \exists \, \bar{i} : Init_{tl_1,tl_2} \wedge Init \wedge \square[\mathcal{N}_{l1} \wedge \mathcal{N}_{l2} \wedge \mathcal{N}_{ctl} \wedge \mathcal{N}_{tl_1,tl_2}]_{(\bar{i},\overline{w},tl_1,tl_2)}$$

Here the $\exists$ operator is a form of existential quantification that is used to hide the state, that is, the internal variables of the boxes are hidden. The first safety property we define is an invariant asserting that both lights cannot be green at the same time:

$$Prog2 \Rightarrow \square(tl_1 \neq (0,0,1) \vee tl_2 \neq (0,0,1))$$

The $\square$-prefix ensures that the property holds throughout execution. This can be strengthened to show, e.g., that if one of the lights is not red, then the other light is red:

$$Prog2 \Rightarrow \square\big((tl_1 \neq (1,0,0) \Rightarrow tl_2 = (1,0,0)) \wedge (tl_2 \neq (1,0,0) \Rightarrow tl_1 = (1,0,0))\big)$$

The final safety property we define is that the *order* of the light changes is correct. This is no longer a state invariant, since we need to compare two states: that before the change and that after the change. We define a pseudo-function Next as follows:

```
Next l = case l of (1,0,0) -> (1,1,0)
                 | (1,1,0) -> (0,0,1)
                 | (0,0,1) -> (0,1,0)
                 | (0,1,0) -> (1,0,0);
```

where Next is a meta-level definition used in the reasoning process and not part of the HW-Hume program. We can then verify that the next-action of *Prog2* implies this change. We use Next tl_1/tl_2 to ensure that there exists a correspondence between changes in the action and the associated value.

$$Prog2 \Rightarrow \square[tl_1' = \text{Next } tl_1]_{tl_1}$$
$$Prog2 \Rightarrow \square[tl_2' = \text{Next } tl_2]_{tl_2}$$

The subscripts to the actions ensure that only those steps where the lights actually change value are considered. This is necessary if the formula is to be valid.

3.2 Liveness Properties

Liveness properties assert that something good will eventually occur [4]. The specification must therefore be constrained to remove non-progress behaviours. We constrain it with a type of liveness called *fairness*. There are two types of fairness, both building on the *enabled* predicate: An action is enabled when it could successfully execute. *Weak* fairness asserts that if an action remains enabled, then it will eventually execute, while *strong* fairness asserts that if an action is enabled infinitely often then it will eventually execute. The scheduling of Hume guarantees both strong and weak fairness of boxes. This is because all boxes that can be executed are always executed. Further, since the only way an executable (enabled) box can become non-executable (disabled) is by executing it, weak and strong fairness are both equivalent for Hume. Note that this notion of fairness is distinct from the notion of fair matching introduced earlier. We only require weak fairness for our proofs, extending *Prog2* with the fairness predicate for all the boxes:

$$Prog3 \triangleq Prog2 \wedge WF_{(\bar{i},\bar{w})}(N_{l1} \wedge N_{l2} \wedge N_{ctl})$$

The first liveness property we show is that at any given time, there will always be a time in the future when the lights are green:

$$Prog3 \Rightarrow \Box\Diamond(tl_1 = (0,0,1)) \wedge \Box\Diamond(tl_2 = (0,0,1))$$

$\Box\Diamond$ is read as "always eventually". One kind of liveness property which is very important for HW-Hume programs is a so-called *leads-to* property. For example, we can specify that if tl_1 is red then tl_2 will eventually become green:

$$Prog3 \Rightarrow tl_1 = (1,0,0) \leadsto tl_2 = (0,0,1) \wedge tl_2 = (1,0,0) \leadsto tl_1 = (0,0,1)$$

where $A \leadsto B$ means that (always) when A is *True* then eventually B will be *True*. Note that this property is strictly weaker than the previous property, which can be specified simply as *True* $\leadsto tl_1 = (0,0,1)$. Note that $\Box\Diamond T$ specifies termination, i.e. the production of some result. This termination property can be strengthened to only check for termination under certain condition P: This is formalised as a leads-to property $P \leadsto T$.

3.3 Real-Time Properties

One of the novel aspects of, and indeed a prime motivation for, the design of Hume is that upper bounds on time and space can be guaranteed for the expression layer. Since HW-Hume is a language of bits, tuples and vectors, it is straightforward to produce precise models of both space and time usage. For brevity, we omit formal definitions of these models here (definitions for FSM-Hume can be found in [23]), but will show how time bounds for the expression layer obtained from such a model can be combined with TLA+ to give time bounds for the Hume coordination layer.

We are interested in properties of the form "if $tl_1 = (1,0,0)$ then $tl_2 = (0,0,1)$ within time *Bound*", that is where *Bound* represents an upper bound on the time usage. Let $T_{l1/l2/ctl}$ be the time bounds guaranteed from the analysis of the expression layer. Further, let T_{con} and T_{write} be respectively the upper bounds on the time it takes to consume and write all values. *Error* indicates that *Bound* has been exceeded and *Disabled* indicates that we are not between $tl_1 = (1, 0, 0)$ and $tl_2 = (0, 0, 1)$. Let t be a variable representing time, and $\mathcal{N}^2$ be the conjunction of all next-actions. We can then define the the real-time specification:

$$Prog4 \triangleq \exists\, \bar{i} : Init_{tl_1, tl_2} \wedge Init \wedge t = Disabled \wedge \Box[\mathcal{N}^2 \wedge t' = NextTime(t)]_{(\bar{i}, \bar{w}, tl_1, tl_2, t)}$$

where t is initially *Disabled*. For each step *NextTime(t)* calculates the new value of t as follows: if $tl_1' = (1, 0, 0)$ then t is set to *Bound*. For all the following steps t is decremented with either $T_{l1} + T_{l2} + T_{ctl} + T_{con}$, if boxes are executed sequentially; or $Max(T_{l1}, T_{l2}, T_{ctl}) + T_{con} + T_{coord}$, if execution is concurrent. T_{coord} is the coordination cost, if applicable. If $tl_2' = (0, 0, 1)$ then t is reset to *Disabled*. Finally, if $t \leq 0$ then t' is set to *Error*. Since we want to verify that our specified time bound is never exceeded, we must prove the property:

$$Prog4 \Rightarrow \Box(t \neq Error)$$

We use *explicit-time* model checking [30] to verify this property. This obviates the use of a special real-time logic or model checker, and may not be much less efficient than such a checker in practice [30]. In our experiment we used the value $T_{l1} = 2, T_{l2} = 2, T_{ctl} = 1, T_{con} = 1, T_{write} = 1$. When executing the boxes sequentially, we found we were unable to guarantee a *Bound* of 30 or 50, but were able to guarantee a *Bound* of 60. In general, concrete time values, such as T_{l1}, T_{l2} and T_{ctl} above, can be obtained by using a worst-case execution time analysis on the expression layer; while T_{con}, T_{write} and, if present, T_{coord} will be platform-dependent, but should be easy to determine. A companion paper [7] shows how this could be done, giving concrete values for a simple architecture, and describes the construction of a worst-case execution time analysis for Full-Hume. Note that these values are not fixed in the TLA$^+$ specification, but can be supplied to TLC as part of the configuration of the model that must be checked.

4   A Software Implementation of HW-Hume

This section describes a high-performance software implementation of HW-Hume that can be used as the basis for software/hardware codesigns (where some HW-Hume boxes are implemented as described and others are replaced by hardware equivalents). The implementation also serves as a low-memory, high-performance implementation of Hume, where the source program is either restricted to the HW-Hume level, or can be transformed from a higher level of Hume into HW-Hume, for example as shown in [21]. We discuss hardware/software integration at the end of the section.

4.1   HW-Hume Abstract Machine Instructions

HW-Hume programs are compiled to a simple abstract machine which has a single accumulator plus some temporary memory locations, and which is designed to be easily implementable using simple logical operations. Each box is compiled independently, with each rule compiled into a sequence of abstract machine instructions. For the pattern-part the abstract machine first determines the availability of the required inputs, then if sufficient inputs are available, matches these inputs against the patterns, and finally consumes the inputs; and for the expression-part, it constructs each non-ignored output by selecting any necessary parts of the inputs (so binding variables) and combining these with any required literal values before writing the result to one of the output wires. Finally, rules may be reordered according to fairness criteria, and control then returned to the scheduler.

Expression-Level Instructions: There are two main instructions. **Load** *lit* loads literal *lit* into the accumulator. **Select** *i pos size shift* loads *size* bits into the accumulator from input *i* starting at bit *pos*, offsetting these in the accumulator by *shift* bits. So:

```
Load 4
Select 1 5 2 0
```

will load three bits into the accumulator, where the top bit is the constant 1 (specified by **Load 4**), and the first and second bits are selected from the fifth and sixth bits of input number 1, respectively (specified by the **Select** instruction). The result can then be written to the appropriate output wire using a **Write** instruction.

Pattern-Matching Instructions: The **Match** *fail i nlits lits nvars vars* instruction matches input *i* against literal pattern *lits* (whose size in bits is specified by *nlits*), disregarding any input positions that will be bound to variables according to *vars* (whose size in bits is specified by *nvars*). If the input doesn't match, execution continues at label *fail*, usually corresponding to the next rule.

```
Match next 2 3 5 3 2
```

requires the first and third bits of input 2 to be constant ones (as specified by the literal 5), but accepts any value for the second bit (as specified by the value 2 for *vars*). Both literals and variables are three bits wide. Each set of **Match** instructions is preceded by a **CanConsume** instruction which determines whether the necessary inputs are available, and followed by a **Consume** instruction which unlatches the corresponding input. For example,

```
CanConsume next 4 6
Consume 4 6
```

checks whether the second and third input can be consumed (specified by the bit pattern 6), consuming them if so, and otherwise branching to the label **next**. For example, we can compile the simple selector box below:

```
box sel in (s :: Bit, x1, x2 :: Byte) out (y :: Byte)
match
    (0,x1,_) -> x1
|   (1,_,x2) -> x2;
```

into the following sequence of instructions (which have beeen wrapped in a pair of **Box/EndBox** pseudo-instructions):

```
Box "sel" "sel" 3 1 2 "sel_init"
```

```
Label "sel"                          Label "sel_1"
CanConsume "sel_1" 3 7               CanConsume "sel_2" 3 7
Match "sel_1" 0 1 0 1 0             Match "sel_2" 0 1 1 1 0
Match "sel_1" 1 8 255 8 255        Match "sel_2" 1 8 255 8 255
Match "sel_1" 2 8 255 8 255        Match "sel_2" 2 8 255 8 255
Consume 3 7                          Consume 3 7
Load 0                              Load 0
Select 1 0 8 0                      Select 2 0 8 0
Write 0                             Write 0
Schedule                            Schedule
Label "sel_2"
EndBox "sel"
```

4.2 Compilation

We have produced a template-compiler that translates each abstract machine instruction into portable C source code. This can then be compiled to give a native implementation of HW-Hume. Each box is compiled as a void C function. We also define an associated set of output wire buffers and a set of pointers that define the box's inputs. Boxes are placed in a scheduler queue and scheduled using a simple round-robin scheduler, where qrem simply removes and returns the next function from the queue if there is one, or else returns NULL. Boxes are added to the scheduler queue when they have sufficient inputs to be able to execute. When no boxes can execute, termination occurs.

```
void runHume () { while((next=qrem()) != NULL) (void) (*next)(); }
```

The main function adds the _initial function to the scheduling queue. This ensures that wires are properly initialised with any required values. It then adds the checkavails function, which will check input availability for each box and add it to the scheduler queue. Finally the main function enters the scheduler runHume, shown above.

Individual abstract machine instructions are defined as C macros, with Hume Abstract Machine (HAM) labels translated directly into C labels that can be branched to using a goto. For the **Match** instruction, we define the macro shown below. By xoring the input against the literal pattern, we will obtain a value which is 1 for each bit where the pattern matches the input and 0 otherwise. We then complete the match by setting each bit that is matched by a variable to 1. In this way, wherever the pattern matches, we will obtain a 1, and wherever it does not match, we will obtain a 0. We then check this against a mask that is all 1s for the number of input bits, branching to the fail label if unsuccessful.

```
#define Match(fail,input,nlits,lits,nvars,vars) \
    { unsigned match = ~(~thisbox->inp[input] ^ ~lits) | vars; \
      const unsigned mask = (1<<nlits)-1; \
      if((match & mask) != mask) goto fail; \
    }
```

Finally, the **Load** instruction simply loads the literal value into the accumulator and the **Select** instruction is used to select the appropriate bits from the required input position.

```
#define Load(val) { accum = val; }

#define Select(input,posn,size,shift)\
      { accum |= ((thisbox->inp[input] & ((1<<(posn+size))-1)) >> posn) << shift; }
```

4.3 Performance Results

Table 1 shows performance results for a number of HW-Hume programs running under three different implementations: t_{hami} gives execution times for the prototype Hume Abstract Machine [20], a bytecode interpreter written in portable C; t_{humec} gives corresponding times under the general Hume to C template-compiler we are constructing as part of the EmBounded project; and t_{HW} gives times under the HW-Hume implementation we have described here. Space usage is given for the HAM interpreter, s_{hami} and for the implementation described here, s_{HW}. Figures in brackets are those predicted by the cost model. All timings were obtained on a 1.67GHz Apple Powerbook G4 running MacOSX 10.4.8 and represent the average of 10 executions. Timings were recorded from box start to box end, and all C compilation was performed using gcc 4.0.0 using -O2 optimisation. Our results show that, for these examples, the template compiler is slightly more than ten times faster than the bytecode compiler, and that the HW-Hume implementation is between 2.8 and 10.9 times faster than the latter implementation. While dynamic memory usage is low for the HAM interpreter at between 130B and 740B, it represents only a few words of memory for the HW-Hume implementation, being between 11 and 60 bits. Binary program size is also acceptably small. On an Intel Pentium IV running Linux, the total binary size for the HW-Hume multiplexor program, including all static and dynamic data and program code is 3526 bytes.

Table 1. Performance Comparisons

Program	t_{hami}	t_{humec}	t_{HW}	s_{hami}	s_{HW}
adder	442μs	–	7.0μs	130B (130B)	17b
multiplexer	149μs	12.9μs	4.62μs	732B (740B)	60b
multiplexer2	275μs	24.4μs	5.25μs	660B (664B)	56b
lights	286μs	21.5μs	1.96μs	136B (240B)	11b

5 Hardware Implementation from HW-Hume

A hardware implementation can be obtained from HW-Hume in one of two main ways. Firstly, *netlists* can be generated directly from the description of Hume boxes and wires. Netlists, such as the widely-used EDIF [1], describe a collection of hardware devices, in terms of instances of master definitions, plus the interconnections between those devices, in terms of the *ports* associated with each device. It is then necessary to refine these netlists to include timing, placement and detailed functional behaviour, so that a hardware implementation can be obtained. Although substantial manual intervention may be required in later stages, there is considerable flexibility over the form of the final hardware implementation. In HW-Hume terms, a *template* is a master definition, a *box* is an instance, box inputs/outputs are ports, and *wires* define interconnections. Alternatively, the C we have produced from our software implementation above could be passed as input to Handel-C [9] or a similar FPGA notation. This will then generate netlists and other required information so that an FPGA implementation can be produced. An example EDIF netlist for the half-adder above might be:

```
(edif halfadder

  -- version info
  (edifVersion 2 0 0) (edifLevel 0) (keywordMap (keywordLevel 0))

-- this library
(library humeprogram
  (edifLevel 0) (technology (numberDefinition )          -- preamble
    (simulationInfo (logicValue H) (logicValue L)))

  (cell (rename HALFADDER "halfadder")(cellType GENERIC)  -- half-adder
    (view COMPASS_mde_view (viewType NETLIST)             -- netlist
      (interface
        (port a (direction INPUT))                        -- in/out ports
        (port b (direction INPUT))
        (port s (direction OUTPUT))
        (port c (direction OUTPUT)))))


  -- export the design
  (design HALFADDER (cellRef HALFADDER (libraryRef humeprogram)))))
```

It is also necessary to construct any required instances of HALFADDER and link these into a coherent network.

5.1 Hardware/Software Integration Issues

Hardware components can be integrated into HW-Hume software programs either by completely replacing some box, where they are equivalent to the HW-Hume source, or as unspecified "pseudo-boxes". In either case, it is necessary to provide linkages between software and hardware so that such boxes will react to (possibly software) inputs and produce outputs that can be directed to software boxes. For example

```
operation "count1" to "74HC393/1"  :: vector 2 of Bit -> vector 4 of Bit;
operation "count2" to "74HC393/2"  :: vector 2 of Bit -> vector 4 of Bit;
```

might specify two pseudo-boxes count1 and count2, one attached to each half of a 74HC393 four-bit binary counter. The two one-bit inputs are a clock signal and a master reset input in each case. These boxes can be connected to software in the usual way. Note that in this case, an explicit clock signal must be threaded as an additional input to each HW-Hume box where it is required.

6 Related Work

Declarative hardware description languages are an attractive approach, allowing clean separation of functionality from behavioural detail, supporting automatic circuit generation, and promoting much higher level of abstraction than found in the industry-standard VHDL notation, for example. One early declarative approach, Ruby [27], was based on relational calculus. While there is an obvious link between logic gates and logical relations, in practice, most hardware circuits map some inputs to some outputs. It follows that functional approaches to hardware description are not only possible, but also completely appropriate, and several examples have been described previously.

There have been several approaches to developing functionally-based notations for hardware. Lava [6,11], produced in association with Xilinx Corporation, uses an embedded domain-specific language approach, extending Haskell with operations that allow the high-level description of FPGA circuits. Where Lava uses non-strictness to specify links between hardware components, in Hume, boxes/wires serve the same purpose. Other similar approaches include Intel's ReFL^{ect} language [19], which is used commercially to verify properties of their processor designs; the Hawk hardware verification language [26]; the Hydra system for logic circuit specification; the *functional derivation* approach, for deriving FPGA circuits from Haskell specifications [25]; the lenient, purely functional language Confluence for designing synchronous circuits [2], the imperative HDCaml hardware design/verification language [3]; the SAFL hardware description language [31]; and the same authors' Flash notation for hardware/software codesign [32]. Compared with HW-Hume, the most obvious differences in these notations are their use of a single-level language rather than a separation between coordination and expression, their inclusion of high-level features such as higher-order functions and direct recursion (though these may be mapped from higher levels of Hume into HW-Hume programs), and the general absence of asynchronous constructs. The decision to include asynchronous constructs in Hume is a careful one. The advantage of a synchronous language design such as Lustre [10] is in terms of a simpler semantic model, that consequently simplifies the construction of cost models. However, while asynchronous systems can generally be restricted to synchronous cases, and this can be detected using model-checking as we have done in this paper, it is considerably more difficult to describe asynchronous systems starting from a purely synchronous basis. Recent work has therefore seen hybrid notations, such as Lucid-Synchrone [14], which combines finite-state-automata and a synchronous communication model, or notations that explicitly expose clocks as additional inputs to otherwise synchronous systems [13].

While model checking has been successfully applied to several imperative languages, for example in the shape of NASA's Java Pathfinder [24] or Microsoft's Terminator [15] tools, there are fewer systems combining functional languages with model checking. Apart from our own work on HW-Hume and Spin [18], the most relevant work of which we are aware is that on ReFL^{ect} [19], on verifying SAFL programs [16], and on verifying resource properties in Erlang [33]. A key difference from our work is that we deal with real-time properties as well as liveness and safety. Since we have constructed a formal model of the Hume coordination layer, which is identical to all Hume levels, we are also able, in principle, to work at arbitrary levels of Hume and to prove properties on transformed code.

7   Conclusions and Future Work

This paper represents a first exploration of HW-Hume. HW-Hume targets low-level system descriptions, using a declarative notation combining purely functional expressions with a high-level process notation. We have shown how essential safety, liveness and real-time properties of HW-Hume programs can be specified in TLA$^+$ and how they can automatically verified with the TLC model checker. In doing this, we have provided the first example of using TLA$^+$ to model check properties in a programming language. The combination of time analysis on boxes with temporal logic is also novel, and reveals the advantage of using a layered language when performing static analysis, allowing clear separation between different aspects of the time analysis.

Since TLA$^+$ is a much higher level notation than supported by most model checkers, this allows a more direct embedding of HW-Hume semantics, and also helps mitigate the "state-space explosion problem", a major bugbear of model checking, where the checker fails because too many states have been generated. Even more interestingly, we have been able to extend the work reported here to model-check that the safety-part of a property is preserved when transforming from a higher-level into a lower-level Hume program.

We have also shown how an efficient software implementation can be produced for HW-Hume, using a template-based compiler compiling through C. This implementation is highly space efficient. For example, for the `sel` box above, we can determine a total dynamic memory usage of 42 bits (including all wiring requirements), and the complete C program in which it is embedded has a total dynamic memory requirement of 620 bytes, including all system data structures and runtime queues. HW-Hume may therefore be the world's most space-efficient functional language.

7.1   Further Work

In addition to producing a concrete hardware implementation for HW-Hume, as discussed above, a number of important issues remain to be addressed. Firstly, hardware/software co-design is becoming increasingly important as an approach to building embedded computer systems. As we have shown above, it is possible to produce both hardware and software implementations from a single HW-Hume definition. We believe this gives a powerful tool for developing combined hardware/software implementations from a single source specification, and intend to investigate this further. Secondly, we have already developed a powerful transformational framework allowing higher levels of Hume to be mapped into HW-Hume programs. In this way, programmers have access to higher-order combinators, repetition and other abstractions. We need to investigate whether this approach gives an effective way to provide high-level abstractions over hardware circuits. Thirdly although TLA$^+$ has proved effective for HW-Hume, when dealing with more expressive levels of Hume, it is likely to prove insufficiently powerful, since we will need to deal with more sophisticated forms of data structures, for example. We are therefore working on formalising TLA in a theorem prover. Fourthly, TLC supports a form of state-space reduction technique called symmetry which may yield further performance benefits. We intend to address how we may exploit this in HW-Hume. Fiftly, we have developed a specification language for HW-Hume, based on [18], which captures all properties we have shown. We plan to create a translator from HW-Hume and this specification language into TLA$^+$ which automatically verifies the properties. We believe this should be a trivial thing to do. Finally, although we have defined box templates and wiring macros to reduce repetition in describing collections of boxes, we have not developed a complete hierarchy of box-combining forms. This would effectively involve constructing a higher-order calculus of boxes, and would allow more modular and scalable verification of properties.

References

1. Electronic Design Interchange Format Version 2.0.0,Technical ANSI/EIA-548-1988 (1988)
2. Confluence: http://www.confluent.org/wiki/doku.php?id=confluence (2006)
3. Hdcaml: http://www.confluent.org/wiki/doku.php (2006)
4. Alpern, B., Schneider, F.B.: Defining liveness. Information Processing Letters 21, 181–185 (1985)
5. Apt, K.R., Olderog, E.-R.: Verification of Sequential and Concurrent Programs, 2nd edn. Springer, Heidelberg (1997)
6. Bjesse, P., Claessen, K., Sheeran, M., Singh, S.: Lava: Hardware design in Haskell. ACM SIGPLAN Notices 34(1), 174–184 (January 1999)
7. Bonenfant, A., Ferdinand, C., Hammond, K., Heckmann, R.: Worst-Case Execution Times for a Purely Functional Language. In: This volume. Springer, Heidelberg (2007)
8. Boussinot, F., de Simone, R.: The Esterel Language. Proceedings of the IEEE 79(9), 1293–1304 (September 1991)
9. Butterfield, A., Woodcock, J.: prialt in Handel-C: an operational semantics. Int. J. Softw. Tools Technol. Transf. 7(3), 248–267 (2005)
10. Caspi, P., Pilaud, D., Halbwachs, N., Place, J.: Lustre: a Declarative Language for Programming Synchronous Systems. In: Proc. POPL '87 – 1987 Symposium on Principles of Programming Languages, München, Germany, pp. 178–188 (January 1987)
11. Claessen, K., Pace, G.: An Embedded Language Framework for Hardware Compilation. In: Proc. Conf. on Designing Correct Circuits (DCC 2002) (2002)
12. Clarke, E.M., Grumberg, O., Peled, D.A.: Model Checking. MIT Press, Cambridge (1999)
13. Cohen, A., Duranton, M., Eisenbeis, C., Pagetti, C., Plateau, F., Pouzet, M.: N-Synchronous Kahn Networks: a Relaxed Model of Synchrony for Real-Time Systems. In: Proc. POPL '06: ACM Symposium on Principles of Programming Languages, pp. 180–193. ACM Press, New York (2006)
14. Colaço, J.-L., Pagano, B., Pouzet, M.: A Conservative Extension of Synchronous Data-flow with State Machines. In: Proc. ACM International Conference on Embedded Software (EMSOFT'05), Jersey City, New Jersey, USA (September 2005)
15. Cook, B., Podelski, A., Rybalchenko, A.: Terminator: Beyond Safety. In: Ball, T., Jones, R.B. (eds.) CAV 2006. LNCS, vol. 4144, Springer, Heidelberg (2006)
16. Foster, J.N.: Model Checking for a Functional Hardware Description Language, BSc Dissertation, Cambridge University. PhD thesis (2002)
17. Gautier, T., Le Guernic, P., Besnard, L.: SIGNAL: A Declarative Language For Synchronous Programming of Real-Time Systems. In: Kahn, G. (ed.) Functional Programming Languages and Computer Architecture. LNCS, vol. 274, pp. 257–277. Springer, Heidelberg (1987)
18. Grov, G., Ireland, A., Michaelson, G.J., Hammond, K.: Verifying Temporal Properties in HW-Hume. Technical report, Heriot-Watt University, School of Mathematical and Computer Sciences (February 2006)

19. Grundy, J., Melham, T., O'Leary, J.: A Reflective Functional Language for Hardware Design and Theorem Proving. J. Funct. Program 16(2), 157–196 (2006)
20. Hammond, K.: Exploiting Purely Functional Programming to Obtain Bounded Resource Behaviour: the Hume Approach. In: Central European Summer School on Functional Programming, July 2005, Springer, Heidelberg (to appear)
21. Hammond, K., Michaelson, G.: Bounded Space Programming using Finite State Machines and Recursive Functions: the Hume Approach. Submitted to ACM Transactions on Software Engineering and Methodology (TOSEM), in preparation(2006)
22. Hammond, K., Michaelson, G.J.: Hume: a Domain-Specific Language for Real-Time Embedded Systems. In: Pfenning, F., Smaragdakis, Y. (eds.) GPCE 2003. LNCS, vol. 2830, pp. 37–56. Springer, Heidelberg (2003)
23. Hammond, K., Michaelson, G.J.: Predictable Space Behaviour in FSM-Hume. In: Peña, R., Arts, T. (eds.) IFL 2002. LNCS, vol. 2670, Springer, Heidelberg (2003)
24. Havelund, K., Pressburger, T.: Model Checking JAVA Programs using JAVA PathFinder. Int. Journal on Software Tools for Technology Transfer 2(4), 366–381 (2000)
25. Hawkins, J., Abdallah, A.E.: Behavioural Synthesis of a Parallel Hardware JPEG Decoder from a Functional Specification. In: Monien, B., Feldmann, R.L. (eds.) Euro-Par 2002. LNCS, vol. 2400, pp. 615–619. Springer, Heidelberg (August 2002)
26. Launchbury, J., Matthews, J., Cook, B.: Microprocessor Specification in Hawk. In: Proc. International Conference on Computer Languages, pp. 90–101 (1998)
27. Jones, G., Sheeran, M.: Circuit design in Ruby. In: J. Staunstrup, editor, Formal Methods for VLSI Design, pp. 13–70. North-Holland (1990)
28. Lamport, L.: The Temporal Logic of Actions. ACM TOPLAS 16(3), 872–923 (1994)
29. Lamport, L.: Specifying Systems — The TLA+ Language and Tools for Hardware and Software Engineers, Reading, Massachusetts. Addison-Wesley, London (2002)
30. Lamport, L.: Real-Time Model Checking Is Really Simple. In: Borrione, D., Paul, W. (eds.) CHARME 2005. LNCS, vol. 3725, pp. 162–175. Springer, Heidelberg (2005)
31. Mycroft, A., Sharp, R.: A Statically Allocated Parallel Functional Language. Automata, Languages and Programming, pp. 37–48 (2000)
32. Mycroft, A., Sharp, R.: Hardware/Software Co-Design Using Functional Languages. In: Margaria, T., Yi, W. (eds.) ETAPS 2001 and TACAS 2001. LNCS, vol. 2031, pp. 236–251. Springer, Heidelberg (2001)
33. Earle, C.B., Arts, T., Derrick, J.: Verifying Erlang Code: a Resource Locker Case-Study. In: Eriksson, L.-H., Lindsay, P.A. (eds.) FME 2002. LNCS, vol. 2391, pp. 184–203. Springer, Heidelberg (2002)
34. Vasconcelos, P.B.: Cost Inference and Analysis for Recursive Functional Programs. PhD thesis, University of St Andrews, in preparation (2006)
35. Vasconcelos, P.B., Hammond, K.: Inferring Costs for Recursive, Polymorphic and Higher-Order Functional Programs. In: Trinder, P., Michaelson, G.J., Peña, R. (eds.) IFL 2003. LNCS, vol. 3145, pp. 86–101. Springer, Heidelberg (2004)

A Conference Management System Based on the iData Toolkit

Rinus Plasmeijer and Peter Achten

Software Technology, Nijmegen Institute for Computing and Information Sciences,
Radboud University Nijmegen
{rinus,P.Achten}@cs.ru.nl

Abstract. The iData Toolkit is a purely functional toolkit for the Clean programming language to create highly dynamic, interactive, thin client web applications on a high level of abstraction. Its main building block is the iData element. With this element the programming effort of the application programmer is reduced significantly because it takes care of state handling, rendering, user interaction, and storage management automatically. In this paper we show that it can be used for even more tasks: handle *destructively shared model data*, perform *version management*, and *state consistency management*. This can be done entirely on top of the iData Toolkit. The toolkit comes with a new programming paradigm. We illustrate the extended power of the toolkit and programming paradigm by a case study of a conference management system.

1 Introduction

The purely functional language Clean has a library to create highly dynamic, interactive, thin client web applications on a high level of abstraction. This library is the iData Toolkit [11,13,12].It is based on the language support for generic programming [2,3]. The toolkit's main building block is the iData element, which is a versatile unit that automates a great deal of things for the programmer:

- it manages a state of arbitrary type;
- it renders an HTML form representation of its state;
- it handles user actions made with these forms in a type safe way;
- it stores its state either in the page or at the server side on disk.

Web applications are created by interconnecting an arbitrary collection of iData elements via their states and rendered forms. In the past years we have obtained experience in programming applications with iData elements, and their desktop GUI predecessors, the GEC elements of the GEC Toolkit [1]. This has resulted in a new programming paradigm. In the iData Toolkit programming paradigm the application programmer *models* the application as an *information system*, by identifying the entities and entity-relations and specify them as pure functional data structures and pure functions. The generic power of the toolkit is used subsequently to handle as much as possible automatically. Human intervention is still required, but the power of generic programming is that it allows application programmers to specialize the generic scheme where needed.

Z. Horváth, V. Zsók, and A. Butterfield (Eds.): IFL 2006, LNCS 4449, pp. 108–125, 2007.

When constructing programs with the programming paradigm, it turns out that the 'classic' version of the toolkit has a number of limitations:

- Model types are pure functional data structures. Although functional languages can define and handle *shared* data structures, they cannot handle *destructively shared* data because this destroys referential transparency. However, in information systems destructive sharing is a natural phenomenon, because data should not be stored redundantly. Hence, an iData Toolkit application programmer can not model destructive sharing directly, but instead has to program this on top of the functional data structures and for each and every edit operation. This is cumbersome, error-prone, and an example of boilerplate code that should be automated once and for all.
- It is important in multi-user web applications with several persistent shared states to manage *versions* of these states correctly. Again, the programmer might be able to program this, but it should be dealt with once and for all.
- The final limitation concerns the *consistency of states*. The iData Toolkit is *edit driven*, i.e.: it reacts to (type safe) edit operations of the application user who can alter a part of the state of one of the iData elements. In general, it may well be the case that during a sequence of edit operations, the set of states is *inconsistent*. In that case, the application should not commit this configuration of states to disk, but rather work on a local version.

In this paper we show that the above concerns can be handled automatically by the iData elements, on top of the 'classic' iData Toolkit. We believe that this provides further evidence to the fact that iData elements form a powerful abstraction mechanism to create highly interactive and dynamic web applications with. We illustrate the use of the new techniques by studying the case of a *conference management system*. Conference management systems are software systems that support conference managers, programme committee members, and authors with a number of tasks, such as the electronic paper submission process, paper distribution and reviewing process, deadline management, and the paper discussion process. They serve as a good example of the domain of web applications that suffer from the limitations that have been presented above. We show that the resulting system widens the application domain of the toolkit while still adhering to its programming paradigm.

This paper is structured as follows: we first briefly present the iData Toolkit in Sect. 2. Next, in Sect. 3, we discuss the case study of a conference management system. Implementation details are presented in Sect. 4. Finally, related work is discussed in Sect. 5, and we conclude in Sect. 6.

2   The iData Toolkit

In this section we present the 'classic' iData Toolkit, i.e. the toolkit without the extensions that are discussed in the next sections. First, we give an informal explanation of iData elements, which are the building blocks of the iData Toolkit (Sect. 2.1). Second, we present the programming paradigm (Sect. 2.2).

2.1   iData **Elements**

iData elements are the fundamental building blocks of the iData Toolkit. An iData element is a typed unit that provides the application user with a GUI (an HTML form) that allows him to edit values of that given type only. The GUI is derived automatically from the type and value using the generic programming facilities of Clean. In this paper, we use one toolkit function to create iData elements:

```
class iData d | gForm{|*|}, gUpd{|*|}, gPrint{|*|}, gParse{|*|} d

mkEditForm :: (InIDataId d) → HStIO d | iData d
:: HStIO d :== *HSt → (Form d,*HSt)
```

The function `mkEditForm` uses four generic cornerstone functions that are collected in the type class `iData`. The `(InIDataId d)` argument of `mkEditForm` describes the type and value of the iData element that is to be created:

```
:: InIDataId d :== (Init,FormId d)
:: Init          = Const | Init | Set
:: FormId   d    = { id::String, ival::d, lifespan::Lifespan, mode::Mode }
:: Lifespan      = Persistentᵖ | PersistentROʳ | Sessionˢ | Pageⁿ | Tempᵗ
:: Mode          = Edit | Displayᵈ | NoFormˣ
```

Here it suffices to state that it is a pair of an `Init` value that specifies the use of the `ival::d` value inside the `(FormId d)` record. The `lifespan` and `mode` fields control the lifespan and rendering mode of the iData element. An iData element can be stored persistently (`Persistent(RO)`) on the server side on disk, or locally in the page (`Session`, `Page`, `Temp`). Although the default mode of an iData element is `Edit`, it can also be used to display its state (`Display`), or even without any rendering at all (`NoForm`). For each of these variants, a `FormId` constructor function $\{p,r,s,n,t\}[d,x]$`FormId :: String d → FormId d` has been defined. `*HSt` is an opaque environment that contains the internal administration that is required to create HTML pages and form handling. It can be updated destructively, hence the *uniqueness type attribute* `*`. (Please consult [13] for details.)

When evaluated, `mkEditForm` basically performs the following actions: it first checks whether an earlier incarnation of the iData element (identified by the `id::String`[1] label) exists. If this is not the case, or the `Init` value is `Set`, then the `ival` value of the `FormId` argument is used. If it already existed, then it contains a possibly user-edited value. This value is used subsequently. Hence, the final iData element is up-to-date. This is recorded in the `(Form d)` record:

```
:: Form d = { changed :: Bool, value :: d, form :: [BodyTag] }
```

The `changed` field records the fact if the application user has edited the value of the iData element; the `value` is the up-to-date value, and `form` is the HTML rendering of this iData element that can be used within an arbitrary HTML page.

---

[1] We are aware that the use of strings for form identification can be a source of (hard to locate) errors, but we have yet to find a better system of equal expressiveness.

As an example, the following code snippet creates an iData element for Int values that, initially, looks as `42          `:

```
# (intF,hst) = mkEditForm (Init,nFormId "My first iData!" 42) hst
```

If included in a web page, the application user can only create integer values with this iData element. A web application is any function that computes an HTML page, using an *HSt environment. Hence, its type is (HStIO Html). The wrapper function doHtmlServer transforms it into a real Clean interactive function:

```
doHtmlServer :: (HStIO Html) *World → *World
```

As an example, the following, complete code, creates a web application that allows users to edit integer values (Fig. 1(a)):

```
Start world = doHtmlServer tiny world
where tiny :: (HStIO Html)
      tiny hst
        # (intF,hst) = mkEditForm (Init,nFormId "My first iData!" 42) hst
        = mkHtml "Simple Example" intF.form hst
```

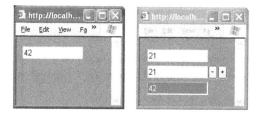

Fig. 1. (a) A single integer editor. (b) Display the sum of two integer input fields.

2.2   The iData Toolkit **Programming Paradigm**

The iData Toolkit programming paradigm advocates the use of pure data types and pure functions to model the UoD (Universe of Discourse) of the application that is to be constructed. From these types, the iData Toolkit derives the required forms automatically that can be used in the HTML pages of the application. The application programmer can specialize the derived GUI where needed, and in the end interconnect all iData elements that are relevant to his application. This amounts to the following four-step programming paradigm:

1. Model the UoD with pure data types and pure functions.
2. Derive iData from the data types generically.
3. Specialize iData where needed.
4. Define the logic of the application by interconnecting iData functionally.

Below, we illustrate the paradigm by constructing a small program that allows the application user to enter two integer values, and display their sum (Fig.1(b)). The same technique can be used to construct real-world applications such as a CD shop and a work administration [12].

1. Modelling the UoD. In this step the application programmer *models* the entities and their relations by means of pure data types and pure functions over these data domains. For the sake of the example, the second integer editor is modeled distinctively as `IntCounter`, accompanied by two conversion functions:

```
::  IntCounter = IntCounter Int
```

```
instance toInt   IntCounter where toInt (IntCounter i) = i
instance fromInt IntCounter where fromInt i = IntCounter i
```

2. Deriving iData. In this step the application programmer unleashes the generative power of the toolkit, and automatically derives instances for the four cornerstone functions of the toolkit. In the example the model types are either the basic `Int` type for which instances are already defined, or the integer counter type, that is specialized below.

3. Specializing iData. In general, the created GUI of an iData element displays the structure of the type. For many types, this is sufficient. However, this is not always the case, and the generically derived GUI needs to be overruled by the application programmer. Overruling a generic recipe is known as *specialization*. Specialization is a delicate task, and hence the iData Toolkit provides a function that aids the application programmer with this:

```
specialize :: ((InIDataId a) → HStIO (Form a))
              (InIDataId a) → HStIO (Form a) | gUpd{|*|} a
```

As an example, assume that there is a function

```
counterIData :: (InIDataId Int) → HStIO (Form Int)
```

that renders `Int` iData elements as `[0          |·|·|]` (in [12] we show how such a function is implemented). If we decide that from now on all `Int` iData elements should be rendered in this way, then this is enforced by:

```
gForm{|Int|} iDataId hst = specialize counterIData iDataId hst
```

In the example, however, we want to *model* the integer counter with the model type `IntCounter`. This amounts to calling `counterIData`, except that the `Int` values need to be converted to `IntCounter` values and vice versa. This is done with:

```
gForm{|IntCounter|} iDataId hst
  = specialize (coerceWith (toInt,fromInt) counterIData) iDataId hst
```

The `coerceWith` function is just a higher-order wrapper function that applies the conversion functions just before and immediately after the core function.

```
coerceWith :: (a → b,c → d) ((InIDataId b) → HStIO (Form c))
                             (InIDataId a) → HStIO (Form d)
coerceWith (f_ab,f_cd) f (init,formId=:{ival}) hst
  # ({changed,value,form},hst) = f (init,{formId & ival=f_ab ival}) hst
  = ({changed=changed,value=f_cd value,form=form},hst)
```

4. Interconnecting iData. The final step is to *interconnect* iData elements. Interconnecting means that we define a functional dependency relation between the iData elements. The application programmer can exploit two important aspects of iData elements. First, the behavior of iData elements (discussed in Sect. 2.1) implies that they can be *shared*, i.e.: referring to the same iData element within the interconnection relation refers to the same iData element. In this way *cyclic dependency relationships* can be defined. Second, every iData element has a rendering that can be used subsequently arbitrarily many times, or even not at all. Each rendering refers to the same iData element. In the example, interconnecting the iData elements is straightforward:

```
Start world = doHtmlServer add world                                    1.
where add :: (HStIO Html)                                               2.
      add hst                                                           3.
      ♯ (i1F,hst) = mkEditForm (Init,nFormId "i1"    0)           hst    4.
      ♯ (i2F,hst) = mkEditForm (Init,nFormId "i2"    (IntCounter 0)) hst 5.
      ♯ (i3F,hst) = mkEditForm (Set, ndFormId "sum"                     6.
                               (toInt i1F.value + toInt i2F.value)) hst 7.
      = mkHtml "Sum" [STable [] [i1F.form,i2F.form,i3F.form]]      hst   8.
```

The input elements are activated in lines 4–5. Their values are used by the sum display in line 7. Their forms are displayed in a single column in line 8. The resulting HTML page is displayed in Fig. 1(b).

3   A Conference Management System

In this section we show how to design a conference management system with the 'classic' iData Toolkit, its new tools, and the programming paradigm. The new tools are: **(i)** modeling *destructively shared data* with *reference types*; **(ii)** automatically *guard the consistency* of database and reference type values; **(iii)** automatic *version management*. Fig. 2(a) shows the initial screen of the system.

3.1   Modelling a Conference Management System

Examples of the logical entities of a conference management system are *members*, *accounts*, *papers*, and *discussions*. Appendix A.1 is a self-explanatory and self-contained subset of the collection of data types that have been defined. The types PasswordBox, HtmlDate, and HtmlTime are 'classic' iData Toolkit data types that have been specialized to model standard GUI elements. The types Account and Login are generally useful types for login handling. Examples of the entity-relations are determining the status of a member, determine the reviews of a programme committee member, and setting conflicts of interest. Appendix A.2 gives a subset of the functional relations between these entities.

In the modeling step, the application programmer can use two of the above mentioned features **(i)** and **(ii)** of the 'non-classic' iData Toolkit.

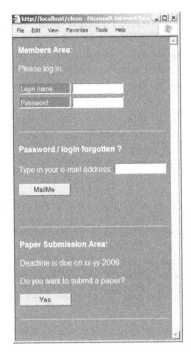
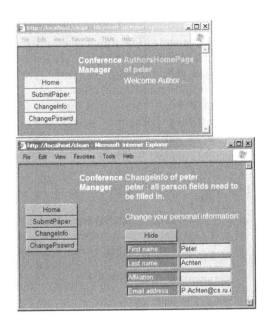

Fig. 2. (a) The initial system look. **(b)** The initial author page look. **(c)** An exception in the author page look when editing personal information.

Modelling Destructively Shared Data. In Sect. 1, we have argued that *destructive sharing* of entities is a natural phenomenon when modeling information systems. In case of the conference management system, the programmer wants to model the fact that *members*, *papers*, *reports*, and *discussions* are destructively shared. As a result, whenever the application user alters a destructively shared (sub)value in any iData element, then this (sub)value should be altered everywhere where it appears in a destructively shared context. Clearly, destructive sharing cannot be handled directly with pure data types in pure functional languages. For this purpose *reference types* have been introduced.

A reference type (**Ref2 d**) is a *phantom* type that creates a reference to a value of type **d**. Using the same reference value in a collection of data values results in a destructively shared occurrence of that value. (Sect. 4.2 discusses the implementation.) Briefly, a reference type 'connects' a type with an identifier:

```
:: Ref2 a = Ref2 String
```

Just as iData identifiers, this identifier is required to be unique. Hence, the application programmer needs to set up an additional name space for reference type identifiers. In the conference management system, this has been done by the function **setInvariantAccounts :: ConfAccounts → ConfAccounts** that traverses the complete administration for reference type occurrences, and assigns unique identifiers in such a way that the same entity obtains the desired destructive sharing structure. For reasons of space, we omit its code. It implements the following rules: persons are identified by their unique login name; refereed reports are identified by the identifier of the referee and their unique paper number; discussions by the author identifier and unique paper number; papers by author name and paper number.

Guarding Consistency of iData. In Sect. 1, we have argued that due to the edit-driven evaluation mechanism of the iData Toolkit, the *consistency* of the iData states cannot be guaranteed. We have included a mechanism to *judge* the consistency of destructively shared and persistent data. A `Judgement` is either `Ok` (`Nothing`), or raises an issue (`Just (id,issue)`) where `id` is the identifier of the judging entity, and `issue` a text that describes the issue. The value of an entity is committed to disk only if the corresponding judgement is `Ok`. Judgements can be rather syntactic. For instance, for `Person`, `Paper`, and `Login`, the judgements basically state that every field has to have a non-empty value:

```
invariantPerson :: String Person → Judgement
invariantPerson id {firstName,lastName,affiliation,emailAddress}
 | any ((==) "") [firstName,lastName,affiliation,emailAddress]
             = Just (id,"all person fields need to be filled in.")
 | otherwise = Ok
```

A more challenging example of a judgement is given below.

```
invariantConfAccounts :: String ConfAccounts → Judgement               1.
invariantConfAccounts id accs                                          2.
 | any ((≥) 0) papers  = Just (id,"paper number must be positive")     3.
 | not (noDups papers) = Just (id,"paper number in use")               4.
 | not uniqConflicts    = Just (id,"conflict already assigned to referee")  5.
 | not uniqAssigns      = Just (id,"paper already assigned to referee")     6.
 | conflicting          = Just (id,"assigned paper in conflict")       7.
 | not (allMembers reports papers)                                     8.
                       = Just (id,"non-existing assigned paper")       9.
 | not (allMembers conflicts papers)                                   10.
                       = Just (id,"non-existing assigned conflict")    11.
 | otherwise           = Ok                                            12.
where                                                                  13.
   papers        =          [nr  \\ (nr,_) ← getRefPapers    accs]    14.
   conflicts     = flatten  [nrs \\ (_,nrs) ← getConflicts   accs]    15.
   reports       = flatten  [nrs \\ (_,nrs) ← getAssignments accs]    16.
   uniqConflicts = and [noDups nrs \\ (_,nrs) ← getConflicts   accs]  17.
   uniqAssigns   = and [noDups nrs \\ (_,nrs) ← getAssignments accs]  18.
   conflicting   = or  [isAnyMember cNrs aNrs                          19.
                      \\ (_,cNrs,aNrs) ← getConflictsAssign accs]     20.
```

This is a judgement over the complete content of the conference management system's database. Paper numbers should be positive (line 3) and uniquely identify a paper (line 4). The list of conflicts and assigned papers should contain no duplicates (lines 5–6). Referees should not review papers for which they have a conflicting interest (line 7). Finally, the set of reports and conflicts should be a subset of the set of papers (line 8 and 10).

Judgements are connected with reference type values and database values by the following two new functions that have been built on top of the iData Toolkit:

```
universalRefEditor
            :: (InIDataId (Ref2 a))   (a → Judgement) → HStIO (Form a)
                                                              | iData a
universalDB :: (Init,a,String) (String a → Judgement) → HStIO a | iData a
```

Their implementation is discussed in Sect. 4. Applications of `universalRefEditor` are all alike, and proceed as in the case of persons:

```
editorRefPerson :: (InIDataId RefPerson) → HStIO (Form Person)
editorRefPerson (init,formid=:{ival=RefPerson refp=:(Ref2 name)})
  = universalRefEditor (init,{formid & ival=refp}) (invariantPerson name)
```

As an example of `universalDB`, we create the main conference database:

```
AccountsDB :: Init ConfAccounts → HStIO ConfAccounts
AccountsDB init accounts
  = universalDB (init,setInvariantAccounts accounts,uniqueDBname)
                invariantConfAccounts
```

3.2   Deriving iData

We can be very brief about this step, as this simply involves enumerating all instances to derive of almost all types for the generic cornerstone functions `gForm`, `gUpd`, `gPrint`, and `gParse`. The exceptions are that `gForm` needs to be specialized for the four reference types, the four custom types `Reports`, `Conflicts`, `Co_authors`, and `Discussion`, and the standard list type (display only the elements, not the list data constructors). In total, derivation concerns 27 data types, hence there are 99 derived instances and 9 specialized `gForm` instances.

3.3   Specializing iData

Reference types are specialized in boilerplate style, as illustrated with `RefPerson` (`editorRefPerson` is given above; `invokeRefEditor` is discussed in Sect. 4):

```
gForm{|RefPerson|} iDataId hst
  = specialize (invokeRefEditor editorRefPerson) iDataId hst
```

The four model types that need to be specialized are `Reports`, `Conflicts`, `Co_authors`, and `Discussion`. The first three are all basically list structures, but the application designer wants to display them in a column. They all proceed as given here for the case of `Co_authors`:

```
gForm{|Co_authors|} inIDataId hst
  = specialize (coerceWith (toList,fromList) vertlistFormButs) inIDataId hst
  where toList (Co_authors authors) = authors
        fromList authors = Co_authors authors
```

Discussions are displayed in a table:

```
gForm{|Discussion|} inIDataId hst = specialize discussion inIDataId hst
where
  discussion (init,formid=:{ival=Discussion d}) hst
    = ({changed=False,form=flatten (map htmlOf d),value=formid.ival},hst)
  where
    htmlOf {messageFrom,date,time,message}
      = [ mkTable [ [ Txt "date: ", toHtml date, Txt "time: ", toHtml time]
                  , [ Txt "from: ", B [] messageFrom ] ]
        , Txt "message:", Txt message, Hr [] ]
```

3.4 Interconnecting iData

The conference management system basically proceeds along the following steps:
it reads in the current accounts database, and then attempts to establish the
identity of the application user. If this is a known user, then the application
needs to present the current application page that the application user was
visiting. This is determined by means of a *conference portal*, that determines
and produces the correct page. If the user is unknown, then he is a guest, and
should attempt to login to the system.

As shown in Sect. 2, the main entry of every iData Toolkit application is a
function of type (HStIO Html):

```
Start world              = doHtmlServer mainEntrance world          1.

mainEntrance :: (HStIO Html)                                        2.
mainEntrance hst                                                    3.
  # (body,hst)           = loginhandling hst                        4.
  = mkHtml "Conference Manager" body hst                            5.

loginhandling :: (HStIO [BodyTag])                                  6.
loginhandling hst                                                   7.
  # (accounts,hst)       = AccountsDB Init                          8.
                           [initManagerAccount initManagerLogin] hst 9.
  = case loginHandlingPage accounts hst of                         10.
      (Left account,hst) = doConfPortal account accounts hst       11.
      (Right body,  hst) = (body,hst)                              12.
```

The loginhandling function checks the current user account. In order to do so,
first the main accounts database needs to be accessed (lines 8–9). This is done
with the function AccountsDB that was presented in Sect. 3.1. Initially, the accounts database contains a single entry for the conference manager. Later on, it
contains all current member accounts. Hence, at this stage the application has the
complete current accounts information. Second, the application needs to know
the current user and his status (conference manager, program committee member, author, or guest) in order to generate the correct HTML page. The function
loginHandlingPage :: ConfAccounts → HStIO (Either ConfAccount [BodyTag]) either yields the valid account of the current user or the HTML code body of the

login page that is displayed in Fig. 2(**a**). For conciseness, we omit its code. In case of an unknown user, body is displayed (line 12); otherwise the application uses account to switch to the proper page (line 11) using the function doConfPortal:

```
doConfPortal :: ConfAccount ConfAccounts → HStIO [BodyTag]              1.
doConfPortal account accounts hst                                       2.
  ♯ (navButtons,hst) = navigationButtons account.state hst              3.
  ♯ (currPage,  hst) = currPageStore     (homePage account.state)       4.
                                         navButtons.value hst            5.
  ♯ (navBody,   hst) = handleCurrPage currPage.value account accounts hst  6.
  ♯ (exception, hst) = eStore id hst                                     7.
  = ( [ mkSTable2 [[EmptyBody,B [] "Conference" <.||.> B [] "Manager "   8.
                  ,oops exception currPage.value]                        9.
                  ,[mkColForm navButtons.form,EmptyBody,BodyTag navBody] 10.
                  ]                                                       11.
    ], hst )                                                             12.
```

This function creates a page that consists of four areas (lines 8–12): **1.** a set of navigation buttons (navButtons.form) that depend dynamically on the user status; **2.** the static "Conference Manager" title; **3.** the user status and page in case of no issues, and the issue otherwise (line 9); **4.** the actual page content that the user is visiting (navBody). Fig. 2(**b**) shows the initial look in case of an author; Fig. 2(**c**) shows a failing judgement (empty entry in the person data). The navigation buttons are created by navigationButtons simply by enumerating the buttons, that, when pressed, yield the corresponding page that should be displayed. If no button is pressed, then its function result is the identity function. Here we only show the code for the author case:

```
navigationButtons :: Member → HStIO (Form (CurrPage → CurrPage))
navigationButtons member
  = ListFuncBut (Init, sFormId "navigation" (navButtons member))
where navButtons :: Member → [(Button,a → CurrPage)]
      navButtons (Authors _)
        = [ (LButton defpixel "Home",       const AuthorsHomePage)
          , (LButton defpixel "SubmitPaper", const SubmitPaper)
          , (LButton defpixel "ChangeInfo",  const ChangeInfo)
          , (LButton defpixel "ChangePsswrd",const ChangePassword) ]
      navButtons ...
```

CurrPage enumerates the possible pages that can be visited:

```
:: CurrPage = RootHomePage    | AssignPapers | ModifyStates  // root pages
            | AuthorsHomePage | SubmitPaper                  // authors
            | ChangePassword  | ChangeInfo                   // common
            | ListPapers      | ListReports  | DiscussPapers // referees + root
                              | ShowPapersStatus | RefereeForm
            | RefereeHomePage                                // referees
            | GuestHomePage                                  // guests
```

The current page is stored in an iData element. The function currPageStore uses the iData Toolkit library function mkStoreForm for this purpose, which extends the library function mkEditForm with a function argument that is applied to the current value. Hence, when combined with the function result of the navigation buttons, this is the page that should be displayed.

```
currPageStore :: CurrPage → (CurrPage → CurrPage) → HStIO (Form CurrPage)
currPageStore currpage = mkStoreForm (Init, sFormId "cf_currPage" currpage)
```

The functions homePage and handleCurrPage enumerate the default starting pages and page content creation functions:

```
homePage :: Member → CurrPage
homePage (ConfManager _)    = RootHomePage
homePage (Referee    _)     = RefereeHomePage
homePage (Authors    _)     = AuthorsHomePage
homePage (Guest      _)     = GuestHomePage


handleCurrPage :: CurrPage → ConfAccount → ConfAccounts → HStIO [BodyTag]
handleCurrPage RootHomePage  = rootHomePage
                        ⋮
handleCurrPage ChangeInfo     = changeInfo
```

These functions define the final content of the HTML pages. As an example, here is the function that computes the page that is displayed in Fig. 2(c) in which members can modify their personal information:

```
changeInfo :: ConfAccount ConfAccounts → HStIO [BodyTag]
changeInfo {state} _ hst
  ♯ ({form},hst) = mkEditForm (Init,nFormId "sh_changeInfo"
                                   (fromJust (getRefPerson state))) hst
  = ([Br, Txt "Change your personal information:", Br, Br] ++ form,hst)
```

As this example demonstrates, some of these page generating functions are very short, and basically use one iData element; others can be rather extensive. The 14 page generating functions consume 232 lines of code, three of which consume the largest part: guestHomePage (55 loc), assignPapersConflictsPage (52 loc), and discussPapersPage (44 loc). Hence, this amounts to an average of 6–7 loc for the remaining 11 functions.

3.5 Summary

In the above sections we have given an impression of working with the iData Toolkit and its programming paradigm. We would like to emphasize the fact that the data types and functions that are created in the modeling step of the programming paradigm belong to the programming repertoire of any novice functional programmer. We also note that the relatively largest programming effort is in the interconnection step of the paradigm. The application logic is guided using local stores of application state to determine the proper status of the application. The current version of the conference management system consumes 945 loc.

4 Implementation

In this section we present the implementation of the new iData Toolkit tools. In Sect. 3 we enumerated them as (**i**) *reference types*; (**ii**) *guarding consistency*; (**iii**) *version management*. We first explain how to implement (**ii**) and (**iii**) for database values in Sect. 4.1. Due to their complexity, *reference types* earn a separate discussion in Sect. 4.2.

4.1 Universal Database

In Sect. 2, we have seen that an iData can store its value persistently by using the `Persistent(RO)` Lifespan value. This implies that we can readily use iData elements as primitive databases:

```
universalDB₁ :: (Init,a,String) → HStIO a | iData a              1.
universalDB₁ (init,v,file) hst                                   2.
 ♯ (dbf,hst)        = mkEditForm (init,pxFormId file v) hst      3.
 = (dbf.value,hst)                                               4.
```

It is rather easy to add version handling to this scheme:

```
universalDB₂ :: (Init,a,String) → HStIO a | iData a              1.
universalDB₂ (init,v,file) hst                                   2.
 ♯ (dbf,hst)        = mkEditForm (Init,rxFormId file (0,v)) hst  3.
 ♯ (dbversion,dbvalue)= dbf.value                                4.
 ♯ (versionf,hst)   = versionNr Init dbversion hst               5.
 | init == Init || dbversion ≠ versionf.value                    6.
                    = (dbvalue,snd (versionNr Set dbversion hst))7.
 ♯ (versionf,hst)   = versionNr Set (dbversion+1) hst            8.
 = (v,snd (mkEditForm (Set, pxFormId file (versionf.value,v)) hst))  9.
where                                                            10.
 versionNr init c = mkEditForm (init,txFormId ("vrs_db_"+++file) c)  11.
```

Instead of storing a single value, we store a pair of the version number and the value (line 3). In addition, we maintain a version counter per database that keeps track of the correct version. The version counter is accessible by all applications that refer to this database. This storage is defined in line 11, and read in line 5. If we are only reading the database, or in case of a conflicting version (line 6), we always adhere to the database version and store its version number (line 7). In any other case, we increase the version number, and store it in both the global version counter (line 8) and the database (line 9).

The final addition is consistency handling:

```
universalDB₃ :: (Init,a,String) (String a → Judgement) → HStIO a  1.
              | iData a                                           2.
universalDB₃ (init,v,file) invariant hst                         3.
 ♯ (dbf,hst)     = mkEditForm (Init,rxFormId file (0,v)) hst     4.
 ♯ (dbversion,dbvalue)                                           5.
                 = dbf.value                                     6.
 ♯ (versionf,hst) = versionNr Init dbversion hst                 7.
```

```
| init == Init                                                          8.
  = (dbvalue,snd (versionNr Set dbversion hst))                        9.
| dbversion ≠ versionf.value                                           10.
  ♯ (_,hst)      = versionNr Set dbversion hst                         11.
  ♯ (_,hst)      = eStore ((+) (Just (file,"Screen out of date."))) hst 12.
  = (dbvalue,hst)                                                      13.
♯ exception      = invariant file v                                   14.
| isJust exception                                                     15.
  = (v,snd (eStore ((+) exception) hst))                              16.
♯ (versionf,hst) = versionNr Set (dbversion+1) hst                    17.
= (v,snd (mkEditForm (Set, pxFormId file (versionf.value,v)) hst))    18.
where                                                                 19.
  versionNr init c = mkEditForm (init,txFormId ("vrs_db_"+++file) c)   20.
```

The second argument in line 1 and 3 of universalDB is the consistency check of the database data. It is checked in line 14 just before updating the database. If it raises an exception (line 15), then the new value is not stored in the database, but instead the exception is passed on to a global exception store (line 16). This exception store is again a simple storage iData element:

```
eStore :: (Judgement → Judgement) → HStIO Judgement
eStore f hst
  ♯ ({value},hst) = mkStoreForm (Init,{txFormId "handle_exception" Ok})f hst
  = ( value, hst)
```

Exceptions are also stored here in case of conflicting version numbers (line 10–13). Any exception thus raised is reported to the application user as explained in Sect. 3.4 (doConfPortal).

4.2   Reference Types

Reference types are used by application programmers to model *destructively shared data*. Recall that a reference type is defined as :: Ref2 a = Ref2 String. Suppose we want to destructively share values of some type A. In Sections 3.1 and 3.4 we have shown what needs to be programmed. Recapitulating:

```
:: RefA = RefA (Ref2 A)                                                1.

gForm{|RefA|} id hst = specialize (invokeRefEditor editorRefA) id hst   2.

editorRefA :: (InIDataId RefA) → HStIO (Form A)                        3.
editorRefA (init,formid=:{ival=(RefA ref=:(Ref2 name))})              4.
  = universalRefEditor (init,{formid & ival=ref}) (invariantA name)    5.
```

The new type RefA serves as a reference to A values (line 1). For each RefA value within a model data type, the user wants an iData element of A values. Clearly, this requires specialization (line 2). The new library function universalRefEditor handles this 'dereferencing'. It is provided with the appropriate consistency checking function invariantA (line 3–5).

The function invokeRefEditor evaluates its higher-order argument, and substitutes the given value parameter in the resulting iData:

```
invokeRefEditor :: ((InIDataId b) → HStIO (Form d))
                    (InIDataId b) → HStIO (Form b)
invokeRefEditor f (init,{ival}) = coerceWith (id,const ival) f
```

The function `universalRefEditor` puts everything together.

```
universalRefEditor :: (InIDataId (Ref2 a)) → HStIO (Form a) | iData a        1.
universalRefEditor (init,ref2Id=:{ival=Ref2 filename}) hst                   2.
  # ({value},hst) = mkEditForm (Init,databaseId createDefault) hst           3.
  # (valueF, hst) = mkEditForm (Init,copyId      value)            hst        4.
  # (_,      hst) = mkEditForm (Set, databaseId valueF.value) hst            5.
  = ({valueF & changed = True},hst)                                          6.
where                                                                        7.
  databaseId v  = {pxFormId "" v  &  id = filename}                          8.
  copyId     v  = {ref2Id & ival = v,id = "copy_r_"+++filename}              9.
```

The clue of the implementation is that a *persistent* iData element `databaseId` is created that is identified by the reference label `filename` (line 8). For this iData a default value is generated using the function `createDefault` (line 3). The application user never edits this iData, but instead is offered an iData on a copy iData, that is identified by `copyId` (line 9). The altered value is written back to the database (line 5), and the altered user iData is returned by `universalRefEditor` (line 6).

We can extend `universalRefEditor` with version and consistency handling as described in Sect. 4.1. For reasons of space, we omit these steps.

4.3 Summary

We have shown how the new tools can be implemented on top of the 'classic' iData Toolkit. We use existing toolkit capabilities: elementary storages that can be destructively shared, specialization, and the flexibility of name space management. It allows us to manipulate persistent storage in a way that cannot be done directly in a functional language without special structures such as heaps or mutable variables. The toolkit itself has not been changed, but applications can now use the new tools for their purposes.

5 Related Work

In the realm of functional programming, many solutions have been proposed to program web applications. We mention just a few of them in a number of languages: the Haskell CGI library by Meijer [10]; the Curry approach by Hanus [6] (the *CurryWeb* application [7] shares a number of application concerns as the conference management system described in this paper); writing XML applications [5] by Elsman and Larsen in *SMLserver* [4]. One sophisticated system is Thiemann's WASH/CGI [14], based on Haskell. Here, HTML is produced as an effect of the CGI monad whereas we consider HTML as first-class citizens, using data types. Instead of storing state, WASH/CGI logs all user responses and I/O operations. These are replayed when needed to bring the application to its desired, most recent state. Forms are programmed explicitly in HTML, and their elements may, or may not, contain values. In the iData Toolkit, forms are generated from arbitrary data types, and always have value. Interconnecting forms in WASH/CGI is done by adding callback actions to submit fields, whereas the iData Toolkit uses a functional dependency relation. The above systems have proven to be highly inspiring. Our contribution is the identification of a single versatile unit, the iData element, that provides an integrated handling of all of their concerns while maintaining a high level of abstraction. In addition, we have shown that the programming paradigm advocates "classic" style functional programming.

The popular framework Rails [15] is based on the object oriented programming language Ruby [8]. With Rails, database front-end applications can be quickly developed. The application programmer is provided with scripts to configure directories and initial class files. The database tabling structure is used as a data structure specification language. A Rails application is a set of classes structured as a classic model-controller-view [9] application. Browser-server communication is based on urls that adhere to the configured directory structure, and the Ruby controller classes that are supposed to reside there. Server-database communication is realized by the model classes. These reflect on the database table structure, and generate the appropriate methods for the class scripts. Views are created via HTML templates that contain Ruby code to manipulate its content. This is similar to WASH/CGI in which HTML code is defined as an effect of the CGI monad. Rails shares with the iData Toolkit the goal of generating as much as possible from data structures. In Rails these are limited to table structures of basic types. The iData Toolkit can handle arbitrary, recursive, higher-order data structures. Rails applications are extremely vulnerable to configuration changes, in contrast with iData Toolkit applications. These are single executables that maintain their own state. (One can even remove all persistent files on-the-fly. Any iData Toolkit application recreates them in their initial state.)

6   Conclusions

In this paper we have presented the programming paradigm of the iData Toolkit. This four-step paradigm advocates the use of traditional, well-known, functional programming techniques to model information systems, and uses the generative power of the toolkit to automatically create interactive applications from these models. When modeling information systems, programmers need tools to model destructively shared data structures, deal with versions in a transparent way, and guard the consistency of the data. We have shown how these tools can be added on top of the 'classic' iData Toolkit, thus demonstrating its expressive power. As a representative example, we have developed a prototype conference management system, using the programming paradigm. The system is a single, compact (1kloc), application.

References

1. Achten, P., van Eekelen, M., Plasmeijer, R., van Weelden, A.: GEC: a toolkit for Generic Rapid Prototyping of Type Safe Interactive Applications. In: Vene, V., Uustalu, T. (eds.) AFP 2004. LNCS, vol. 3622, pp. 210–244. Springer, Heidelberg (August 2005)
2. Alimarine, A.: Generic Functional Programming - Conceptual Design, Implementation and Applications. PhD thesis, University of Nijmegen, The Netherlands, ISBN 3-540-67658-9, (2005)
3. Alimarine, A., Plasmeijer, R.: A Generic Programming Extension for Clean. In: Arts, T., Mohnen, M. (eds.) IFL 2002. LNCS, vol. 2312, pp. 168–186. Springer, Heidelberg (September 2002)
4. Elsman, M., Hallenberg, N.: Web programming with SMLserver. In: Dahl, V., Wadler, P. (eds.) PADL 2003. LNCS, vol. 2562, Springer, Heidelberg (January 2003)
5. Elsman, M., Larsen, K.F.: Typing XHTML Web applications in ML. In: Jayaraman, B. (ed.) PADL 2004. LNCS, vol. 3057, pp. 224–238. Springer, Heidelberg (June 2004)
6. Hanus, M.: High-Level Server Side Web Scripting in Curry. In: Ramakrishnan, I.V. (ed.) PADL 2001. LNCS, vol. 1990, pp. 76–92. Springer, Heidelberg (2001)
7. Hanus, M., Huch, F.: An Open System to Support Web-based Learning. In: Proc. of the 12th International Workshop on Functional and (Constraint) Logic Programming (WFLP 2003), Valencia (Spain) (2003)
8. Hunt, A., Thomas, D.: Programming Ruby: The Pragmatic Programmer's Guide, 1st edn. Addison Wesley Professional, London (2000)
9. Krasner, G., Pope, S.: A cookbook for using the Model-View-Controller user interface paradigm in Smalltalk-80. Journal of Object-Oriented Programming 1(3), 26–49 (August 1988)
10. Meijer, E.: Server Side Web Scripting in Haskell. Journal of Functional Programming 10(1), 1–18 (2000)
11. Plasmeijer, R., Achten, P.: Generic Editors for the World Wide Web. In: Central-European Functional Programming School, Eötvös Loránd University, Budapest, Hungary, Jul 4-16 (2005)
12. Plasmeijer, R., Achten, P.: iData For The World Wide Web - Programming Interconnected Web Forms. In: Hagiya, M., Wadler, P. (eds.) FLOPS 2006. LNCS, vol. 3945, Springer, Heidelberg (April 2006)
13. Plasmeijer, R., Achten, P.: The Implementation of iData - A Case Study in Generic Programming. In: Butterfield, A., Grelck, C., Huch, F. (eds.) IFL 2005. LNCS, vol. 4015, Springer, Heidelberg (September 2006)
14. Thiemann, P.: WASH/CGI: Server-side Web Scripting with Sessions and Typed, Compositional Forms. In: Krishnamurthi, S., Ramakrishnan, C.R. (eds.) PADL 2002. LNCS, vol. 2257, pp. 192–208. Springer, Heidelberg (January 2002)
15. Thomas, D., Hansson, H. D.: Agile Web Development with Rails. The Pragmatic Programmers, 1st edition (August 2005)

A Appendix

A.1 A Sample of the UoD Model Types Specified as Pure Data Types

```
:: ConfAccounts    := [ConfAccount]
:: ConfAccount     := Account Member
:: Account s        = { login           :: Login,  state    :: s              }
:: Login            = { loginName        :: String, password :: PasswordBox }
:: Member           = ConfManager     ManagerInfo | Authors  PaperInfo
                    | Referee         RefereeInfo | Guest    Person
:: ManagerInfo      = { person          :: RefPerson                          }
:: PaperInfo        = { person          :: RefPerson,      nr    :: PaperNr
                    , discussion      :: RefDiscussion, paper :: RefPaper
                    , status          :: PaperStatus                        }
:: PaperNr         := Int
:: PaperStatus      = Accepted | CondAccepted | Rejected | Submitted
                    | UnderDiscussion DiscussionStatus
:: DiscussionStatus = ProposeAccept | ProposeCondAccept | ProposeReject
                    | DoDiscuss
:: RefereeInfo      = { person          :: RefPerson, reports    :: Reports
                    , conflicts       :: Conflicts                          }
:: Reports          = Reports          [(PaperNr, RefReport)]
:: Conflicts        = Conflicts        [PaperNr]
:: Person           = { firstName       :: String, lastName     :: String
                    , affiliation     :: String, emailAddress :: String  }
:: Discussion       = Discussion [Message]
:: Message          = { messageFrom     :: String, date :: HtmlDate
                    , message         :: String, time :: HtmlTime        }
:: Paper            = { title           :: String, first_author :: Person
                    , abstract        :: String, co_authors   :: Co_authors
                    , pdf             :: String                          }
:: Co_authors       = Co_authors [Person]
:: Report           = { recommendation:: Recommendation
                    , familiarity   :: Familiarity                       }
:: Recommendation   = StrongAccept | Accept | WeakAccept | Discuss
                    | StrongReject | Reject | WeakReject
:: Familiarity      = Expert | Knowledgeable | Low
:: RefPerson        = RefPerson      (Ref2 Person)
:: RefPaper         = RefPaper       (Ref2 Paper)
:: RefReport        = RefReport      (Ref2 (Maybe Report))
:: RefDiscussion    = RefDiscussion  (Ref2 Discussion)
```

A.2 A Sample of the Entity-Relations Specified as Functions

```
getRefPapers       :: ConfAccounts → [(PaperNr,RefPaper)]
getConflicts       :: ConfAccounts → [(RefPerson,[PaperNr])]
getAssignments     :: ConfAccounts → [(RefPerson,[PaperNr])]
getConflictsAssign :: ConfAccounts → [(RefPerson,[PaperNr],[PaperNr])]
```

A Pattern Logic for Prompt Lazy Assertions in Haskell[*]

Olaf Chitil[1] and Frank Huch[2]

[1] University of Kent, UK
oc@kent.ac.uk
[2] CAU Kiel, Germany
fhu@informatik.uni-kiel.de

Abstract. Assertions test expected properties of run-time values without disrupting the normal computation of a program. Here we present a library for enriching programs in the lazy language Haskell with assertions. Expected properties are written in an expressive *pattern logic* that combines pattern matching with logical operations and predicates. The presented assertions are lazy: they do not force evaluation but only examine what is evaluated by other parts of the program. They are also prompt: assertion failure is reported as early as possible, before a faulty value is used by the main computation.

1 Introduction

Large programs are composed of algorithms and numerous (more or less) abstract data types which interact in complex ways. A bug in the implementation of a basic data structure can result in the whole program going wrong. Such a bug can be hard to locate, because the faulty data structure may not be part of the wrong result, it may just be an intermediate data structure. Even worse, the program may produce wrong results for a long time before the user even notices.

Testing abstract data types exhaustively is difficult. However, interesting test cases often occur when data structures are used within other algorithms. Hence it is a good idea to check for bugs in basic data structures and functions during the execution of larger programs. Using *assertions* is a common approach to do so. The programmer specifies *intended properties* of data structures and functions by writing assertions. During program execution, these assertions are tested and failure of an assertion is reported to the programmer. Examples of assertions are restricting the square root function to positive arguments or the property of being sorted for a search tree.

The Glasgow Haskell Compiler (GHC) already provides the possibility to define assertions:

```
assert :: Bool -> a -> a
```

---

[*] This work has been partially supported by the German Research Council (DFG) under grant Ha 2457/5-2 and by the United Kingdom under EPSRC grant EP/C516605/1.

Z. Horváth, V. Zsók, and A. Butterfield (Eds.): IFL 2006, LNCS 4449, pp. 126–144, 2007.

The first argument is the asserted property. If this property evaluates to True, then **assert** behaves like the identity function. Otherwise, an error is reported with detailed information about the source code position of the failed assertion. For example, consider an assertion that checks whether a list is sorted:

```
checkSorted :: Ord a => [a] -> [a]
checkSorted xs = assert (sorted xs) xs

sorted :: Ord a => [a] -> Bool
sorted (x:y:ys) = x<=y && sorted (y:ys)
sorted _        = True
```

Unfortunately **assert** is strict in its Boolean argument which clashes with Haskell's laziness. The asserted property is evaluated and the tested data structure is evaluated as far as necessary to decide the property. Hence, programming with assertions will result in strict programs with loss of the expressive power of laziness, e.g., the use of infinite data structures.

We conclude that assertions in lazy languages should respect laziness. They should only be evaluated as far as possible, i.e., an assertion should only be checked for the part of the data structure which is evaluated during the computation. A first approach for lazy assertions is [2]. It is based on

```
assert :: String -> (a -> Bool) -> a -> a
```

The first parameter is a label naming the assertion. When an assertion fails, the computation aborts with an appropriate message that includes the assertion's label. As further parameters **assert** takes the property and the value on which it behaves as a partial identity.

To prevent an assertion from evaluating too much, the property has to be defined as a predicate on the tested data structure. The implementation of **assert** ensures that only the context in which the application of **assert** appears determines how far the tested data structure is evaluated. Only the evaluated part is passed as argument to the predicate.

We can redefine **checkSorted** as follows:

```
checkSorted xs = assert "sorted" sorted xs
```

Applying **checkSorted** to the list [1,3,2,4] yields:

```
Assertion (sorted) failed: 1:3:2:_
```

The failure is reported as early as possible, before the whole list is evaluated. However, the approach of [2] has a major drawback. If we evaluate only the tail of the observed list, no failure occurs, although the evaluated part of the observed data structure is not sorted:

```
> tail (checkSorted [1,3,2,4])
[3,2,4]
```

The reason for this behaviour is that the function (&&) used in the definition of the predicate **sorted** is sequentially defined. The assertion is suspended on checking the sorted property for the first two elements of the list. The conjunction is never evaluated to `False`, although there are two elements in the evaluated part which are not in order.

In practice, many lazy assertions are suspended exactly for this reason. Many asserted properties may not hold for evaluated parts of data structures, but the assertions do not fail and hence, the programmer wrongly believes their program to be correct. The evaluation of an assertions involves a *sequential* evaluation order, which may not be related to the evaluation order of the program generating/evaluating the data structures.

In this paper we introduce a new approach for lazy assertions. The basic idea is to define assertions by means of a pattern logic instead of arbitrary Haskell functions. In this logic, we express properties with parallel versions of (`&&`) and (`||`). If any of the arguments of such a parallel operator makes the whole assertion fail, then this is reported independently of the other parts of the assertion. Furthermore, our assertions are checked as early as possible, which we call *promptness*. Whenever a new part of a data structure is required by the main computation, assertions are checked for this part and any assertion failure is reported before a faulty value is used by the main computation.

Although in some cases this approach may be more complicated than defining assertions within the programming language Haskell itself, there is also an opportunity. Our pattern logic is more a specification language than a programming language. Hence, properties are asserted in a style that is completely different to ordinary programs. So it is unlikely that programmers will make the same mistakes in the assertions as in the program, which may happen easily using the same language for programming as for specifying properties.

Beside reporting failed assertions, reporting how many and which assertions have succeeded may also be useful. We collect succeeded assertions in a file, so that the programmer can later analyse which assertions succeeded. However, not every assertion is supposed to succeed in the presence of laziness. The user must be aware that in many cases checking assertions suspends and cannot be decided on the evaluated parts of the data structures. This behaviour is even required when a property shall be tested on a never fully evaluated infinite data structure. However, if an assertion fails because of any part of an evaluated data structure, then this is reported immediately.

Our assertions have the following properties:

- They do not modify the lazy behaviour of a program.
- Whenever some part of a data structure is evaluated and this part violates an asserted property, this is promptly reported to the programmer.
- Assertions are implemented as a library and do not need any compiler or run-time modifications; the only extension to Haskell 98 used for the implementation are `unsafePerformIO` and `IORefs`.

In Sections 2 to 5 we explain how to use our pattern logic by means of examples. Section 6 outlines how the implementation works. In Section 7 we discuss related work and we close in Section 8.

2   Patterns and Quantification

In the following sections we introduce our pattern logic step by step and justify our design decisions through examples.

2.1   Patterns

Pattern matching is a powerful feature of modern functional languages. The pattern is a kind of prototype of a function's argument. For example, it allows a simple definition of a function that tests whether a list has exactly two elements:

```
hasTwoElements :: [Int] -> Bool
hasTwoElements (_:_:[]) = True
hasTwoElements _        = False
```

We can define a function that is basically the identity function on lists but additionally asserts that the argument has exactly two elements as follows:

```
twoElements :: [Int] -> [Int]
twoElements = assert "two elements" (p_ <:> p_ <:> pNil)
```

So what are the new functions used in this definition? We cannot use built-in pattern matching for prompt lazy assertions and we do not want to extend the language Haskell. Therefore, we implement our pattern logic using an abstract type constructor `Pat`. We provide functions for constructing `Pat`s:

`p_ :: Pat a` is the wildcard pattern that matches everything;

`pNil :: Pat [a]` and `(<:>) :: Pat a -> Pat [a] -> Pat [a]`

construct patterns that match the two data constructors of the list type. Using these pattern constructors we can write `p_ <:> p_ <:> pNil` to express a `Pat` similar to the pattern `_:_:[]` used in the definition of `hasTwoElements`. For every predefined data type appropriate patterns are defined, e.g., `pNothing` and `pJust` for matching `Maybe` values and `pPair` for matching pairs.

The assertion itself is expressed with

```
assert :: Observe a => String -> Pat a -> a -> a
```

The type of any value we make assertions about has to be an instance of class `Observe`, whose rôle is explained later.

Whereas `hasTwoElements` forces the evaluation of the list constructors of its argument to perform pattern matching, `twoElements` is lazy: the argument is only evaluated as far as its result is demanded by the caller of `twoElements`.

In many cases it will be useful to combine patterns by means of the logical conjunction and disjunction operators:

```
(|||) :: Pat a -> Pat a -> Pat a        (&&&) :: Pat a -> Pat a -> Pat a
```

For instance, we can now define an assertion which expresses that a list contains less than two elements:

```
shortList :: [a] -> [a]
shortList = assert "length less than two" (pNil ||| p_ <:> pNil)
```

2.2 Context Patterns

When specifying properties of large data structures, it is not sufficient to match a finite initial part of the data structure. We would like to be able to match patterns in arbitrarily deep contexts, for example, to select an arbitrary element of a list. Hence we provide *context patterns* within our pattern logic. The pattern constructor

```
pListC :: Pat [a] -> Pat [a]
```

matches its argument pattern against arbitrary sublists of a list. For example

```
oneTrue :: [Bool] -> [Bool]
oneTrue = assert "True in list" (pListC (pTrue <:> p_))
```

asserts that there exists an element `True` in the argument list.

2.3 Universal and Existential Quantification

Why does the preceding example assert that there *exists* an element `True`? Could it not mean that *all* elements should be `True`? Indeed we will sometimes want to assert a property for all sublists and sometimes want to assert that there exists a sublist with a given property. Hence we introduce the quantifier patterns

```
forAll, exists :: Pat a -> Pat a
```

which change the meaning of context patterns within their scope. So

```
exists (pListC (pTrue <:> p_))
```

asserts that there exists an element `True` whereas

```
forAll (pListC ((exists pTrue) <:> p_))
```

asserts that all list elements are `True`.

Why is there a nested `exists` in the last example? Because quantifiers do not only change the semantics of context patterns, but also of normal patterns. Within the scope of `forAll` a constructor pattern such as `pTrue` matches any other constructor. Because of the quantifier `forAll` the context pattern `pListC` has to match *all* sublists with its argument pattern. In any finite list one sublist will be `[]`. We could list this alternative in our definition:

```
forAll (pListC (pTrue <:> p_ ||| pNil))
```

This is acceptable for lists, but not for more complex types with more constructors, such as abstract syntax trees. We would have to add a disjunction for every constructor and the size of assertions would blow-up unacceptably. Therefore we decided that within the scope of `forAll` a pattern built from (`<:>`) also matches the empty list. In contrast, in an existential context the pattern describes which structure is supposed to exist. Hence, non-matching sub-data-structures should not match the pattern inside `exists`. So within the scope of `forAll` the pattern `exists pTrue <:> p_` matches both the empty list and a non-empty list that does start with `True`. In contrast, the pattern `pTrue <:> p_` also matches a non-empty list starting with `False`. Additionally, the dependence of the pattern semantics on quantification becomes crucial in the context of predicates with several arguments, as we will show in Section 3.4.

The function `assert` implicitly surrounds its pattern by `exists`. Hence in the preceding subsection the pattern context is existentially quantified.

3   Predicates

Pattern matching cannot express properties of primitive types, such as a number being positive or a number being greater than another. For expressing such properties, Haskell enriches standard pattern matching with guards, in which the programmer specifies restrictions for the bound variables.

3.1   Unary Predicates

Because we cannot define a new variable binding construct within Haskell, we cannot bind normal variables in our patterns. Instead, we introduce a new pattern `val` that represents binding a variable to a value. To check a property of such a "variable" we provide a function `check`.

For example, we define an assertion that checks whether a number is positive:

```
posInt :: Int -> Int
posInt = assert "positive" (check val (>0))
```

Similarly, we can define a more complex assertion that checks whether all elements of a list are positive:

```
allPos :: [Int] -> [Int]
allPos =
  assert "all positive" (forAll (pListC ((check val (>0)) <:> p_)))
```

3.2   Predicates with Several Arguments

Unary predicates are not very expressive. For instance, it is not possible to compare two elements of a data structure, as it is necessary for expressing the property of being sorted. Hence we extend the function `check` so that values from different `val`s can be compared in a predicate:

```
sortedList :: [Int] -> [Int]
sortedList = assert "sorted"
      (forAll (check (pListC (val <:> (pListC (val <:> p_)))) (<=)))
```

We select two elements within a list (respecting their positions in the list) by means of two list contexts, and check whether these two elements are in order. The assertion is checked for every possible combination of elements in the list. Evaluating `sortedList [2,4,6,3,5]`, the following failure is reported:

```
Assertion (sorted) failed: 2:█:6:█:_
```

The result of the application is the list itself. For printing this list, the list has to be evaluated from left to right. When the list element 3 is evaluated, the assertion fails. The list elements which cause the assertion to fail are highlighted. Because the remaining list is not evaluated at all, an underscore is presented to the user for the unevaluated tail of the list. With a different evaluation order of the values within the list other failure positions may be reported. However, our assertions are prompt. When an assertion fails during the evaluation of a data structure, this is directly reported to the user. The data structure is not evaluated any further.

Checking `sortedList` is expensive in time ($\mathcal{O}(n^2)$, where n is the length of the list). Using the transitivity of (`<=`), we can define a linear variant instead:

```
sortedLin :: [Int] -> [Int]
sortedLin = assert "sortedLin"
     (forAll (check (pListC (val <:> val <:> p_)) (<=)))
```

However, assertions should be seen as high-level specifications for which it is more important to be understandable and correct than to be efficient. Furthermore, this more efficient implementation has another drawback. If only every second element of the list is evaluated, then `sortedLin` will not compare any list element, i.e., for a list which is only evaluated to `1:_:2:_:1:_` `sortedLin` does not fail, whereas the less efficient assertion `sortedList` would fail. On the other hand, in practice evaluation orders like this one are uncommon and failure of `sortedLin` will in most cases be detected as early as failure of `sorted`.

3.3   The Pattern Type

When introducing predicates with more than one argument, we have to extend the definition of patterns (`Pat`) as well. Applying `check` to a pattern and a predicate function, we have to guarantee that the predicate takes as many arguments as `vals` occur in the pattern. Furthermore, the type of each value matched by `val` and the corresponding argument of the predicate must agree. In other words, `check` should have a type like

```
check :: Pat a (b_1,...,b_n) -> (b_1->...->b_n->Bool) -> Pat a ()
```

where $b_1,\ldots,b_n$ are the types of the values matched by `vals`. How can such a type be expressed within Haskell 98? We want `check` to work with predicates of any arity. Even a set of `check` functions indexed by arity would not do as a first take at the type of a simple constructor pattern demonstrates:

```
(<:>) :: Pat a (b_1,...,b_n) -> Pat [a] (b_{n+1},...,b_m)
           -> Pat [a] (b_1,...,b_m)
```

How shall we handle all these varying numbers of arguments collected by `val` for the predicate tested by `check`? The solution is to extend the type constructor `Pat` not by one but by two type arguments. The first is the type of a predicate passed as input to the pattern and the second is the type of a predicate resulting from the pattern. We revise the types as follows:

```
check :: Pat a (b_1->...->b_n->Bool) Bool -> (b_1->...->b_n->Bool)
          -> Pat a Bool Bool

(<:>) :: Pat a (b_1->...->b_m->Bool) (b_{n+1}->...->b_m->Bool) ->
         Pat [a] (b_{n+1}->...->b_m->Bool) Bool
         -> Pat [a] (b_1->...->b_m->Bool) Bool
```

These are still not Haskell 98 types, but they are instances of types that we can use:

```
check :: Pat a b Bool -> b -> Pat a c c
(<:>) :: Pat a b c -> Pat [a] c d -> Pat [a] b d
```

So the second type argument of `Pat` is the type of a value passed into the pattern and the third type argument is the type of a value passed back out of the pattern, if the pattern matches. We always use patterns for which these passed values are predicates or simply Boolean values.

The type of `check` expresses that the predicate of type b has to be applied to all its arguments in the pattern to return a Boolean value. The variable bindings within `check` are encapsulated. Also, while `check` tests the predicate for its argument pattern, it also accepts a predicate as input which it passes back unchanged, if the pattern matches.

We have the following type for the variable pattern:

```
val :: Pat a (a -> b) b
```

This type expresses that the input function is applied to the matched value and the result is passed back. *We do not discuss all modified type signatures here.*

To make our assertions lazy, `val` can only be performed if the selected data structure is fully evaluated. Otherwise the predicate would be tested on partially evaluated values, which could involve further evaluation destroying the laziness of our assertions. However, the pattern `val` is usually used for values of primitive types, which cannot be evaluated partially at all.

3.4   Example: Equal Sets

Let us define the property that two sets (implemented as unordered lists without repeated items) contain the same elements. A simple way to describe this property would be the following:

> For each element of the first list, there exists an equal element in the second list and
> for each element of the second list, there exists an equal element in the first list.

Using our quantifiers, the first of these two assertions can easily be defined as follows:

```
subset :: ([Int],[Int]) -> ([Int],[Int])
subset = assert "already subset"
    (check (pPair (forAll (pListC (val <:> p_)))
                  (exists (pListC (val <:> p_))))
           (==))
```

The quantifiers are nested with respect to the order in which they appear within the linearly written formula. Hence, for every element of the first list an equal element within the second list has to exist. Expressing the other direction is more difficult, because the nesting of quantifiers (`forAll exists`) has to be applied in the reverse order of the tuple elements. We need to first select any element of the second list and then check whether there exists the same element within the first list. This can be expressed by matching the same data structure twice, by means of a modified conjunction operator

```
(+++) :: Pat a b c -> Pat a c d -> Pat a b d
```

which applies both argument patterns to the same data structure and collects all `val`s within the two argument patterns (all combinations — like a product) to apply a predicate to these by means of `check`. Using this operator, we can define the complete assertion as:

```
equalSets :: ([Int],[Int]) -> ([Int],[Int])
equalSets = assert "equal sets"
  (check (    pPair (forAll (pListC (val <:> p_)))
                    (exists (pListC (val <:> p_)))
          &&& (    pPair p_ (forAll (pListC (val <:> p_)))
               +++ pPair (exists (pListC (val <:> p_))) p_)))
          (==))
```

Evaluation of `equalSets ([1,2,3],[3,2,2,1])` just yields the tuple of sets, whereas the call `equalSets ([1,2,3],[3,2,4,2,1])` aborts with the message:

  Assertion (equal sets) failed: (1:(2:(3: ▓)),3:(2:(▓ :_)))

For the element 4 of the second list, no element was found in the first list. In the presence of existential properties it is not so easy to show the programmer where an assertion failed. The first list does not contain the element 4. Marking the first list completely would present the reason for the failure of the existentially quantified part. However, this would often mean that the whole data structure is marked. Hence, we decided to mark only that part of the data structure, at which the failure of the existential pattern is observed. To distinguish these sub-terms from those causing failure of a universally quantified `val` we use a lighter colour for marking. In this application the lists were evaluated from left to right. As a consequence, the empty list made the decision that the assertion fails possible and we mark it. If the elements of the list were evaluated in another order, another element might be highlighted.

This example also shows why the design decision of making the constructor pattern semantics dependent on quantification is crucial. If the constructor pattern `<:>` does not match the empty list within a `forAll` context, then we have to add patterns for all other constructors (the empty list), i.e., replace the pattern

        (forAll (pListC (val <:> p_)))

by the disjunction

        (forAll (pListC ((val <:> p_) ||| pNil)))

Unfortunately, this is not possible and results in a type error. The pattern `pNil` does not yield a value for which we can check whether it occurs in the other list.

4   Further Patterns and Assertion Features

4.1   Functions

So far, our approach allows programmers to annotate arbitrary data structures with assertions. However, where should a programmer add such assertions? To express pre- and post-conditions, it would be nice to add assertions directly to functions. Furthermore, in a higher-order language, it should be possible to add assertions to functional arguments, functional return values, and functions within data structures as well.

In our pattern logic we handle functions just like any other data structure. The idea is that a function can be seen as a set of argument/result pairs which are matched by the function pattern

    (-->) :: Pat a c d -> Pat b d e -> Pat (a -> b) c e

The first argument of (-->) is matched against the argument the function is applied to. The second argument is matched against the function result. An assertion for functions will usually contain predicates relating arguments and results. Hence, its type is similar to any pattern constructor of arity two.

Because again b can be a functional type, patterns for functions with higher arity can be defined by nested (-->) applications. As an example we consider the greatest common divisor (*gcd*) of two numbers. A reasonable assertion for gcd is that the result is a factor of both arguments:

```
gcd :: Int -> Int -> Int
gcd = assert "result is factor of arguments"
  (forAll (check (val --> val --> val)
                (\x y res -> mod x res==0 && mod y res==0))) gcd'

gcd' :: Int -> Int -> Int
gcd' n m = let r = n `mod` m in if r == 0 then m else gcd n r
```

The algorithm is implemented by the function gcd'. For the assertion, we add a wrapper gcd which checks every application of gcd'. The function works correctly for many arguments, but we finally get a report like:

```
Assertion (result is factor of arguments) failed: █ -> █ -> █
```

The function gcd applied to the arguments 6 and 9 yields 6, which is wrong, because 6 is not a factor of 9. The reason is the wrong argument of gcd in the recursive call to gcd: we wrote n instead of m. After fixing the bug, the assertion is always satisfied.

In contrast to data structures, which are only evaluated once during the computation, functions can be applied many times. The assertion is checked for each application and any failure is reported to the programmer.

The definition of gcd demonstrates how programmers should add assertions to their functions. The defined function is renamed (here to gcd') and a wrapper with the original name (gcd) is defined.

Because (-->) is just a standard pattern constructor, its usage is not restricted to top-level function definitions. We can also use it for asserting properties of functional arguments and results as well as for functions occurring within data structures.

4.2   Negation and Implication

Finally we add negation to the logic: `neg :: Pat a b Bool -> Pat a b Bool`

We restrict negation to Boolean formulas, because using values selected by both negated and non-negated patterns in the same predicate does not make sense. We can, for example, define implication in the common way:

```
(==>) :: Pat a b Bool -> Pat a b Bool -> Pat a b Bool
(==>) pat1 pat2 = neg pat1 ||| pat2
```

4.3 Positions in Data Structures

For tree-like data structures it can be useful to compare positions of selected values in the structure. We provide positional information by means of

```
valPos :: Pat a ((Pos,a) -> b) b
```

where Pos is an abstract data type which can be compared by functions such as

```
moreLeft :: Pos -> Pos -> Bool          above :: Pos -> Pos -> Bool
```

p1 'moreLeft' *p2* is true iff in an in-order traversal of the data structure *p1* is reached before *p2* is reached. *p1* 'above' *p2* is true iff position *p2* is within the substructure at position *p1*. For example, using positions, the property of being sorted can be defined as follows:

```
sortedPos = assert "sortedPos"
    (forAll (check (pListC (valPos <:> p_) +++ pListC (valPos <:> p_))
                 (\ (p1,x1) (p2,x2) -> p2 'moreLeft' p1 || x1<=x2))
```

We non-deterministically select two elements of the list and compare them taking their positions into account.

4.4 Deactivating Assertions

Any system supporting assertions enables the programmer to easily deactivate assertions. Hence we provide a module AssertWithoutCheck with a function assert that is just implemented as the identity function on its third argument and does not check any assertion. To deactivate assertions the programmer replaces import Assert by import AssertWithoutCheck in their program.

While it may be advisable to leave simple assertions ("argument greater zero") in production code, our pattern logic encourages the formulation of properties of large data structures. Testing these properties is inherently time consuming. For example, it is infeasible in practice to check in a compiler after every update of the symbol table that the whole table is sorted with respect to a key.

5 Defining New Patterns

Using our library does not come for free. The user has to define pattern constructors for their own data types. For each algebraic data type they usually have to define – a context pattern,

> – pattern constructors for all its constructors, and
> – an instance of the class Observe.

To make these definitions as simple as possible, we provide a set of combinators, shown in Figure 1. The implementation of observers and the abstract data type Obs a, will be discussed in more detail in Section 6. Here we concentrate on what a programmer has to do to assert properties for their data types. As an example, we introduce a data type Tree for polymorphic trees in Figure 2 and show the definitions the programmer has to write for the pattern logic.

First, the programmer has to define an instance of the class Observe: for each constructor, they have to define an observation function. We provide generic

```
class Observe a where
  observe :: a -> Obs a

o0 :: a -> String -> Obs a
o1 :: Observe a => (a -> b) -> String -> a -> Obs b
o2 :: (Observe a,Observe b) => (a -> b -> c) ->
      String -> a -> b -> Obs c
o3 :: (Observe a,Observe b,Observe c) => (a -> b -> c -> d) ->
      String -> a -> b -> c -> Obs d
...
pat0 :: (a -> Maybe ()) -> Pat a b b
pat1 :: (a -> Maybe b) -> Pat b e f -> Pat a e f
pat2 :: (a -> Maybe (b,c)) -> Pat b e f -> Pat c f g -> Pat a e g
pat3 :: (a -> Maybe (b,c,d)) -> Pat b e f -> Pat c f g -> Pat d g h ->
        Pat a e h
...
patContext :: (a -> [(Int,a)]) -> Pat a b c -> Pat a b c
```

Fig. 1. Combinators for defining patterns for new types

```
data Tree a = Node (Tree a) a (Tree a) | Empty

instance Observe a => Observe (Tree a) where
  observe (Node lt n rt) = o3 Node "Node" lt n rt
  observe Empty = o0 Empty "Empty"

pNode :: Pat (Tree a) b c -> Pat a c d -> Pat (Tree a) d e
         -> Pat (Tree a) b e
pNode = pat3 (\t -> case t of Node tl n tr -> Just (tl,n,tr)
                             _             -> Nothing)

pEmpty :: Pat (Tree a) b b
pEmpty = pat0 (\t -> case t of Empty -> Just ()
                              _     -> Nothing)

pTreeC :: Pat (Tree a) b c -> Pat (Tree a) b c
pTreeC = patContext (\t -> case t of Node tl n tr -> [(0,tl),(2,tr)]
                                    Empty -> [])
```

Fig. 2. Extending the pattern logic for polymorphic trees

observers for constructors of any reasonable arity. These observers have to be applied to the constructor function itself, a string representation of the constructor and the arguments obtained from pattern matching. The programmer also has to define the pattern constructors. Again, we provide generic versions for pattern constructors (pat$n$) for each arity. The only argument of these generic patterns is a function which makes pattern matching a total function by means of a Maybe type and a tuple of the same arity as the constructor. Finally, the programmer has to define the context pattern for their new type. They should use the generic function patContext, which takes a function that determines all arguments in which the type is recursive. We encode these arguments as a list of the argument number and the corresponding actual argument. Note, that descending within a data type only makes sense for arguments of the same data type. Whenever we want to descend another type, we have to add a context of this type. For instance, consider a tree of lists of `Int`s. An arbitrary `Int` within this tree can be selected by the pattern

```
pTreeC (pNode p_ (pListC (val <:> p_)) p_)
```

Although a user has to generate some boilerplate code, we minimised the required amount of work and possible mistakes by defining the abstractions *on*, pat*n* and `patContext`. In practice the effort for introducing observers and patterns for each user defined datatype should be small. For GHC users we additionally provide a module that enables fully automatic derivation of such instances and functions by means of Template Haskell [14].

5.1   Example: Clausify

The program `clausify` by Colin Runciman takes a propositional formula of type

```
data Prop = Sym Char | Neg Prop | Dis Prop Prop |
            Con Prop Prop | Imp Prop Prop | Eqv Prop Prop
```

and transforms it into clausal form. The program is a composition of several simple transformation stages. After each successive stage, the following properties should hold, cumulatively:

1. `neg . exists $ pPropC (pImp p_ p_ ||| pEqv p_ p_)`
   Implication (`Imp`) and equivalence (`Eqv`) have been eliminated.
2. `forAll (pPropC (exists (pNeg p_) ==> exists (pNeg (pSym p_))))`
   `Neg (Sym _)` is the only permitted form of negation. Note, that `==>` matches its argument patterns against the same data.
3. `neg . exists $ pPropC (pDis (pCon p_ p_) p_ |||`
   `                        pDis p_ (pCon p_ p_))`
   No conjunction occurs within a disjunction.

Intentionally introduced faults usually cause the program to abort with a pattern-match failure at a later stage. Our assertions always report a failed assertion before such a pattern-match failure occurs, in contrast to [2], where the same properties are asserted.

6   Implementation

We have space to give only a rough outline of how our assertion library works. The implementation combines two ideas: We use the technique of the Haskell Object Observation Debugger (HOOD) [6] to observe when a part of a value is demanded and get access to this part of the value. We check assertion patterns in coroutines that are implemented via continuations.

We have to check an assertion pattern for the argument of **assert** before the argument is used by the context of the assertion application, but we cannot evaluate the argument further than the context of the assertion application

```
instance Observe a => Observe [a] where
  observe [] r = ...
  observe (x:xs) r = unsafePerformIO $ do
    Uneval routines <- readIORef r
    rx <- newIORef (Uneval (return ()))
    rxs <- newIORef (Uneval (return ()))
    writeIORef r (Cons "(:)" [rx,rxs])
    routines                         -- activate suspended assertions
    return (observe x rx : observe xs rxs)
```

Fig. 3. Observe instance for lists

demands. So we use the technique of HOOD and wrap the argument with a function observe :: Observe a => a -> EvalTreeRef -> a. This function is a non-strict identity, except that as a side-effect it records how far the value of the argument has been demanded by the context. This information is recorded in an evaluation tree[1]:

```
data EvalTree = Cons String [EvalTreeRef] | Uneval (IO ())
type EvalTreeRef = IORef EvalTree
```

Every time the argument is further evaluated, the evaluation tree grows at a leaf via a mutable variable EvalTreeRef.

All suspended assertions (pattern matches) are stored as IO actions in unevaluated leaves. When the corresponding part is evaluated, the IO actions are executed and thus checking continues, as the non-empty list case of the Observe instance declaration for lists in Figure 3 shows. Checking an assertion pattern is performed on the evaluation tree. The checking functions are defined in continuation style. So when a checking function comes across a leaf of the tree that indicates a yet unevaluated part, the IO action is extended by further checks (which themselves can again extend other actions when executed). So we have implemented a scheduler for coroutines with waiting coroutines stored in the evaluation tree. Assuming that the predicates used in patterns terminate, all pattern checking terminates and hence we do not need preemptive concurrency but cooperating coroutines suffice. The observe function ensures that all checking coroutines run before a part of an argument is returned to the program context. Thus an assertion will always report failure before a faulty value is returned to the program context.

To illustrate the mechanism of extending suspended checks in more detail, we briefly discuss the code of some patterns. The type Pat is defined as a function with result type IO() which is stored in the initially unevaluated EvalTreeRef within assert[2]:

```
type Join = Bool -> IO ()
type Pat a b c = Bool -> EvalTreeRef -> a -> b -> Join ->
                 (Join -> c -> IO ()) -> IO ()
```

---

[1] Hence, the type Obs already used in Figure 1 can be defined as:
```
type Obs a = EvalTreeRef -> a
```
[2] To obtain better type error messages, Pat is defined as an abstract datatype guarded by a constructor in the real implementation.

Successively, the arguments of the `Pat` function have the following meanings

- a Boolean value distinguishing the two quantification contexts,
- the evaluation tree on which the pattern is supposed to be checked,
- the real value (which may not be evaluated further),
- the partially applied check function,
- a join function which combines results of parallel pattern matching by means of (&&&) or (|||) and which depends on quantification,
- and a continuation passing a join function and the remaining checks (c) to be performed in `val` patterns.

The pattern matching itself can be illustrated with the definition of (<:>):

```
(<:>) :: Pat a b c -> Pat [a] c d -> Pat [a] b d
(patx <:> patxs) ex r y p join c = do
  evalT <- readIORef r
  case evalT of
    Uneval routines ->        -- extend suspended assertions
      writeIORef r (Uneval (routines >> patx <:> patxs ex r y p join c))
    Cons _ rs -> case y of
                   (y:ys) -> let [rx,rxs] = rs in
                             patx ex rx x p join
                               (\join2 p2 -> patxs ex rxs xs p2 join2 c)
                   _      -> join (not ex)
```

If the data structure to be matched has not been evaluated yet, then the suspended check action is extended with the actual matching. Otherwise, pattern matching is performed. If it succeeds, the sub-patterns are matched (in continuation style). If it fails, no further pattern matches have to be performed; the local result of pattern matching can be combined with other pattern matches executed in "parallel", which should become clearer from the definition of the parallel conjunction and disjunction of patterns. Both can be defined by means of a more general function (***) which stores two patterns within the evaluation tree:

```
(***) :: Pat a b c -> Pat a b c -> Pat a b c
(***) pat1 pat2 ex r x p join c = do
  rcount <- newIORef 2
  pat1 ex r x p (newJoin rcount join) c
  pat2 ex r x p (newJoin rcount join) c
  where
    newJoin = if ex then ... else ...

forAll :: Pat a b c -> Pat a b c
forAll pat _ = pat False

exists :: Pat a b c -> Pat a b c
exists pat _ = pat True

(&&&) :: Pat a -> Pat a -> Pat a
pat1 &&& pat2 = forAll (pat1 *** pat2)

(|||) :: Pat a -> Pat a -> Pat a
pat1 ||| pat2 = exists (pat1 *** pat2)
```

The initial value of `join` is a function that prints that the assertion succeeded or failed, depending on the Boolean value. In the definition of the combinator (***) the `join` continuation is extended. The `newJoin` applied in both coroutines uses a common reference so that a coroutine can determine if it is the first to do the join. Thus a parallel conjunction or disjunction can be implemented. When the first coroutine yields `False` for an argument of a conjunction, the result of the conjunction is determined and the coroutine evaluates the remaining `join`. When the first coroutine yields `True` for an argument of a conjunction, it updates the common reference accordingly and terminates. The second coroutine will evaluate the remaining `join`. We obtain a parallel implementation of conjunction and disjunction.

Unlike [2] our implementation of assertions does not use any features of Concurrent Haskell [12], which is a substantial extension of Haskell that is fully implemented only in GHC. Like [2] we need references to mutable variables in the IO monad (`IORefs`) and the function `unsafePerformIO :: IO a -> a`. These two language extension are provided by all Haskell systems. Using the function `unsafePerformIO` is dangerous, because it bypasses the safety net of the type system. The alternative would be to modify a compiler and its run-time system, which would be non-portable and far more complex.

7   Related Work

Assertions have been used in programs since the 1970s [11,13] and are directly supported by many programming languages. In particular the object-oriented programming language Eiffel is based on a "Design by Contract" philosophy and language constructs directly support assertions to express contracts [8,9].

Assertion-based contracts have been introduced into the Scheme community [5]. Findler and Felleisen motivate how assertions enable the programmer to express interesting properties that they cannot express in existing type systems. The two issues dealt with here, ensuring that assertions are both lazy and prompt, do not arise for a strict language such as Scheme, because all expressions are fully evaluated before an asserted property needs to be checked. Hence arbitrary Scheme expressions can be used to express properties, but a pattern logic might increase the usability of such contracts as well. Properties of functions are also expressed as properties of the argument-result pairs. A major concern of [5] is to determine which part of a program has to be blamed for the failure of an assertion. For example, when the pre-condition of a function fails, the caller of the function is to blame, when the post-condition fails, the function itself is to blame. Because in a lazily evaluated language the runtime stack does not reflect the call-structure, assigning blame is more complex. A cooperation with the Haskell tracer Hat [4] and its redex trail view may provide a solution in the future. Recently the contracts for Scheme have been transferred to Haskell [7], but without taking account of its lazy semantics.

Chitil, McNeill and Runciman [2] previously expressed the need for assertions to be lazy in a lazy language. They give several implementations but because properties are expressed as arbitrary Boolean-valued functions, assertions are not prompt but often get stuck. Their most advanced implementation requires Concurrent Haskell and their synchronisation that gives assertion threads higher priority than the main computation can cause deadlocks. Properties of functions can only be asserted by a special assertion combinator for functions with limited expressibility. We can define a similar combinator with our pattern logic as well:

```
assertFun :: (Observe a, Observe b) => String ->
             Pat a c d -> Pat b d Bool -> c -> (a -> b) -> (a -> b)
assertFun label patA patB p fun a = b'
    where (a',b') = assert label (check (pPair patA patB) p) (a,fun a')
```

To make assertions lazy, we have adapted the lazy observation technique of the Haskell Object Observation Debugger (HOOD) [6]. In every application area we know of it is used slightly differently. So the original HOOD records a linear trace of events, in [2] a copy of the observed value is recorded, and here we record the evaluation tree. We also intimately link scheduling of coroutines with observations. Nonetheless we believe that it is possible to wrap up this useful technique once and for all in a library that can then be used for the listed and future application areas.

There are numerous proposals in the literature for extending the pattern matching facilities of functional programming languages. Our context pattern combinators were inspired by [10] and the pattern logic is similar to regular expressions [1]. All these proposals aim to extend the expressiveness of the programming language and the semantics of extended patterns is similar to that of normal patterns. The pattern logic for prompt lazy assertions requires a different semantics. Previous papers propose language extensions that require compiler modifications or preprocessors, whereas we provide a portable library. Also, each of our context pattern combinators matches only the data constructors of a single type. Thus they are more specific and easier to use.

Basically our patterns describe a grammar and our pattern combinators are parser combinators [15]. They do not parse a string or list of tokens but tree-structured data. Hence our combinators have to leave the sequential structure of normal parser combinators. As grammars describe context-free properties, the similarity to parsing combinators gives an indication of the expressiveness of our pattern logic; however, the combinator `check` used with several arguments goes beyond grammars and allows the specification of context-sensitive properties.

QuickCheck is a library for testing Haskell programs with random data [3]. Properties are expressed as Haskell functions. For example, the property that the function `insert` preserves order can be expressed as follows:

```
prop :: Int -> [Int] -> Property
prop x xs = sorted xs ==> sorted (insert x xs)
```

QuickCheck properties can use normal pattern matching and Boolean functions, because they are only checked for total, finite data structures that are randomly generated. Testing with random data and testing with real data as our assertions do are two different methods which complement each other. A combined tool is feasible, but to handle laziness it would need to use our pattern logic.

QuickCheck and assertions handle preconditions (like `sorted xs` in the example) in distinct ways. In QuickCheck a precondition is a filter on the test data, so that a strong precondition makes it hard to obtain a sufficient amount of test data. When that is the case, the user is left with the difficult task of defining a special test generator that generates data fulfilling the precondition (for example generate sensible abstract syntax trees for testing compiler phases). In contrast, our assertions check for every call of a function that its preconditions are met by the caller. So assertions naturally support the contract between caller and callee whereas for QuickCheck preconditions cause additional problems.

8   Conclusions

We have presented a new approach for assertions in lazy functional programming languages such as Haskell. Our assertions do not modify the run-time behaviour of lazy execution (unless a predicate used by check fails to terminate). Assertions are implemented by means of a pattern logic, a high level, abstract specification language. Assertions provide a parallel implementation of conjunction and disjunction, which makes it possible to report failure of assertions promptly, before faulty values can effect the rest of the computation. Our approach is implemented as a library, without any modification of the compiler or the run-time system, and only needs common extensions of Haskell 98.

For future work, we plan to add assertions to more real-life programs. The practical experience we will gain will guide us in improving our pattern logic. We may revise some design decisions and possibly add further combinators to make the logic more expressive and/or easier to use.

We will also investigate which function should be blamed when an assertion fails. Combining assertions with the Haskell tracer Hat [4] should enable the programmer to locate the function to blame and even the precise fault location.

References

1. Broberg, N., Farre, A., Svenningsson, J.: Regular expression patterns. In: ICFP '04: Proceedings of the ninth ACM SIGPLAN international conference on Functional programming, pp. 67–78. ACM Press, New York (2004)
2. Chitil, O., McNeill, D., Runciman, C.: Lazy assertions. In: Trinder, P., Michaelson, G., Peña, R. (eds.) IFL 2003. LNCS, vol. 3145, pp. 1–19. Springer, Heidelberg (November 2004)
3. Claessen, K., Hughes, R.J.M.: QuickCheck: a lightweight tool for random testing of Haskell programs. In: Proc. 5th Intl. ACM Conference on Functional Programming, pp. 268–279. ACM Press, New York (2000)
4. Claessen, K., Runciman, C., Chitil, O., Hughes, J., Wallace, M.: Testing and Tracing Lazy Functional Programs using QuickCheck and Hat. In: Jeuring, J., Jones, S.L.P. (eds.) AFP 2002. LNCS, vol. 2638, pp. 59–99. Springer, Heidelberg (August 2003)
5. Findler, R.B., Felleisen, M.: Contracts for higher-order functions. In: ICFP '02: Proceedings of the seventh ACM SIGPLAN international conference on Functional programming, pp. 48–59. ACM Press, New York (2002)

6. Gill, A.: Debugging Haskell by observing intermediate datastructures. Electronic Notes in Theoretical Computer Science, In: Proc. 2000 ACM SIGPLAN Haskell Workshop. vol. 41(1), (2001)
7. Hinze, R., Jeuring, J., Löh, A.: Typed contracts for functional programming. In: Hagiya, M., Wadler, P. (eds.) FLOPS 2006. LNCS, vol. 3945, pp. 208–225. Springer, Heidelberg (2006)
8. Meyer, B.: Applying "design by contract". Computer 25(10), 40–51 (1992)
9. Meyer, B.: Eiffel: The Language. Prentice-Hall, Inc, Englewood Cliffs (1992)
10. Mohnen, M.: Context patterns, part II. In: Clack, C., Hammond, K., Davie, T. (eds.) IFL 1997. LNCS, vol. 1467, pp. 338–357. Springer, Heidelberg (1998)
11. Parnas, D.L.: A technique for software module specification with examples. Commun. ACM 15(5), 330–336 (1972)
12. Jones, S.P., Gordon, A., Finne, S.: Concurrent Haskell. In: Conference Record of POPL '96: The 23rd ACM SIGPLAN-SIGACT Symposium on Principles of Programming Languages, pp. 295–308, 21–24 (January 1996)
13. Rosenblum, D.S.: A practical approach to programming with assertions. IEEE Trans. Softw. Eng. 21(1), 19–31 (1995)
14. Sheard, T., Jones, S.P.: Template metaprogramming for haskell. In: Haskell Workshop 2002, (October 2002)
15. Swierstra, Alcocer.: Fast, error correcting parser combinators: A short tutorial. In: Bartosek, M., Tel, G., Pavelka, J. (eds.) SOFSEM 1999. LNCS, vol. 1725, Springer, Heidelberg (1999)

Ivor, a Proof Engine

Edwin Brady

School of Computer Science,
University of St Andrews, St Andrews, Scotland
Tel.: +44-1334-463253; Fax: +44-1334-463278
eb@cs.st-andrews.ac.uk

Abstract. Dependent type theory has several practical applications in the fields of theorem proving, program verification and programming language design. Ivor is a Haskell library designed to allow easy extending and embedding of a type theory based theorem prover in a Haskell application. In this paper, I give an overview of the library and show how it can be used to embed theorem proving technology in an implementation of a simple functional programming language; by using type theory as a core representation, we can construct and evaluate terms and prove correctness properties of those terms within the *same* framework, ensuring consistency of the implementation and the theorem prover.

1 Introduction

Type theory based theorem provers such as Coq [7] and Agda [8] have been used as tools for verification of programs (e.g. [20,13,28]), extraction of correct programs from proofs (e.g. [21]) and formal proofs of mathematical properties (e.g. [14,16]). However, these tools are designed with a human operator in mind; the interface is textual which makes it difficult for an external program to interact with them. In contrast, the Ivor library is designed to provide an implementation of dependent type theory (i.e. dependently typed λ-calculus) and tactics for proof and program development to a Haskell application programmer, via a stable, well-documented and lightweight (as far as possible) API. The goal is to allow: i) easy embedding of theorem proving tools in a Haskell application; and ii) easy extension of the theorem prover with *domain specific* tactics, via a domain specific embedded language (DSEL) for tactic construction.

1.1 Motivating Examples

Many situations can benefit from a dependently typed proof and programming framework accessible as a library from a Haskell program. For each of these, by using an implementation of a well understood type theory, we can be confident that the underlying framework is sound.

Programming Languages. Dependent type theory is a possible internal representation for a functional programming language. Correctness properties

Z. Horváth, V. Zsók, and A. Butterfield (Eds.): IFL 2006, LNCS 4449, pp. 145–162, 2007.

of programs in purely functional languages can be proven by equational reasoning, e.g. with Sparkle [11] for the Clean language [32], or Cover [1] for translating Haskell into AGDA [8]. However these tools separate the language implementation from the theorem prover — every language feature must be translated into the theorem prover's representation, and any time the language implementation is changed, this translation must also be changed. In section 4.2, we will see how IVOR can be used to implement a language with a built-in theorem prover, with a common representation for both.

Verified DSL Implementation. We have previously implementated a verified domain specific language [5] with IVOR. The abstract syntax tree of a program is a dependent data structure, and the type system guarantees that invariant properties of the program are maintained during evaluation. Using staging annotations [36], such an interpreter can be specialised to a translator. We are continuing to explore these techniques in the context of resource aware programming [4].

Formal Systems. A formal system can be modelled in dependent type theory, and derivations within the system can be constructed and checked. A simple example is propositional logic — the connectives $\wedge$, $\vee$ and $\rightarrow$ are represented as types, and a theorem prover is used to prove logical formulae. Having an implementation of type theory and an interactive theorem prover accessible as an API makes it easy to write tools for working in a formal system, whether for educational or practical purposes. In section 4.1, I will give details of an implementation of propositional logic.

In general, the library can be used wherever formally certified code is needed — evaluation of dependently typed IVOR programs is possible from Haskell programs and the results can be inspected easily. Domain specific tactics are often required; e.g. an implementation of a programming language with subtyping may require a tactic for inserting coercions, or a computer arithmetic system may require an implementation of Pugh's Omega decision procedure [34]. IVOR's API is designed to make implementation of such tactics as easy as possible.

In IVOR's dependent type system, types may be predicated on arbitrary values. Programs and properties can be expressed within the same self-contained system — properties are proved by construction, at the same time as the program is written. The tactic language can thus be used not only for constructing proofs but also for interactive program development.

2   The Type Theory, TT

2.1   The Core Calculus

The core type theory of IVOR is a strongly normalising dependently typed λ-calculus with inductive families [12], similar to Luo's UTT [22], the Calculus of Inductive Constructions in COQ [7], or EPIGRAM's ETT [6]. This language, which I call TT [3], is an enriched lambda calculus, with the usual reduction rules, and properties of subject reduction, Church Rosser, and uniqueness of types up to conversion. More details on programming in TT are given in [3,4]. The strong normalisation property (i.e. that evaluation always terminates) is guaranteed by allowing only primitive recursion over strictly positive inductive datatypes. The syntax of terms (t) and binders (b) in this language is:

$$
\begin{array}{ll}
t ::= \star_i & \text{(type universes)} \\
\mid x & \text{(variable)} \\
\mid b.\ t & \text{(binding)} \\
\mid t\ t & \text{(application)}
\end{array}
\qquad
\begin{array}{ll}
b ::= \lambda x\!:\!t & \text{(abstraction)} \\
\mid \underline{\text{let}}\ x \mapsto t\ :\ t & \text{(let binding)} \\
\mid \forall x\!:\!t & \text{(function space)}
\end{array}
$$

We may also write the function space $\forall x\!:\!S.\ T$ as $(x\ :\ S) \to T$, or abbreviate it to $S \to T$ if x is not free in T. This is both for readability and a notation more consistent with traditional functional programming languages. Universe levels on types (e.g. $\star_0$ for values, $\star_1$ for types, etc.) may be inferred as in [33]. Contexts (Γ) are collections of binders.

The typing rules, given below, depend on a conversion relation $\Gamma \vdash x \simeq y$, which holds if and only if x and y have a common reduct. This requires the typechecker to normalise terms, to find the common reduct, so it is important for decidability of typechecking that the language is strongly normalising.

$$
\frac{\Gamma \vdash \text{valid}}{\Gamma \vdash \star_n\ :\ \star_{n+1}} \ \ \text{Type}
$$

$$
\frac{(\lambda x\!:\!S) \in \Gamma}{\Gamma \vdash x\ :\ S}\ \text{Var}_1 \qquad
\frac{(\forall x\!:\!S) \in \Gamma}{\Gamma \vdash x\ :\ S}\ \text{Var}_2 \qquad
\frac{(\underline{\text{let}}\ x\ :\ S \mapsto s) \in \Gamma}{\Gamma \vdash x\ :\ S}\ \text{Val}
$$

$$
\frac{\Gamma \vdash f\ :\ (x\ :\ S) \to T \quad \Gamma \vdash s\ :\ S}{\Gamma \vdash f\ s\ :\ T[s/x]}\ \text{App}
$$

$$
\frac{\Gamma;\lambda x\!:\!S \vdash e\ :\ T \quad \Gamma \vdash (x\ :\ S) \to T\ :\ \star_n}{\Gamma \vdash \lambda x\!:\!S.e\ :\ (x\ :\ S) \to T}\ \text{Lam}
$$

$$
\frac{\Gamma;\forall x\!:\!S \vdash T\ :\ \star_n \quad \Gamma \vdash S\ :\ \star_n}{\Gamma \vdash (x\ :\ S) \to T\ :\ \star_n}\ \text{Forall}
$$

$$
\frac{\begin{array}{c}\Gamma \vdash e_1\ :\ S \quad \Gamma;\underline{\text{let}}\ x \mapsto e_1\ :\ S \vdash e_2\ :\ T \\ \Gamma \vdash S\ :\ \star_n \quad \Gamma;\underline{\text{let}}\ x \mapsto e_1\ :\ S \vdash T\ :\ \star_n\end{array}}{\Gamma \vdash \underline{\text{let}}\ x \mapsto e_1\ :\ S.\ e_2\ :\ T[e_1/x]}\ \text{Let}
$$

$$
\frac{\Gamma \vdash x\ :\ A \quad \Gamma \vdash A'\ :\ \star_n \quad \Gamma \vdash A \simeq A'}{\Gamma \vdash x\ :\ A'}\ \text{Conv}
$$

2.2 Inductive Families

Inductive families [12] are a form of simultaneously defined collection of algebraic data types (such as Haskell **data** declarations) which can be parametrised over *values* as well as types. An inductive family is declared in a similar style to a Haskell GADT declaration [31] as follows, using the de Bruijn telescope notation, $\vec{x}$, to indicate a sequence of zero or more x:

$$\underline{\text{data}}\ \mathsf{T}\ (\vec{x}\ :\ \vec{t})\ :\ t \quad \underline{\text{where}} \quad \mathsf{c}_1\ :\ t\ \mid\ ...\ \mid\ \mathsf{c}_n\ :\ t$$

Constructors may take recursive arguments in the family T. Furthermore these arguments may be indexed by another type, as long it does not involve T — this restriction is known as **strict positivity** and ensures that recursive arguments of a constructor are structurally smaller than the value itself.

The Peano style natural numbers can be declared as follows:

$\underline{\text{data}}\,\mathbb{N}\ :\ \star\quad\underline{\text{where}}\quad 0\ :\ \mathbb{N}\ |\ \text{s}\ :\ (k\ :\ \mathbb{N})\to\mathbb{N}$

A data type may have zero or more parameters (which are invariant across a structure) and a number of indices, given by the type. For example, a list is parametrised over its element type:

$\underline{\text{data}}\,\text{List}\,(A\ :\ \star)\ :\ \star\quad\underline{\text{where}}\ \text{nil}\ :\ \text{List}\,A$
$\qquad\qquad\qquad\qquad\qquad\qquad\quad |\ \text{cons}\ :\ (x\ :\ A)\to(xs\ :\ \text{List}\,A)\to\text{List}\,A$

Types can be parametrised over values. Using this, we can declare the type of vectors (lists with length), where the empty list is statically known to have length zero, and the non empty list is statically known to have a non zero length. Vect is parametrised over its element type, like List, but *indexed* over its length.

$\underline{\text{data}}\,\text{Vect}\,(A\ :\ \star)\ :\ \mathbb{N}\to\star\quad\underline{\text{where}}$
$\qquad\text{vnil}\ :\ \text{Vect}\,A\,0$
$\qquad |\ \text{vcons}\ :\ (k\ :\ \mathbb{N})\to(x\ :\ A)\to(xs\ :\ \text{Vect}\,A\,k)\to\text{Vect}\,A\,(\text{s}\,k)$

2.3   Elimination Rules

When we declare an inductive family D, we give the constructors which explain how to build objects in that family. IVOR generates from this an **elimination operator** D-Elim and corresponding reductions, which implements the reduction and recursion behaviour of terms in the family — it is a fold operator. The method for constructing elimination operators automatically is well documented, in particular by [12,22,24]. For Vect, IVOR generates the following operator:

$$\begin{aligned}
\textbf{Vect-Elim}\ :\ &(A\ :\ \star)\to(n\ :\ \mathbb{N})\to(v\ :\ \text{Vect}\,A\,n)\to\\
&(P\ :\ (n\ :\ \mathbb{N})\to(v\ :\ \text{Vect}\,A\,n)\to\star)\to\\
&(m_{\text{vnil}}\ :\ P\,0\,(\text{vnil}\,A))\to\\
&(m_{\text{vcons}}\ :\ (k\ :\ \mathbb{N})\to(x\ :\ A)\to(xs\ :\ \text{Vect}\,A\,k)\to\\
&\qquad\qquad (ih\ :\ P\,k\,xs)\to P\,(\text{s}\,k)\,(\text{vcons}\,A\,k\,x\,xs))\to\\
&P\,n\,v
\end{aligned}$$

$\textbf{Vect-Elim}\,A\ 0\qquad(\text{vnil}\,A)\qquad P\ m_{\text{vnil}}\ m_{\text{vcons}}\rightsquigarrow m_{\text{vnil}}$
$\textbf{Vect-Elim}\,A\,(\text{s}\,k)\,(\text{vcons}\,A\,k\,x\,xs)\,P\,m_{\text{vnil}}\,m_{\text{vcons}}$
$\qquad\qquad\rightsquigarrow m_{\text{vcons}}\,k\,x\,xs\,(\textbf{Vect-Elim}\,A\,k\,xs\,P\,m_{\text{vnil}}\,m_{\text{vcons}})$

The arguments are the **parameters** and **indices** (A and n here), the **target** (the object being eliminated; v here), the **motive** (a function which computes the return type of the elimination; P here) and the **methods** (which describe how to achieve the motive for each constructor form). Note the distinction between parameters and indices — the parameter A is invariant across the structure so is not passed to the methods as an argument, but n does vary, so is passed. A more detailed explanation of this distinction can be found in [22,3]. A case analysis operator **D-Case**, is obtained similarly, but without the induction hypotheses.

2.4 The Development Calculus

For developing terms interactively, the type theory needs to support *incomplete* terms, and a method for term construction. We extend TT with the concept of **holes**, which stand for the parts of constructions which have not yet been instantiated; this largely follows McBride's OLEG development calculus [24].

The basic idea is to extend the syntax for binders with a *hole* binding and a *guess* binding. The *guess* binding is similar to a <u>let</u> binding, but without any computational force, i.e. the bound names do not reduce:

$$b ::= \dots \mid ?x:t \text{ (hole binding)} \mid ?x:t \approx t \text{ (guess)}$$

Using binders to represent holes as discussed in [24] is useful in a dependently typed setting since one value may determine another. Attaching a "guess" to a binder ensures that instantiating one such value also instantiates all of its dependencies. The typing rules for binders ensure that no ? bindings leak into types, and are given below.

$$\frac{\Gamma; ?x:S \vdash e : T}{\Gamma \vdash ?x:S.\, e \; : \; T} \; x \notin T \;\; \text{Hole} \qquad \frac{\Gamma; ?x:S \approx e_1 \vdash e_2 \; : \; T}{\Gamma \vdash ?x:S \approx e_1.\, e_2 \; : \; T} \; x \notin T \;\; \text{Guess}$$

3 The Ivor Library

The IVOR library allows the incremental, type directed development of TT terms. In this section, I will introduce the basic tactics available to the library user, along with the Haskell interface for constructing and manipulating TT terms. This section includes only the most basic operations; the API is however fully documented on the web[1].

3.1 Definitions and Context

The central data type is `Context` (representing Γ in the typing rules), which is an abstract type holding information about inductive types and function definitions as well as the current proof state. All operations are defined with respect to the context. An empty context is contructed with `emptyContext :: Context`.

Terms may be represented several ways; either as concrete syntax (a `String`), an abstract internal representation (`Term`) or as a Haskell data structure (`ViewTerm`). A typeclass `IsTerm` is defined, which allows each of these to be converted into the internal representation. This typeclass has one method:

```
class IsTerm a where
    check :: Monad m => Context -> a -> m Term
```

---

[1] http://www.cs.st-andrews.ac.uk/~eb/Ivor/doc/

The check method parses and typechecks the given term, as appropriate, and if successful returns the internal representation. Constructing a term in this way may fail (e.g. due to a syntax or type error) so check is generalised over a monad m — it may help to read m as Maybe. In this paper, for the sake of readability we will use the syntax described in section 2.1, and assume an instance of IsTerm for this syntax.

Similarly, there is a typeclass for inductive families, which may be represented either as concrete syntax or a Haskell data structure.

```
class IsData a where
    addData :: Monad m => Context -> a -> m Context
```

The addData method adds the constructors and elimination rules for the data type to the context. Again, we assume an instance for the syntax presented in section 2.2.

The simplest way to add new function definitions to the context is with the addDef function. Such definitions may not be recursive, other than via the automatically generated elimination rules, ensuring termination:

```
addDef :: (IsTerm a, Monad m) => Context -> Name -> a -> m Context
```

However, IVOR is primarily a library for constructing proofs; the Curry-Howard correspondence [10,18] identifies programs and proofs, and therefore such definitions can be viewed as proofs; to prove a theorem is to add a well-typed definition to the context. We would like to be able to construct more complex proofs (and indeed programs) interactively — and so at the heart of IVOR is a theorem proving engine.

3.2   Theorems

In the emptyContext, there is no proof in progress, so no proof state — the theorem function creates a proof state in a context. This will fail if there is already a proof in progress, or the goal is not well typed.

```
theorem::(IsTerm a, Monad m) => Context -> Name -> a -> m Context
```

A proof state can be thought of as an incomplete term, i.e. a term in the development calculus. For example, calling theorem with the name **plus** and type $\mathbb{N} \to \mathbb{N} \to \mathbb{N}$, an initial proof state would be:

plus $= ?plus : \mathbb{N} \to \mathbb{N} \to \mathbb{N}$

This theorem is, in fact, a specification (albeit imprecise) of a program for adding two unary natural numbers, exploiting the Curry-Howard isomorphism. Proving a theorem (i.e. also writing a program interactively) proceeds by applying tactics to each unsolved hole in the proof state. The system keeps track of which subgoals are still to be solved, and a default subgoal, which is the next subgoal to be solved. I will write proof states in the following form:

bindings in the context of the subgoal x_0

...

$?x_0 : default\ subgoal\ type$

...

$?x_i : other\ subgoal\ types$

...

Functions are available for querying the bindings in the context of any subgoal. A tactic typically works on the bindings in scope and the type of the subgoal it is solving.

When there are no remaining subgoals, a proof can be lifted into the context, to be used as a complete definition, with the `qed` function:

```
qed :: Monad m => Context -> m Context
```

This function typechecks the entire proof. In practice, this check should never fail — the development calculus itself ensures that partial constructions as well as complete terms are well-typed, so it is impossible to build ill-typed partial constructions. However, doing a final typecheck of a complete term means that the soundness of the system relies only on the soundness of the typechecker for the core language, e.g. [2]. We are free to implement tactics in any way we like, knowing that any ill-typed constructions will be caught by the typechecker.

3.3   Basic Tactics

A tactic is an operation on a goal in the current system state; we define a type synonym `Tactic` for functions which operate as tactics. Tactics modify system state and may fail, hence a tactic function returns a monad:

```
type Tactic = forall m . Monad m => Goal -> Context -> m Context
```

A tactic operates on a hole binding, specified by the `Goal` argument. This can be a named binding, `goal :: Name -> Goal`, or the default goal `defaultGoal :: Goal`. The default goal is the first goal generated by the most recent tactic application.

Hole Manipulations. There are three basic operations on holes, **claim**, **fill**, and **abandon**; these are given the following types:

```
claim :: IsTerm a => Name -> a -> Tactic
fill :: IsTerm a => a -> Tactic
abandon :: Tactic
```

The `claim` function takes a name and a type and creates a new hole. The `fill` function takes a guess to attach to the current goal. In addition, `fill` attempts to solve other goals by unification. Attaching a guess does not necessarily solve the goal completely; if the guess contains further hole bindings, it cannot yet have any computational force. A guess can be removed from a goal with the `abandon` tactic.

Introductions. A basic operation on terms is to introduce λ bindings into the context. The `intro` and `introName` tactics operate on a goal of the form $(x : S) \rightarrow T$, introducing $\lambda x : S$ into the context and updating the goal to T.

That is, a goal of this form is solved by a λ-binding. `introName` allows a user specified name choice, otherwise IVOR chooses the name.

```
intro :: Tactic
introName :: Name -> Tactic
```

For example, to define our addition function, we might begin with

$$\overline{?plus : \mathbb{N} \to \mathbb{N} \to \mathbb{N}}$$

Applying `introName` twice with the names x and y gives the following proof state, with x and y introduced into the local context:

$$\begin{array}{l} \lambda x : \mathbb{N} \\ \lambda y : \mathbb{N} \\ \hline ?plus\_H : \mathbb{N} \end{array}$$

Refinement. The `refine` tactic solves a goal by an application of a function to arguments. Refining attempts to solve a goal of type T, when given a term of the form $t : (\vec{x} : \vec{S}) \to T$. The tactic creates a subgoal for each argument x_i, attempting to solve it by unification.

```
refine :: IsTerm a => a -> Tactic
```

For example, given a goal

$$\overline{?v : \mathsf{Vect}\,\mathbb{N}\,(\mathsf{s}\,n)}$$

Refining by vcons creates subgoals for each argument, attaching a guess to v:

$$\begin{array}{l} \hline ?A : \star \\ ?k : \mathbb{N} \\ ?x : A \\ ?xs : \mathsf{Vect}\,A\,k \\ ?v : \mathsf{Vect}\,\mathbb{N}\,(\mathsf{s}\,n) \approx \mathsf{vcons}\,A\,k\,x\,xs \end{array}$$

However, for vcons $A\,k\,x\,xs$ to have type $\mathsf{Vect}\,\mathbb{N}\,(\mathsf{s}\,n)$ requires that $A = \mathbb{N}$ and $k = n$. Refinement unifies these, leaving the following goals:

$$\begin{array}{l} \hline ?x : \mathbb{N} \\ ?xs : \mathsf{Vect}\,\mathbb{N}\,n \\ ?v : \mathsf{Vect}\,\mathbb{N}\,(\mathsf{s}\,n) \approx \mathsf{vcons}\,\mathbb{N}\,n\,x\,xs \end{array}$$

Elimination. Refinement solves goals by constructing new values; we may also solve goals by deconstructing values in the context, using an elimination operator as described in section 2.3. The `induction` and `cases` tactics apply the D-**Elim** and D-**Case** operators respectively to the given target:

```
induction, cases :: IsTerm a => a -> Tactic
```

These tactics proceed by refinement by the appropriate elimination operator. The motive for the elimination is calculated automatically from the goal to be solved. Each tactic generates subgoals for each method of the appropriate elimination rule.

An example of **induction** is in continuing the definition of our addition function. This can be defined by induction over the first argument. We have the proof state

$$\lambda x : \mathbb{N}$$
$$\underline{\lambda y : \mathbb{N}}$$
$$?plus\_H : \mathbb{N}$$

Applying **induction** to x leaves two subgoals, one for the case where x is zero, and one for the inductive case[2]:

$$\lambda x : \mathbb{N}$$
$$\lambda y : \mathbb{N}$$
$$?plus\_O : \mathbb{N}$$
$$?plus\_S : (k \ : \ \mathbb{N}) \rightarrow (k\_H \ : \ \mathbb{N}) \rightarrow \mathbb{N}$$

By default, the next goal to solve is $plus\_O$. However, the **focus** tactic can be used to change the default goal. The k_H argument to the $plus\_S$ goal is the result of a recursive call on k.

Rewriting. It is often desirable to rewrite a goal given an equality proof, to perform equational reasoning. The **replace** tactic replaces occurrences of the left hand side of an equality with the right hand side. To do this, it requires:

1. The equality type; for example $\mathsf{Eq} \ : \ (A \ : \ \star) \rightarrow A \rightarrow A \rightarrow \star$.
2. A replacement lemma, which explains how to substitute one term for another; for example
   repl $: \ (A \ : \ \star) \rightarrow (a, b \ : \ A) \rightarrow \mathsf{Eq}\_a\,b \rightarrow (P \ : \ A \rightarrow \star) \rightarrow P\,a \rightarrow P\,b$
3. A symmetry lemma, proving that equality is symmetric; for example
   sym $: \ (A \ : \ \star) \rightarrow (a, b \ : \ A) \rightarrow \mathsf{Eq}\_a\,b \rightarrow \mathsf{Eq}\_b\,a$
4. An equality proof.

The IVOR distribution contains a library of TT code with the appropriate definitions and lemmas. Requiring the lemmas to be supplied as arguments makes the library more flexible — for example, heterogeneous equality [24] may be preferred. The tactic will fail if terms of inappropriate types are given; recall from sec. 2.4 that the development calculus requires that incomplete terms are also well-typed, so that all tactic applications can be typechecked. The type is:

```
replace :: (IsTerm a, IsTerm b, IsTerm c, IsTerm d) =>
             a -> b -> c -> d -> Bool -> Tactic
```

The **Bool** argument determines whether to apply the symmetry lemma to the equality proof first, which allows rewriting from right to left. This **replace** tactic is similar to LEGO's **Qrepl** tactic [23].

---

[2] c.f. the Haskell function **natElim** :: Nat -> a -> (Nat -> a -> a) -> a).

For example, consider the following fragment of proof state:

$$\cdots$$
$$\lambda x : \text{Vect } A \,(\textbf{plus } x \, y)$$
$$\overline{?vect\_H : \text{Vect } A \,(\textbf{plus } y \, x)}$$

Since **plus** is commutative, x ought to be a vector of the correct length. However, the type of x is not convertible to the type of *vect_H*. Given a lemma **plus_commutes** : $(n, m \,:\, \mathbb{N}) \rightarrow \text{Eq}_-\,(\textbf{plus } n \, m)\,(\textbf{plus } m \, n)$, we can use the `replace` tactic to rewrite the goal to the correct form. Applying `replace` to Eq, **repl**, **sym** and **plus_commutes** $y \, x$ yields the following proof state, which is easy to solve using the `fill` tactic with x.

$$\cdots$$
$$\lambda x : \text{Vect } A \,(\textbf{plus } x \, y)$$
$$\overline{?vect\_H : \text{Vect } A \,(\textbf{plus } x \, y)}$$

3.4   Tactic Combinators

IVOR provides an embedded domain specific language for building tactics, in the form of a number of combinators for building more complex tactics from the basic tactics previously described. By providing an API for basic tactics and a collection of combinators, it becomes easy to extend the library with more complex domain specific tactics. We will see examples in sections 4.1 and 4.2.

Sequencing Tactics. There are three basic operators for combining two tactics to create a new tactic:

```
(>->), (>+>), (>=>) :: Tactic -> Tactic -> Tactic
```

1. The `>->` operator constructs a new tactic by sequencing two tactic applications to the *same* goal.
2. The `>+>` operator constructs a new tactic by applying the first, then applying the second to the next *default* goal.
3. The `>=>` operator constructs a new tactic by applying the first tactic, then applying the second to every subgoal generated by the first.

Finally, `tacs` takes a list of tactics and applies them in turn to the default goal:

```
tacs :: Monad m => [Goal -> Context -> m Context] ->
                   Goal -> Context -> m Context
```

Note that the type of this is better understood as `[Tactic] -> Tactic`, but the Haskell typechecker requires that the same monad be abstracted over all of the combined tactics.

Handling Failure. Tactics may fail (for example a refinement may be ill-typed). Recovering gracefully from a failure may be needed, for example to try a number of possible ways of rewriting a term. The `try` combinator is an exception handling combinator. The identity tactic, `idTac`, is often appropriate on success.

```
try :: Tactic -> -- apply this tactic
       Tactic -> -- apply if the tactic succeeds
       Tactic -> -- apply if the tactic fails
       Tactic
```

4 Examples

In this section we show two examples of embedding Ivor in a Haskell program. The first shows an embedding of a simple theorem prover for propositional logic. The second example extends this theorem prover by using the same logic as a basis for showing properties of a functional language.

4.1 A Propositional Logic Theorem Prover

Propositional logic is straightforward to model in dependent type theory; here we show how Ivor can be used to implement a theorem prover for propositional logic. The full implementation is available from http://www.cs.st-andrews. ac.uk/ eb/Ivor/. The language of propositional logic is defined as follows, where x stands for an arbitrary free variable:

$$L ::= x \mid L \wedge L \mid L \vee L \mid L \rightarrow L \mid \neg L$$

There is a simple mapping from this language to dependent type theory — the $\wedge$ and $\vee$ connectives can be declared as inductive families, where the automatically derived elimination rules give the correct elimination behaviour, and the $\rightarrow$ connective follows the same rules as the function arrow. Negation can be defined with the empty type.

The $\wedge$ connective is declared as an inductive family, where an instance of the family gives a proof of the connective. The and_intro constructor builds a proof of $A \wedge B$, given a proof of A and a proof of B:

<u>data</u> And $(A, B : \star) : \star$ <u>where</u>
  and_intro $: (a : A) \rightarrow (b : B) \rightarrow$ And $A B$

Similarly, $\vee$ is declared as an inductive family; an instance of $A \vee B$ is built either from a proof of A (inl) or a proof of B (inr):

<u>data</u> Or $(A, B : \star) : \star$ <u>where</u>
  inl $: (a : A) \rightarrow$ Or $A B$
  $\mid$ inr $: (b : B) \rightarrow$ Or $A B$

I will write $[\![e]\!]$ to denote the translate from an expression $e \in L$ to an implementation in TT; in the implementation, this is a parser from strings to ViewTerms:

$$[\![e_1 \wedge e_2]\!] = \text{And } [\![e_1]\!] \, [\![e_2]\!]$$
$$[\![e_1 \vee e_2]\!] = \text{Or } [\![e_1]\!] \, [\![e_2]\!]$$
$$[\![e_1 \rightarrow e_2]\!] = [\![e_1]\!] \rightarrow [\![e_2]\!]$$

To implement negation, we declare the empty type:

<u>data</u> False : $\star$ <u>where</u>

Then $\llbracket\neg e\rrbracket = \llbracket e\rrbracket \to$ False. The automatically derived elimination shows that a value of *any* type can be created from a proof of the empty type:

False-**Elim** : $(x : \text{False}) \to (P : \text{False} \to \star) \to P\,x$

In the implementation, we initialise the Context with these types (using addData) and propositional variables $A \ldots Z$ (using addAxiom[3]).

Domain Specific Tactics. Mostly, the implementation of a propositional logic theorem prover consists of a parser and pretty printer for the language L, and a top level loop for applying introduction and elimination tactics. However, some domain specific tactics are needed, in particular to deal with negation and proof by contradiction.

To prove a negation $\neg A$, we assume A and attempt to prove False. This is achieved with an assumeFalse tactic which assumes the negation of the goal. Negation is defined with a function **not**; the assumeFalse tactic then unfolds this name so that a goal (in TT syntax) **not** A is transformed to $A \to$ False, then A can be introduced.

```
assumeFalse :: Tactic
assumeFalse = unfold (name "not") >+> intro
```

The proof by contradiction tactic is implemented as follows:

```
contradiction :: String -> String -> Tactic
contradiction x y = claim (name "false") "False" >+>
                    induction "false" >+>
                    (try (fill $ x ++ " " ++ y)
                         idTac
                         (fill $ y ++ " " ++ x))
```

This tactic takes the names of the two contradiction premises. One is of type $A \to$ False for some A, the other is of type A. The tactic works by claiming there is a contradiction and solving the goal by induction over that assumed contradiction (which gives no subgoals, since False-**Elim** has no methods). Finally, using >+> to solve the next subgoal (and discharge the assumption of the contradiction), it looks for a value of type False by first applying y to x then, if that fails, applying x to y.

4.2   Funl, a Functional Language with a Built-In Theorem Prover

Propositional logic is an example of a simple formal system which can be embedded in a Haskell program using IVOR; however, more complex languages can be implemented. FUNL is a simple functional language, with primitive recursion

---

[3] This adds a name with a type but no definition to the context.

over integers and higher order functions. It is implemented on top of IVOR as a framework for both language representation and correctness proofs in that language. By using the same framework for both, it is a small step from implementing the language to implementing a theorem prover for showing properties of programs, making use of the theorem prover developed in sec. 4.1. An implementation is available from `http://www.cs.st-andrews.ac.uk/~eb/Funl/`; in this section I will sketch some of the important details of this implementation. Like the propositional logic theorem prover, much of the detail is in the parsing and pretty printing of terms and propositions, relying on IVOR for typechecking and evaluation.

Programs and Properties. The FUNL language allows programs and statements of the properties those programs should satisfy to be expressed within the same input file. Functions are defined as in the following examples, using `rec` to mark a primitive recursive definition:

```
fac : Int -> Int =
    lam x . rec x 1 (lam k. lam recv. (k+1)*recv);
myplus : Int -> Int -> Int =
    lam x. lam y. rec x y (lam k. lam recv. 1+recv);
```

The `myplus` function above defines addition by primitive recursion over its input. To show that this really is a definition of addition, we may wish to show that it satisfies some appropriate properties of addition. In the FUNL syntax, we declare the properties we wish to show as follows:

```
myplusn0 proves
    forall x:Int. myplus x 0 = x;
myplusnm1 proves
    forall x:Int. forall y:Int. myplus x (1+y) = 1+(myplus x y);
myplus_commutes proves
    forall x:Int. forall y:Int. myplus x y = myplus y x;
```

On compiling a program, the compiler requires that proofs are provided for the stated properties. Once built, the proofs can be saved as proof terms, so that properties need only be proved once.

Building Terms. Terms are parsed into a data type `Raw`; the name `Raw` reflects the fact that these are raw, untyped terms; note in particular that `Rec` is an operator for primitive recursion on arbitrary types, like the **D-Elim** operators in TT — it would be fairly simple to write a first pass which translated recursive calls into such an operator using techniques similar to McBride and McKinna's labelled types [27], which are implemented in IVOR. Using this, we could easily extend the language with more primitive types (e.g. lists) or even user defined data types. The representation is as follows:

```
data Raw = Var String | Lam String Ty Raw | App Raw Raw
         | Num Int | Boolval Bool | InfixOp Op Raw Raw
         | If Raw Raw Raw | Rec Raw [Raw]
```

Building a FUNL function consists of creating a theorem with a goal representing the function's type, then using the buildTerm tactic to traverse the structure of the raw term, constructing a proof of the theorem — note especially that rec translates into an application of the appropriate elimination rule via the induction tactic:

```
buildTerm :: Raw -> Tactic
buildTerm (Var x) = refine x
buildTerm (Lam x ty sc) = introName (name x) >+> buildTerm sc
buildTerm (Language.App f a) = buildTerm f >+> buildTerm a
buildTerm (Num x) = fill (mkNat x)
buildTerm (If a t e) =
    cases (mkTerm a) >+> buildTerm t >+> buildTerm e
buildTerm (Rec t alts) =
    induction (mkTerm t) >+> tacs (map buildTerm alts)
buildTerm (InfixOp Plus x y) =
    refine "plus" >+> buildTerm x >+> buildTerm y
buildTerm (InfixOp Times x y) = ...
```

A helper function, mkTerm, is used to translate simple expressions into ViewTerms. This is used for the scrutinees of if and rec expressions, although if more complex expressions are desired here, it would be possible to use buildTerm instead.

```
mkTerm :: Raw -> ViewTerm
mkTerm (Var x) = (Name Unknown (name x))
mkTerm (Lam x ty sc) = Lambda (name x) (mkType ty) (mkTerm sc)
mkTerm (Apply f a) = App (mkTerm f) (mkTerm a)
mkTerm (Num x) = mkNat x
mkTerm (InfixOp Plus x y) =
    App (App (Name Free (name "plus")) (mkTerm x)) (mkTerm y)
mkTerm (InfixOp Times x y) = ...
```

IVOR handles the typechecking and any issues with renaming, using techniques from [26]; if there are any type errors in the Raw term, this tactic will fail (although some extra work is required to produce readable error messages). By using IVOR to handle typechecking and evaluation, we are in no danger of constructing or evaluating an ill-typed term.

Building Proofs. We also define a language of propositions over terms in FUNL. This uses propositional logic, just like the theorem prover in section 4.1, but extended with equational reasoning. For the equational reasoning, we use a library of equality proofs to create tactics for applying commutativity and associativity of addition and simplification of expressions.

A basic language of propositions with the obvious translation to TT is:

```
data Prop = Eq Raw Raw
          | And Prop Prop | Or Prop Prop
          | All String Ty Prop | FalseProp
```

This allows equational reasoning over FUNL programs, quantification over variables and conjunction and disjunction of propositions. A more full featured prover may require relations other than Eq or even user defined relations.

5 Related Work

The ability to extend a theorem prover with user defined tactics has its roots in Robin Milner's LCF [29]. This introduced the programming language ML to allow users to write tactics; we follow the LCF approach in exposing the tactic engine as an API. The implementation of IVOR is based on the presentation of OLEG in Conor McBride's thesis [24]. We use implementation techniques from [26] for dealing with variables and renaming.

The core language of EPIGRAM [27,6] is similar to TT, with extensions for observational equality. EPIGRAM is a dependently typed functional programming language, where types can be predicated on arbitrary values so that types can be read as precise specifications. Another recent language which shares the aim of begin theorem proving technology closer to programers is Sheard's Ωmega [35]. While IVOR emphasises interactive theorem proving, Ωmega emphasises programming but nevertheless allows more precise types to be given to programs through Generalised Algebraic Data Types [31] and extensible kinds.

Other theorem provers such as COQ [7], AGDA [8] and Isabelle [30] have varying degrees of extensibility. COQ includes a high level domain specific language for combining tactics and creating new tactics, along the lines of the tactic combinators presented in section 3.4. This language is ideal for many purposes, such as our `contradiction` tactic, but more complex examples such as `buildTerm` would require extending COQ itself. Using a DSEL [19] as provided by IVOR gives complete flexibility in the construction of tactics, and allows a close relationship between the tactics and the structures on which they operate (e.g. Raw).

Isabelle [30] is a generic theorem prover, in that it includes a large body of object logics and a meta-language for defining new logics. It includes a typed, extensible tactic language, and can be called from ML programs, but unlike IVOR is not based on a dependent type theory. There is therefore no *proof term* associated with an Isabelle proof — the proof term gives a derivation tree for the proof, allowing easy and independent rechecking without referring to the tactics used to build the proof.

The implementation of FUNL allows a theorem prover to be attached to the language in a straightforward way, using IVOR's tactics directly. This would be a possible method of attaching a theorem prover to a more full featured programming language such as the Sparkle [11] prover for Clean [32]. Implementing a full language in this way would require some extra work to deal with general recursion and partial definitions (in particular, dealing with ⊥ as a possible value), but the general method remains the same.

6   Conclusions and Further Work

We have seen an overview of the IVOR library, including the term and tactic language. By exposing the tactic API and providing an interface for term construction and evaluation, we are able to embed theorem proving technology in a Haskell application. This in itself is not a new idea, having first been seen as far back as the LCF [29] prover — however, the theorem proving technology is not an end in itself, but a mechanism for constructing domain specific tools such as the propositional logic theorem prover in section 4.1 and the programming language with built in equational reasoning support in section 4.2.

The library includes several features we have not been able to discuss here, e.g. dependently typed pattern matching [9], which gives a better notation for *programming* as well as proof. There is experimental support for multi-stage programming with dependent types, exploited in [5]. The term language can be extended with primitive types and operations, e.g. integers and strings with associated arithmetic and string manipulation operators. Such features would be essential in a representation of a real programming language. In this paper, we have stated that TT is strongly normalising, with no general recursion allowed, but again in the representation of a real programming language general recursion may be desirable — however, this means that correctness proofs can no longer be total. The library can optionally allow general recursive definitions, but such definitions cannot be reduced by the typechecker. Finally, a command driven interface is available, which can be accessed as a Haskell API or used from a command line driver program, and allows user directed proof scripts in the style of other proof assistants. These and other features are fully documented on the web site[4].

Development of the library has been driven by the requirements of our research into Hume [17], a resource aware functional language. We are investigating the use of dependent types in representing and verifying resource bounded functional programs [4]. For this, automatic generation of injectivity and disjointness lemmas for constructors will be essential [25]. Future versions will include optimisations from [3] and some support for compiling TT terms; this would not only improve the efficiency of the library (and in particular its use for evaluating certified code) but also facilitate the use of IVOR in a real language implementation. Finally, an implementation of coinductive types [15] is likely to be very useful; currently it can be achieved by implementing recursive functions which do not reduce at the type level, but a complete implementation with criteria for checking productivity would be valuable for modelling streams in Hume.

---

[4] http://www.cs.st-andrews.ac.uk/~eb/Ivor/

Acknowledgements

My thanks to Kevin Hammond and James McKinna for their comments on an earlier draft of this paper, and to the anonymous reviewers for their helpful comments. This work is generously supported by EPSRC grant EP/C001346/1.

References

1. Cover translator. http://coverproject.org/CoverTranslator/
2. Barras, B., Werner, B.: Coq in Coq (1997)
3. Brady, E.: Practical Implementation of a Dependently Typed Functional Programming Language. PhD thesis, University of Durham (2005)
4. Brady, E., Hammond, K.: A dependently typed framework for static analysis of program execution costs. In: Butterfield, A., Grelck, C., Huch, F. (eds.) IFL 2005. LNCS, vol. 4015, pp. 74–90. Springer, Heidelberg (2006)
5. Brady, E., Hammond, K.: A verified staged interpreter is a verified compiler. In: Proc. Conf. Generative Programming and Component Engineering (GPCE '06) (2006)
6. Chapman, J., Altenkirch, T., McBride, C.: Epigram reloaded: A standalone typechecker for ETT. In: Trends in Functional Programming, 2005. To appear (2006)
7. Coq Development Team. The Coq proof assistant — reference manual. (2001) http://coq.inria.fr/
8. Coquand, C.: Agda. (2005) http://agda.sourceforge.net/
9. Coquand, T.: Pattern matching with dependent types. Available from (1992) http://www.cs.chalmers.se/~coquand/type.html
10. Curry, H.B., Feys, R.: Combinatory Logic, vol. 1. North Holland, Amsterdam (1958)
11. de Mol, M., van Eekelen, M., Plasmeijer, R.: Theorem proving for functional programmers. In: Arts, T., Mohnen, M. (eds.) IFL 2002. LNCS, vol. 2312, Springer, Heidelberg (2002)
12. Dybjer, P.: Inductive families. Formal Aspects Of. Computing 6, 440–465 (1994)
13. Filliâtre, J.-C.: Why: a multi-language multi-prover verification tool. Research Report 1366, LRI, Université Paris Sud (March 2003)
14. Geuvers, H., Wiedijk, F., Zwanenburg, J.: A constructive proof of the fundamental theorem of algebra without using the rationals. In: TYPES 2000, pp. 96–111 (2000)
15. Giménez, E.: An application of co-inductive types in coq: Verification of the alternating bit protocol. In: Berardi, S., Coppo, M. (eds.) TYPES 1995. LNCS, vol. 1158, pp. 135–152. Springer, Heidelberg (1996)
16. Gonthier, G.: A computer-checked proof of the Four Colour Theorem. (2005) http://research.microsoft.com/~gonthier/4colproof.pdf
17. Hammond, K., Michaelson, G.: Hume: a Domain-Specific Language for Real-Time Embedded Systems. In: Proc. Conf. Generative Programming and Component Engineering (GPCE '03), Springer, Heidelberg (2003)
18. Howard, W.A.: The formulae-as-types notion of construction, A reprint of an unpublished manuscript from 1969. In: Seldin, J.P., Hindley, J.R. (eds.) To H.B.Curry: Essays on combinatory logic, lambda calculus and formalism, Academic Press, San Diego (1980)
19. Hudak, P.: Building domain-specific embedded languages. ACM Computing Surveys, 28A(4) (December 1996)

20. Leroy, X.: Formal certification of a compiler back-end. In: Principles of Programming Languages 2006, pp. 42–54. ACM Press, New York (2006)
21. Letouzey, P.: A new extraction for Coq. In: Geuvers, H., Wiedijk, F. (eds.) TYPES 2002. LNCS, vol. 2646, pp. 200–219. Springer, Heidelberg (2003)
22. Luo, Z.: Computation and Reasoning – A Type Theory for Computer Science. Intl. Series of Monographs on Comp. Sci. OUP (1994)
23. Luo, Z., Pollack, R.: Lego proof development system: User's manual. Technical report, Department of Computer Science, University of Edinburgh (1992)
24. McBride, C.: Dependently Typed Functional Programs and their proofs. PhD thesis, University of Edinburgh (May 2000)
25. McBride, C., Goguen, H., McKinna, J.: Some constructions on constructors. In: Filliâtre, J.-C., Paulin-Mohring, C., Werner, B. (eds.) TYPES 2004. LNCS, vol. 3839, Springer, Heidelberg (2006)
26. McBride, C., McKinna, J.: I am not a number, I am a free variable. In: Proceedings of the ACM SIGPLAN Haskell Workshop (2004)
27. McBride, C., McKinna, J.: The view from the left. Journal of Functional Programming 14(1), 69–111 (2004)
28. McKinna, J., Wright, J.: A type-correct, stack-safe, provably correct, expression compiler in Epigram. Journal of Functional Programming. To appear (2007)
29. Milner, R.: LCF: A way of doing proofs with a machine. In: Winkowski, J. (ed.) Mathematical Foundations of Computer Science 1978. LNCS, vol. 64, pp. 146–159. Springer, Heidelberg (1978)
30. Nipkow, T., Paulson, L.C., Wenzel, M.: Isabelle/HOL - A proof assistant for higher order logic. In: Nipkow, T., Paulson, L.C., Wenzel, M. (eds.) Isabelle/HOL. LNCS, vol. 2283, Springer, Heidelberg (2002)
31. Jones, S.P., Vytiniotis, D., Weirich, S., Washburn, G.: Simple unification-based type inference for GADTs. In: Proc. 2006 International Conf. on Functional Programming (ICFP 2006) (2006)
32. Plasmeijer, R., van Eekelen, M.: The Concurrent CLEAN language report (draft). Available from http://www.cs.kun.nl/~clean/ (2003)
33. Pollack, R.: Implicit syntax. Informal Proceedings of First Workshop on Logical Frameworks, Antibes (May 1990)
34. Pugh, W.: The Omega Test: a fast and practical integer programming algorithm for dependence analysis. Communication of the ACM, pp. 102–114 (1992)
35. Sheard, T.: Languages of the future. In: ACM Conference on Object Orientated Programming Systems, Languages and Applications (OOPSLA'04) (2004)
36. Taha, W.: A gentle introduction to multi-stage programming. Available from (2003) http://www.cs.rice.edu/~taha/publications/journal/dspg04a.pdf

Proving Program Properties Specified with Subtype Marks[*]

Tamás Kozsik

Department of Programming Languages and Compilers,
Eötvös Loránd University, Budapest, Hungary
tamas.kozsik@elte.hu

Abstract. This paper presents a method that facilitates formal reasoning about the correctness of programs. In this method, properties of programs (e.g. pre- and postconditions of functions) are described in terms of type invariants. Subtype marks are annotations attached to types and denote type invariants. A large amount of program properties expressed with subtype marks are verifiable fully automatically by an appropriate type system; the rest can be proven with a proof system. In this paper an eager pure functional language with a type system supporting subtype marks is briefly described. By assigning an interpretation to subtype marks, a concept of program correctness is introduced. The soundness of the presented type system is investigated.

1 Introduction

The development of safety-critical applications may be facilitated with programming environments in which formal reasoning about the correctness of programs can be accomplished. Such a programming environment may include a proof system that helps the programmer formally prove properties of the program code. Sparkle [1] is such a proof system, integrated into the IDE of Clean [2]. An advantage of this tool is that it is based on and optimized for the semantics of Clean. This paper proposes a possible extention to Clean and Sparkle which could further improve the collaboration between the language and the proof tool in the course of formal reasoning about the correctness of Clean programs. The concept of subtype marks [3–7] can be used to bind a proof tool to the type system of a programming language; here a Sparkle to Clean binding is being studied.

Subtype marks provide a means to express properties of programs in terms of type invariants. They appear as annotations attached to types, and each subtype mark corresponds to a logical predicate describing the legal values of a type. The argument and return types of functions may contain subtype marks. This is how the specification of pre- and postconditions becomes feasible.

Proving those properties of programs which are specified with subtype marks can be performed with the collaboration of a type system and a proof system.

* Supported by GVOP-3.2.2-2004-07-0005/3.0 ELTE IKKK.

Z. Horváth, V. Zsók, and A. Butterfield (Eds.): IFL 2006, LNCS 4449, pp. 163–180, 2007.

Certain properties of programs can be proven fully automatically by the type system. Other properties might require an automatic, semi-automatic or manual proof carried out in the proof system.

Currently the presented technique supports only a subset of Clean: an eager, explicitly typed language without parametric polymorphism is considered. (Type classes, lazy evaluation and type inference is left as future work.) The extention of this subset of Clean with subtype marks is called SENYV. For improved readability, the syntax used for SENYV slightly differs from that of Clean. The dynamic semantics of SENYV is independent of subtype marks, and it is defined by a translation from SENYV to Clean. This translation removes subtype marks and takes care of the syntactic differences.

The paper is structured as follows. In Sect. 2 the syntax and the semantics of types with subtype marks in SENYV are given. Sect. 3 describes the rest of SENYV. Type correctness is defined in Sect. 4. Sect. 5 presents the concept of program correctness with respect to the properties specified with subtype marks. A theorem formulating the soundness of the introduced type system is given in Sect. 6. Finally, Sect. 7 provides some concluding remarks and the discussion of related and future work.

2   Subtype Marks

Type invariants are predicates that select the legal values of types from a broader set. The predicates are defined in a typed universe. For example, predicate $N(x) = (x \geq 0)$ selects natural numbers, and predicate $E(x) = (2|x)$ selects even numbers from the set of integer numbers. Subtype marks provide a way to describe type invariants in a programming language.

In a type system supporting subtype marks, annotations can be attached to types. An annotation may consist of a set of subtype marks. Suppose that the type of integer numbers is called `Int`; then the type of natural numbers can be written as `Int{N}`. The type of even natural numbers is `Int{E,N}`, which is the same as `Int{N,E}`. Note that `Int` is used as a shorthand for `Int{}`. Sect. 2.2 explains how a subtype mark (e.g. `N`) is assigned a meaning (like predicate N).

Sect. 2.1 introduces a syntax-based subtype/supertype relation (denoted by $<:$) among the annotated types. For example, the type of even natural numbers is a subtype of the type of natural numbers, which is, in turn, a subtype of the type of integer numbers: `Int{N,E}` $<:$ `Int{N}` $<:$ `Int`.

The subtype relation induces subtype polymorphism in the type system. This paper focuses on subtype marks, hence the utilized type system is kept very simple; it even lacks for type inference and parametric polymorphism. Type constructors, all nullary, come from algebraic type definitions. The only exception is the (binary) built-in "function space" type constructor.

Besides subtype marks, annotations attached to types have another constituent: "believe-me marks". Believe-me marks annotate subtype marks; they are used to describe the division of labour between the type system and the proof system. On the one hand, properties that are specified with subtype marks without believe-me marks will be proven by the type system. On the other hand, properties specified with subtype marks annotated with believe-me marks will be proven with the proof system: the type system "believes" in these properties without trying to prove them. (The compiler should generate the verification conditions corresponding to the believe-me marks.) The type of natural numbers where the subtype mark is annotated with a believe-me mark is written as Int{N!}. Believe-me marks have no effect on the subtype relation.

2.1 The Syntax of Subtype Marked Types

Let $\mathfrak{T}$ denote the set of the type constructor symbols introduced by a system of algebraic type definitions. Furthermore, let $\mathfrak{M}$ be a fixed set of symbols; subtype marks are chosen from this set. (Variable m is used to run through $\mathfrak{M}$.) It is assumed that subtype marks are used in a "clean" manner, namely that a subtype mark is never used to annotate two different types.

Definition 1 (Monomorphic subtype annotation). *Monomorphic subtype annotations are functions from $\mathfrak{M}$ to the set $\{\uparrow, \downarrow, !\}$. The values $\uparrow$, $\downarrow$ and $!$ are read as "present", "dubious" and "believe-me", respectively.*

Definition 2 (Abstract syntax of types). *Types with monomorphic subtype marks are defined inductively as follows.*

$$T \quad ::= \quad \mathbf{T}^\alpha \quad | \quad T_1 \xrightarrow{\beta} T_2 \ ,$$

where T, T_1, T_2 are types, $\mathbf{T} \in \mathfrak{T}$ and α, β are monomorphic subtype annotations.

In the concrete syntax, as seen in earlier examples, only non-dubious subtype marks are recorded. For instance, Int{N,E!} stands for $\mathbf{Int}^\gamma$, where

$$\gamma(m) = \begin{cases} \uparrow & \text{if } m = \mathtt{N}, \\ ! & \text{if } m = \mathtt{E}, \\ \downarrow & \text{otherwise.} \end{cases}$$

Definition 3 (Subtype relation).

- $\mathbf{T}^\alpha <: \mathbf{T}^\beta$, *if* $\{m \in \mathfrak{M} \mid \alpha(m) \neq \downarrow\} \supseteq \{m \in \mathfrak{M} \mid \beta(m) \neq \downarrow\}$.
- $(T_1 \xrightarrow{\alpha} T_2) <: (T_1' \xrightarrow{\beta} T_2')$, *if* $\{m \in \mathfrak{M} \mid \alpha(m) \neq \downarrow\} \supseteq \{m \in \mathfrak{M} \mid \beta(m) \neq \downarrow\}$ *and* $T_1' <: T_1$ *and* $T_2 <: T_2'$.
- *In all other cases two types are not in subtype relation.*

2.2 The Semantics of Subtype Marks

When reasoning about programs, a key question, in general statically undecidable, is how to manage the undefinedness of programs: run-time errors or exceptions and infinite computations. To alleviate the difficulties arisen from undefinedness, the method presented here is based on an eager language. Hence the only sources of undefinedness are partially defined functions and infinite recursion. In an eager language, for instance, there are no infinite or partially defined data structures.

Algebraic type definitions in SENYV are similar to those in Clean, but type constructors are always nullary, and the data structures are implicitly strict: the translation from SENYV to Clean (which defines the dynamic semantics of SENYV) should insert strictness annotations into these definitions.

Example 1 (The algebraic data type `List`*).* The type of lists of integer numbers in SENYV (to the left), and the definition translated to Clean (to the right) are shown below. The definition in Clean contains strictness annotations.

```
:: List = Nil | Cons Int List        :: List = Nil | Cons !Int !List
```

The intended interpretation of a subtype mark is a predicate over the corresponding data type. There are many possibilities to define such a predicate, e.g. in a first-order or a higher-order logic—the choice may depend on the programming language and proof system in use. In the case of SENYV the predicates are defined as `Bool`-functions with strict arguments written in Clean. (`Bool` is the standard algebraic data type with data constructors `True` and `False`.) This approach – albeit that other choices might result in more expressive interpretations – is advantageous because it is in compliance with the capabilities of Sparkle, the proof system to be adapted to SENYV. Since no subtype marks will be used in the interpretation of subtype marks, these `Bool`-functions need not be defined in SENYV, but rather in Clean; therefore the power of full Clean can be exploited in these definitions. Note that Clean is used for defining both the interpretation of subtype marks in SENYV and the dynamic semantics of SENYV.

Example 2 (Sorted lists). Subtype mark `S` characterizes sorted lists of integer numbers. Its interpretation is the following Clean function.

```
S :: !List -> Bool | S (Cons x Nil) = True
S Nil = True        | S (Cons x xs=:(Cons y ys)) = (x<=y) && (S xs)
```

The Clean function which interprets a subtype mark attached to a function type usually requires more than one argument. The additional arguments are considered universally quantified. (The introduction of existential quantification is also possible, but not yet supported in the current version of SENYV.)

Example 3 (Monotonically increasing functions). Let `M` be the subtype mark characterizing monotonically increasing functions from `Int` to `Int`. It is interpreted with a Clean function with two (strict) arguments. The first argument is the function concerned, and the second one is an element from its domain. Assume that `MAX_INT` is the largest representable value of `Int`.

```
M :: !(Int->Int)  !Int  ->  Bool
M f x   =   (x == MAX_INT) || f x <= f (x+1)
```

The formal definition of the meaning of subtype marks and that of subtype marked types is given in Sect. 5.

3   A Language Supporting Subtype Marks

Programs written in SENYV are made up of algebraic type definitions (see Ex. 1), type declarations for (function and data constructor) symbols and function definitions. Function definitions contain one or more alternatives. The program is started with the evaluation of the nullary function `Start`.

Example 4 (Function type declarations and function definitions). Assume that `Zero` is a (nullary) data constructor for `Int`, furthermore `Succ` and `Pred` are functions from `Int` to `Int`.

```
Length :: List -> Int{N}
Length Nil = Zero
Length (Cons x xs) = Succ (Length xs)

Repeat :: Int{N} -> Int -> List{S!}
Repeat Zero e = Nil
Repeat     n e = let n_minus_one :: Int{N!} = Pred n
                 in  Cons e (Repeat n_minus_one e)
```

The meaning of these two functions is obtained by the translation to Clean. The translation removes subtype annotations, introduces strictness annotations, removes type declarations for local variables and modifies symbol type declarations to reflect the arity of the symbol. The last transformation is necessary because in SENYV the arity of a symbol can be found out from its definition, and not from its type declaration. For instance, `Repeat`, the arity of which is two, is translated into Clean in the following way.

```
Repeat :: !Int  !Int  -> List
Repeat Zero e = Nil
Repeat     n e = let n_minus_one = Pred n
                 in  Cons e (Repeat n_minus_one e)
```

Before formalizing the syntactical and semantic rules of SENY, the concept of polymorphic subtype marks has to be introduced.

3.1   Polymorphic Subtype Marks

The `Length` function presented in Ex. 4 is polymorphic. Due to subtype polymorphism, it belongs into all of the following types.

```
Length :: List -> Int{N}    |    Length :: List{S} -> Int
Length :: List -> Int       |    Length :: List{S} -> Int{N}
```

However, SENYV supports another kind of polymorphism as well. Polymorphic subtype marks may contain "subtype mark variables", which may be instantiated with the values ↑ and ↓ (present and dubious).

Example 5 (Polymorphic subtype marks).

```
Tail :: List{s:S} -> List{s:S}    |    Tail (Cons x xs) = xs
```

Instantiating the subtype mark variable s with ↑ and ↓ yields two types with monomorphic subtype marks.

```
Tail :: List{S} -> List{S}    |    Tail :: List -> List
```

These two types tell us that the tail of a sorted list is a sorted list, and that the tail of a not necessarily sorted list is not necessarily sorted. Further types for Tail can be obtained by subtype polymorphism, e.g. "Tail :: List{S} -> List". Another popular function is Map, which can be defined in SENYV as follows.

```
Map :: (Int ->{s:M} Int) -> List{s:S} -> List{s:S!}
Map f Nil = Nil
Map f (Cons x xs) = Cons (f x) (Map f xs)
```

The types obtained by instantiating the subtype mark variable are the following.

```
Map :: (Int ->{M} Int) -> List{S} -> List{S!}
Map :: (Int -> Int) -> List -> List
```

In types with polymorphic subtype marks the subtype mark variables are universally quantified. SENYV supports only prenex (rank 1) quantification. Similarly to the uniqueness type system of Clean [8], a type with polymorphic subtype marks may contain "inequalities" over its subtype mark variables. Examples of such types can be found in [7]. Without any further details on the structure of inequalities and types with polymorphic subtype marks, the concept of substituting subtype mark variables is introduced.

Definition 4 (Substitution of subtype mark variables). *Let T be a type with polymorphic subtype marks, and let V_T denote the subtype mark variables occurring in it. The function "$\mu : V_T \to \{\uparrow, \downarrow\}$" is a legal substitution for T if it does not violate the inequalities in T. The type with monomorphic subtype marks obtained from T by μ is denoted by $T[\mu]$.*

In SENYV every function is equipped with a single type declaration—with one that may contain polymorphic subtype marks. The type system of SENYV utilizes a type checking algorithm that works directly with such types. However, the meaning of a type with polymorphic subtype marks is given as a set of types with monomorphic subtype marks. Therefore, the type-correctness and the correctness of programs will be defined in terms of types with monomorphic subtype marks.

3.2   Expressions and Function Definitions

Expressions are made up of (function and data constructor) symbols and variables, using application and (non-cyclic) sharing.

Definition 5 (Expressions). *The abstract syntax of expressions is defined as:*

$$E \;:=\; \mathrm{S} \;\mid\; x \;\mid\; E_1\,E_2 \;\mid\; \mathbf{let}\; y :: T = E' \;\mathbf{in}\; E'' \,,$$

where S *is a (function or data constructor) symbol,* x, y *are variables,* E, E_1,
E_2, E' *and* E'' *are expressions, and* T *is a type with polymorphic subtype marks.*

*Let-expressions are not recursive: the variable bound by the let-expression does
not occur free in the expression assigned to it. The declared type of a local variable
may not contain inequalities, and all of its subtype mark variables must occur in
the declared type of the function that contains the let-expression.*

A substitution μ of subtype mark variables that turn the declared type of a
function into a type with monomorphic subtype marks will also turn the declared types of the local variables into ones with monomorphic subtype marks.
The application of μ on an expression E is denoted by $E[\mu]$, and it is defined
inductively in such a way that μ is applied on the declared type of each local
variable.

The concrete syntax for expressions follows the conventions: applications are
left-associative, and have higher precedence than let-expressions. Subexpressions
can be delimited by parentheses.

Definition 6 (Function definitions). *A function* F *is defined as a non-empty
sequence of alternatives:* F $\overline{P} = E$, *and pattern expressions are* $P := x \mid \mathrm{C}\,\overline{y}$,
where C *is a data constructor symbol, and* x *and* y *are variables.* $|\overline{P}|$ *must be
equal for every pattern: this is the arity of* F. *Each pattern* $\overline{P}$ *must be linear,
and the free variables in* E *must occur in the corresponding* $\overline{P}$.

The dynamic semantics of function definitions are similar in SENYV *and in
Clean: patterns are matched from top to bottom.*

3.3   Type Declarations

In SENYV there is a type declaration for every function. A type declaration
assigns a type with (possibly polymorphic) subtype marks to a function, see e.g.
`Length` and `Repeat` in Ex. 4, and `Tail` and `Map` in Ex. 5.

Type declarations assign types to data constructors as well. In contrast to
functions, there are two types with polymorphic subtype marks (hence two sets
of types with monomorphic subtype marks) assigned to each data constructor.
"Composition types" (introduced with the token `:>:`) describe the behaviour
of data constructors in expressions occurring in the right-hand side of function definitions, while "decomposition types" (introduced with `:<:`) are used
for occurrences in patterns. Data constructor types never contain believe-me
marks.

Example 6 (Types declared for data constructors). The composition and decomposition types for the data constructors of `List` can be the following.

```
Nil :>: List{S}       |   Cons :>: Int -> List -> List
Nil :<: List{S}       |   Cons :<: Int -> List{s:S} -> List{s:S}
```

The most interesting type here is the decomposition type of `Cons`: if a function (say `Tail` in Ex. 5) has an argument that is a sorted list, and the function definition pattern matches on this argument, then the types deduced for the two variables occurring in a `Cons` pattern expression (`x` and `xs` in the example) are `Int` and `List{S}`, respectively. This is how the type system checks that the tail of a sorted list is indeed a sorted list. On the other hand, the deduced type for the tail of a not necessarily sorted list is "not necessarily sorted list", viz. `List`.

The composition type for `Cons` cannot say anything about sortedness. If a list is constructed from an integer number and a sorted list, then the result is not guaranteed to be sorted. This is why the believe-me mark is necessary in the declared type of `Repeat` (see Ex. 4). The type checker can guarantee the sortedness of the result in the first alternative (according to the composition type of `Nil`), but cannot guarantee it in the second one.

Decomposition types differ from composition types and from types declared for functions in an important respect. If a subtype mark does not appear in the right-hand side of the decomposition type of a data constructor, then this fact does not mean dubiety of the corresponding property: it means that values constructed with that data constructor *never* have the property. This approach, as it will be shown later, enhances the capabilities of the type checker.

Example 7 (Non-empty lists). Let subtype mark `C` mean that a list is non-empty, namely that it is constructed with a `Cons` data constructor.

```
C :: !List -> Bool  │  C Nil = False
                    │  C _   = True
```

The declared type for the `List` data constructors can be adjusted for this subtype mark in the following way.

```
Nil :>: List{S}     │  Cons :>: Int -> List -> List{C}
Nil :<: List{S}     │  Cons :<: Int -> List{s:S} -> List{s:S,C}
```

`C` is present in the right-hand side of the decomposition type for `Cons`, but it is missing from that of `Nil`. This informs the type checker that values constructed with `Nil` are "not non-empty" lists.

The introduced subtype mark can be used to describe a pre-condition for function `Tail`. The type system can enforce the safe use of this function if its declared type from Ex. 5 is changed to `Tail :: List{C,s:S} -> List{s:S}`.

Before talking about type-correctness, some more semantic rules about type declarations – enforcing meaningful use of subtype marks – should be established.

Definition 7 (Legal type declaration). *Type declarations is a* SENYV *program are legal, if they satisfy the following four rules.*

1. *In a declared type of a function, believe-me marks are not allowed "to the left of" a function space type constructor. Namely, if a declared type is in the form $T \xrightarrow{\alpha} T'$, then T is not allowed to contain believe-me marks, and – recursively – no believe-me marks are allowed in T' to the left of a function space type constructor.*

2. *Let n be the arity of a function. The types with monomorphic subtype marks obtained from the declared type of that function must be in the form $T_1 \xrightarrow{\alpha_1} \cdots \xrightarrow{\alpha_{n-1}} T_n \xrightarrow{\alpha_n} T$. The declaration of the type of the function is legal, only if for all such types with monomorphic subtype marks, for all $i \in [1..n]$ and for all $m \in \mathfrak{M}$: $\alpha_i(m) \neq \uparrow$.*

3. *Let n be the arity of a data constructor. The types with monomorphic subtype marks obtained from the decomposition type of that data constructor must be in the form $T_1 \xrightarrow{\alpha_1} \cdots \xrightarrow{\alpha_{n-1}} T_n \xrightarrow{\alpha_n} \mathbf{T}^\alpha$. The decomposition type of the data constructor is legal, if for all such types with monomorphic subtype marks, for all $i \in [1..n]$ and for all $m \in \mathfrak{M}$: $\alpha_i(m) = \downarrow$.*

4. *Those types with polymorphic subtype marks from which no type with monomorphic subtype marks can be obtained are illegal in a type declaration.*

The first rule is necessary because types with subtype marks correspond to theorems: theorems to prove some properties of a certain program. In these theorems, subtype annotations occurring to the left of a function space type constructor will be part of some hypotheses, while annotations not to the left of any "$\to$" will be part of a goal. Subtype marks annotated with believe-me marks denote properties that the type system might use, but need not prove. Therefore believe-me marks are meaningless (and considered illegal) for subtype marks corresponding to hypotheses.

The second rule is necessary because the type system has no possibility to prove properties described by those subtype marks that occur in the mentioned annotations. The typing rules (to be presented soon) ignore these subtype annotations, therefore the proof of the corresponding properties should be prepared with a proof system. The third rule is necessary because decomposition types are used to type patterns, and in patterns non-dubious subtype marks in the mentioned annotations make no sense. Finally, the fourth rule can be violated by types with polymorphic subtype marks containing inequalities.

Example 8 (Legal and illegal type declarations). Consider the monotonically increasing function `Succ`, which preserves non-negativeness. The only believe-me mark appearing in the declared type of this function annotates M, attached to the top-level type constructor, "$\to$". Hence it is not to the left of any "$\to$".

```
Succ :: Int{n:N} ->{M!} Int{n:N}
Succ x = ...
```

The arity of `Succ` (as its sketched definition reveals) is 1, hence the annotation of the top-level "$\to$" type constructor should be examined with respect to the second part of Def. 7. There is a single non-dubious subtype mark in this annotation, namely M. Since it is annotated with a believe-me mark, the given type declaration satisfies the second rule as well. Finally, notice that two types with monomorphic subtype marks can be obtained from the declared type of `Succ` by substituting the subtype mark variable n, therefore the fourth rule is also satisfied. Now let us show some illegal type declarations.

```
Bad    :: (Int->Int{N!}) -> Int       Baaad  :: Int ->{M} Int
Baad   :<: Int ->{M} Int              Baaad x = Succ x
```

4   Type Correctness

The type system of SENYV is based on type checking: the type of every symbol and every variable is provided by the programmer. The type checker has to deal with those subtype marks which are not annotated with believe-me marks. In order to formalize this, two transformations that manage believe-me marks are defined; one that *ignores* believe-me marks and another that *removes* subtype marks annotated with believe-me marks.

Definition 8 (i_b and r_b). *Transformations i_b and r_b can be applied on types with monomorphic subtype marks and on monomorphic subtype annotations. Applying them on a type means applying them on all the annotations occurring in the type. Furthermore, for any α monomorphic subtype annotation, $i_b(\alpha)$ and $r_b(\alpha)$ are also monomorphic subtype annotations.*

$$i_b(\alpha)(m) = \begin{cases} \downarrow & \text{if } \alpha(m) = \downarrow \\ \uparrow & \text{otherwise} \end{cases} \qquad r_b(\alpha)(m) = \begin{cases} \uparrow & \text{if } \alpha(m) = \uparrow \\ \downarrow & \text{otherwise} \end{cases}$$

The type checker of SENYV uses three type environments for symbols: $\mathcal{C}$, $\mathcal{D}$ and $\mathcal{F}$. These environments contain information about the declared composition and decomposition types of data constructors, and the declared type of functions.

Definition 9 (Type environments)

$\mathcal{C} \ni C : T$ *means that $\mathcal{C}$ contains a type T with monomorphic subtype marks for the data constructor C. All the types obtained from the declared composition type of C (which is a type with polymorphic subtype marks) are stored in $\mathcal{C}$.*

$\mathcal{D} \ni C : T$ *is defined in a similar way, but before computing the types with monomorphic subtype marks from the declared decomposition type of C, the result type (with structure $\mathbf{T}^\alpha$, where α is a polymorphic subtype annotation) of the declared decomposition type must be generalized: if $\alpha(m) = \uparrow$ for some $m \in \mathfrak{M}$, then $\alpha(m)$ should be set to a fresh subtype mark variable.*

$\mathcal{F} \ni F : (T, \mu)$ *means that not only the types with monomorphic subtype marks are stored in $\mathcal{F}$, but also the substitutions that were used to create those types from the declared type of F.*

Example 9 (Generalization in decomposition types). Generalization in the declared decomposition type of a data constructor C expresses that known subtype invariants of a value constructed with C can be ignored when the value is pattern matched against a function alternative. When creating the $\mathcal{D}$ type environment, the decomposition types for `Nil` and `Cons` given in Ex. 7 are generalized:

```
Nil :>: List{S}       |  Cons :>: Int -> List -> List{C}
Nil :<: List{s:S}     |  Cons :<: Int -> List{s:S} -> List{s:S,c:C}
```

During typing, type information about variables will be stored in a basis. A basis $\mathcal{B}$ is a partial function from variables to types with monomorphic subtype marks. The type of a variable x in the basis $\mathcal{B}$ is denoted by $\mathcal{B}(x)$.

Table 1. Typing rules for SENYV

$$\frac{\mathcal{F} \ni F : (T,\mu)}{\mathcal{B},\mathcal{F},\mathcal{C} \vdash F : i_b(T)} \qquad \frac{\mathcal{C} \ni C : T}{\mathcal{B},\mathcal{F},\mathcal{C} \vdash C : T} \qquad \frac{\mathcal{D} \ni C : T}{\mathcal{B},\mathcal{D} \vdash C : T}$$

$$\frac{}{\mathcal{B},\mathcal{F},\mathcal{C} \vdash x : i_b(\mathcal{B}(x))} \qquad \frac{\mathcal{B},\mathcal{F},\mathcal{C} \vdash E : T, \quad T <: T'}{\mathcal{B},\mathcal{F},\mathcal{C} \vdash E : T'}$$

$$\frac{\mathcal{B},\mathcal{F},\mathcal{C} \vdash E_1 : T_1 \xrightarrow{\alpha} T_2, \quad \mathcal{B},\mathcal{F},\mathcal{C} \vdash E_2 : T_1}{\mathcal{B},\mathcal{F},\mathcal{C} \vdash (E_1 \; E_2) : T_2}$$

$$\frac{\mathcal{B},\mathcal{F},\mathcal{C} \vdash E' : r_b(T'), \quad \mathcal{B} \cup x : T',\mathcal{F},\mathcal{C} \vdash E : T}{\mathcal{B},\mathcal{F},\mathcal{C} \vdash (\textbf{let } x :: T' = E' \textbf{ in } E) : T}$$

$$\frac{}{\mathcal{B},\mathcal{D} \vdash x : \mathcal{B}(x)} \qquad \frac{\begin{array}{c}\mathcal{B},\mathcal{D} \vdash x_i : T_i \text{ for all } i \in [1..n], \\ \mathcal{B},\mathcal{D} \vdash C : T_1 \xrightarrow{\beta_1} \cdots \xrightarrow{\beta_{n-1}} T_n \xrightarrow{\beta_n} T\end{array}}{\mathcal{B},\mathcal{D} \vdash C \; x_1 \ldots x_n : T}$$

Definition 10 (Type-correctness)

- *A* SENYV *program is type-correct, if all the alternatives of its function definitions are type-correct with respect to the type environments $\mathcal{C}$, $\mathcal{D}$ and $\mathcal{F}$ created from the type declarations of the program.*
- *An alternative "F $P_1 \ldots P_n = E$" is type-correct with respect to $\mathcal{C}$, $\mathcal{D}$, $\mathcal{F}$, if:*
  - *there is at least one (T,μ) such that $\mathcal{F} \ni F : (T,\mu)$ and $r_b(T)$ matches the pattern $\langle P_1 \ldots P_n \rangle$, and*
  - *for all $\mathcal{F} \ni F : (T,\mu)$ such that $r_b(T)$ matches $\langle P_1 \ldots P_n \rangle$, the alternative can be typed with $\big(r_b(T),\mu\big)$.*
- *The type "$T_1 \xrightarrow{\alpha_1} \cdots \xrightarrow{\alpha_{n-1}} T_n \xrightarrow{\alpha_n} T$" matches the pattern $\langle P_1 \ldots P_n \rangle$ if there is a basis $\mathcal{B}$ such that for all $i \in [1..n]$ the judgement $\mathcal{B},\mathcal{D} \vdash P_i : T_i$ can be derived with the rules in Table 1.*
- *An alternative "F $P_1 \ldots P_n = E$" can be typed with $(T_1 \xrightarrow{\alpha_1} \cdots \xrightarrow{\alpha_{n-1}} T_n \xrightarrow{\alpha_n} T,\mu)$, if there is a basis $\mathcal{B}$ such that the judgements $\mathcal{B},\mathcal{F},\mathcal{C} \vdash E[\mu] : T$ and $\mathcal{B},\mathcal{D} \vdash P_i : T_i$ (for all $i \in [1..n]$) can be derived with the rules in Table 1.*

Notice that in the above definition the composition and decomposition types of data constructors are used as axioms during typing.

The concept of "types that match patterns" is sensible because of the special treatment of missing subtype marks in the right-hand side of decomposition types, illustrated by Ex. 7. This concept makes it possible to type-check e.g. Reverse.

Example 10 (Types that match patterns). Function Snoc is the opposite to Cons: it adds an element to the *end* of a list. Reverse reverses a list, hence it preserves the non-emptiness property of its argument.

```
Snoc :: List -> Int -> List{C}
Snoc Nil e = Cons e Nil
Snoc (Cons x xs) e = Cons x (Snoc xs e)

Reverse :: List{c:C} -> List{c:C}
Reverse Nil = Nil
Reverse (Cons x xs) = Snoc (Reverse xs) x
```

The first alternative of Reverse does not match the type List{C} -> List{C}, because Nil does not match List{C}. However, due to the generalization of decomposition types in Def. 9, Nil matches List: see Ex. 9. Hence List -> List, the other type with monomorphic subtype marks obtained from the declared type of Reverse is required to type the first alternative of this function.

Remark 1. If a SENYV program is type-correct, then the Clean program describing its dynamic semantics is also type-correct (according to the definition of type-correctness in Clean). Hence "conventional type-correctness" (namely, which is based on the translation to Clean) is a necessary condition for type-correctness in SENYV.

Definition 11 (Conventional types, $\mathcal{E}_{|T|}$ and $|\mathcal{E}_{|T|}|$). *Let T be a type. $|T|$ is called the conventional type created from T, where*

$$|T| = \begin{cases} \mathbf{T} & \text{if } T = \mathbf{T}^\alpha \ , \\ |T_1| \to |T_2| & \text{if } T = T_1 \xrightarrow{\beta} T_2 \ . \end{cases}$$

Given a conventionally type-correct SENYV program, let $\mathcal{E}_{|T|}$ denote the set of SENYV expressions (meaningful in that program) which can be conventionally typed with $|T|$. Furthermore, let $|\mathcal{E}_{|T|}|$ denote the set of Clean expressions obtained by translating the expressions in $\mathcal{E}_{|T|}$ into Clean.

5   Correctness of Programs

Subtype marks in SENYV are interpreted as Bool-functions written in Clean.

Definition 12 (The meaning of a subtype mark). *Consider a subtype mark, say $M \in \mathfrak{M}$. Assume that it is used to annotate the conventional type $|T|$. The meaning of this subtype mark is described by the Clean function M with the following properties.*

  - *The arity of M is at least one.*
  - *The first argument type of M is $|T|$.*
  - *The return type of M is Bool.*
  - *The argument types of M are strict.*

Let $|T|$, $|T_1|$, ... $|T_n|$ *be the argument types of* M. *Let* $\mathbb{L} = \{\mathbf{f}, \mathbf{t}\}$ *denote the set of logical values. Predicate* $P_M : \mathcal{E}_{|T|} \rightarrow \mathbb{L}$ *is introduced in such a way that for any* $E \in \mathcal{E}_{|T|}$, $P_M(E) = \mathbf{t}$ *if and only if the following holds. Let* $E' \in |\mathcal{E}_{|T|}|$ *denote the Clean expression obtained by transforming* E *into Clean; for every* $E_i \in |\mathcal{E}_{|T_i|}|$ *(where* $i \in [1..n]$*), the Clean expression* M E' E_1 ... E_n *must reduce to* True.

Remark 2. In Sparkle the symbol "=" corresponds to reduction. (More precisely, A = B holds, if the reduction of A and B results in the same observable behaviour.) Since True is in normal form, E = True means that the normal form of E is True. Therefore, adopting the notations of Def. 12, $P_M(E) = \mathbf{t}$ if the following theorem holds in Sparkle.

$$\forall p_1 :: |T_1| \ ... \ \forall p_n :: |T_n| : \big(M \ E' \ p_1 \ ... \ p_n \ = \ \texttt{True} \big) \tag{1}$$

A program is considered correct, if it uses subtype annotations in a proper way. First a couple of examples illustrate this concept, then the formal definition is presented. The focus is on the relation between the meaning of subtype marks (Def. 12) and type-correctness (Def. 10). In accordance with Remark 1, in what follows it is assumed that concerned programs and expressions are always conventionally type-correct.

The meaning of subtype marks is irrelevant with respect to type-correctness. The type system uses the composition and decomposition types as axioms. One aspect of program correctness is the correctness of these axioms with respect to Def. 12.

Example 11. Consider the composition and decomposition types of Nil in Ex. 7. Ex. 2 tells us that S Nil reduces to True. By Remark 2 this can be rewritten to $P_S(\text{Nil})$. Hence Nil is sorted, and the composition type is correct.

The decomposition type requires a different point of view: those subtype marks are interesting that do not appear in the right-hand side of the decomposition type; in this case C is such a subtype mark. According to Ex. 7, C Nil reduces to False, not True. Hence $\neg P_C(\text{Nil})$. Therefore the decomposition type of Nil is also correct.

The second aspect of program correctness is the correctness of the declared type of functions. For example, it has to be proven that if k is the integer number equal to Length list, then $P_N(k)$. (This shifty phrasing is intentional.) Finally, the third aspect of program correctness is the correctness of the declared type of local variables. Consider, for instance, the variable n_minus_one in the second alternative of Repeat. It has to be proven that P_N holds on this variable.

Now a notation capturing the meaning of subtype marked types is presented. The proof system used for SENYV should support this notation. (Currently no machine support exists for this notation; it is expanded for Sparkle by hand.)

Definition 13. *Given a (conventionally type-correct)* SENYV *program, let* T *be a type with monomorphic subtype marks, and* $E \in \mathcal{E}_{|T|}$ *an expression that are sensible with respect to this program. The formula* $E \in T$ *denotes the following.*

- If $T = \mathbf{T}^\alpha$, then *"either E has no normal form, or $P_m(E) = \mathbf{t}$ for each $m \in \mathfrak{M}$ such that $\alpha(m) \neq \downarrow$."*
- If $T = T_1 \xrightarrow{\alpha} T_2$, then *"either E has no normal form, or $P_m(E) = \mathbf{t}$ for each $m \in \mathfrak{M}$ such that $\alpha(m) \neq \downarrow$ and $(E\ E') \in T_2$ for all $E' \in T_1$."*

Remark 3. The formula $E \in T$ can be formalized in Sparkle style in the following way: (2) for $T = \mathbf{T}^\alpha$, and (3) for $T = T_1 \xrightarrow{\alpha} T_2$.

$$E = \perp\ \vee\ \left(\bigwedge_{\alpha(m) \neq \downarrow} P_m(E) \right) \tag{2}$$

$$E = \perp\ \vee\ \left(\left(\bigwedge_{\alpha(m) \neq \downarrow} P_m(E) \right)\ \wedge\ \left(\forall x : x \in T_1 \rightarrow (E\ x) \in T_2 \right) \right) \tag{3}$$

Undefined computations are denoted by the $\perp$ symbol: $E = \perp$ means that E has no normal form. The empty conjunction is considered $\mathbf{t}$ (true).

The method presented here is not aiming at reasoning about termination and undefinedness. It attempts to avoid the problems related to these issues by being very permissive towards infinite and undefined computations. This is reflected in the above definition.

Example 12. Let us prove that `Length` $\in$ `List->Int{N}`. This formula can be rewritten to

$$\texttt{Length} = \perp\ \vee\ \left(\forall x : \texttt{Length}\ x = \perp \vee \texttt{N}\ (\texttt{Length}\ x) = \texttt{True} \right).$$

In Sparkle (version 0.0.4b, 20-Apr-2004), using the definition of `Length` which is transformed to Clean (as given in Ex. 4), it is possible to prove this theorem in 34 steps.

Definition 14 (Correct type environments). *The type environment $\mathcal{F}$ is correct, if for each function symbol F and for all judgements $\mathcal{F} \ni F : (T, \mu)$ the formula $F \in T$ is valid.*

The type environment $\mathcal{C}$ is correct, if for each data constructor C and for all judgements $\mathcal{C} \ni C : T$ the formula $C \in T$ is valid.

The type environment $\mathcal{D}$ is correct, if for each data constructor C the following holds. Let n denote the arity of C, and for all $i \in [1..n]$ let C_i be an auxiliary projection function defined in this way: "$C_i\ (C\ p_1\ \ldots\ p_i\ \ldots\ p_n) = p_i$". For all judgements "$\mathcal{D} \ni C : T_1 \xrightarrow{\alpha_1} \cdots \xrightarrow{\alpha_{n-1}} T_n \xrightarrow{\alpha_n} \mathbf{T}^\alpha$" the formula $C_i \in \mathbf{T}^\alpha \rightarrow T_i$ should be valid. Furthermore, if β is a monomorphic subtype annotation such that there is no judgement "$\mathcal{D} \ni C : T_1 \xrightarrow{\beta_1} \cdots \xrightarrow{\beta_{n-1}} T_n \xrightarrow{\beta_n} \mathbf{T}^\beta$", then the formula "$\neg(\exists x_1 \ldots \exists x_n : (C\ x_1\ \ldots\ x_n) \in \mathbf{T}^\beta)$" should also be valid.

Finally, the correct use of local variables should be investigated. For analyzing let-expressions, the variables occurring in it must be identified first. These variables are introduced in the patterns of the function alternative containing the let-expression, and the local variables introduced by the surrounding let-expressions.

Then the conditions that can be used during the proof of the correctness should be collected. These conditions come from three sources: firstly, from the declared type (the pre-condition) of the containing function; secondly, from the fact that the alternatives preceeding the containing alternative did not match; and thirdly, from the bindings of the surrounding let-expressions.

Definition 15 (Correct use of local variables). *Local variables are used in a correct way in a program, if for all function definitions of the program and all let-expressions occurring in the function definitions satisfy the following.*

Let function F *with arity* n *be defined with* m *alternatives. Let* $P_{i,j}$ *be a pattern expression, and* E_i *is an expression* $(i \in [1..m], \; j \in [1..n])$*; alternative number* i *is:* F $P_{1,1}$ ... $P_{1,n}$ = E_1.

For the sake of simplicity, assume that all variables (formal arguments and local variables) occurring in this function definition are called differently. (This can be achieved in a way that preserves the meaning of the program by renaming variables.) Consider a let-expression in the rth *alternative:* let $x :: T'=E'$ in E. *Assume that this let-expression occurs in a context where the local variables* $x_1, \ldots, x_u$ *are bound with values* $E'_1, \ldots, E'_u$. *Let* $y_1, \ldots, y_{v(i,j)}$ *denote the variables introduced by the patterns* $P_{1,1}, \; P_{1,2} \; \ldots \; P_{i,j}$. *The following formula must be valid for all judgements* $\mathcal{F} \ni$ F $: T_1 \xrightarrow{\alpha_1} \cdots \xrightarrow{\alpha_{n-1}} T_n \xrightarrow{\alpha_n} (T, \mu)$.

$$\forall y_1 \; \ldots \; \forall y_{v(r,n)} \; \forall x_1 \; \ldots \; \forall x_u : \; (P_{r,1} \in T_1 \wedge \cdots \wedge P_{r,n} \in T_n) \; \rightarrow$$
$$\neg(P_{r,1} = P_{1,1} \wedge \cdots \wedge P_{r,n} = P_{1,n}) \; \rightarrow \qquad (4)$$
$$\cdots$$
$$\neg(P_{r,1} = P_{r-1,1} \wedge \cdots \wedge P_{r,n} = P_{r-1,n}) \; \rightarrow$$
$$(x_1 = E'_1[\mu] \wedge \cdots \wedge x_u = E'_u[\mu]) \; \rightarrow$$
$$E'[\mu] \in T'$$

Example 13. Consider function Repeat from Ex. 4. The let-expression in its second alternative is correct, if the following formula is valid.

$$\forall e1 \; \forall n \; \forall e : \; (\texttt{N } n = \texttt{True}) \rightarrow$$
$$\neg(n = \texttt{Zero} \wedge e = e1) \rightarrow$$
$$(\texttt{Pred } n = \bot \; \vee \; \texttt{N (Pred } n) = \texttt{True})$$

The validity of this formula can indeed be proven in Sparkle in 40 proof steps.

Definition 16 (Correct program). *A program is called correct with respect to the subtype annotations, if the type environments* $\mathcal{F}$, $\mathcal{C}$ *and* $\mathcal{D}$ *built up from the program and the use of local variables in the program are correct (Def. 14 and 15).*

6   The Soundness of the Type System

The idea of dividing labour between the SENYV type checker and a proof system when reasoning about the correctness of programs with respect to subtype marks is supported by believe-me marks. For type-correct programs it is sufficient to restrict the use of a proof system for analyzing believe-me marked subtype marks. First a transformation s_b is introduced that selects believe-me marked subtype marks.

Definition 17 (s_b). *Transformation s_b can be applied on types with monomorphic subtype marks and on monomorphic subtype annotations. Applying it on a type means applying on all the annotations occurring in the type. Furthermore, for any α monomorphic subtype annotation, $s_b(\alpha)$ is also a monomorphic subtype annotation.*

$$s_b(\alpha)(m) = \begin{cases} \uparrow & \text{if } \alpha(m) = ! \\ \downarrow & \text{if } \alpha(m) = \uparrow \vee \alpha(m) = \downarrow \end{cases}$$

Now a notion of correctness similar to Def. 14 and Def. 15 is introduced.

Definition 18 (Believe-me correct programs). *A* SENYV *program is called "believe-me correct", if its C and D type environments are correct, and for functions the following holds.*

1. *For each function symbol* F *and for each judgement* $\mathcal{F} \ni$ F $: (T, \mu)$, *the formula* F $\in s_b(T)$ *is valid.*
2. *Same as Def. 15, apart from that in the formula the validity of which is to be proven (namely in formula (4)), T' must be replaced by $s_b(T')$. (That is the consequence part of the formula becomes $E'[\mu] \in s_b(T')$.)*

The soundness of the SENYV type system is phrased with the following theorem. The proof of the theorem can be found in [9].

Theorem 1 (Sufficient condition for correctness). *If a* SENYV *program is type-correct and believe-me correct, then it is correct with respect to the subtype annotations.*

7   Conclusions

This paper described SENYV, an eager functional language with a type system supporting subtype marks. Subtype marks provide a mechanism to denote type invariants, and this way express pre- and postconditions and – through subtype mark variables – the preservation of invariants. They also induce subtype polymorphism in the type system. Similar type systems were proposed by [3, 4], and a limited form of subject reduction and principal typing were proved in [5, 6]. Another such type system was presented and illustrated with several meaningful examples in [7], which improved expressive power by introducing inequalities on subtype mark variables – similarly to Clean uniqueness typing [8] –, and by providing special rules for typing patterns. The concept of "types match patterns" in this latter is similar to type refinement in case alternatives for GADTs [10].

SENYV should be regarded as a subset of Clean extended with subtype marks: its dynamic semantics is defined by a translation to Clean. The aim of this paper is to explore a method to facilitate reasoning about Clean programs. According to this method each subtype mark is assigned an interpretation, a `Bool` function written in Clean. Therefore belonging to a subtype marked type can be defined as a predicate representable in Sparkle, the proof tool designed for and integrated with Clean. Correctness of SENYV/Clean programs with respect to such predicates is defined. The paper investigates the conditions required for the soundness of the type system of SENYV, and formulates the soundness theorem. This theorem guarantees that correctness of programs can be proved with the collaboration of the SENYV type checker (full automation) and of a proof system (Sparkle, semi-automation). The verification conditions passed to the proof system are to be generated by the SENYV compiler.

The main alternative approach to subtype marks is the use of dependently typed programming languages [11, 12]. Since subtype marks cannot depend on values, dependent types are more powerful. They provide an elegant and consistent way to reason about programs, even without using additional proof systems. In some dependently typed programming languages it is possible to specify program properties at the type level, and use the compiler to check the proof of correctness – or use an interactive IDE to design those proofs. However, one might claim that they are too complex to learn and to use by a not highly educated, average programmer. Subtype marks add less to traditional types, and they can be introduced gradually: proving the VCs can be optional; therefore they are easier to learn, and they can make their way into practice faster.

Hoare Type Theory [13] integrates dependent types with a Hoare-style logic. In HTT it is possible to specify Hoare-triples in types, thus pre- and postconditions are expressible. It is used mainly for creating correct effectful programs. HTT splits reasoning into two phases similarly to SENYV: first a decidable combination of type checking and verification condition generation, and then an optional phase for proving the VCs either manually or with a theorem prover.

Type refinements of [14] primarily target effectful programming: they support reasoning about values produced by computations as well as about the changes in program state. Some of the examples given in [14] can also be written and type-checked in SENYV. However, type refinements use a first-order specification language and are based on linear logic.

There are many further static type systems that provide means to reason about safety properties of high-level programs, typically in a specific domain. To mention but a few: ownership types [15] and the alike let the programmer reason about aliasing, the system described in [16] can be used for resource usage analysis, and the dependently typed framework in [17] is capable of expressing dynamic execution costs of programs.

Experiments [7] with subtype marks show that they are best at describing data with multiple abstract states, when certain operations are permissible in some, but not all states. In the future it should be analyzed how subtype marks work together with parametric polymorphism, and especially with type classes. Inference of subtype annotations would also be a nice feature, but – holding with [11] – considered a less important goal. Supporting subtype marks in

Distributed Clean [18] and in a mainstream language such as C++ is also subject to future work.

References

1. de Mol, M., van Eekelen, M., Plasmeijer, R.: Theorem Proving for Functional Programmers, Sparkle: A Functional Theorem Prover. In: Arts, T., Mohnen, M. (eds.) IFL 2002. LNCS, vol. 2312, pp. 55–71. Springer, Heidelberg (2002)
2. Plasmeijer, R., van Eekelen, M.: Concurrent Clean Version 2.0 Language Report. (2001) http://www.cs.ru.nl/~clean/Manuals/manuals.html
3. Koopman, P.: Language support to enforce constraints on data types. Technical Report 96-37, Computer Science, Leiden University, The Netherlands (1996)
4. van Arkel, D.F.R.: Annotated Types. M.Sc. thesis, Rijksuniversiteit te Leiden, Vakgroep Informatica (1998)
5. Kozsik, T., van Arkel, D., Plasmeijer, R.: Subtyping with strengthening type invariants. In: Mohnen, M., Koopman, P., eds.: Proceedings of the 12th International Workshop on Implementation of Functional Languages. Aachener Informatik-Berichte, Aachen, Germany pp. 315–330 (2000)
6. Kozsik, T.: Subtyping with subtype marks. Technical Report 2003-P05, Eötvös Loránd University, Faculty of Informatics, Budapest, Hungary (2003)
7. Kozsik, T.: Tutorial on Subtype Marks. In: Horváth, Z. (ed.) CEFP 2005. LNCS, vol. 4164, pp. 191–222. Springer, Heidelberg (2006)
8. Barendsen, E., Smetsers, S.: Uniqueness typing for functional languages with graph rewriting semantics. Mathematical Structures in Comp. Sci. 6, 579–612 (1996)
9. Kozsik, T.: Soundness of the type system of Senyv. Technical Report, Eötvös Loránd University, Faculty of Informatics, Budapest, Hungary (2007) To appear
10. Peyton Jones, S., Washburn, G., Weirich, S.: Wobbly types: type inference for generalised algebraic data types. Technical Report MS-CIS-05-26, Computer and Information Science Department, University of Pennsylvania (2004)
11. McBride, C.: Epigram: Practical Programming with Dependent Types. In: Vene, V., Uustalu, T. (eds.) AFP 2004. LNCS, vol. 3622, pp. 130–170. Springer, Heidelberg (2005)
12. Chen, C., Xi, H.: Combining Programming with Theorem Proving. In: ACM SIGPLAN Int'l Conf. on Functional Programming. pp. 66–77 (2005)
13. Nanevski, A., Morrisett, G., Birkedal, L.: Polymorphism and Separation in Hoare Type Theory. In: ACM SIGPLAN Int'l Conf. on Functional Programming. pp. 62–73 (2006)
14. Mandelbaum, Y., Walker, D., Harper, R.: An Effective Theory of Type Refinements. In: ACM SIGPLAN Int'l Conf. on Functional Programming. pp. 213–225 (2003)
15. Clark, D., Potter, J., Noble, J.: Ownership types for flexible alias protection. In: Proceedings of Conference on Object-Oriented Programming, Languages, and Applications, ACM Press, New York (1998)
16. Igarashi, A., Kobayashi, N.: Resource usage analysis. In: Symposium on Principles of Programming Languages. pp. 331–342 (2002)
17. Brady, E., Hammond, K.: A dependently typed framework for static analysis of program execution costs. In: Butterfield, A., Grelck, C., Huch, F. (eds.) IFL 2005. LNCS, vol. 4015, pp. 74–90. Springer, Heidelberg (2006)
18. Horváth, Z., Hernyák, Z., Zsók, V.: Control Language for Distributed Clean. Acta Cybernetica 17, 247–271 (2005)

Uniqueness Typing Redefined

Edsko de Vries[1,*], Rinus Plasmeijer[2], and David M. Abrahamson[1]

[1] Trinity College Dublin, Ireland
{devriese,david}@cs.tcd.ie
[2] Radboud Universiteit Nijmegen, Netherlands
rinus@cs.ru.nl

Abstract. We modify *Clean*'s uniqueness type system in two ways. First, while Clean functions that are partially applied to a unique argument are *necessarily* unique (they cannot lose their uniqueness), we just require that they must be unique *when applied*. This ultimately makes subtyping redundant. Second, we extend the type system to allow for higher-rank types. To be able to do this, we explicitly associate type constraints (attribute inequalities) with type schemes. Consequently, types in our system are much more precise about constraint propagation.

1 Background

The problem of modelling side effects in pure functional languages, without losing referential transparency, is well-known. Consider the function `freadi` that reads the next integer from a file. The type of this function might be

```
freadi :: File → Int
```

To be able to return the *next* integer on every invocation, `freadi` advances the file pointer before returning. This side effect causes a loss of referential transparency. For instance, `f` and `g` are not interchangeable[1]:

```
f₁ file = (freadi file) + (freadi file)
g₁ file = (freadi file) * 2
```

One way to make `freadi`'s side effect explicit is modifying its signature to

```
freadi :: World → File → (World, Int)
```

where `World` is some data type representing "the world". We must then redefine `f` and `g` as

```
f₂ world file =
    let (world1, a) = freadi world file in
    let (world2, b) = freadi world1 file in
    (a + b, world2)
```

---

* Supported by the Irish Research Council for Science, Engineering and Technology: funded by the National Development Plan.

[1] The subscripts of f and g are used only to be able to refer to particular versions of f and g, and are not part of the code.

Z. Horváth, V. Zsók, and A. Butterfield (Eds.): IFL 2006, LNCS 4449, pp. 181–198, 2007.
© Springer-Verlag Berlin Heidelberg 2007

```
g₂ world file =
    let (world1, a) = freadi world file in
    (a * 2, world1)
```

which makes it clear that f and g are different functions. But the problem has not gone away, because nothing is stopping us from writing f as

```
f₃ world file =
    let (world1, a) = freadi world file in
    let (world2, b) = freadi world file in
    (a + b, world2)
```

In the language *Haskell* this problem is essentially solved by hiding the "state threading" in a monad and never giving direct access to the World object. This makes programs "correct by construction", but rather affects the style of programming. By contrast, uniqueness typing enforces correct state threading in the type system. The main idea is to ensure that there is never more than one reference to a particular world state. This is reflected in the type of freadi:

$$\texttt{freadi :: World}^\bullet \to \texttt{File} \to \texttt{(World}^\bullet\texttt{, Int)}$$

The bullets (•) indicate that freadi requires a unique reference to the World, and in turn promises to return a unique reference. When the compiler type-checks f_3, it finds that there are two references to world, which violates the uniqueness requirements; f_2 however is accepted.

The type system presented in this paper depends on a sharing analysis of the program, which is explained briefly in Sect. 2. Since the typing rules for rank-1 are easier to understand than the typing rules for arbitrary rank, we first present the rank-1 typing rules in Sect. 3 and then extend them to arbitrary rank in Sect. 4. We consider a few examples in Sect. 5, outline a type inference algorithm in Sect. 6, compare our system to the original Clean type system in Sect. 7, and present our conclusions and list future work in Sect. 8.

2   Sharing Analysis

The typing rules that we will present in this paper depend on a sharing analysis that marks variable uses as exclusive (⊙) or shared (⊗). This sharing analysis could be more or less sophisticated [1], but if in any derivation of the program the same variable could be evaluated twice, it must be marked as shared. In this paper, we assume sharing analysis has been done, leaving a formal definition to future work. Here we look at an example only. Compare again the definitions of f_2 and f_3 from Sect. 1. In the correct definition (f_2), the variable marking indicates that the reference to world is indeed unique (as required by freadi)[2]:

---

[2] The sharing analysis does not make a distinction between variables that happen to be functions and other variables.

```
f₂ world file =
    let (world1, a) = freadi⊗ world⊙ file⊗ in
    let (world2, b) = freadi⊗ world1⊙ file⊗ in
    (a⊙ + b⊙, world2⊙)
```

The marking in the incorrect definition indicates that there is more than one reference to the same world state, violating the uniqueness requirement:

```
f₃ world file =
    let (world1, a) = freadi⊗ world⊗ file⊗ in
    let (world2, b) = freadi⊗ world⊗ file⊗ in
    (a⊙ + b⊙, world2⊙)
```

In Sect. 5, we will look at an example that can be typed only if a more sophisticated sharing analysis is applied.

3   Introducing Uniqueness Typing

We will present a uniqueness type system that allows for rank-1 types only, before showing the full type system in Sect. 4. Although both the expression language and the type language must be modified to support arbitrary rank types, the typing rules as presented in this section are easier to understand and provide a better way to introduce the type system.

3.1   The Language

We define our type system over a core lambda calculus:

$e ::=$	expression
$x^{\odot}, x^{\otimes}$	variable (exclusive, shared)
$\lambda x \cdot e$	abstraction
$e_1 \, e_2$	application
i	integer

The typing rules assign an attributed type τ^{ν} to an expression e, given a type environment Γ and a uniqueness attribute u_{γ} (explained in Sect. 3.4), denoted

$$\Gamma, u_{\gamma} \vdash e : \tau^{\nu}$$

The language of types and uniqueness attributes is defined as

$\tau ::=$	type	$\nu ::=$	uniqueness attribute
a, b	type variable	u, v	variable
$\tau_1^{\nu_1} \xrightarrow{\nu_a} \tau_2^{\nu_2}$	function	$\bullet$	unique
Int	constant type	$\times$	non-unique

The syntax for arrows (function space constructor) warrants a closer look. The domain and codomain of the arrow are two attributed types $\tau_1^{\nu_1}$ and $\tau_2^{\nu_2}$. The arrow itself has an *additional* attribute ν_a, whose role will become apparent when we discuss the rule for abstractions. We will adopt the notational convention of writing $(\tau_1^{\nu_1} \xrightarrow[\nu_a]{} \tau_2^{\nu_2})^{\nu_f}$, where ν_f is "normal" uniqueness attribute of the arrow, as $(\tau_1^{\nu_1} \xrightarrow[\nu_a]{\nu_f} \tau_2^{\nu_2})$.

As is customary, all type and attribute variables in an attributed type τ^ν are implicitly universally quantified at the outermost level (of course, this will not be true for the arbitrary rank system). In this section, a type environment maps variable names to attributed types (in Sect. 4, it will map variable names to type schemes).

3.2   Integers

We can specify two alternative rules for integers (only one of which is required):

$$\frac{}{\Gamma, u_\gamma \vdash i : \mathrm{Int}^\nu} \;\; \textsc{Int} \qquad \frac{}{\Gamma, u_\gamma \vdash i : \mathrm{Int}^\bullet} \;\; \textsc{Int}'$$

INT says that integers have type Int^ν, for an arbitrary ν: the programmer is free to assume the integer is unique or non-unique. Alternatively, INT' states that an integer is always unique. We will discuss why we prefer INT in Sect. 3.4.

3.3   Variables

To find the type of the variable, we look up the variable in the environment, correcting the type to be non-unique for shared variables:

$$\frac{}{(\Gamma, x : \tau^\nu), u_\gamma \vdash x^\odot : \tau^\nu} \;\; \textsc{Var}^\odot \qquad \frac{}{(\Gamma, x : \tau^\nu), u_\gamma \vdash x^\otimes : \tau^\times} \;\; \textsc{Var}^\otimes$$

Note that $\textsc{Var}^\otimes$ leaves the uniqueness attribute of the variable *in the environment* arbitrary. This means that variables can "lose" their uniqueness. For example, the function $\mathtt{mkPair}$ defined as $\lambda x \cdot (x^\otimes, x^\otimes)$ has type $a^u \to (a^\times, a^\times)$ (assuming a product type); in other words, no matter what the uniqueness of a on input is, each a in the pair will be non-unique.

3.4   Abstractions

Before we discuss the typing rule for abstractions, we must return to the example discussed in Sect. 1 and point out a subtlety. Consider f_3 again:

```
f₃ world file =
    let (world1, a) = freadi⊗ world⊗ file⊗ in
    let (world2, b) = freadi⊗ world⊗ file⊗ in
    (a⊙ + b⊙, world2⊙)
```

The compiler is able to reject this definition because $\mathtt{world}$ is marked as shared, which will cause its type to be inferred as non-unique by rule $\textsc{Var}^\otimes$. But what happens if we "curry" $\mathtt{freadi}$?

```
f world file =
    let curried = freadi⊙ world⊙ in
    let (world1, a) = curried⊗ file⊗ in
    let (world2, b) = curried⊗ file⊗ in
    (a⊙ + b⊙, world2⊙)
```

Both programs are semantically equivalent, so the type-checker should reject both. However, the argument `world` to `freadi` is in fact exclusive in the second example, so how can we detect the type error? The general principle is

> *when a function accesses unique objects from its closure, that closure (i.e., the function) must be unique itself* (∗)

In the example above, `curried` accesses the unique world state from its closure, and must therefore be unique itself—but is not, resulting in a type error. We can approximate[3] (∗) by

> *if a function is curried, and its curried argument is unique, the resulting function must be unique when applied* (∗′)

In the lambda calculus, functions only take a single argument, and the notion of currying translates into lambda abstractions returning new lambda abstractions. Thus, we can rephrase (∗′) as

> *if a lambda abstraction returns a new lambda abstraction, and the argument to the outer lambda abstraction is unique, the inner lambda abstraction must be unique when applied* (∗″)

In our type language, the additional attribute ν_a in the arrow type $\tau_1^{\nu_1} \xrightarrow{\nu_a} \tau_2^{\nu_2}$ indicates whether the function is required to be "unique when applied". The purpose of u_γ in the typing rules is to indicate whether we are currently in the body of an (outer) lambda abstraction whose argument must be unique. Thus we arrive at rule ABS:

$$\frac{(\Gamma, x : \tau_1^{\nu_1}), u_{\gamma'} \vdash e : \tau_2^{\nu_2} \qquad \nu_a \leq u_\gamma, u_{\gamma'} \leq \nu_1, u_{\gamma'} \leq u_\gamma}{\Gamma, u_\gamma \vdash \lambda x \cdot e : \tau_1^{\nu_1} \xrightarrow[\nu_a]{\nu_f} \tau_2^{\nu_2}} \text{ABS}$$

This rule is very similar to the normal rule for abstractions in a Hindley/Milner type system, with the exception of the attribute inequalities in the premise of the rule. The $u \leq v$ operator can be read as an implication: if v is unique, then u must be unique (v implies u, $u \leftarrow v$)[4].

---

[3] This is an approximation since the function may not use the curried argument. In $\lambda x \cdot \lambda y \cdot y^\odot$, x is not used in the body of the function, so its uniqueness need not affect the type of the function.

[4] Perhaps the choice of the symbol $\leq$ is unfortunate. In logic $a \leq b$ denotes $ab' = 0$ (i.e., a implies b), whereas here we use $u \leq v$ to mean v implies u. We use it here to conform to *Clean* conventions.

The first constraint establishes the conclusion of $(*'')$: if we are in the body of an outer lambda abstraction whose argument must be unique (u_γ), then the inner lambda abstraction must be unique when applied (ν_a). The second constraint $u_{\gamma'} \leq \nu_1$ is a near direct translation of the premise of $(*'')$. Finally, $u_{\gamma'} \leq u_\gamma$ simply propagates u_γ: if the premise of $(*'')$ already holds (u_γ), it will continue to do so in the body of the abstraction $(u_{\gamma'})$. Note that ABS is the only rule that changes the value of u_γ; all the other rules simply propagate it. When typing an expression, u_γ is initially assumed to be non-unique.

It is instructive to consider an example at this point. We show the type derivation for $\lambda x \cdot \lambda y \cdot x^\odot$, the function that returns the first of its two arguments:

$$\cfrac{\cfrac{(x : \tau_1^{\nu_1}, y : \tau_2^{\nu_2}), u_{\gamma''} \vdash x^\odot :: \tau_1^{\nu_1} \qquad \nu_{a'} \leq u_{\gamma'}, u_{\gamma''} \leq \nu_2, u_{\gamma''} \leq u_{\gamma'}}{(x : \tau_1^{\nu_1}), u_{\gamma'} \vdash \lambda y \cdot x^\odot :: \tau_2^{\nu_2} \xrightarrow[\nu_{a'}]{\nu_f'} \tau_1^{\nu_1} \qquad \nu_a \leq \times, u_{\gamma'} \leq \nu_1, u_{\gamma'} \leq \times}\text{ABS}}{\emptyset, \times \vdash \lambda x \cdot \lambda y \cdot x^\odot :: \tau_1^{\nu_1} \xrightarrow[\nu_a]{\nu_f} (\tau_2^{\nu_2} \xrightarrow[\nu_{a'}]{\nu_f'} \tau_1^{\nu_1})}\text{ABS}$$

Noting that $\nu_a \leq \times$ and $u_{\gamma'} \leq \times$ are vacuously true, that $u_{\gamma''} \leq \nu_2$ and $u_{\gamma''} \leq u_{\gamma'}$ are irrelevant as $u_{\gamma''}$ does not constrain any other attributes, and that $\nu_{a'} \leq u_{\gamma'}$ and $u_{\gamma'} \leq \nu_1$ imply that $\nu_{a'} \leq \nu_1$ (by transitivity), we arrive at the type

$$\lambda x \cdot \lambda y \cdot x^\odot :: \tau_1^{\nu_1} \xrightarrow[\nu_a]{\nu_f} (\tau_2^{\nu_2} \xrightarrow[\nu_{a'}]{\nu_f'} \tau_1^{\nu_1}) \qquad \nu_{a'} \leq \nu_1$$

where the constraint $\nu_{a'} \leq \nu_1$ says that if we curry the function (specify x but not y), and x happens to be unique, the result function must be unique on application (its attribute $\nu_{a'}$ must be $\bullet$).

If we now consider rule INT$'$, which says that integers are always unique, this definition of ABS would imply that if we curry a function by passing in an integer, the result function must be unique on application, which is unnecessary. For example, we want the following expression to be type correct:

$$\text{let fst} = \lambda x \cdot \lambda y \cdot x \text{ in let one} = \text{fst } 1 \text{ in } (\text{one } 2, \text{one } 3)$$

For the same reason, nothing in ABS constrains ν_f, and the actual uniqueness of the function is left free.

3.5   Application

The rule for function application is relatively straightforward. The only difference between the rule as presented here and the usual definition is that APP enforces the constraint that functions that must be unique when applied, are unique when applied $(\nu_f \leq \nu_a)$:

$$\cfrac{\Gamma, u_\gamma \vdash e_1 : \tau_1^{\nu_1} \xrightarrow[\nu_a]{\nu_f} \tau_2^{\nu_2} \qquad \Gamma, u_\gamma \vdash e_2 : \tau_1^{\nu_1} \qquad \nu_f \leq \nu_a}{\Gamma, u_\gamma \vdash e_1 \, e_2 : \tau_2^{\nu_2}}\text{APP}$$

4   Arbitrary Rank Types

The rank of a type is the depth at which universal quantifiers appear in the domain of functions. In most cases, universal quantifiers appear only at the outermost level, for example

$$\text{id} :: \forall a.a \to a$$

which is a type of rank 1. In higher-rank types, we have nested universal quantifiers. For example [2],

$$g :: (\forall a.[a] \to [a]) \to ([\text{Bool}], [\text{Int}]) = \lambda f. (f \, [\text{True}, \text{False}], f \, [1, 2, 3])$$

In this example, g requires a function f that works on lists of type $[a]$ for all a (the rank of the type of g is 2). Type *inference* is undecidable for types with rank $n > 2$, but we can support type inference by combining type inference with type checking. Thus, higher-rank types are only supported when function arguments are given an explicit type signature. We extend the expression language with annotated lambda expressions (and `let` expressions):

$e \mathrel{+}=$	expression *(ctd.)*
$\lambda x :: \sigma \cdot e$	annotated abstraction
$\text{let } x = e \text{ in } e'$	local definition

In the rank-1 system presented in section 3 (as well as in Clean's type system), constraints are never explicitly associated with types, but are left implicit in the typing rules. Although this makes the types simpler, we can no longer do so if we want to support arbitrary rank types. When we generalize a type τ^ν to a type scheme σ, τ^ν may be constrained by a set of constraints $\mathcal{C}$. Those constraints should be associated with the type scheme σ, because if at a later stage we instantiate σ to get a type $\tau^{\nu\prime}$, the same set of constraints should apply to $\tau^{\nu\prime}$ as well. This makes the types more complicated, but it also makes them more precise (see sections 7 and 8). So, we define a type scheme as

$$\sigma ::= \forall \vec{x}.\tau^\nu, \mathcal{C} \qquad \text{type scheme}$$

where $\vec{x}$ is a set of type and uniqueness variables, and $\mathcal{C}$ is set of constraints or a constraint variable. We modify the type language to allow for type schemes in the domain of the arrow. We follow [2] and do not allow for type schemes in the codomain:

$\tau ::=$	type
a, b	type variable
$\sigma \xrightarrow[\nu_a]{} \tau_2^{\nu_2}$	arrow type (functions)
Int	constant type

$$\overline{\Gamma, u_\gamma \vdash i : \mathrm{Int}^\nu \mid \emptyset} \qquad \text{INT}$$

$$\frac{\vdash^{\mathrm{inst}} \sigma \preceq \tau^\nu \mid \mathcal{C}}{(\Gamma, x : \sigma), u_\gamma \vdash x^\odot : \tau^\nu \mid \mathcal{C}} \qquad \text{VAR}^\odot$$

$$\frac{\vdash^{\mathrm{inst}} \sigma \preceq \tau^\nu \mid \mathcal{C}}{(\Gamma, x : \sigma), u_\gamma \vdash x^\otimes : \tau^\times \mid \mathcal{C}} \qquad \text{VAR}^\otimes$$

$$\frac{(\Gamma, x : \forall.\tau_1^{\nu_1}, \mathcal{C}_1), u_{\gamma'} \vdash e : \tau_2^{\nu_2} \mid \mathcal{C}_2}{\Gamma, u_\gamma \vdash \lambda x \cdot e : (\forall.\tau_1^{\nu_1}, \mathcal{C}_1) \xrightarrow[\nu_a]{\nu_f} \tau_2^{\nu_2} \mid \mathcal{C}_2, \nu_a \le u_\gamma, u_{\gamma'} \le u_\gamma, u_{\gamma'} \le \nu_1} \qquad \text{ABS}$$

$$\frac{\Gamma, u_\gamma \vdash e_1 : \sigma_1 \xrightarrow[\nu_a]{\nu_f} \tau_2^{\nu_2} \mid \mathcal{C} \qquad \Gamma, u_\gamma \vdash^{\mathrm{gen}} e_2 : \sigma_2 \qquad \vdash^{\mathrm{subs}} \sigma_2 \preceq \sigma_1}{\Gamma, u_\gamma \vdash e_1 \, e_2 : \tau_2^{\nu_2} \mid \mathcal{C}, \nu_f \le \nu_a} \qquad \text{APP}$$

$$\frac{\Gamma, u_\gamma \vdash^{\mathrm{gen}} e : \sigma \qquad (\Gamma, x : \sigma), u_\gamma \vdash e' : \tau^\nu \mid \mathcal{C}}{\Gamma, u_\gamma \vdash \mathrm{let}\ x = e\ \mathrm{in}\ e' : \tau^\nu \mid \mathcal{C}} \qquad \text{LET}$$

$$\frac{(\Gamma, x : \sigma), u_{\gamma'} \vdash e : \tau_2^{\nu_2} \mid \mathcal{C}}{\Gamma, u_\gamma \vdash \lambda x :: \sigma \cdot e : \sigma \xrightarrow[\nu_a]{\nu_f} \tau_2^{\nu_2} \mid \mathcal{C}, \nu_a \le u_\gamma, u_{\gamma'} \le u_\gamma, u_{\gamma'} \le \lceil \sigma \rceil} \qquad \text{ANNOT}$$

$$\frac{\Gamma, u_\gamma \vdash e : \tau^\nu \mid \mathcal{C} \qquad \vec{x} = \mathrm{freevars}(\tau^\nu) - \mathrm{freevars}(\Gamma)}{\Gamma, u_\gamma \vdash^{\mathrm{gen}} e : \forall \vec{x}.\tau^\nu, \mathcal{C}} \qquad \text{GEN}$$

$$\overline{\vdash^{\mathrm{inst}} \forall \vec{x}.\tau^\nu, \mathcal{C} \preceq \mathcal{S}_x \tau^\nu \mid \mathcal{S}_x \mathcal{C}} \qquad \text{INST}$$

$$\frac{\vec{y} \notin \mathrm{freevars}(\forall \vec{x}.\tau_1^{\nu_1}) \qquad \vdash^{\mathrm{subs}} \mathcal{S}_x \tau_1^{\nu_1} \preceq \tau_2^{\nu_2} \qquad \mathcal{C}_2 \vDash \mathcal{S}_x \mathcal{C}_1}{\vdash^{\mathrm{subs}} \forall \vec{x}.\tau_1^{\nu_1}, \mathcal{C}_1 \preceq \forall \vec{y}.\tau_2^{\nu_2}, \mathcal{C}_2} \qquad \text{SUBS}^\sigma$$

$$\frac{\vdash^{\mathrm{subs}} \sigma_2 \preceq \sigma_1 \qquad \vdash^{\mathrm{subs}} \forall.\tau_1^{\nu_1}, \emptyset \preceq \forall.\tau_2^{\nu_2}, \emptyset}{\vdash^{\mathrm{subs}} \sigma_1 \to \tau_1^{\nu_1} \preceq \sigma_2 \to \tau_2^{\nu_2}} \qquad \text{SUBS}^\to$$

$$\overline{\vdash^{\mathrm{subs}} \tau^\nu \preceq \tau^\nu} \qquad \text{SUBS}^\tau$$

Fig. 1. Uniqueness Typing Rules

Typing derivations now have the structure

$$\Gamma, u_\gamma \vdash e : \tau^\nu \mid \mathcal{C}$$

which says that e has type τ^ν, given an environment Γ and uniqueness attribute u_γ (see Sect. 3.4), provided constraints $\mathcal{C}$ are satisfied (where environments now map variable names to type schemes). The full typing rules are listed in Fig. 1; we will explain them separately below.

4.1 Variables

Because the type environment now associates variable names with type schemes rather than types, to find the type of a variable we must look up the associated type scheme in the environment, and instantiate it. Instantiation is defined as

$$\frac{}{\vdash^{\text{inst}} \forall \vec{x}.\tau^\nu, \mathcal{C} \preceq S_x \tau^\nu \mid S_x \mathcal{C}} \quad \text{INST}$$

where S_x is some substitution $[\vec{x} \mapsto \ldots]$ mapping all variables $\vec{x}$ to fresh variables. Since we associate a set of constraints $\mathcal{C}$ with a type scheme, a type $S_x \tau^\nu$ is only an instance of a type scheme σ if those constraints are satisfied.

4.2 Abstraction

The rule for abstraction remains unchanged except for the domain of the arrow operator which is now a type scheme. However, since we can only infer rank-1 types, the type scheme for unannotated lambda expressions must be a "degenerate" type scheme with no quantified variables $(\forall.\tau^\nu, \mathcal{C})$—in other words, a type[5].

4.3 Application

The rule for application looks slightly different from the rank-1 version. Previously, with APP the type of the actual parameter had to equal the type of the formal parameter of the function:

$$\frac{\Gamma, u_\gamma \vdash e_1 : \tau_1^{\nu_1} \xrightarrow[\nu_a]{\nu_f} \tau_2^{\nu_2} \quad \Gamma, u_\gamma \vdash e_2 : \tau_1^{\nu_1} \quad \nu_f \leq \nu_a}{\Gamma, u_\gamma \vdash e_1 \, e_2 : \tau_2^{\nu_2}} \quad \text{APP}_1$$

In the rank-n case, the only requirement is that the type of the actual parameter is an instance of the type of the formal parameter. To this end, we infer a type scheme for the actual parameter, and do a subsumption check:

$$\frac{\Gamma, u_\gamma \vdash e_1 : \sigma_1 \xrightarrow[\nu_a]{\nu_f} \tau_2^{\nu_2} \mid \mathcal{C} \quad \Gamma, u_\gamma \vdash^{\text{gen}} e_2 : \sigma_2 \quad \vdash^{\text{subs}} \sigma_2 \preceq \sigma_1}{\Gamma, u_\gamma \vdash e_1 \, e_2 : \tau_2^{\nu_2} \mid \mathcal{C}, \nu_f \leq \nu_a} \quad \text{APP}$$

(We will explain subsumption separately in section 4.5.) To infer a type scheme, we first infer a type, and then generalize over all the free variables in the type, excluding the free variables in the environment:

$$\frac{\Gamma, u_\gamma \vdash e : \tau^\nu \mid \mathcal{C} \quad \vec{x} = \text{freevars}(\tau^\nu) - \text{freevars}(\Gamma)}{\Gamma, u_\gamma \vdash^{\text{gen}} e : \forall \vec{x}.\tau^\nu, \mathcal{C}} \quad \text{GEN}$$

---

[5] In [2] the arrow $\rightarrow$ is overloaded; there is an arrow $\tau \rightarrow \tau$ and an arrow $\sigma \rightarrow \tau$. Since we do not use the notion of ρ–types, our arrows always have type $\sigma \rightarrow \tau^\nu$.

4.4 Annotated Lambda Abstractions

The rule for annotated lambda abstractions is similar to the rule for "ordinary" lambda abstractions, except that programmers can now specify a type scheme manually, allowing for higher-rank types:

$$\frac{(\Gamma, x : \sigma), u_{\gamma'} \vdash e : \tau_2^{\nu_2} \mid \mathcal{C}}{\Gamma, u_\gamma \vdash \lambda x :: \sigma \cdot e : \sigma \xrightarrow[\nu_a]{\nu_f} \tau_2^{\nu_2} \mid \mathcal{C}, \nu_a \leq u_\gamma, u_{\gamma'} \leq u_\gamma, u_{\gamma'} \leq \lceil \sigma \rceil} \quad \text{ANNOT}$$

We have to be careful defining $\lceil \forall \vec{x}.\tau^\nu \rceil$, used to constrain $u_{\gamma'}$. The obvious answer (ν) is only correct if ν is not itself universally quantified. For example, consider

$$\lambda x :: \forall u.a^u \cdot \lambda y \cdot x^\odot :: (\forall u.a^u) \xrightarrow[u_a]{u_f} b^v \xrightarrow[u_{a'}]{u_{f'}} a^w, ?$$

(Note that this is a rank-2 type.) What should the constraint at the question mark be? One possible solution is

$$\forall u \cdot u_{a'} \leq u$$

which is equivalent to saying

$$u_{a'} \leq \bullet$$

So, to avoid unnecessary complication by introducing universal quantification into the constraint language, we define $\lceil \ \rceil$ as

$$\lceil \forall \vec{x}.\tau^\nu \rceil = \begin{cases} \nu & \text{if } \nu \notin \vec{x} \\ \bullet & \text{otherwise} \end{cases}$$

4.5 Subsumption

The rules for subsumption are defined as in [2], except that we have collapsed rules SKOL and SPEC into one rule (SUBS$^\sigma$) and added one additional premise. SUBS$^\sigma$ is the main rule that checks whether one type scheme is a (generic) instance of another.

$$\frac{\vec{y} \notin \text{freevars}(\forall \vec{x}.\tau_1^{\nu_1}) \qquad \vdash^{\text{subs}} S_x \tau_1^{\nu_1} \preceq \tau_2^{\nu_2} \qquad \mathcal{C}_2 \vDash S_x \mathcal{C}_1}{\vdash^{\text{subs}} \forall \vec{x}.\tau_1^{\nu_1}, \mathcal{C}_1 \preceq \forall \vec{y}.\tau_2^{\nu_2}, \mathcal{C}_2} \quad \text{SUBS}^\sigma$$

In a standard type system, as here, a type scheme $\sigma_1 = \forall \vec{x}.\tau_1$ is at least as polymorphic as another type scheme $\sigma_2 = \forall \vec{y}.\tau_2$ if a unifier S_x can be found that instantiates τ_1 to an *arbitrary* instantiation of τ_2 (guaranteed by $\vec{y} \notin \text{freevars}(\forall \vec{x}.\tau_1^{\nu_1})$). In our system, however, we need an additional constraint $\mathcal{C}_2 \vDash S_x \mathcal{C}_1$, which is best explained by example. Suppose we have two functions f, g

$$f :: (\forall u, v.a^u \xrightarrow[u_a]{u_f} b^v) \to \ldots$$

$$g :: a^u \xrightarrow[u_a]{u_f} b^v, [u \leq v]$$

Should the application $f\,g$ type-check? Intuitively, f expects to be able to use the function it is passed to obtain a b with uniqueness v (say, a unique b), independent of the uniqueness of a. However, g only promises to return a unique b if a is also unique! Thus, the application $f\,g$ should be disallowed. Conversely, if we instead define f' and g' as

$$f' :: (\forall u, v. a^u \xrightarrow[u_a]{u_f} b^v, [u \leq v]) \to \ldots$$

$$g' :: a^u \xrightarrow[u_a]{u_f} b^v$$

the application $f'\,g'$ *should* be allowed because the type of g' is more general than the type expected by f'. The condition $\mathcal{C}_2 \vDash S_x \mathcal{C}_1$, where the $\vDash$ symbol stands for logical entailment from propositional logic, means that if constraints $\mathcal{C}_2$ are satisfied, constraints $\mathcal{C}_1$ must also be satisfied[6]. In other words, the constraints of the offered type must be the same or less restrictive than the constraints of the requested type.

5   Examples

In this section we consider a few example expressions and their associated types. We start with very simple expressions and slowly build up from there. First, we consider a single integer:

$$5 :: \forall u.\text{Int}^u, \emptyset$$

Rule INT says that integers have type Int with an arbitrary uniqueness, hence the universally quantified u. Next we consider the identity function id:

$$\lambda x.x^\odot :: \forall a, u, u_f, u_a, c.(\forall.a^u, c) \xrightarrow[u_a]{u_f} a^u, c$$

This type may appear more complicated than it really is, because we show top-level attributes and degenerate type schemes; we can be slightly less formal:

$$\lambda x.x^\odot :: (a^u, c) \xrightarrow[u_a]{u_f} a^u, c$$

Either way, this is the type one would expect an identity function to have. Note that this function is polymorphic in the constraints of its argument: if the argument has type a^u under constraints c, then the result has type a^u only if the same set of constraints is satisfied.

The function apply (\$ in Haskell) behaves like id restricted to function types:

$$\lambda f.\lambda x.f^\odot\, x^\odot :: \left((a^u, c_1) \xrightarrow[u_{a''}]{u_{f''}} b^v, c_2 \right) \xrightarrow[u_a]{u_f} \left((a^u, c_1) \xrightarrow[u_{a'}]{u_{f'}} b^v \right), [c_2,$$

$$u_{a'} \leq u_{a''}, u_{a'} \leq u_{f''}, u_{f''} \leq u_{a''}]$$

---

[6] If either $\mathcal{C}_1$ or $\mathcal{C}_2$ in $\mathcal{C}_1 \vDash \mathcal{C}_2$ is a constraint variable, we apply unification instead of the entailment check.

With the exception of the constraints, this type should be self-explanatory. We consider each constraint in turn:

c_2 If f has type $(a^u, c_1) \xrightarrow[u_{a''}]{u_{f''}} b^v$ only when constraints c_2 are satisfied, then $\mathtt{apply}\, f$ also has that type only when those constraints are satisfied (*cf.* the constraint c in the type of $\mathtt{id}$.)

$u_{a'} \leq u_{a''}$ If f can only be executed once (in other words, if f must be unique on application, if $u_{a''}$ is unique), then $\mathtt{apply}\, f$ can also only be executed once.

$u_{a'} \leq u_{f''}$ If f is unique, then $\mathtt{apply}\, f$ can only be executed once; this is a direct consequence of the "currying rule" from Sect. 3.4.

$u_{f''} \leq u_{a''}$ Finally, $\mathtt{apply}\, f$ applies f, so if f must be unique on application, we require that it is unique.

The next example emphasises a point with respect to the sharing analysis. Suppose that we have a primitive type Array and two functions *resize* to (destructively) resize the array, and *size* to return the current size of the array:

$$resize :: \text{Array}^\bullet \xrightarrow[u_a]{u_f} \text{Int}^v \xrightarrow[\bullet]{u_{f'}} \text{Array}^\bullet$$

$$size :: \text{Array}^u \xrightarrow[u_a]{u_f} \text{Int}^v$$

Then the following expression is correctly marked and type correct:

$$\lambda arr \cdot \text{if } size^\odot arr^\otimes < 10 \text{ then } resize^\otimes arr^\odot 20 \text{ else } resize^\otimes arr^\odot 30$$

This expression is marked correctly, because only one of the two branches of the conditional expression will be executed, and the shared mark $arr^\otimes$ in the condition guarantees that the condition cannot modify *arr*.

To conclude this section, we consider two examples that contain a type error, which in both cases will be detected in the subsumption check (although for different reasons). The first example shows a simple case of an argument not being polymorphic enough:

$$\text{let } id_\mathsf{f} = \lambda f :: \forall u.a^u \xrightarrow[u_a]{u_f} a^u \cdot f^\odot$$

$$\text{in let } id_\text{int} = \lambda i :: \text{Int}^\bullet \cdot i^\odot$$

$$\text{in } id_\mathsf{f}^\odot \, id_\text{int}^\odot$$

Here, id_f demands that its argument is polymorphic in u, but id_int is not (it works only on unique integers). The problem is detected when we do the subsumption check

$$\vdash^{\text{subs}} \forall.\text{Int}^\bullet \xrightarrow[u_a]{u_f} \text{Int}^\bullet \preceq \forall u.a^u \xrightarrow[u_{a'}]{u_{f'}} a^u$$

We have to check that we can unify $Int^\bullet$ and a^u for *an arbitrary instantiation* of u, but that will clearly fail[7]. The second "incorrect" example that we consider fails due to the entailment check explained in section 4.5:

$$\text{let } first = \lambda f :: a^u \xrightarrow[u_a]{u_f} b^v \xrightarrow[u_{a'}]{u_{f'}} a^u \cdot \lambda x \cdot \lambda y \cdot f^{\odot} x^{\odot} y^{\odot}$$
$$\text{in } first^{\odot} (\lambda x \cdot \lambda y \cdot x^{\odot})$$

The function that is passed as an argument to *first* has type[8]

$$\lambda x \cdot \lambda y \cdot x^{\odot} :: a^u \xrightarrow[u_a]{u_f} b^v \xrightarrow[u_{a'}]{u_{f'}} a^u, [u_{a'} \leq u]$$

whereas the type specified for the argument f of *first* does not allow for the constraint $u_{a'} \leq u$; so, the type-checker will fail with

[] `does not entail` $[u_{a'} \leq u]$

6 Type Inference

We have written a prototype implementation of the type system presented in this paper. The typing rules as presented in Fig. 1 allow for a relatively straightforward translation to an algorithm $\mathcal{W}$ [3] style type-checker (our prototype is just under a thousand lines long) once the following subtleties have been observed.

When doing unification, a unification goal, $\tau_1^{\nu_1} \equiv \tau_2^{\nu_2}$ should be expanded into two subgoals $\tau_1 \equiv \tau_2$ and $\nu_1 \equiv \nu_2$. In other words, the base types and the uniqueness attributes should be unified independently.

Unification should not be used to unify functions because, as far as unification is concerned, $\sigma_1 \rightarrow \tau_1^{\nu_1} \equiv \sigma_2 \rightarrow \tau_2^{\nu_2}$ is the same as $\sigma_2 \rightarrow \tau_2^{\nu_2} \equiv \sigma_1 \rightarrow \tau_1^{\nu_1}$, but to compare two type schemes we need to use subsumption, which clearly gives different answers for $\vdash^{\text{subs}} \sigma_1 \preceq \sigma_2$ and $\vdash^{\text{subs}} \sigma_2 \preceq \sigma_1$. However, when properly implemented, by the time we need unification, the subsumption rules (in particular, SUBS$^{\rightarrow}$) will have taken care of all arrows[9].

To implement the subsumption check, the technique suggested by Peyton Jones [2] of using skolem constants can be applied, introducing skolem constants both type and uniqueness variables.

Logical entailment of two sets of constraints $\mathcal{C}_1$ and $\mathcal{C}_2$ can be implemented as a validity check for the propositional logic formula $C_1 \rightarrow C_2$, where the

---

[7] The implementation of SUBS$^{\sigma}$ will have instantiated u with a fresh "skolem constant": an unknown, but fixed, uniqueness attribute. These skolem constants are the "rigid variables" known from, for example, `ghc`, and the type error the user will get is `Cannot unify rigid attribute` u `and` $\bullet$.

[8] There are additional "polymorphic" constraint variables in these types that we are leaving out for conciseness.

[9] In [2], due to the distinction between ρ functions and τ functions, unification must still deal with arrows $\tau \rightarrow \tau$; since we only have one arrow type, this is unnecessary in our approach.

$u \leq v$ operator is regarded as an implication $v \rightarrow u$. Although the complexity of checking the validity of functions in propositional logic is exponential, that will not matter much in practice since the formulae generated by the type-checker will be small (most type schemes will not have many associated constraints). A simple algorithm (the one we have implemented) to check the validity of a formula in propositional logic is to convert the formula to conjunctive normal form. Then inspect every conjunct and search for atoms in the conjunct such that the conjunct contains the atom and its negation. If such a match is found for all conjuncts, the formula is valid (see [4, Sect. 1.5] for details).

Finally, when generalizing a type τ^{ν} with respect to a set of constraints $\mathcal{C}$, the set should be checked for inconsistencies; these should be reported as type errors. For improved readability of types, it is also useful to take the transitive closure of $\mathcal{C}$ instead of $\mathcal{C}$ itself, and add only the "relevant" inequalities to the type scheme (rule ABS might generate unnecessary constraints $[u_{\gamma'} \leq u_{\gamma}, u_{\gamma'} \leq \nu_1]$ if $u_{\gamma'}$ is never used to constrain other attributes); this is demonstrated in the example in Sect. 3.4.

7   Comparison with Clean

The uniqueness type system presented here is based on that of the programming language *Clean* [1,5], which is in turn strongly related to substructural logics (see [6] for an accessible introduction to linear logic; [7] is a good introduction to substructural type systems). However, there are a number of important differences, one being that Clean's system is defined over graph rewrite rules rather than the lambda calculus; this gives the type system a very different "feel".

A rather more important difference is the treatment of curried functions. In Clean, a function that is (partially) applied to a unique argument, is itself unique. Moreover, unique functions are *necessarily unique*: they cannot lose their uniqueness. In the curry example in Sect. 3.4, there are two references to `curried`, causing `curried` to be marked as $\otimes$. The type correction in rule VAR$^{\otimes}$ (a trivial operation in our system) must check whether the variable represents a function, and if so, reject the program. While this solves the curried function problem, it has far reaching consequences for the type system.

The first is that type variables, as well as functions, are not allowed to lose their uniqueness, since a type variable can be instantiated to a function type. In Clean, for example, the function `mkPair` has type

$$\lambda x \cdot (x^{\otimes}, x^{\otimes}) :: a^{\times} \rightarrow (a^{\times}, a^{\times})$$

and not

$$\lambda x \cdot (x^{\otimes}, x^{\otimes}) :: a^{u} \rightarrow (a^{\times}, a^{\times})$$

The type assigned by Clean is not as restrictive at is seems, however, due to Clean's subtyping relation: a unique type is considered to be *subtype* of its non-unique counterpart. For example, the following is a correct Clean program:

```
five :: Int•
five = 5

mkPair :: a× → (a×, a×)
mkPair x = (x, x)

Start = mkPair five
```

where Start is assigned the type $(\text{Int}^\times, \text{Int}^\times)$. Of course, the subtyping relation is adapted for arrows [5]:

$$S \xrightarrow{u} S' \leq T \xrightarrow{v} T' \qquad \text{iff} \qquad u = v \text{ and } T \leq S \text{ and } S' \leq T'$$

There are two things to note about this definition: a unique function is never a subtype of its non-unique version (condition $u = v$), since functions are not allowed to lose their uniqueness (a similar restriction applies to type variables); and subtyping is contravariant in the function argument. Although this is not surprising, it complicates the type system—especially in the presence of algebraic data types. We have not discussed ADTs in this paper (see Sect. 8), but they are easy to add to our system. However, algebraic data constructors can include arrows, for example

```
data Fun a b = Fun (a → b)
```

which means that arguments to constructors must be analysed to check whether they have covariant, contravariant or invariant subtyping behaviour.

By contrast, in our system we do not have the notion of "necessarily unique"; instead, we add a single additional attribute ν_a as explained before, and the condition that (some) curried functions can only be executed once becomes a local constraint $\nu_f \leq \nu_a$ in the rule for function application. There are no global effects (for example, type variables are unaffected) and we do not need subtyping[10].

That last point is worth emphasizing. The subtyping relation in Clean is very shallow. The only advantage of subtyping is that we can pass in a unique object to a function that expects a non-unique object. So, in Clean, marking a formal parameter as non-unique really means, "I do not care about the uniqueness of this parameter". However, in our system, we can always use an attribute variable to mean the same thing. That is not always possible in Clean, since type variables are not allowed to lose their uniqueness (the type we assign to the function mkPair above would be illegal in Clean).

Since we do not have subtyping, functions can specify that their arguments must be unique $(a^\bullet)$, non-unique $(a^\times)$, or indicate that the uniqueness of the input does not matter (a^u). In Clean, it is only possible to specify that arguments must be unique $(a^\bullet)$ or that the uniqueness of an argument does not matter $(a^u$ or, due to subtyping, $a^\times)$. Experience will tell whether this extra functionality is useful.

---

[10] One might argue that subsumption introduces subtyping between type schemes; however, due to the predicative nature of our type system, this does not have an effect on algebraic data type arguments; see the discussion in [2, Sect. 7.3].

Another consequence is mentioned in [5, Sect. *Uniqueness Type Inference*]:

> *However, because of our treatment of higher-order functions (involving a restriction on the subtype relation w.r.t. variables), it might be the case that lifting this most general solution fails, whereas some specific instance is attributable. (...) Consequently, there is no "Principal Uniqueness Type Theorem".*

The authors hope that the system presented here *does* have principal types, although a formal proof is future work.

An additional benefit of allowing for type schemes in the domain of arrows (necessary to support higher-rank types) is that we can be more conscientious about associating uniqueness inequalities (constraints) with types. For example, in Clean, the function `apply` from Sect. 5 has type

$$\lambda f \cdot \lambda x \cdot f\, x :: (a^u \to b^v) \to a^u \to b^v$$

But given a function f with type

$$f :: a^u \to b^v, [u \le v]$$

the Clean type-checker assigns the following type to `apply` f:

$$\mathtt{apply}\, f :: a^u \to b^v, [u \le v]$$

This type is quite reasonable, and similar to the type we would assign. However, it contains constraints that do not appear in the type of `apply`, which suggests that the type of `apply` as assigned by the Clean type-checker is somehow "incomplete". The type we assign to `apply` is explicit about the propagation of constraints[11]:

$$\lambda f \cdot \lambda x \cdot f\, x :: ((a^u, c_1) \to b^v, c_2) \to (a^u, c_1) \to b^v, c_2$$

8   Future Work and Conclusions

We have designed a uniqueness type system for the lambda calculus that can be used to add side effects to a pure functional language without losing referential transparency. This type system is based on the type system of the functional programming language *Clean*, but modifies it in a number of ways. First, it is defined over the lambda calculus rather than a graph rewrite system. Second, our treatment of curried functions is completely different and makes the type system much simpler; in particular, there is no need for subtyping. Third, our system supports arbitrary rank types, and it is much more careful about associating constraints with types.

---

[11] Not showing the attributes on the arrows.

The system as presented in this paper deals only with the core lambda calculus; however, extensions to deal with algebraic data types and recursive definitions are straightforward. For recursive definitions $\mu \cdot e$, the type of e is corrected to be non-unique (this is the same approach as taken in [5] for `letrec` expressions). The main principle in dealing with algebraic data types is that if a unique object is extracted from an enclosing container, the enclosing container must in turn be unique (this is a slightly more permissive definition than the one used in Clean, which requires that a container must be unique *when it is constructed* if any of its elements are unique).

We need to define a semantics for our small core language and show that a number of standard properties of the type system hold with respect to the semantics (in particular, subject reduction). Also, we would like to prove that our system has principal types. Given an appropriate semantics with an explicit representation of sharing (for example, Launchbury's natural semantics for lazy evaluation [8], or perhaps a graph rewriting semantics), we should also prove that our type system guarantees that there is never more than one reference to an object with a unique type.

The inference algorithm described briefly in Sect. 6 is based on algorithm $\mathcal{W}$ and inherits its associated problems, in particular unhelpful error messages. We are planning to investigate the feasibility of other approaches—the constraint based algorithm proposed by Heeren looks promising [9].

The formalization of the constraint language in this paper is not as precise as it could be, but a more precise definition is difficult to give. Moreover, constraints considerably complicate the type system and the types assigned to terms. We are currently investigating the possibility of removing the constraints altogether by replacing the inequalities in the constraints with equalities. This will make the type system more restrictive, but will also make it much simpler. It remains to be seen whether this trade-off between simplicity and generality is desirable.

In the explanation of the rule for abstractions ABS in Sect. 3.4, we mentioned that our method of constraining ν_a is conservative. For example, the constraint $u_{a'} \leq u$ in

$$\lambda x.\lambda y.y^{\odot} :: (a^u, c_1) \xrightarrow[u_a]{u_f} (b^v, c_2) \xrightarrow[u_{a'}]{u_{f'}} b^v, [c_2, u_{a'} \leq u]$$

is not actually necessary since x is not referenced in $\lambda y \cdot x$. Hence, it may be possible to relax the rules to be less conservative. This would only affect how ν_a in ABS is established; it would not change the type language.

Finally, the original motivation for wanting to extend Clean's uniqueness system to arbitrary rank is the fact that generic programming [10] frequently generates higher-rank types. We plan to extend our prototype implementation of the system to support generics, with the ultimate goal of proving that if a function defined generically is type correct (with respect to some "generic" uniqueness type system), then the functions derived from the generic function will also be type correct. This will give us some experience with the type system, which may provide more insights into whether the extra power that our uniqueness system gives over Clean's system (see Sect. 7) is useful in practice.

Acknowledgements

We thank Bastiaan Heeren, Dervla O'Keeffe, John Gilbert, Wendy Verbruggen, and Sjaak Smetsers for their comments on various drafts of this paper, and the anonymous referees for their thorough reviews and helpful suggestions.

References

1. Barendsen, E., Smetsers, S.: Conventional and uniqueness typing in graph rewrite systems. Technical Report CSI-R9328, University of Nijmegen (1993)
2. Peyton Jones, S., Shields, M.: Practical type inference for arbitrary rank types. Under consideration for publication in J. Functional Programming (2004)
3. Damas, L., Milner, R.: Principal type-schemes for functional programs. In: POPL '82: Proceedings of the 9th ACM SIGPLAN-SIGACT symposium on Principles of programming languages, pp. 207–212. ACM Press, New York (1982)
4. Huth, M., Ryan, M.: Logic in Computer Science: Modelling and Reasoning about Systems. Cambridge University Press, New York (2004)
5. Barendsen, E., Smetsers, S.: Uniqueness typing for functional languages with graph rewriting semantics. Mathematical Structures in Computer Science 6, 579–612 (1996)
6. Wadler, P.: A taste of linear logic. In: Borzyszkowski, A.M., Sokolowski, S. (eds.) MFCS 1993. LNCS, vol. 711, pp. 185–210. Springer, Heidelberg (1993)
7. Walker, D.: Substructural type systems. In: Pierce, B. (ed.) Advanced Topics in Types and Programming Languages, MIT Press, Cambridge (2005)
8. Launchbury, J.: A natural semantics for lazy evaluation. In: POPL '93: Proceedings of the 20th ACM SIGPLAN-SIGACT symposium on Principles of programming languages, pp. 144–154. ACM Press, New York (1993)
9. Heeren, B., Hage, J., Swierstra, S.D.: Generalizing Hindley-Milner type inference algorithms. Technical Report UU-CS-2002-031, Institute of Information and Computing Science, University Utrecht, Netherlands (2002)
10. Alimarine, A., Plasmeijer, M.J.: A generic programming extension for Clean. In: Arts, T., Mohnen, M. (eds.) IFL 2002. LNCS, vol. 2312, pp. 168–185. Springer, Heidelberg (2002)

Heuristics for Type Error Discovery and Recovery

Jurriaan Hage and Bastiaan Heeren

Department of Information and Computing Sciences, Universiteit Utrecht
P.O.Box 80.089, 3508 TB Utrecht, The Netherlands
{jur,bastiaan}@cs.uu.nl

Abstract. Type error messages that are reported for incorrect functional programs can be difficult to understand. The reason for this is that most type inference algorithms proceed in a mechanical, syntax-directed way, and are unaware of inference techniques used by experts to explain type inconsistencies. We formulate type inference as a constraint problem, and analyze the collected constraints to improve the error messages (and, as a result, programming efficiency). A special data structure, the type graph, is used to detect global properties of a program, and furthermore enables us to uniformly describe a large collection of heuristics which embed expert knowledge in explaining type errors. Some of these also suggest corrections to the programmer. Our work has been fully implemented and is used in practical situations, showing that it scales up well. We include a number of statistics from actual use of the compiler showing us the frequency with which heuristics are used, and the kind and number of suggested corrections.

Keywords: type inferencing, type graph, constraints, heuristics, error messages, error recovery.

1 Introduction

Type inference algorithms for Hindley-Milner type systems typically proceed in a syntax-directed way. The main disadvantage of such a rigid and local approach is that the reported type error messages not always reflect the actual problem. Over the last five years we have developed the TOP framework to support flexible and customizable type inference. This framework has been used to build the Helium compiler [6], which implements almost the entire Haskell 98 standard, and which is especially designed for learning the programming language.

An important issue is that the order in which constraints on types are resolved can strongly influence at which point an inconsistency is detected. In existing compilers (which tend to solve constraints as they go), this has the disadvantage that a bias exists for finding errors towards the end of a program. In this paper we discuss a constraint solver that uses type graphs, a data structure that allows a global analysis of the types in a program. More importantly, type graphs naturally support heuristics, which embed expert knowledge in explaining type errors.

Some of these heuristics correspond closely to earlier proposals for improving error messages. Some are new, such as heuristics which can discover commonly made mistakes (like confusing addition + and append ++), and a sophisticated heuristic which considers function applications in detail to discover incorrectly ordered, missing, or superfluous arguments.

Z. Horváth, V. Zsók, and A. Butterfield (Eds.): IFL 2006, LNCS 4449, pp. 199–216, 2007.

A number of these heuristics are tried in parallel, and a voting mechanism decides which constraints will be blamed for the inconsistency. These constraints are then removed from the type graph, and each of them results in a type error message reported back to the programmer. The use of type graphs thus leads naturally to reporting multiple, possibly independent type error messages.

The contributions we make in this paper are the following: we have integrated a large collection of heuristics into a comprehensive and extensible framework. Although some of these are known from the literature, this is the first time, to our knowledge, that they have been integrated into a full working system. In addition, we have defined a number of new heuristics based on our experiences as teachers of Haskell. Our work has been fully implemented into the Helium compiler which shows that it scales to a full programming language. Helium has been used in a course of functional programming at Universiteit Utrecht since 2002, comprising several hundreds of students. It is freely available for download [6]. Furthermore, we have applied the compiler to a large collection of programs written by students, and considered how often the various heuristics influence the outcome. Many of the examples in this paper are taken from this collection of programs.

This paper is organized as follows. After setting the scene in the next section, we introduce each heuristic in turn in Section 3. In Section 5 we show how the heuristics are put together in the Helium compiler, and Section 6 gives statistical information about the usage of heuristics based on a large collection of programs compiled by first-year students. Section 4 considers the type graph data structure on which the implementation of our heuristics in Helium are based. In Section 7 we consider related work, after which we conclude.

2   Constraints

In this paper we consider only sets of equality constraints. Naturally, polymorphism is part of the language, but it is used only For every such use, the polymorphic type will be replaced by a fresh instance of that type. The major consequence of this approach is that definitions from previous binding groups are considered given and can not be blamed for a type error, only their use can. Due to space restrictions, we refer the reader to [2] for more details of this process.

For the purposes of this paper, we can thus simply assume that constraints are of the form $\tau_1 \equiv \tau_2$, in which τ_1 and τ_2 are monomorphic types, either type variables $v_1, v_2, \ldots$, type constants (such as Int and $\rightarrow$), or the application of a type to another. For example, the type of functions from integers to booleans is written $(((\rightarrow) \ Int) \ Bool)$. Type application is left-associative, and we omit parentheses where allowed. We often write the function constructor infix, resulting in $Int \rightarrow Bool$. We assume the types are well-kinded: types like $Int \ Bool$ do not occur.

3   Heuristics

In principle, all the constraints that contribute to an error are candidates for removal. However, some constraints are better candidates for removal than others. To select the "best" candidate for removal, we use a number of heuristics. These heuristics are usually based on common techniques used by experts to explain type errors. In addition to selecting what is reported, heuristics can specialize error messages, for instance by including hints and probable fixes. For each removed constraint, we create a single type error message using the constraint information stored with that constraint. The approach naturally leads to multiple, independent type error messages being reported.

Many of our heuristics are considered in parallel, so we need some facility to co-ordinate the interaction between them. The Helium compiler uses a voting mechanism based on weights attached to the heuristics, and the "confidence" that a heuristic has in its choice. Some heuristics, the tie-breakers, are only considered if none of the other heuristics came up with a suggestion.

A consideration is how to present the errors to a user, taking into consideration the limitations imposed by the used output format. In this paper we restrict ourselves to simple textual error messages.

In the following we shall consider a number of heuristics, a subset of what is currently available in Helium. Heuristics available in Helium have been omitted for various reasons: some of the heuristics are still in their experimental stages (e.g., the repair heuristics developed as part of a Master Thesis project by Langebaerd [7]), some have been considered elsewhere (e.g., the type inference directives [5]), and some deal exclusively with overloading, an issue we considered in an earlier paper [4]. Note, however, that all of the heuristics described do work in the presence of type classes, as evidenced by the Helium implementation (with overloading turned on).

We have grouped the heuristics into three major groups: the general heuristics that apply to constraint solving in general, the language dependent heuristics that are specific for functional programming languages and Haskell in particular, and, finally, a number of program correcting heuristics that include a probable fix as part of the type error message.

We illustrate the heuristics by means of examples. The ones that are followed by an error message are taken from a collection of 11,256 actual compiles made by students in the course year 2004/2005. For reasons of brevity we only include the parts of the program that are involved in the error, and in some cases have translated identifiers to English and removed some unimportant aspects of the code, for reasons of clarity and concision.

3.1 General Heuristics

The heuristics in this section are not restricted to type inference, but they can be used for other constraint satisfaction problems as well.

Participation Ratio Heuristic. Our first heuristic applies some common sense reasoning: if a constraint is involved in more than one conflict, then it is a better candidate for removal. The set of candidates is thus reduced to the constraints that occur most often in conflicts. This heuristic is driven by a ratio r (typically at least 95%): only constraints that occur in at least r percent of the conflicts are retained as candidates. This percentage is computed relative to the maximum number of conflicts any of the constraints in the set was involved in.

Note that this heuristic also helps to decrease the number of reported error messages, as multiple conflicts are resolved by removing a single constraint. However, it does not guarantee that the compiler returns the minimum number of error messages.

The participation-ratio heuristic implements the approach suggested by Johnson and Walz [14]: if we have three pieces of evidence that a value should have type *Int*, and only one for type *Bool*, then we should focus on the latter.

First Come, First Blamed Heuristic. The next heuristic we present is used as a final tie-breaker since it always reduces the number of candidates to one. This is an important task: without such a selection criteria, it would be unclear (even worse: arbitrary) what is reported. We propose a tie-breaker heuristic which considers the position of a constraint in the constraint list.

In [1] we address how to flatten an abstract syntax tree decorated with constraints into a constraint list L. Although the order of the constraints is irrelevant while constructing the type graph, we store it in the constraint information, and use it for this particular heuristic: for each error path, we take the constraint which completes the path – i.e., which comes *latest* in L. This results in a list of constraints that complete an error path, and out of these constraints we pick the one that came *first* in L.

3.2 Language Dependent Heuristics

The second class of heuristics involves those that are driven by domain knowledge. Although the instances we give depend to some extent on the language under consideration, it is likely that other programming languages allow similarly styled heuristics.

Trust Factor Heuristic. The trust factor heuristic computes a trust factor for each constraint, which reflects the level of trust we have in the validity of a constraint. Obviously, we prefer to report constraints with a low trust factor. We discuss four cases that we found to be useful.

(1) Some constraints are introduced *pro forma*: they trivially hold. An example is the constraint expressing that the type of a let-expression equals the type of its body. Reporting such a constraint as incorrect would be highly inappropriate. Thus, we make this constraint highly trusted. The following definition is ill-typed because the type signature declared for *squares* does not match with the type of the body of the let-expression.

$$squares :: Int$$
$$squares = \textbf{let } f\ i = i * i$$
$$\textbf{in } map\ f\ [1 .. 10]$$

Dropping the constraint that the type of the let-expression equals the type of the body would remove the type inconsistency. However, the high trust factor of this constraint prevents us from doing so. In this case, we select a different constraint, and report, for instance, the incompatibility between the type of *squares* and its right-hand side.

(2) The type of a function imported from the standard Prelude, that comes with the compiler, should not be questioned. Ordinarily, such a function can only be *used* incorrectly.

(3) Although not mandatory, type annotations provided by a programmer can guide the type inference process. In particular, they can play an important role in the reporting of error messages. These type annotations reflect the types expected by a programmer, and are a significant clue where the actual types of a program differ from his perception. We can decide to trust the types that are provided by a user. In this way, we can mimic a type inference algorithm that pushes a type signature into its definition. Practice shows, however, that one should not rely too much on type information supplied by a novice programmer: these annotations are frequently in error themselves.

(4) A final consideration for the trust factor of a constraint is in which part of the program the error is reported. Not only types of expressions are constrained, but errors can also occur in patterns, declarations, and so on. Hence, patterns and declarations can be reported as the source of a type conflict. Whenever possible, we report an error for an expression. In the definition of *increment*, the pattern $(\_ : x)$ (x must be a list) contradicts with the expression $x + 1$ (x must be of type *Int*).

$$increment \ (\_ : x) = x + 1$$

We prefer to report the expression, and not the pattern. If a type signature supports the assumption that x must be of type *Int*, then the pattern can still be reported as being erroneous.

Avoid Folklore Constraints Heuristic. Some of the constraints restrict the type of a subterm (e.g., the condition of a conditional expression must be of type *Bool*), whereas others constrain the type of the complete expression at hand (e.g., the type of a pair is a tuple type). These two classes of constraints correspond very neatly to the unifications that are performed by algorithm $\mathcal{W}$ and algorithm $\mathcal{M}$ [8], respectively. We refer to constraints corresponding to $\mathcal{M}$ as *folklore* constraints. Often, we can choose between two constraints – one which is folklore, and one which is not. In the following definition, the condition should be of type *Bool*, but is of type *String*.

$test :: Bool \rightarrow String$
$test \ b = $ **if** `"b"` **then** `"yes!"` **else** `"no!"`

Algorithm $\mathcal{W}$ detects the inconsistency at the conditional, when the type inferred for `"b"` is unified with *Bool*. As a consequence, it mentions the entire conditional and complains that the type of the condition is *String* instead of *Bool*. Algorithm $\mathcal{M}$, on the other hand, pushes down the expected type *Bool* to the literal `"b"`, which leads to a similar error report, but now only the literal `"b"` will be mentioned. The former gives more context information, and is thus easier to understand for novice programmers. For this reason we prefer not to blame folklore constraints for an inconsistency.

Avoid Application Constraints Heuristic. This heuristic is surprising in the sense that we only found out that we needed it after using our compiler, and discovering that some programs gave counterintuitive error messages. Consider the following fragment

if *plus* 1 2 **then** ... **else** ...

in which *plus* has type *Int* $\rightarrow$ *Int* $\rightarrow$ *Int*.

The application heuristic (a program correcting heuristic discussed in Section 3.3) finds that the arguments to *plus* indeed fit the type of the function. However, the result of the application does not match the expected *Bool* for the condition. In this situation, algorithm $\mathcal{W}$ would put the blame on the condition, while $\mathcal{M}$ would blame the use of *plus*. Because our constraints are very fine-grained and introduce some intermediary constraints, there is (unfortunately) another possibility: the application itself is blamed. However, given that the arguments do fit, it is quite unlikely that the application as a whole is at fault, and such an error message becomes unnatural. The task of this heuristic is to remove these constraints from the candidate set.

Unifier Vertex Heuristic. At this point, the reader may have the impression that heuristics always put the blame on a single location. If we have only two locations that contradict, however, then preferring one over another introduces a bias. Our last heuristic illustrates that we can also design heuristics to restore balance and symmetry in error messages, by reporting multiple program locations with contradicting types. This technique is comparable to the approach suggested by Yang [15].

The design of our type rules (Chapter 6 of [2]) accommodates such a heuristic: at several locations, a fresh type variable is introduced to unify two or more types, e.g., the types of the elements in a list. We call such a type variable a *unifier*. In our heuristic, we use unifiers in the following way: we remove the edges from and to a unifier type variable. Then, we try to determine the types of the program fragments that were equated via this unifier. With these types we create a specialized error message. In the following example, the type of the context is also a determining factor.

All the elements of a list should be of the same type, which is not the case in f's definition.

$$f \ x \ y = [x, y, id, "\backslash\mathtt{n}"]$$

In the absence of a type signature for f, we choose to ignore the elements x and y in the error message, because their types are unconstrained. We report that id, which has a function type, cannot appear in the same list as the string $"\backslash\mathtt{n}"$. By considering how f is applied in the program, we could obtain information about the types of x and y. In our system, however, we never let the type of a function depend on the way it is used. An example from the collection of logged programs is the following.

$$simplify :: Prop \rightarrow Prop$$
$$simplify = (...)$$
$$simplifyAnd :: [Prop] \rightarrow [Prop]$$
$$simplifyAnd \ (p : ps) = [simplify \ p, simplifyAnd \ ps]$$

yields the error message

```
(5,22): Type error in list (elements have different types)
    expression  : [simplify p, simplifyAnd ps]
    1st element : simplify p
       type     : Prop
    2nd element : simplifyAnd ps
       type     : [Prop]
```

which simply lists all the participating uses and the types inferred for these uses, and leaves putting the blame in the hands of the programmer.

Without the unifier heuristic, Helium returns the following message

```
(5,22): Type error in element of list
   expression        : [simplify p, simplifyAnd ps]
   term              : simplifyAnd ps
     type            : [Prop]
   does not match : Prop
```

which puts the blame squarely on the second element in the list.

3.3 Program Correcting Heuristics

A different direction in error reporting is trying to discover what a user was trying to express, and how the program could be corrected accordingly. Given a number of possible edit actions, we can start searching for the closest well-typed program. An advantage of this approach is that we can report locations with more confidence. Additionally, we can equip our error messages with hints how the program might be corrected. However, this approach has a disadvantage too: suggesting program fixes is potentially harmful since there is no guarantee that the proposed correction is the semantically intended one (although we can guarantee that the correction will result in a well-typed program). Furthermore, it is not immediately clear when to stop searching for a correction, nor how we could present a complicated correction to a programmer.

An approach to automatically correcting ill-typed programs is that of type isomorphisms [10]. Two types are considered isomorphic if they are equivalent under (un)currying and permutation of arguments. Such an isomorphism is witnessed by two morphisms: expressions that transform a function of one type to a function of the other type, in both directions. For each ill-typed application, one may search for an isomorphism between the type of the function and the type expected by the arguments and the context of that function. The heuristics described in this section elaborate on this idea.

the application, the permutation and the sibling heuristics take into account that class predicates that need to be satisfied due to program corrections can indeed be resolved [3]. These heuristics can therefore be said to work correctly in the presence of overloading.

The Application Heuristic. Function applications are often involved in type inconsistencies. Hence, we introduce a special heuristic to improve error messages involving applications. It is advantageous to have *all* the arguments of a function available when analyzing such a type inconsistency. Although mapping n-ary applications to a number of binary ones simplifies type inference, it does not correspond to the way most programmers view their programs.

The heuristic behaves as follows. First, we try to determine the type of the function. We can do this by inspecting the type graph after having removed the constraint created for the application. In some cases, we can determine the maximum number of arguments that a function can consume. However, if the function is polymorphic in its result, then it can receive infinitely many arguments (since a type variable can always be instantiated to a function type). For instance, every constant has zero arguments, the function $map :: (a \to b) \to [a] \to [b]$ has two, and the function $foldr :: (a \to b \to b) \to b \to [a] \to b$ a possibly infinite number.

If the number of arguments passed to a function exceeds the maximum, then we can report that too many arguments are given – without considering the types of the arguments. In the special case that the maximum number of arguments is zero, we report that *it is not a function*.

To conclude the opposite, namely that not enough arguments have been supplied, we do not only need the type of the function, but also the type that the context of the application is expecting. An example follows.

The following definition is ill-typed: *map* should be given more arguments (or *xs* should be removed from the left-hand side).

$$doubleList :: [Int] \rightarrow [Int]$$
$$doubleList\ xs = map\ (*2)$$

At most two arguments can be given to *map*: only one is supplied. The type signature for *doubleList* provides an expected type for the result of the application, which is $[Int]$. Note that the first $[Int]$ from the type signature belongs to the left-hand side pattern *xs*. We may report that not enough arguments are supplied to *map*, but we can do even better. If we are able to determine the types inferred for the arguments (this is not always the case), then we can determine at which position we have to insert an argument, or which argument should be removed. We achieve this by unification with *holes*. First, we have to establish the type of *map*'s only argument: $(*2)$ has type $Int \rightarrow Int$. Because we are one argument short, we insert one hole (•) to indicate a forgotten argument. (Similarly, for each superfluous argument, we would insert one hole in the function type.) This gives us the two configurations depicted in Figure 1.

Configuration 1 does not work out, since column-wise unification fails. The second configuration, on the other hand, gives us the substitution $S = [a := Int, b := Int]$. This informs us that our function (*map*) requires a second argument, and that this argument should be of type $S([a]) = [Int]$.

The final technique we discuss attempts to blame one argument of a function application in particular, because there is reason to believe that the other arguments are all right. If such an argument exists, then we put extra emphasis on this argument in the reported error message.

$$evaluate :: Prop \rightarrow [String] \rightarrow Bool$$
$$evaluate\ (And\ [p:q])\ xs = all\ [p\ |\ p \leftarrow xs]$$

```
(2,27): Type error in application
   expression        : all [p | p ← xs]
   term              : all
     type            : (a → Bool) → [a] → Bool
     does not match  : [String] → Bool
   probable fix      : insert a first argument
```

The Tuple Heuristic. Many of the considerations for the application heuristic also apply to tuples. As a result, this heuristic can suggest that elements of a tuple should be permuted, or that some component(s) should be inserted or removed.

configuration 1 :

	function	$(a \to b)$	$\to$	$[a]$	$\to$	$[b]$
	arguments + context	$\bullet$	$\to$	$(Int \to Int)$	$\to$	$[Int]$

configuration 2 :

	function	$(a \to b)$	$\to$	$[a]$	$\to$	$[b]$
	arguments + context	$(Int \to Int)$	$\to$	$\bullet$	$\to$	$[Int]$

Fig. 1. Two configurations for column-wise unification

The Permutation Heuristic. A mistake that is often made is the simple exchange of one or more arguments to a function. The permutation heuristic considers applications which are type incorrect, and tries to determine whether there is a *single* permutation that makes the application correct. For this to work, we need the type of the application expected by the context, and the types of the arguments (if any of these cannot be typed, then it makes no sense to apply this heuristic). By local changes to the type graph, the compiler then determines how many permutations result in a correctly typed application. If there is only one, then a fix to the program is suggested (in addition to the usual error message). If there are more, then we deem it impossible to suggest a probable fix, and no additional hint is given.

$$zero :: (Float \to Float) \to Float \to Float$$
$$zero\ f\ y0 = until\ (\lambda b \to b -. f\ b\ /.\ diff\ f\ b)$$
$$(\lambda b \to f\ b <. 0.000001)\ y0$$

with the following error message as a result

```
(2,13): Type error in application
  expression      : until (λb → b −. f b /. ...) (λb → ...) y0
  term            : until
    type          : (a → Bool) → (a → a) → a → a
  does not match  : (Float → Float) → (Float → Bool) → Float → Float
  probable fix    : re-order arguments
```

The Sibling Function Heuristic. Novice students often have problems distinguishing between specific functions, e.g., concatenate two lists (++) and insert an item at the front of a list (:). We call such functions *siblings*. If we encounter an error in an application in which the function that is applied has a sibling, then we can try to replace it by its sibling to see if this solves the problem (naturally only at the type level). This can be done quite easily and efficiently on type graphs by a local modification of the type graph. The main benefit is that the error message may include a hint suggesting to replace the function with its sibling. (Helium allows programmers to add new pairs of siblings, which the compiler then takes into account [5].)

$$smash :: [a] \to [a]$$
$$smash\ [] = []$$
$$smash\ [a] = head\ [a] ++ smash\ (tail\ [a])$$

with the following error message as a result

```
(3,22): Type error in variable
   expression    : ++
      type       : [a] → [a] → [a]
      expected type : b → [b] → [b]
   because       : unification would give infinite type
   probable fix  : use : instead
```

The Sibling Literal Heuristic. A similar kind of confusion that students have is that they mix floating points numbers with integers (in Helium we distinguish the two), and characters with strings. This gives rise to a heuristic that may replace a string literal `"c"` with a character literal `'c'` if that resolves the inconsistency.

$$writeRow :: [[String]] \rightarrow Int \rightarrow String$$
$$writeRow\ tab\ n = \textbf{if}\ n == (length\ tab + 3)\ \textbf{then}\ ""$$
$$\textbf{else}\ replicate\ (columnWidth\ tab\ n)\ "\ " ++ "\ " ++ ....$$

results in

```
(3,61): Type error in literal
   expression    : " "
      type       : String
      expected type : Char
   probable fix  : use a char literal instead
```

4   Type Graphs

The heuristics of the previous section share the characteristic that they have all been implemented in Helium as functions that work on type graphs. Essentially, a type graph represents a set of constraints, and as such is similar to a substitution. The main difference is that type graphs can also represent inconsistent sets of constraints. In this section, we first describe what type graphs are, and then describe for a few of the previously described heuristics how they can be handled in terms of operations on type graphs. Due to lack of space we only try to convey the essential ideas, intuitions, and features of type graphs and how they may be used. For a complete description we refer the reader to Chapter 7 of the PhD thesis of the second author [2].

Our type graphs resemble the path graphs that were proposed by Port [11], and which can be used to find the cause of non-unifiability for a set of equations. However, we follow a more effective approach in dealing with derived equalities (i.e., equalities obtained by decomposing terms, and by taking the transitive closure).

McAdam has also used graphs to represent type information [9]. In his case, parts of the graph are duplicated to handle let-constructs, which implies a lot of duplication of effort, and, worse, it can give rise to duplication of errors if the duplicated parts themselves are inconsistent. We avoid this complication by first handling the definitions of a let (which gives us the complete types of those definitions), before continuing with the let body. This implies that in case of a mismatch between the definition and the use of an identifier, the blame is always on the latter.

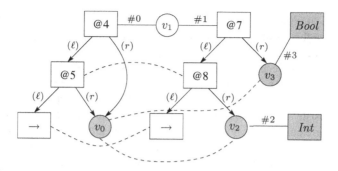

Fig. 2. An inconsistent type graph

We consider a set of equality constraints as a running example and show how type graphs may be used to determine which constraints should be removed to make the set of constraints consistent. The resulting constraint set can then be converted into a substitution (the usual outcome of the type inference process). As explained in Section 2, we may assume that we deal with equality constraints exclusively: polymorphism is handled at a different level.

Consider the following set of equality constraints.

$$\{v_1 \overset{\#0}{\equiv} v_0 \rightarrow v_0,\ v_1 \overset{\#1}{\equiv} v_2 \rightarrow v_3,\ v_2 \overset{\#2}{\equiv} Int,\ v_3 \overset{\#3}{\equiv} Bool\}$$

Annotations like $\#0$ are used for reference purpose only. For each left and right hand side of a constraint we construct a term graph, which reflects the hierarchical structure of type terms. These term graphs consist of vertices and directed edges, as shown on the left and right hand side of Figure 2. Recall that the type $v_0 \rightarrow v_0$ is represented by a binary type application $((\rightarrow)\ v_0)\ v_0$, and it is this type that is used in type graph construction. For readability, we continue to use $v_0 \rightarrow v_0$ in the text.

The equality constraints between terms introduce undirected edges in the type graph. Thus each constraint results in a single undirected edge (with its number as a label), called an initial edge. When we equate two structured types, we implicitly equate the subtypes of these types. In the example, v_0 and v_2 become equated, because through v_1, $v_0 \rightarrow v_0$ and $v_2 \rightarrow v_3$ become equated. This gives rise to the derived edges, occurring as dashed edges in Figure 2. The connected components that arise when considering all vertices that are connected via an initial or derived edge, are called equivalence groups. Clearly, each vertex in an equivalence groups should represent the same type. This is not the case in Figure 2, because *Int* and *Bool* end up in the same equivalence group. The paths between such clashing constants are called error paths, which may contain both initial and derived edges. When we encounter such an error path, we unfold the derived edges until we end up with a path that consists solely of initial edges (remember that these relate directly to the constraints from which the type graph was built).

The example type graph has only a single error path, but can in principle contain many. The task of the type graph solver is to dissolve all error paths and it may do so by selecting a constraint from each error path. This is exactly where the heuristics discussed earlier in this paper come in: they operationalize what are the best places to cut. After a set of constraints is selected, the removal of which dissolves all error paths, then we can use the resulting type graph to construct a substitution as the end result of the solving process.

In the example, there are a number of possibilities to dissolve the error path. This is generally the case, and this is where the heuristics play a role in selecting the most likely candidate for removal. We can choose to remove any of the four constraints to make the type graph consistent, each choice leading to a substitution obtained from the remaining type graph. For example, if we remove #0, then the resulting substitution maps v_1 to $Int \rightarrow Bool$, v_2 to Int, and v_3 to $Bool$. If we choose to remove #3 instead, then the substitution maps v_0, v_2 and v_3 to Int, and v_1 to $Int \rightarrow Int$. In our implementation, the constraint is provided with enough information to be able to generate a precise error message that tells the user why it was removed, in terms of types computed from the remainder of the type graph. For example, in the latter case it will contrast the type it expected for v_3, which is Int, with the type it found for v_3, which is $Bool$.

Thus far, we have explained rather informally how type graphs are built and handled, but in practice there are a number of complications: The number of vertices in a type graph grows quickly, as does the number of derived edges. The number of error paths in any given type graph can be very large, even when one disregards error paths that may be considered superfluous. Furthermore, how can one effectively deal with infinite types, which occur as a result of constraints such as $v_1 \equiv v_1 \rightarrow Int$? How does one deal with type synonyms, that introduce new type constants as abbreviations for existing types? Detailed descriptions of solutions to these complications can be found in [2].

The Implementation of Heuristics

The type graph data structure is well-suited for implementing the heuristics we have defined. Because it is important for many heuristics to know what kind of constraint we are dealing with, this information is included explicitly during the constraint generation process. For example, this is how the heuristics can tell that a certain constraint is a so-called folklore constraint. Implementing the avoid folklore constraints heuristic is then simply a matter of removing these constraints from the current candidate set.

A slightly more complicated example is the implementation of the siblings heuristic. When applied to a given edge e, it first decides whether that edge directly relates to the type of some identifier, say id. Then it considers whether siblings were defined for id. If so, then it tries to discover whether replacing id with any of its siblings resolves the type error. This is accomplished by removing the edge e, computing the type id is supposed to have based on the context in which it was used, and determining whether any of the candidates fit this context. If so, then a hint is given that suggests to use any of the matching candidates (there may be more than one). Care must be taken to verify that the possible class predicates generated by the context, and by the use of the candidate are satisfied.

The application heuristic works in a similar fashion: we remove and add a few edges in the type graph and consider whether that removes the error paths we are currently considering. Indeed, the idea of adding and removing edges is central to many of the heuristics.

5 Putting It All Together

The Helium compiler includes all the heuristics we have discussed (and more), and has been used for a number of years to teach students to program in Haskell. Reactions in the first year were very promising (some of these students had used Hugs before and indicated that the quality of error messages was much improved). Since then we have improved the compiler in many ways, adding new language features and new heuristics. Unfortunately, the students who currently do the course have never encountered any other system for programming in Haskell and thus cannot compare their experiences.

Another issue we would like to address here is that of efficiency of the compiler. We have constructed a special kind of solver that partitions the program into a number of relatively independent chunks (in a first approximation, every top level definition is a chunk), applies a fast greedy solver to each, and only when it finds a type error in one of the chunks, does it apply the slower but more sophisticated type graph solver to this erroneous chunk (but *not* to the foregoing chunks). This means that the type graph solver is only used when a type error is encountered, and only on a small part of the program. Additionally, there is a maximum to the number of error paths that the type graph solver will consider in a single compile. Still, constructing and inspecting a type graph involves additional overhead, which slows down the inference process. In a practical setting (teaching Haskell to students), we have experienced that the extra time spent on type inference does not hinder programming productivity.

To give the reader some idea how the ideas of the previous section take form in an actual compiler, we have included the function *listOfHeuristics* in Figure 3. It takes a (partially user specified) list of siblings to generate the list of available heuristics for this compilation.

Each heuristic can be categorized as either a filtering heuristic or a selector heuristic. The heuristic *avoidTrustedConstraints* is an example of the former: it filters out all the constraints from the candidate set that have a high trust value, thus making sure that these are never reported. Note that *avoidForbiddenConstraints* avoids constraints of the sort described under (1) of the trust factor heuristic, only (3) and (4) are part of *avoidTrustedConstraints* (case (2) is already taken care of by our choice that the use of an identifier can never influence its type). It is easy to make the distinction between selectors and filters in *listOfHeuristics*: all the heuristics that are part of the *Voting* construct in the middle are selectors, the others are filters.

A voting heuristic is built out of a number of subsidiary heuristics, each of which looks to see whether it can suggest a constraint likely to be responsible for the type inconsistency. Each voting heuristic also returns a value that gives a measure of trust the heuristic has in its suggestion. Based on these measures the combined voting heuristic will decide which constraint to select, if any.

Most of the heuristics in Figure 3 are connected directly with heuristics discussed in the paper. There are a few special cases, however: *variableFunction* has largely the same functionality as the *applicationHeuristic*, but the latter is only triggered on applications (a function followed by at least one argument). Instead, *variableFunction* is triggered on identifiers that have a function type, but that do not have arguments at all. It may for instance suggest to insert certain arguments to make the program type

$listOfHeuristics\ siblings\ path =$
  $earlyFilters \mathbin{+\!\!+} [Heuristic\ (Voting\ selectors)] \mathbin{+\!\!+} tiebreakers$
    where
      $earlyFilters = [\,avoidForbiddenConstraints, highParticipation\ 0.95\ path\,]$
      $selectors \quad = [\,siblingFunctions\ siblings, similarNegation$
                   $, applicationHeuristic, fbHasTooManyArguments$
                   $, siblingLiterals, variableFunction, tupleHeuristic\,]$
      $tiebreakers = [\,avoidApplicationConstraints, avoidNegationConstraints$
                   $, avoidTrustedConstraints, avoidFolkloreConstraints$
                   $, firstComeFirstBlamed\,]$

Fig. 3. The list of heuristics taken from the Helium compiler

correct. Another thing to remark is that the permutation of arguments in applications is implemented as part of the *applicationHeuristic* as well.

The heuristic *similarNegation* provides the same functionality as *siblingFunctions*, but specifically for the negation function, which is a syntactic construct in Haskell and must be treated somewhat differently. The heuristic *fbHasTooManyArguments* (fb is short for function binding) tries to discover whether the type inconsistency can be explained by a discrepancy between the number of formal arguments, and the expected number of arguments derived from the function's explicit type signature.

The heuristics in the final block, starting with *avoidApplicationConstraints* are low priority heuristics that are used as tie-breakers. Note that *avoidNegationConstraints* provides the same functionality as *avoidApplicationConstraints*, but specifically for negation.

The function that applies the list of heuristics starts with a set of constraints that lie on an error path. It considers the heuristics in *listOfHeuristics* in sequence. A filtering heuristic may remove any number of candidates from the set, but never all. If a constraint is selected by a selector heuristic, all other constraints will be removed from the set of candidates leaving only the selected constraint.

6   Validation and Statistics

The existence of an actual implementation of our work immediately raises another issue: it should be possible to establish whether the implemented heuristics are effective by means of this implementation. However, the "quality" of a type error message is not likely to get a precise definition any time soon, which means that the usability of Helium can only be verified empirically. To perform such experiments is a difficult problem in itself and beyond the scope of this paper.

The best way to judge the quality of the improved error messages of Helium is, simply, by using it. Still, to give the reader an idea of how often heuristics are applied, we indicate for each kind of heuristics how often it was responsible for choosing or contributing to finding what Helium considered to be the erroneous constraint. We present a number of statistics computed from programs collected by logging Helium compilations in a first year programming course. Each logging corresponds to a unique compile

heuristic	type	contributing	deciding
Avoid forbidden constraints	filter	3756	22
Participation ratio (ratio=0.95)	filter	3791	202
Function siblings	selector	479	433
Similar negation	selector	0	0
Literal siblings	selector	196	145
Application heuristic	selector	2229	1891
Variable function	selector	123	111
Tuple heuristic	selector	5	5
Function binding has too many arguments	selector	35	35
Avoid application constraints	filter	726	15
Avoid negation constraints	filter	0	0
Avoid trusted constraints	filter	2371	1146
Avoid folklore constraints	filter	1298	922
First come, first blamed	filter	963	963

Fig. 4. The frequency of heuristics for the loggings of 2004/2005

performed by a student in the student network. We use the data sets collected for the course year 2004-2005, with a total of $11,256$ loggings of which $3,448$ resulted in one or more type errors. In total, the type incorrect programs produced $5,890$ type error messages.

Figure 4 shows how often each heuristic contributed to eliminating candidate constraints, and in how many cases it was also decisive in bringing the number of candidates down to one. In other words, it was responsible for selecting the constraint to be removed and as such strongly influences the error message reported to the programmer. Note that the contributing count includes the deciding count. One thing that can be noted from the results is that the tuple heuristic and the special heuristics for negation are hardly used. The reason for this is that the programming assignments in 2004/2005 did not call for heavy use of tuples and negation.

Note that the heuristics below are applied in the given order, starting with *Avoid forbidden constraints*. Note that a filter heuristic such as this contributes often, but only rarely is the deciding factor. This should not be surprising, because it can only be decisive if all but one of the candidate constraints is forbidden, and this is not very likely. In many programs there are cases of forbidden constraints, such as the one that says that the body of the let and the let-expression as a whole have the same type. In the case of the selector heuristics, the number of contributing and deciding occurrences should be quite close, because typically they select a single candidate to remain.

Figure 5 focuses on the type of probable fixes given to the programmer. Of the 5,890 error messages, a total of 1,116 actually gave such a probable fix (in addition to the standard error message). Note that for example the application heuristic in Figure 4 may result in a variety of probable fixes: re-order arguments, insert missing argument, and so on. On the other hand, some of the fixes suggested by the variable function heuristic are the same as those of the application heuristic. As explained before, the variable function heuristic is conceptually the same as the application heuristic. For reasons of brevity, we have kept the table compact, lumping a number of similar probable fixes of

probable fix	generated by	frequency
insert a first/second/... argument	application/variable function	142
insert one/two/three/... argument(s)	application/variable function	107
remove a first/second/... argument	application	139
swap the two arguments	application	57
re-order arguments	application	56
re-order elements of tuple	tuple	3
use a char/int/float/string literal instead	sibling literals	154
use ++ instead	sibling functions	100
use : instead instead	sibling functions	142
use concatMap instead	sibling functions	62
use eqString instead	sibling functions	45
other sibling fixes	sibling functions	109

Fig. 5. Probable fix frequency for the loggings of 2004/2005

lesser frequency together. For example "insert a first and second argument" falls into the category of "insert a first/second/... argument". We do make the distinction between "insert a first argument" and "insert one argument". In the former case, the compiler was able to conclude unambiguously that the first argument was missing.

7   Related Work

There is quite a large body of work on improving type error messages for polymorphic, higher-order functional programming languages such as Haskell, cf. [14,11,9,10,15]. The drawback of these papers is that they have not led to full scale implementations and in many cases disregard issues such as efficiency and scalability. Since we refer to the articles who have influenced our choice of heuristic where we discuss the heuristic, we shall consider only some of the more current approaches in the remainder of this section. For a very detailed description of the literature in this area, see Chapter 3 of the PhD thesis of the second author [2].

In recent years, there is a trend towards implementation. One of these systems is Chameleon [12] which is an interactive system for type-debugging Haskell. The view-point here is that no static type inference process will come up with a good message in every possible situation. For this reason, they prefer to support an interactive dialogue to find the source of the error. A disadvantage of such a system is that is not very easy to use by novice programmers, and more time consuming as well. An advantage is that the process itself may give the programmer insight into the process of type inferencing, helping him to avoid repeating the mistake. In a later paper, the authors move in the di-rection of type error reporting [13], using the same algorithm to compute the locations contributing to the error. As far as we know, Chameleon has not been used on groups of (non-expert) programmers.

Ideally, a compiler provides a combination of feedback and interaction: if the pro-vided heuristics are reasonably sure that they have located the source of error, then a type error message may suffice, otherwise an interactive session can be used to examine the situation in detail. Our unifier heuristic occupies a middle point: it makes no judgment on who is to blame, but only describes which types clash and where they arise from. It only applies if there is no overwhelming amount of evidence against one of the candidates for removal (for a particular choice of "overwhelming").

Finally, our focus on expert knowledge was inspired by work of Jun, Michaelson, and Trinder [16]. Their idea of interviewing experts has appeal, but a drawback of their work is that the resulting algorithm $\mathcal{H}$ is very incomplete (only 10 out of 40 rules are given), and we have not been able to find an implementation.

8   Conclusion

We have discussed heuristics for the discovery of and the recovery from type errors in Haskell. Knowledge of our problem domain allows us to define special purpose heuristics that can suggest how to change parts of the source program so that they become type correct. Although there is no guarantee that the hints always reflect what the programmer intended, we do think that they help in many cases. Moreover, we have shown that it is possible to integrate various heuristics known from the literature with our own resulting in a full scale, practical system that can be easily extended with new heuristics as the need arises. We have applied our compiler to a large body of programs that have been compiled by students during a first year functional programming course, resulting in information about the frequency of hints and particular heuristics. Many of the examples in the paper are taken from this body of programs, lending additional strength to our work.

References

1. Hage, J., Heeren, B.: Ordering type constraints: A structured approach. Technical Report UU-CS-2005-016, Department of Information and Computing Science, Utrecht University, Netherlands, Technical Report (April 2005)
2. Heeren, B.: Top Quality Type Error Messages. PhD thesis, Universiteit Utrecht, The Netherlands, http://www.cs.uu.nl/people/bastiaan/phdthesis (2005)
3. Heeren, B., Hage, J.: A first attempt at type class directives. Technical Report UU-CS-2002-031, Department of Information and Computing Science, University Utrecht, Netherlands, Technical Report (September 2004)
4. Heeren, B., Hage, J.: Type class directives. In: Seventh International Symposium on Practical Aspects of Declarative Languages, pp. 253–267. Springer, Heidelberg (2005)
5. Heeren, B., Hage, J., Swierstra, S.D.: Scripting the type inference process. In: Eighth ACM Sigplan International Conference on Functional Programming, pp. 3–13. ACM Press, New York (2003)
6. Heeren, B., Leijen, D., van IJzendoorn, A.: Helium, for learning Haskell. In: ACM Sigplan 2003 Haskell Workshop, pp. 62–71. ACM Press, New York (2003)
7. Langebaerd, A.: Repair systems, automatic correction of type errors in functional programs. http://www.cs.uu.nl/wiki/Top/Publications
8. Lee, O., Yi, K.: Proofs about a folklore let-polymorphic type inference algorithm. ACM Transanctions on Programming Languages and Systems 20(4), 707–723 (July 1998)

 9. McAdam, B.J.: Generalising techniques for type debugging. In: Trinder, P.,Michaelson, G., Loidl, H-W. (eds.), Trends in Functional Programming, Bristol, UK, Intellect, vol. 1, pp. 50–59 (2000)
10. McAdam, B.J.: How to repair type errors automatically. Trends in Functional Programming 3, 87–98 (2002)
11. Port, G.S.: A simple approach to finding the cause of non-unifiability. In: Kowalski, R.A., Bowen, K.A. (eds.) Proceedings of the Fifth International Conference and Symposium on Logic Programming, pp. 651–665. The MIT Press, Cambridge (1988)
12. Stuckey, P.J., Sulzmann, M., Wazny, J.: Interactive type debugging in Haskell. In: Haskell'03: Proceedings of the ACM SIGPLAN Workshop on Haskell, pp. 72–83. ACM Press, New York (2003)
13. Stuckey, P.J., Sulzmann, M., Wazny, J.: Improving type error diagnosis. In: Haskell'04: Proceedings of the ACM SIGPLAN Workshop on Haskell, pp. 80–91. ACM Press, New York (2004)
14. Walz, J.A., Johnson, G.F.: A maximum flow approach to anomaly isolation in unification-based incremental type inference. In: Conference Record of the 13th Annual ACM Symposium on Principles of Programming Languages, pp. 44–57, St. Petersburg, FL (January 1986)
15. Yang, J.: Explaining type errors by finding the sources of type conflicts. In: Greg Michaelson, Phil Trindler, and Hans-Wolfgang Loidl, editors, Trends in Functional Programming, pp. 58–66. Intellect Books (2000)
16. Yang, J., Michaelson, G., Trinder, P.: Explaining polymorphic types. The. Computer Journal 45(4), 436–452 (2002)

Testing Properties of Generic Functions

Patrik Jansson[1], Johan Jeuring[2], Laurence Cabenda, Gerbo Engels[3],
Jacob Kleerekoper[3], Sander Mak[3], Michiel Overeem[3], and Kees Visser[3]

[1] CSE, Chalmers University of Technology, Sweden
patrikj@chalmers.se
[2] ICS, Utrecht University, the Netherlands
johanj@cs.uu.nl
[3] Students of the Utrecht University Generic Programming class

Abstract. A datatype-generic function is a family of functions indexed by (the structure of) a type. Examples include equality tests, maps and pretty printers. Property based testing tools like QuickCheck and Gast support the definition of properties and test-data generators, and they check if a monomorphic property is satisfied by the test cases. Generic functions satisfy generic properties and this paper discusses specifying and testing such properties. It shows how generic properties and generators can be expressed, and explains three bugs we found and corrected in the Generic Haskell library.

1 Introduction

Software testing aims to find faults in software by comparing its behaviour with a specification. Testing comes in many flavours: validation testing, integration testing, system testing, unit testing, etc. We focus on property-based unit testing for datatype-generic functional programs.

In property-based testing, a specification is expressed in terms of executable properties. Together with a function a programmer writes one or more properties that should be satisfied by the function. Such properties can be used both as documentation (executable specifications) and as part of a test suite for regression testing. For example, consider the following excerpt from a Haskell module for manipulating bits.

```
data Bit = O | I deriving (Show, Eq)
bits2int    :: [Bit] → Int
bits2int bs  = bits2int' bs (length bs − 1)
    where bits2int' []       n = 0
          bits2int' (x : xs) n = bits2int' xs (n − 1) + bit2int x * 2 ^ n
int2bits   :: Int → [Bit]
int2bits n = if n ⩾ 0  then int2bits' n [] else []
    where int2bits' 0 bs = bs
          int2bits' n bs = int2bits' (n ‘div‘ 2) (int2bit (n ‘mod‘ 2) : bs)
bit2int b  = if b == O then 0 else 1
int2bit n  = if n == 0 then O else I
```

Z. Horváth, V. Zsók, and A. Butterfield (Eds.): IFL 2006, LNCS 4449, pp. 217–234, 2007.

Functions *bits2int* and *int2bits* convert a list of bits to an integer and *vice versa*. To see if these functions are inverses we could check the following properties:

$$prop\_int2bits\_bits2int \quad :: [\mathsf{Bit}] \to \mathsf{Bool}$$
$$prop\_int2bits\_bits2int \ bs = (int2bits \,.\, bits2int) \ bs \mathrel{==} bs$$

$$prop\_bits2int\_int2bits \quad :: \mathsf{Int} \to \mathsf{Bool}$$
$$prop\_bits2int\_int2bits \ n \ = (bits2int \,.\, int2bits) \ n \mathrel{==} n$$

Checking with a property checker immediately reveals that they don't hold. A counterexample to the first property is $[\,O, I, I\,]$ (leading zeroes should be ignored in the first property), and to the second property is -3 (negative numbers are not properly encoded). Mistakes like these are common in specifications and programs, and ideas like Design-by-Contract [13] and Test-Driven Development [1] are now widely used in software development. For monomorphic programs and properties this is well understood, but for datatype-generic programs the testing area is largely unexplored.

A datatype-generic function is a family of functions indexed by a type. Examples of generic functions are equality, map, and pretty printers. A generic function can be seen as a template algorithm that can be instantiated with (the structure of) a data type. Similarly, a generic property can be seen as a template property that can be instantiated with a data type to obtain a simple property. A generic library is a highly reusable software component, and by stating and verifying properties for such a library, the effort spent on verification pays off over and over again.

QuickCheck [2] is one of the most advanced tools for testing properties of functional programs. It supports the definition of properties and random test-data generators in Haskell, and checks that a monomorphic property passes the test cases. Gast [8] is a tool similar to QuickCheck, but for property-based testing in Clean [15]. Gast comes with *generic* test-data generators which work for arbitrary data types. But Gast enumerates data which leads to bad coverage for infinite datatypes (we expand on this later).

This paper

- discusses specifying and testing properties of generic functions,
- shows how parts of the Generic Haskell [4] library can be specified and tested using QuickCheck (revealing three bugs), and
- defines generic QuickCheck generators using Generic Haskell. This means we get the best of both worlds — we combine the strengths of QuickCheck with generic support inspired by Gast.

The paper is organised as follows. Section 2 briefly introduces and compares a few property-based testing tools. Section 3 introduces generic programming in Generic Haskell. Section 4 shows how QuickCheck is used to check properties of generic functions. Section 5 discusses verification of the Generic Haskell library and explains the bugs found. Section 6 presents different ways of generating test cases for arbitrary data types. Section 7 concludes and discusses future work.

2   Property-Based Testing Tools

This section introduces the testing tools QuickCheck, Gast and SmallCheck.

QuickCheck
QuickCheck is an automatic testing tool for Haskell programs. The programmer
provides a specification of the program, in the form of executable properties that
functions should satisfy, and QuickCheck then tests that the properties hold
in a large number of randomly generated cases. Specifications are expressed
in Haskell, using combinators defined in the QuickCheck library. The library
provides combinators to define properties, observe the distribution of test data,
and define test-case generators.

Many properties are simple Boolean functions, implicitly universally quantified over all arguments:

$prop\_PlusAssoc$ :: Float $\rightarrow$ Float $\rightarrow$ Float $\rightarrow$ Bool
$prop\_PlusAssoc$ x y $z = (x + y) + z$ == $x + (y + z)$

To test a property it is passed to the function *test*:

```
Main> test prop_PlusAssoc
Falsifiable, after 8 tests:
-4.6
-4.0
3.6
```

Here QuickCheck finds a simple counterexample illustrating that finite precision
Floats don't behave like ideal real numbers.

The QuickCheck library also provides conditional properties, where tests not
satisfying the precondition are discarded:

$prop\_SmallPrime$ :: Integer $\rightarrow$ Property
$prop\_SmallPrime$ $x = prime$ $x \Longrightarrow x < 88$

```
Main> test prop_SmallPrime
OK, passed 100 successful tests.
```

Here QuickCheck has generated a few hundred test cases (randomly chosen numbers x) out of which 100 were prime and all of those were unfortunately <88. In
this case the brute force solution of asking QuickCheck to generate even more
test cases works, but in general the coverage for the default generators is bad for
"sparse" properties. Fortunately, it is also possible to define custom generators
— here is an example using the infinite list of *primes*:

$primeNumbers$ :: Gen Integer
$primeNumbers = \mathbf{do}$ $n \leftarrow arbitrary$
                       $return$ $(primes$!! abs $n)$

$prop\_SmallPrime2$ :: Property
$prop\_SmallPrime2 = forAll$ $primeNumbers$ $(\lambda x \rightarrow x < 88)$

```
Falsifiable, after 39 successful tests:
97
```

QuickCheck also supports a simple but powerful way of searching for small counter examples. When a test case fails, QuickCheck tries to shrink the test case until a "local minimum" is found. As an example, for the first property of the bits example in the introduction we get the following result:

```
Main> test prop_int2bits_bits2int
Falsifiable, after 2 successful tests
(shrunk failing case 3 times):
[0]
```

Gast

Gast (Generic Automated Software Testing) [8] is a property-based testing tool which can be seen as a QuickCheck for Clean. Gast is implemented in the non-strict functional language Clean [15], a close relative to Haskell. From the users perspective, Gast is very similar to QuickCheck — properties can be defined as normal Boolean functions and tests can be run by calling the function *test*:

$$listsAreShort \quad :: [\mathsf{Int}] \rightarrow \mathsf{Bool}$$
$$listsAreShort\ xs = length\ xs < 5$$
$$Start = test\ listsAreShort$$

which in this case results in the answer

```
Passed after 500 tests.
```

This example is chosen to show that some care needs to be taken in interpreting the results from testing: Gast enumerates data in a breadth-first manner, only randomising the order "within each level". For recursive data types this is problematic, because of the exponential growth of the search space — as we can see, the first 500 test cases do not contain a single list with more than four elements. QuickCheck generates lists up to length around 200 in the same situation.

The enumeration approach used by Gast does have a few advantages: it avoids generating the same test case more than once and it makes it possible to actually prove properties over finite domains within the same framework (using exhaustive testing). Gast does not need to shrink failing test cases because they are generated and tested in order of increasing size. The Clean implementation of Gast is fast, but for recursive data types the exponential search space means that reaching reasonably sized test cases just takes too long.

SmallCheck

While finishing this paper we learnt about Runcimans recent work on Small-Check — a combinator library for lightweight testing in Haskell closely based on QuickCheck. SmallCheck tests properties for all values up to some depth, progressively increasing the depth used. The SmallCheck library shares many of the strengths and weaknesses of Gast, but has no generic programming support. Both our generic generators and our methodology for testing generic properties would be useful in combination with SmallCheck, but that is left as future work.

3   Generic Programming in Generic Haskell

In this section we introduce type-indexed functions by means of an example and we explain how type-indexed functions become generic in Generic Haskell.

Type-Indexed Functions
A type-indexed function takes an explicit type argument, and can have behaviour that depends on this type argument. For example, suppose the unit type Unit, sum type :+:, and product type :*: are defined as follows:

data Unit $= U$
data a :+: b $= Inl$ a $\mid Inr$ b
data a :*: b $=$ a :*: b.

We use infix type constructors :+: and :*: and an infix value constructor :*: to ease the presentation. The type-indexed function eq checks equality of two values. We define the function eq on booleans, the unit type, sums, and products as follows in Generic Haskell:

$$
\begin{array}{llll}
eq\{\!|\mathsf{Bool}|\!\} & b_1 & b_2 & = eqBool\ b_1\ b_2 \\
eq\{\!|\mathsf{Unit}|\!\} & U & U & = True \\
eq\{\!|\alpha \text{ :+: } \beta|\!\} & (Inl\ x_1) & (Inl\ x_2) & = eq\{\!|\alpha|\!\}\ x_1\ x_2 \\
eq\{\!|\alpha \text{ :+: } \beta|\!\} & (Inr\ y_1) & (Inr\ y_2) & = eq\{\!|\beta|\!\}\ y_1\ y_2 \\
eq\{\!|\alpha \text{ :+: } \beta|\!\} & \_ & \_ & = False \\
eq\{\!|\alpha \text{ :*: } \beta|\!\} & (x_1 \text{ :*: } y_1) & (x_2 \text{ :*: } y_2) & = eq\{\!|\alpha|\!\}\ x_1\ x_2 \wedge eq\{\!|\beta|\!\}\ y_1\ y_2,
\end{array}
$$

where $eqBool$ is the standard equality function on Booleans. The eq type signature is $eq\{\!|\mathsf{a} :: *|\!\} :: (eq\{\!|\mathsf{a}|\!\}) \Rightarrow \mathsf{a} \to \mathsf{a} \to \mathsf{Bool}$. The context $(eq\{\!|\mathsf{a}|\!\}) \Rightarrow$ in this signature says that eq has a *dependency* [11] on eq. A type-indexed function f depends on another type-indexed function g if g is used on a type argument (a *dependency variable*) α in the definition of f. The occurrences of α and β in the definition of eq are dependency variables.

Generic Functions
A type-indexed function such as eq does not only work on the types that appear as type indices in its definition. To see why eq is in fact *generic* and works on arbitrary data types, we give a mapping from data types to structure types such as units, sums, and products. If there is no specific case for a type in the definition of a generic function, generic behaviour is derived automatically by the compiler by exploiting the structural representation.

For example, the definition of the function eq that is generically derived for lists is equivalent to the following specific definition:

$$
\begin{array}{lll}
eq\{\!|[\alpha]|\!\}\ [] & [] & = True \\
eq\{\!|[\alpha]|\!\}\ (x : xs)\ (y : ys) & = eq\{\!|\alpha|\!\}\ x\ y \wedge eq\{\!|[\alpha]|\!\}\ xs\ ys \\
eq\{\!|[\alpha]|\!\}\ \_ & \_ & = False
\end{array}
$$

To obtain this instance, the compiler needs to know the structural representation of lists, and how to convert between lists and their structural representation. We will describe these components in the remainder of this section.

Structure Types

The structural representation (or structure type) of types is expressed in terms of units, sums, products, and base types such as integers, characters, etc. For example, for the list and tree data types defined by

data [a]   = [] | a : [a]
data Tree a b = *Tip* a | *Node* (Tree a b) b (Tree a b),

we obtain the following structural representations:

type [a]°   = Unit :+: a :*: [a]
type Tree° a b = a   :+: Tree a b :*: b :*: Tree a b,

where we assume that :*: binds stronger than :+: and both type constructors associate to the right. Note that the representation of a recursive type is not recursive, and refers to the recursive type itself: the representation of a type in Generic Haskell only represents the structure of the top level of the type.

Embedding-Projection Pairs

If a type a can be embedded in, or represented by, another type b, a witness of this property can be stored as a pair of functions converting back and forth (an embedding-projection pair):

data EP a b = *Ep*{*from* :: a → b, *to* :: b → a}.

A type T can be embedded in its structure-representation type T°, witnessed by a value $conv_T$ :: EP T T°. For example we get $conv_{[]} = Ep\ from_{[]}\ to_{[]}$:

$from_{[]}$ :: [a] → [a]°
$from_{[]}$ [] = *Inl U*
$from_{[]}$ (x : xs)   = *Inr* (x :*: xs)

$to_{[]}$ :: [a]° → [a]
$to_{[]}$ (*Inl U*)   = []
$to_{[]}$ (*Inr* (x :*: xs)) = x : xs.

The definitions of such embedding-projection pairs are automatically generated by the Generic Haskell compiler for all data types that appear in a program.

Tying the Knot

Using structure-representation types and embedding-projection pairs, a call to a generic function on a data type T is reduced to a call on type T°. The inductive definition of a generic function is used to generate an instance on the structure type T°. For example, for equality we obtain a function of type T° → T° → Bool. To convert this function back to a function of type T → T → Bool we use the function *bimap* [3]. Function *bimap* is a bi-directional generic variant of the well-known map function, of the following type:

$$bimap\{a :: *, b :: *\} :: (bimap\{a, b\}) \Rightarrow EP\ a\ b.$$

When using *bimap*, it is only applied to one type argument which is used both for a and b. So *bimap*{|a|} is an embedding-projection pair of type EP a a. The type index can have higher kind, and the fully generic type for *bimap* is actually kind-indexed. For example, the instance of *bimap* on the type constructor Tree has the following type:

$$bimap\{|\mathsf{Tree}|\} :: \mathsf{EP\ a\ c} \to \mathsf{EP\ b\ d} \to \mathsf{EP\ (Tree\ a\ b)\ (Tree\ c\ d)}$$

Kind-indexed types can be defined in GH but are not used in this paper.

To turn a function of type $\mathsf{T}° \to \mathsf{T}° \to \mathsf{Bool}$ into a function of type $\mathsf{T} \to \mathsf{T} \to \mathsf{Bool}$, we call *bimap*{|$\mathsf{T} \to \mathsf{T} \to \mathsf{Bool}$|} in which we use $conv_\mathsf{T}$ for the T-values. Thus we obtain a function of type $\mathsf{EP\ (T}° \to \mathsf{T}° \to \mathsf{Bool)\ (T} \to \mathsf{T} \to \mathsf{Bool)}$. The *from*-component of this embedding-projection pair is the function that converts the implementation of the generic function on structure types back to a function that works on the original data type values. Hence, if the generic function is defined for structure types such as Unit, :+:, and :*:, we do not need cases for specific data types such as List or Tree anymore. For primitive types such as Int, Float, IO or $\to$, no structure type is available. Therefore, for a generic function to work on these types, specific cases are necessary.

Generic Abstractions, Local Redefinitions, and Default Cases
Generic Haskell supports a number of extensions that simplify defining and using generic functions. First, using a *generic abstraction*, we can define a generic function in terms of another generic function instead of by induction on the structure types. For example, we can test pointwise equality of functions by means of the following generic function:

$$feq\{|\mathsf{b} :: *|\} :: (eq\{|\mathsf{b}|\}) \Rightarrow (\mathsf{a} \to \mathsf{b}) \to (\mathsf{a} \to \mathsf{b}) \to \mathsf{a} \to \mathsf{Bool}$$
$$feq\{|\mathsf{b}|\}\ f\ g = \lambda x \to eq\{|\mathsf{b}|\}\ (f\ x)\ (g\ x)$$

which is a generic abstraction that is defined in terms of, and depends on, the generic equality function. Note that each generic abstraction (including *feq*) works for types of of *fixed kind*. This is in contrast to generic functions defined by induction on the type structure which work for types of arbitrary kinds.

Generic functions may have dependencies. We can use *local redefinition* to redefine the dependencies of generic functions. For example, if we want equality on lists of characters to be case insensitive, we can write

$$equalCaseInsensitive \qquad :: \mathsf{Char} \to \mathsf{Char} \to \mathsf{Bool}$$
$$equalCaseInsensitive\ x\ y = toUpper\ x\ ==\ toUpper\ y$$

let $eq\{|\alpha|\} = equalCaseInsensitive$
in $eq\{|[\alpha]|\}$ `"Generic Programming"` `"GENERIC programming"`

Another way in which we may obtain this behaviour is via a so-called *default case*, which allows us to extend an existing generic function by adding new cases or overriding existing ones.

$cieq\{|a :: *|\} :: (cieq\{|a|\}) \Rightarrow a \to a \to \mathsf{Bool}$
$cieq$ **extends** eq -- default for cieq is eq
$cieq\{|\mathsf{Char}|\}\ x\ y = toUpper\ x == toUpper\ y$

Many more examples of these extensions, and a discussion about the merits and disadvantages of these constructs can be found in Löh's thesis [10].

4   QuickCheck for Generic Functions

This section explains how we use QuickCheck for testing properties of generic functions. The biggest challenge here is to *formulate* generic properties. We start this section with a number of generic properties, and then discuss how we can use QuickCheck to test them.

Minimal and Maximal Values
Haskell's prelude contains a class *Bounded* defined by

   class *Bounded* a **where** $minBound, maxBound :: a$

The methods $minBound$ and $maxBound$ should satisfy

   $prop\_minBound\ x = compare\ minBound\ x \neq GT$
   $prop\_maxBound\ x = compare\ maxBound\ x \neq LT$

that is, $minBound$ is smaller than or equal to any other value, and $maxBound$ is larger than or equal to any other value. The method $compare::a \to a \to \mathsf{Ordering}$, in the class *Ord* (used for totally ordered data types) allows a single comparison to determine the precise ordering of two elements:

   data Ordering $= LT \mid EQ \mid GT$

Haskell allows to derive the bounds automatically for some user-defined data types (enumeration types and single-constructor data types whose constituent types are in *Bounded*). Generic Haskell's library contains definitions of the generic values $gminBound$ and $gmaxBound$ for all algebraic types (not only for those types for which Haskell supports deriving). To formulate generalisations of the properties above, we also need the generic compare function $gcompare$ from Generic Haskell's library. The desired properties now read as follows:

   $prop\_gminBound\{|t :: *|\} :: (gcompare\{|t|\}, gminBound\{|t|\}) \Rightarrow t \to \mathsf{Bool}$
   $prop\_gminBound\{|t|\}\ x\ = gcompare\{|t|\}\ (gminBound\{|t|\})\ x \neq GT$
   $prop\_gmaxBound\{|t :: *|\} :: (gcompare\{|t|\}, gmaxBound\{|t|\}) \Rightarrow t \to \mathsf{Bool}$
   $prop\_gmaxBound\{|t|\}\ x\ = gcompare\{|t|\}\ (gmaxBound\{|t|\})\ x \neq LT$

Note that the properties are formulated as generic abstractions, thus restricting t to types of kind $*$. Later we will see an example of using local redefinition as a work-around.

Properties of gmap

The generic equivalent *gmap* of the well-known *map* function applies zero or more functions (depending on the kind of its data-type argument) to the appropriate elements in a value of the data type.

$$gmap\{|\mathsf{a} :: *, \mathsf{b} :: *|\} :: (gmap\{|\mathsf{a}, \mathsf{b}|\}) \Rightarrow \mathsf{a} \rightarrow \mathsf{b}$$

Function *gmap* is defined as the deep identity function, and local redefinition can be used to obtain *map*-like behaviour. For *tree* :: Tree Int Char we can write

> **let** $gmap\{|\alpha|\} = toEnum$
> $\quad gmap\{|\beta|\} = fromEnum$
> **in** $gmap\{|\mathsf{Tree}\ \alpha\ \beta|\}\ tree$

to convert the integers to characters, and the characters to integers.

Properties of *gmap* can be derived from properties of *map*. Function *map* on lists is a part of a functor, and satisfies the functor laws: it preserves the identity, and distributes over composition:

> $map\ id \quad === id$
> $map\ (f \cdot g) === map\ f \cdot map\ g$

Here (===) is pointwise equality of functions on lists, implemented by $feq\{|[\alpha]|\}$, see Section 3. Generalised versions of these properties should hold for the generic map function *gmap*. We take the composition law as an example.

For a type constructor $\mathsf{c} :: * \rightarrow *$ we have two function arguments (the f and g in the above property), and for a type constructor $\mathsf{d} :: * \rightarrow * \rightarrow *$ we have four function arguments (two functions per type argument):

> $prop\_gmap\_comp1\{|\mathsf{c}|\}\ f\ g \quad = gmap\{|\mathsf{c}|\}\ (f \cdot g) === (gmap\{|\mathsf{c}|\}\ f \cdot gmap\{|\mathsf{c}|\}\ g)$
> $prop\_gmap\_comp2\{|\mathsf{d}|\}\ f\ g\ h\ j = gmap\{|\mathsf{d}|\}\ (f \cdot g)\ (h \cdot j) ===$
> $\qquad\qquad\qquad\qquad\qquad (gmap\{|\mathsf{d}|\}\ f\ h \cdot gmap\{|\mathsf{d}|\}\ g\ j)$

Hinze [3] shows how to generalise this property to types of arbitrary kinds. The resulting, fully generic property is *kind-indexed*, but cannot be expressed in GH.

Testing Generic Properties

As the examples of generic properties for *gmap* show, a generic property may involve kinds, type constructors, polymorphic types, higher-order functions, and plain values. To test a property, we have to supply values for each of the above components. QuickCheck can generate values of monomorphic types and functions, but generating type constructors, let alone kinds, is out of reach. This implies, amongst others, that we have to instantiate the properties on fixed monomorphic types.

Happily, generating type constructors and kinds is not necessary. To *prove* a generic property, it suffices to prove instances of the property on the structure types [3]. Similarly, to *test* the validity of a generic property, it suffices to test the validity of a property on the structure types. To test the validity of a property on all structure types, we would have to write a separate instance of the property for each structure type. Take the property *prop_gminBound* as an example. The simplest structure type is Unit. For this case, the following expression would be tested:

$$gcompare \{\!|Unit|\!\} \ (gminBound \{\!|Unit|\!\}) \ U \neq GT$$

By definition of *gminBound* and *gcompare*, this test, and the equivalent tests for Int and Char trivially pass. For the sum type case QuickCheck would need to test something like

$$prop\_gminBound\_Sum \ cmpa \ cmpb \ mba \ mbb \ x =$$
$$(\forall a \ . \ cmpa \ mba \ a \neq GT) \Longrightarrow$$
$$(\forall b \ . \ cmpb \ mbb \ b \neq GT) \Longrightarrow$$
$$(gminBound\_Sum \ cmpa \ cmpb \ mba \ mbb \ x \neq GT)$$

Since *gminBound* depends on *gcompare* and on itself, *prop_gminBound_Sum* takes five arguments. The last argument is a value of type a :+: b, and the other arguments are instances of *gcompare* and *gminBound* on the types a and b, respectively.

In general, implications $P \Longrightarrow Q$ may be hard to test in QuickCheck. In particular when the condition P is often *False*, Q is only tested for a few of the generated test cases. For many of the properties this turns out to be a problem — for example, for most properties of equality the condition requires independently generated values to be equal. For *prop_gminBound_Sum* the problem is even worse, because the left-hand side of the implication includes a local universal quantification which is not implementable with QuickCheck properties. We can solve this problem by supplying generators: instead of testing $\lambda x \to P \ x \Longrightarrow Q \ x$ we test *forAll genP* $(\lambda x \to Q \ x)$. In general it is hard or impossible to convert a property to a generator, but to obtain testable properties we need at least a good approximation of *genP*.

To avoid some of the problems with implications and local quantification, we define a data type which combines the structure types in a single data type, and use that data type for testing generic functions. The following data type combines the most important structure types, and is easily extended with more cases for basic structure types. (In the code we have also used an infix constructor for *STProd*.)

$$\textbf{data } \mathsf{StructureTypes} \ \mathsf{a} = STUnit$$
$$\mid \ STInt \ \mathsf{Int}$$
$$\mid \ STChar \ \mathsf{Char}$$
$$\mid \ STProd \ (\mathsf{StructureTypes} \ \mathsf{a}) \ (\mathsf{StructureTypes} \ \mathsf{a})$$
$$\mid \ STLabel \{ \ anA :: \mathsf{a} \}$$

The data type StructureTypes contains cases for units, integers, characters, products, and labels. The cases for sums and constructors are implicit, but appear since there is a choice between constructors in the data type, and there are constructor names in the data type. The type is parameterised to make it possible to test *gmap* — in all other tests we instantiate the type parameter (to Int).

To test the validity of the property *prop_gminBound* with this approach we use the QuickCheck function *test* on the data type StructureTypes Int:

test (*prop_gminBound*⟨StructureTypes Int⟩)

QuickCheck generates test cases from the data type StructureTypes Int if we provide a generator (an element of Gen (StructureTypes Int)). We have used an instance of the generic generator *arb3* (defined later in Section 6).

5   Properties of the Generic Haskell Library

The Generic Haskell library consists of a number of basic generic functions that are used often in generic programs. Many functions of the Generic Haskell library are generic versions of Haskell's prelude [14] functions. This includes functions that implement the methods that are derivable in Haskell, and generalisations of list functions such as *map*, *sum*, *prod*, *and*, etc. Another source of inspiration for the Generic Haskell library is PolyLib [7], the library of PolyP, which contains many basic generic functions and some properties.

Since generic functions from the library will often be used as basic building blocks in generic-programming applications, it is important that they are correct. Therefore, the generic functions in the Generic Haskell library are natural candidates for applying our approach to testing generic functions.

The Generic Haskell library consists of twelve modules, of which we will consider the following six: Eq, Compare, Enum, Bounds, and ReadShow, corresponding to the derivable Haskell classes *Eq*, *Ord*, *Enum*, *Bounded*, *Read*, and *Show*, and the module Map, which implements the generic map function *gmap*. We will introduce the generic functions used in this section briefly, often referring to their non-generic Haskell equivalents. More information about the functions in the Generic Haskell library can be found in the user's guide [12].

Properties of gread and gshow
Functions *gread* and *gshow* implement the derivable *read* and *show* functions from Haskell. Just as in Haskell, they are defined in terms of helper functions *gshowsPrec* and *greadsPrec*. Reading a value after showing it should be the identity. Showing after reading need not be the identity: parsing may fail or the original value might contain concrete syntax (spaces, newlines) that is not generated by the *show* function (like the leading zeros in the bits example from the introduction). We have tested the following property:

$$prop\_gread\_gshow\langle\mathsf{t} :: *\rangle :: (eq\langle\mathsf{t}\rangle, greadsPrec\langle\mathsf{t}\rangle, gshowsPrec\langle\mathsf{t}\rangle) \Rightarrow$$
$$\mathsf{t} \to \mathsf{Bool}$$
$$prop\_gread\_gshow\langle\mathsf{t}\rangle \quad = feq\langle\mathsf{t}\rangle \ (gread\langle\mathsf{t}\rangle \ . \ gshow\langle\mathsf{t}\rangle) \ id$$

where *feq* is pointwise equality of functions, see Section 3.

It turned out that *gread* could not cope with named fields in data types. The StructureTypes a data type contains the constructor $STLabel\{\,anA::a\,\}$. The *anA* field triggered a runtime error (pattern match failure) in *gread*. QuickCheck does not trap exceptions, so when a property fails, QuickCheck fails instead of just counting this as a failed test case. Fortunately, the Haskell compiler ghc includes (unsafe) functions to catch exceptions in pure code, so by wrapping the property in an exception handler returning *False* for all exceptions, we have used QuickCheck to find the bug.

```
Main> test (protect prop_gread_gshow_STInt)
Falsifiable, after 3 successful tests
(shrunk failing case 3 times):
STLabel {anA =-2}
```

The problem was actually not in *gread*, but in *gshow*. There was no space character after the equality sign, so when a negative integer was shown, the two characters "=-" were later parsed by *gread* as one token. A one-character change to the source code fixed this problem, but revealed another bug, this time in *gread*. Function *gread* did not allow parentheses around $STLabel\{\,anA=2\,\}$, while *gshow* (and the derived *show* in Haskell) printed parentheses. After this second fix, all tests passed. (Adding infix constructors to StructureTypes *a* we revealed yet another bug, but constructor fixity problems was already noted in the Generic Haskell release notes so we already knew that.)

Properties of gmap

Function *gmap* preserves the identity:

$$prop\_gmap\_id\{t\} :: (eq\{t\}, gmap\{t, t\}) \Rightarrow t \to \mathsf{Bool}$$
$$prop\_gmap\_id\{t\} = feq\{t\} \ (gmap\{t\}) \ id$$

To test this function, we instantiate it on the type StructureTypes a.

$$prop\_gmap\_id\_ST :: (Eq\ a) \Rightarrow \mathsf{StructureTypes\ a} \to \mathsf{Bool}$$
$$prop\_gmap\_id\_ST = \mathbf{let}\ eq\{a\} \quad = (\texttt{==})$$
$$gmap\{a\} = id$$
$$\mathbf{in}\ \ prop\_gmap\_id\{\mathsf{StructureTypes\ a}\}$$

Function *gmap* distributes over composition. We formulate the distributivity property by means of three copies of *gmap*, of which we only define *gmap1* here.

$$gmap1\ \{a :: *, b :: *\} :: (gmap1\ \{a, b\}) \Rightarrow a \to b$$
$$gmap1\ \mathbf{extends}\ gmap$$

$$prop\_gmap\_comp\{a :: *, b :: *, c :: *\} ::$$
$$(eq\{c\}, gmap1\ \{b, c\}, gmap2\ \{a, b\}, gmap3\ \{a, c\}) \Rightarrow a \to \mathsf{Bool}$$
$$prop\_gmap\_comp\{t\} = feq\{t\}\ (gmap1\ \{t\}\ .\ gmap2\ \{t\}) \ (gmap3\ \{t\})$$

To instantiate this property on the data type StructureTypes a, we locally redefine the *gmap* copies.

$prop\_gmap\_comp\_ST\ op\ f\ g =$
  let $eq\{\!|a|\!\}\qquad = op$
     $gmap1\,\{\!|a|\!\} = f;\quad gmap2\,\{\!|a|\!\} = g;\quad gmap3\,\{\!|a|\!\} = f\,.\,g$
  in $prop\_gmap\_comp\{\!|\mathsf{StructureTypes}\ a|\!\}$

We have also tested *gmap* on the structure types (:+:), (:*:), etc.

Properties of enum
Function *enum* exhaustively enumerates all possible instances of a particular data type.

$$enum\{\!|\mathsf{t} :: *|\!\} :: (enum\{\!|\mathsf{t}|\!\}) \Rightarrow [\mathsf{t}]$$

For example, $enum\{\!|\mathsf{Int}|\!\}$ yields the list of all possible (machine-) integers. A property that should hold for this function is the following:

$prop\_enum\{\!|\mathsf{t}|\!\}\qquad :: \mathsf{t} \to \mathsf{Bool}$
$prop\_enum\{\!|\mathsf{t}|\!\}\ value = value \in enum\{\!|\mathsf{t}|\!\}$

This property says that any value of type t should be in the enumeration of that type. Interestingly, checking this property is not really an option — at least for most real-life data types. Recursive data types often have infinitely many values, so using QuickCheck to test whether or not a value appears in the enumeration may take infinitely long. When testing the property instantiated with the StructureTypes Int data type QuickCheck just looped, and at first we thought this was just to be expected. But a more careful examination revealed that the property looped already for the first test case, which should have been small enough to be found early in the enumeration list. It turned out to be a subtle bug in the definition of the generic *enum* function. The enumeration used a version of Cantor diagonalisation which was "non-productive" in the case of infinite lists. By replacing just the diagonalisation function, the generic *enum* implementation worked as expected. Still, the property remains effectively untestable — already some trees built from just seven constructors are more than 10000 elements down the list.

The problem is just another instance of the problem Gast has with coverage for recursive data types (remember that Gast also uses (randomised) enumeration): While every element is *somewhere* in the enumeration list, and will *eventually* be generated by Gast, only small elements are reachable (will be tested by Gast) within reasonable time. Testing the enumeration property with Gast (instead of QuickCheck) is possible but not very useful — it is not very surprising that values (test cases) generated from an enumeration list actually are elements of a very similar enumeration list.

Another property of *enum* relates *enum* to the generic function *empty* that returns the 'least' value of a type. For example, for the List type *empty* would return the empty list.

$prop\_enum\_empty\{\!|\mathsf{t}|\!\} :: \mathsf{Bool}$
$prop\_enum\_empty\{\!|\mathsf{t}|\!\} = empty\{\!|\mathsf{t}|\!\} \in enum\{\!|\mathsf{t}|\!\}$

As the type signature reveals, this is more a unit test than a QuickCheck property. No random value is generated, so QuickCheck tests the same thing in each test. It would be more interesting to range over different types for t, but this does not fit the (current, non-generic) QuickCheck framework.

Properties of gcompare

Function *gcompare* generalises the derivable *compare* function from Haskell. We have tested what corresponds to reflexivity, anti-symmetry and transitivity for *gcompare*. Transitivity can be expressed as a QuickCheck property by:

$$prop\_gcompare\_trans\{\!|t :: *|\!\} \quad :: (gcompare\{\!|t|\!\}) \Rightarrow t \to t \to t \to \mathsf{Property}$$
$$prop\_gcompare\_trans\{\!|t|\!\} \; x \; y \; z = gcompare\{\!|t|\!\} \; x \; y = gcompare\{\!|t|\!\} \; y \; z \Longrightarrow$$
$$gcompare\{\!|t|\!\} \; x \; y = gcompare\{\!|t|\!\} \; x \; z$$

This captures transitivity for ($<$), (==) and ($>$) when $gcompare\{\!|t|\!\} \; x \; y$ has values *LT*, *EQ* and *GT*. We use the QuickCheck conditional operator $\Longrightarrow$ to rule out non-interesting test cases. Reflexivity and anti-symmetry are implemented in a similar fashion.

Another property relates function *gcompare* with the generic equality function *eq*. Function *gcompare* returns *EQ* iff function *eq* returns *True*.

$$prop\_gcompare\_eq\{\!|t :: *|\!\} \quad :: (gcompare\{\!|t|\!\}, eq\{\!|t|\!\}) \Rightarrow t \to t \to \mathsf{Bool}$$
$$prop\_gcompare\_eq\{\!|t|\!\} \; x \; y = (gcompare\{\!|t|\!\} \; x \; y = EQ) = eq\{\!|t|\!\} \; x \; y$$

This concludes the section on properties for generic functions in the Generic Haskell library. Formulating and testing these properties has been useful: we have discovered three bugs in the library.

6   Generic Generators

Normally, QuickCheck requires a user to write a test-case generator for a user-defined data type on which QuickCheck is used. Generic programming allows us to automatically generate test cases for any given data type. This makes testing properties of (generic) functions easier. This section shows the implementation of generic generators in Generic Haskell. We could have chosen any of the approaches to generic programming to implement generic generators. The expressivity and type safety of Generic Haskell, and the recently added generic views feature, are the most important reasons why we use Generic Haskell. A detailed comparison of the different approaches to generic programming in Haskell can be found elsewhere [5].

Porting the Gast Generator to Generic Haskell

For Clean a generic approach to generating test cases is already available: Gast (Generic Automated Software Testing) [8]. We have translated their implementation of pseudo random data generation [9] into Generic Haskell.

$$generate\{\!|g :: *|\!\} :: \mathsf{Int} \to \mathsf{StdGen} \to [g]$$

To make this a generator we can use the same technique as in the *primeNumbers* example — let *gast* be the (often infinite) list from *generate* and pick the value at a random index *n*. We just have to be careful not to index outside the list in case it turns out to be finite.

Thus we obtain a QuickCheck generator, written in Generic Haskell, which works for all Haskell data types. But, unfortunately, it has the same weakness for recursive types as the Gast generator in that it takes very long before any reasonably sized elements are generated. Worse, where Gast can use the systematic generation of test data for exhaustive checking for finite types, QuickCheck cannot guarantee to generate all elements (incompleteness). Still, it is convenient to have a fully generic generator around, and it can be modified with default cases and local redefinitions to customise its behaviour for selected constructors or types.

Non-terminating Generators
Instead of first enumerating and then selecting it should be possible to define a generic generator directly. As a first try we can define the following generic generator:

$$
\begin{array}{ll}
arb1\,\{\!|\,\mathsf{a}::*|\!\} & :: (arb1\,\{\!|\mathsf{a}|\!\}) \Rightarrow \mathsf{Gen\ a} \\
arb1\,\{\!|\,\mathsf{Unit}\,|\!\} & = return\ U \\
arb1\,\{\!|\,\mathsf{Int}\,|\!\} & = arbitrary \\
arb1\,\{\!|\,\mathsf{Char}\,|\!\} & = arbitrary \\
arb1\,\{\!|\,\alpha\ \mathord{:+:}\ \beta\,|\!\} & = arb\_Sum\ (arb1\,\{\!|\alpha|\!\})\ (arb1\,\{\!|\beta|\!\}) \\
arb1\,\{\!|\,\alpha\ \mathord{:*:}\ \beta\,|\!\} & = liftM2\ (\mathord{:*:})\ (arb1\,\{\!|\alpha|\!\})\ (arb1\,\{\!|\beta|\!\})
\end{array}
$$

$$
\begin{array}{ll}
arb\_Sum & :: \mathsf{Gen\ a} \rightarrow \mathsf{Gen\ b} \rightarrow \mathsf{Gen\ (a \mathbin{:+:} b)} \\
arb\_Sum\ ga\ gb & = oneof\ [\,liftM\ Inl\ ga, liftM\ Inr\ gb\,]
\end{array}
$$

This generator is very simple, works for all data types and does generate reasonably sized values, but it has at least two drawbacks: a skewed distribution and possible non-termination.

The first problem is because Generic Haskell encodes multiple-constructor data types with nested binary sums, which means that *arb1* will give a very skewed distribution of the constructors. If p_i denotes the probability of constructor C_i we get $p_i = 1/2^i$ for $i \in \{1..n-1\}$. Here a balanced encoding would help and the next Generic Haskell release will support this as described in the Generic Views [6] paper. It is possible to work around this problem already in the current version of Generic Haskell by first analysing the data type, but we have not done so.

The second problem is more subtle, but it was noted already in the first QuickCheck paper (for a specific Tree data type). For recursive data types that branch into more than one subtree, it is fairly easy to accidentally define a generator that often fails to terminate (or, actually, terminates but with an infinite tree as the result). The problem is that if a branching constructor is often generated, the final tree is only finite if all the subtrees are finite and after a few branches the number of subtrees is high. The skewed distribution offers some degree of protection against these infinite trees, but this Bin data type is an example of the problem:

data Bin = *B1* Bin Bin | *B2* Bin Bin | *L*.

Here the probability to generate *L* is 1/4 and the probability for a finite tree is only 1/3.

A Terminating Generic Generator
The solution to the termination problem is to use *sized* generators — we use a parameter n to limit the size of the generated trees. For a generic function it is not obvious to define what "size" should measure, but one simple choice is the number of constructors in the tree. Using a sized generator, we generate trees of size at most n. The first few cases in the definition are simple generalisations of *arb1*:

$$
\begin{aligned}
&arb2\{\!|a :: *|\!\} && :: (arb2\{\!|a|\!\}, empty\{\!|a|\!\}) \Rightarrow \mathsf{Int} \to \mathsf{Gen\ a} \\
&arb2\{\!|\mathsf{Unit}|\!\} && n = return\ U \\
&arb2\{\!|\mathsf{Int}|\!\} && n = arbitrary \\
&arb2\{\!|\mathsf{Char}|\!\} && n = arbitrary \\
&arb2\{\!|\alpha :+: \beta|\!\} && n = arb\_Sum\ (arb2\{\!|\alpha|\!\}\ n)\ (arb2\{\!|\beta|\!\}\ n)
\end{aligned}
$$

Our size measure tells us that we should reduce the size when passing through a constructor and distribute the size over the two subtrees in the product. In the product case it is tempting to just use

$$
arb2\{\!|\alpha :*: \beta|\!\}\ n = liftM2\ (:*:)\ (arb2\{\!|\alpha|\!\}\ (n\ /\ 2))\ (arb2\{\!|\beta|\!\}\ (n\ /\ 2))
$$

but that would tend to generate almost balanced trees. Instead we divide the size randomly over the two subtree:

$$
\begin{aligned}
&arb2\{\!|\mathsf{Con}\ c\ \alpha|\!\} && n\ = liftM\ Con\ (arb2\{\!|\alpha|\!\}\ (n-1)) \\
&arb2\{\!|\alpha :*: \beta|\!\} && n \\
&\quad | n > 1 = \mathbf{do}\ m \leftarrow choose\ (1, n-1) \\
&\qquad\qquad\qquad\quad x \leftarrow arb2\{\!|\alpha|\!\}\ m \\
&\qquad\qquad\qquad\quad y \leftarrow arb2\{\!|\beta|\!\}\ (n-m) \\
&\qquad\qquad\qquad\quad return\ (x :*: y) \\
&\quad | n \leqslant 1 = return\ (empty\{\!|\alpha|\!\} :*: empty\{\!|\beta|\!\})
\end{aligned}
$$

This generator works for all data types, it always terminates and generates finite trees (if there are any). It still has the skewed constructor distribution and it has a similar problem with a skewed size distribution for nested products. Both these problems can be avoided with a balanced view or with an analysis of the data type. Initial experiments are promising, but messy, so we leave that for future work.

Better Distribution for Regular Data Types

A problem with all the "fully generic" generators is that they cannot treat the recursive case differently from other cases. As an example, the *arb2* generator for a normal list will distribute the size parameter evenly between the element and the tail. This makes long lists very unusual and the sizes of the elements will decrease exponentially along the list. For lists we can include a special case in the definition, but similar problems occur also for other data types. Generic Haskell has been extended with some Generic Views [6], and using the Fix view it is possible to detect the recursive case, at least for regular data types.

Using the latest version of Generic Haskell (1.61) we have implemented yet another (sized) generic generator:

$$arb3 \{| a :: * |\} :: \mathsf{Int} \rightarrow \mathsf{Gen}\ a$$

This generator produces finite elements and has an even distribution of constructor probabilities and subtree sizes. The limitation is that it only works for regular data types (no mutual recursion and recursive occurrences must have the same parameters). The code depends on the generic function

$$children \{| a :: *\ viewed\ \mathsf{Fix} |\} :: a \rightarrow [a]$$

which is the classical example of what could be done in PolyP but cannot be done in the "old" Generic Haskell implementation.

7   Conclusions and Future Work

We have shown how we can formulate and test properties of generic functions, we have used QuickCheck to test the Generic Haskell libraries and we have defined a few generic QuickCheck generators.

Since an inductive proof of a property of a generic function only requires cases for the structure types used to represent data types, it suffices to test properties of generic functions on these structure types. We go one step further and collect the structure types into one representative type, StructureTypes *a*, which we use to instantiate the generic functions before testing them.

We have implemented a number of properties for generic functions in the Generic Haskell library. Formulating and testing these properties has revealed three bugs in the library. We have not yet completed the description of the properties of the functions in the library, so we expect (but do not hope) to find more bugs.

The generic QuickCheck test-case generators produce test data with a much better spread than the Gast generator. We have explored several variants with different random distributions and we have identified the Generic Views extension of GH as an important step towards better generic generators.

While implementing the different tests using QuickCheck we encountered a few problems, in particular with exception handling and a better control of the size of generated test cases. It turned out that the latest version of QuickCheck (obtained from CVS) solves most of these problems.

Future work consists of finishing formulating properties for the functions in the Generic Haskell library, further fine-tuning the generic QuickCheck test-data generators and adding tests of (non-)strictness. Another idea we would like to investigate is to generate random *types* as well as random values, and use these randomly generated types for testing, instead of the StructureTypes a type. It would also be natural to add generic support to SmallCheck.

Acknowledgements. A. Rodriguez, N.A. Danielsson and anonymous referees commented on previous versions of this paper.

References

1. Beck, K.: Test-Driven Development by Example. Addison-Wesley, London (2003)
2. Claessen, K., Hughes, J.: QuickCheck: A lightweight tool for random testing of Haskell programs. In: ICFP'00, pp. 268–279. ACM Press, New York (2000)
3. Hinze, R.: Generic Programs and Proofs. Bonn University, Habilitation (2000)
4. Hinze, R., Jeuring, J.: Generic Haskell: practice and theory. In: Backhouse, R., Gibbons, J. (eds.) Generic Programming. LNCS, vol. 2793, pp. 1–56. Springer, Heidelberg (2003)
5. Hinze, R., Jeuring, J., Löh, A.: Comparing approaches to generic programming in Haskell. In: Technical Report UU-CS-2006-022, ICS, Utrecht University. To appear in Datatype-Generic Programming, LNCS, Springer, Heidelberg (2007)
6. Holdermans, S., Jeuring, J., Löh, A., Rodriguez, A.: Generic views on data types. In: Uustalu, T. (ed.) MPC 2006. LNCS, vol. 4014, Springer, Heidelberg (2006)
7. Jansson, P., Jeuring, J.: PolyLib – a polytypic function library. In: Workshop on Generic Programming, Marstrand (June 1998)
8. Koopman, P., Alimarine, A., Tretmans, J., Plasmeijer, R.: Gast: Generic automated software testing. In: Arts, T., Mohnen, M. (eds.) IFL 2002. LNCS, vol. 2312, pp. 84–100. Springer, Heidelberg (2002)
9. Koopman, P., Plasmeijer, R.: Generic generation of elements of types. In: TFP'05, pp. 167–179. Tallinn (2005)
10. Löh, A.: Exploring Generic Haskell. PhD thesis, Utrecht University (2004)
11. Löh, A., Clarke, D., Jeuring, J.: Dependency-style Generic Haskell. In: Shivers, O. (ed.) ICFP'03, pp. 141–152. ACM Press, New York (August 2003)
12. Löh, A., Jeuring, J., Rodriguez, A.: (editors) et al. The Generic Haskell user's guide, Version 1.60 - Diamond release. Technical Report UU-CS-2006-049, ICS, Utrecht University (2006)
13. Mitchelland, R., McKim, J.: Design by Contract: by example. Addison-Wesley, London (2002)
14. Peyton Jones, S. et al.: Haskell 98, Language and Libraries. In: The Revised Report, Cambridge University Press, Cambridge (2003)
15. Plasmeijer, R., van Eekelen, M.: Clean Language Report version 2.1 (2005)

Worst-Case Execution Times for a Purely Functional Language

Armelle Bonenfant[1], Christian Ferdinand[2], Kevin Hammond[1],
and Reinhold Heckmann[2]

[1] School of Computer Science, University of St Andrews, St Andrews, UK
[2] AbsInt GmbH, Saarbrücken, Germany

Abstract. This paper provides guaranteed bounds on worst-case execution times for a strict, purely functional programming notation. Our approach involves combining time information obtained using a low-level commercial analyser with a high-level source-derived model to give worst-case execution time information. We validate our results using concrete timing information obtained using machine code fragments executing on a Renesas M32C/85 microcontroller development board. Our results confirm experimentally that our worst-case execution time model is a good predictor of execution times.

1 Introduction

Information on worst-case execution time is essential for programming a variety of *dependable systems*, such as those found in safety-critical or mission-critical domains. With their emphasis on functional correctness, functional programming languages would appear to be a good match to dependable systems requirements. However, it is also necessary to provide an equally rigorous approach to behavioural information, especially worst-case execution times. In the functional programming community, there have been some successes in obtaining recursion bounds, typically for linearly-bounded programs (e.g. [20]), and we are working on extending these approaches to non-linear cases [31]. However, without good quality time information, these approaches will not provide strong guarantees of worst-case execution time. Simple timing metrics, based on e.g. step counts [10] are clearly inadequate in this respect.

In this paper, we consider how to obtain *guaranteed* upper bounds on execution time for a strict, purely functional expression notation. Expressions are related to an underlying abstract machine implementation through a formal translation process. We obtain concrete costs for each abstract machine instruction and provide a model to relate these costs to the functional language source. Our work is undertaken in the context of Hume [17,16], a functionally-based language that takes a layered approach to language design. embedding purely functional expressions within a high-level process model. In principle, however, our approach is equally applicable to other strict functional programing languages, or even, by extrapolation, to other paradigms. This paper provides the first set of guaranteed WCET results for a functional language (in fact to our

Z. Horváth, V. Zsók, and A. Butterfield (Eds.): IFL 2006, LNCS 4449, pp. 235–252, 2007.

knowledge, the first set that has been formally related to any high-level programming language), and develops a new approach to WCET based on aggregating costs of individual abstract machine examples. For the simple architecture we have tested (a Renesas M32C/85 microprocessor typical of real-time embedded systems applications), this approach gives a surprisingly good estimate of the actual execution cost.

This paper is structured as follows: the remainder of this section discusses possible approaches to predicting worst-case executions; Section 2 describes the Hume Abstract Machine [14] that forms the target for our measurements; Section 3 introduces AbsInt's **aiT** tool for measuring worst-case execution times of low-level programs; Section 4 discusses experimental results and provides a comparison with the **aiT** tool; Section 5 outlines a cost model for Hume and gives experimental results showing that the cost model correctly predicts upper bounds on worst-case execution times for a compiled implementation of the HAM on a Renesas M32C/85 microcontroller development board; in Section 6, we discuss related work; finally, Section 7 concludes and considers further work.

1.1 Predicting Worst-Case Execution Time (WCET)

Obtaining high-quality WCET results is important in order to avoid seriously over-engineering real-time embedded systems, which would result in considerable and unnecessary hardware costs for the large production runs that are often required. Three competing technologies can be used to obtain worst-case execution times: *experimental* (or testing-based) approaches, *probabilistic measurement* and *static analysis*. Experimental approaches determine worst-case execution costs by (repeated and careful) measurement of real executions, using either software or hardware monitoring. While they may give good estimates of actual execution costs, they cannot usually *guarantee* upper bounds on execution cost. Probabilistic approaches build on experimental measurements by measuring costs for repeated executions over a suite of test cases [2,3]. Under the assumption that the test suite provides representative data, it is then possible to construct statistical profiles that can be used to determine worst-case execution time to some stated probability. Absolute guarantees cannot, however, be provided. Finally, *static analysis* approaches (e.g. [10,23]) construct detailed and precise models of processor instruction timings in order to be able to predict worst-case timings. This typically involves constructing accurate models of the processor state, including cache and pipeline information.

The primary advantage of measurement or probabilistic approaches is that they may be applied to arbitrary computer architectures, without detailed knowledge of the underlying design, and using relatively unsophisticated timing techniques. In contrast, static analyses require detailed architectural knowledge and painstaking effort to construct. Moreover, some architectural features, such as Pseudo-LRU replacement policies for caches present specific difficulties. However static analysis approaches provide the only guaranteed bounds of worst-case execution time, and are therefore to be preferred for use in safety-critical or mission-critical systems.

1.2 Research Methodology

Our approach involves extending recent work on static analysis of space costs for source-level functional programs [18], where we have considered the use of sized types [32] to expose bounds on recursive function definitions, to cover worst-case execution times. This involves combining information about high-level language constructs obtained from source-level analysis with low-level timing information. By basing our time metrics on a high-level abstract machine, the Hume Abstract Machine (HAM), we can provide a strong compilation structure that can easily be re-targeted to different platforms, without restricting future compilation directly to machine code. We also obtain a set of metrics that can be rapidly applied to the analysis of as-yet-unwritten programs, without the need for sophisticated and time-consuming programmer intervention to guide the tools, as is currently required. The disadvantage is that there may be some performance losses compared with the most sophisticated global optimisation techniques. At this point in our research, we feel that this is a reasonable trade, though it is an issue that we intend to revisit in future.

This paper reports results based on comparing the bounds obtained by static analysis against measured execution times for individual HAM instructions on a concrete target architecture: the Renesas M32C/85 microcontroller [7]. This is a microprocessor architecture typical of many used in sensor network and similar embedded systems – desktop processors such as modern Pentium IVs are rarely used in real-time embedded systems, both for cost reasons, and because their architectures make it hard to predict real-time acosts. While not seriously restricting future architectural choices for our analyses, it provides a relatively simple, but realistic architecture on which we may be able to obtain accurate timings. It also exploits an existing Hume port compiling to concrete machine code: we use the ham2c translation, which compiles HAM instructions through C to produce machine code that can be executed directly on a bare-bones development board. The use of bare hardware is important, since it gives us a good real-time experimental framework. The microcontroller board we are using has a total of 16KB of memory. We use a compiled implementation of the HAM for the M32C, and assemble the machine code, the runtime system and all dynamic memory requirements into this space.

2 The Hume Abstract Machine (HAM)

This section outlines a formal compilation scheme for translating Hume programs into HAM instructions. Our intention is to demonstrate that a formal (and ultimately provable) model of compilation can be constructed for Hume. By constructing a formal translation to real machine code from HAM code, it is then possible to verify both correctness of the compiler output and time/space cost models. We provide full information here so that it is possible to properly situate the time cost results given in Section 3.2 and so that the cost model of Section 5 can both be understood and extended by the reader. A formal semantics of the HAM would, of course, clearly be redundant for this purpose (since

$$\mathcal{C}_E \; \rho \; (c \; e_1 \ldots e_n) \quad = \quad \mathcal{C}_E \; \rho \; e_n \; +\!\!+ \ldots +\!\!+ \; \mathcal{C}_E \; \rho \; e_1 \; +\!\!+ \; \langle \; \mathrm{MkCon} \; c \; n \; \rangle$$

$$\mathcal{C}_E \; \rho \; (f \; e_1 \ldots e_n) \quad = \quad \mathcal{C}_E \; \rho \; e_n \; +\!\!+ \ldots +\!\!+ \; \mathcal{C}_E \; \rho \; e_1 \; +\!\!+ \; \langle \; \mathrm{Call} \; f, \mathrm{Slide} \; n \; \rangle$$

$$\mathcal{C}_E \; \rho \; (i) \quad = \quad \langle \; \mathrm{MkInt32} \; i \; \rangle$$

$$\ldots$$

$$\mathcal{C}_E \; \rho \; (*) \quad = \quad \langle \; \mathrm{MkNone} \; \rangle$$

$$\mathcal{C}_E \; \rho \; (var) \quad = \quad \langle \; \mathrm{PushVar} \; (\rho \; var) \; \rangle$$

$$\mathcal{C}_E \; \rho \; (\mathbf{if} \; c \; \mathbf{then} \; t \; \mathbf{else} \; f) \quad = \quad \mathcal{C}_E \; \rho \; c \; +\!\!+ \; \langle \; \mathrm{If} \; lt \; \rangle \; +\!\!+ \; \mathcal{C}_E \; \rho \; f \; +\!\!+$$
$$\langle \; \mathrm{Goto} \; ln, \mathrm{Label} \; lt \; \rangle \; +\!\!+ \; \mathcal{C}_E \; \rho \; t \; +\!\!+$$
$$\langle \; \mathrm{Label} \; ln \; \rangle$$

$$\mathcal{C}_E \; \rho \; (\mathbf{let} \; d_1 \ldots d_n \; \mathbf{in} \; e) \quad = \quad \mathbf{let} \; \rho' = bindDefs \; \langle \; d_1, \; \ldots, \; d_n \; \rangle \; \rho \; \mathbf{in}$$
$$\langle \; \mathrm{Call} \; ll, \mathrm{Goto} \; ln, \mathrm{Label} \; ll, \mathrm{CreateFrame} \; n \; \rangle \; +\!\!+$$
$$\mathcal{C}_{Let} \; \rho \; 0 \; d_1 \; +\!\!+ \ldots +\!\!+ \; \mathcal{C}_{Let} \; \rho \; (n-1) \; d_n \; +\!\!+$$
$$\mathcal{C}_E \; \rho' \; e \; +\!\!+ \; \langle \; \mathrm{Return}, \mathrm{Label} \; ln \; \rangle$$

$$\mathcal{C}_{Let} \; \rho \; n \; (\; id = e \;) \quad = \quad \mathcal{C}_E \; \rho \; e \; +\!\!+ \; \langle \; \mathrm{MakeVar} \; n \; \rangle$$

Fig. 1. Compilation Rules for Expressions

it does not convey time information it would, in fact, be useless), and we therefore omit a description here (a complete description of the HAM may, however, be obtained, if required, from http://www.embounded.org). Figures 1–4 outline rules for compiling Hume abstract syntax forms into the HAM in [14], as a formal compilation scheme similar to that for the G-machine [1]. These rules have been used to construct a compiler from Hume source code to the HAM, whose main component is a 500-line Haskell module translating abstract syntax to HAM instructions. The compilation scheme makes extensive use of a simple sequence notation: $\langle \; i_1, \; \ldots, \; i_n \; \rangle$ denotes a sequence of n items. The $+\!\!+$ operation concatenates two such sequences. Many rules also use an environment ρ which maps identifiers to $\langle \; depth, \; offset \; \rangle$ pairs.

Four auxiliary functions are used, but not defined here: *maxVars* calculates the maximum number of variables in a list of patterns; *bindDefs* augments the environment with bindings for the variable definitions taken from a declaration sequence – the *depth* of these new bindings is 0, whilst the depth of existing variable bindings in the environment is incremented by 1; *bindVars* does the same for a sequence of patterns; and *labels* generates new labels for a set of function/box rules. Note that where labels *lt*, *ln*, *lx* etc. are used, these are assumed to be unique in the obvious way: there is at most one **Label** pseudo-instruction for each label in the translated program. Labels for boxes and function blocks are derived in a standard way from the (unique) name of the box or function. Finally, priming (e.g. ρ') is simply used for naming purposes.

The rules are structured by abstract syntax class. The rules for translating expressions ($\mathcal{C}_E$ etc. – Figure 1) are generally straightforward, but note that function frames are created to deal with *let*-expressions and other similar structures,

$$\mathcal{C}_D \; \rho \; (\textbf{box } b \; ins \; outs \; \textbf{fair } rs \; \textbf{handle } xs) \;\; = \;\; \mathcal{C}_B \; \rho \; true \; b \; ins \; outs \; rs$$
$$\mathcal{C}_D \; \rho \; (\textbf{box } b \; ins \; outs \; \textbf{unfair } rs \; \textbf{handle } xs) \;\; = \;\; \mathcal{C}_B \; \rho \; false \; b \; ins \; outs \; rs$$
$$\mathcal{C}_D \; \rho \; (f \; = \; \langle \; p_1 \; \rightarrow \; e_1 \ldots p_n \; \rightarrow \; e_n \; \rangle \;) =$$
$$\textbf{let } nvars \; = \; maxVars \; \langle \; p_1, \; \ldots, \; p_n \; \rangle \; \textbf{in}$$
$$\langle \; \text{Label } f, \text{CreateFrame } nvars \; \rangle \; \mathbin{+\!\!+}$$
$$\mathcal{C}_F \; \rho \; \langle \; \langle \; p_1 \; \rangle \; \rightarrow \; e_1, \; \ldots, \; \langle \; p_n \; \rangle \; \rightarrow \; e_n \; \rangle \; \mathbin{+\!\!+}$$
$$\langle \; \text{Function } f \; (labels \; f) \; \rangle$$

$$\mathcal{C}_B \; \rho \; f \; b \; (in_1, \ldots, in_i) \; (out_1, \ldots, out_m) \; rs \;\; =$$
$$\textbf{let } nvars \; = \; maxVars \; \langle \; in_1, \; \ldots, \; in_i \; \rangle \; \textbf{in}$$
$$\langle \; \text{Label } b \; \rangle \; \mathbin{+\!\!+}$$
$$\langle \; \text{CopyInput } (i - 1), \; \ldots, \; \text{CopyInput } 0 \; \rangle \; \mathbin{+\!\!+}$$
$$\langle \; \text{Push } 2, \text{CreateFrame } nvars \; \rangle \; \mathbin{+\!\!+}$$
$$(if \; f \; then \; \langle \; \text{StartMatches} \; \rangle \; else \; \langle \; \rangle) \; \mathbin{+\!\!+} \; \mathcal{C}_R \; \rho \; f \; m \; rs \; \mathbin{+\!\!+}$$
$$\langle \; \text{Box } b \ldots \rangle$$

Fig. 2. Compilation Rules for Declarations and Box Bodies

which then exploit the function calling mechanism. This allows the creation of local stack frames. It would obviously be possible to eliminate the function call for *let*-expressions provided the stack frame was properly set up in order to allow access to non-local definitions.

Hume programs define a number of concurrent processes. Each process is defined in terms of a "box" that maps some inputs to some outputs [17]. Box inputs/outputs are connected to form a static process network. The rules for translating box and function declarations are shown in Figure 2. These rules create new stack frames for the evaluation of the box or function, label the entry points and introduce appropriate pseudo-instructions. In the case of box declarations, it is also necessary to copy inputs to the stack using **CopyInput** instructions and to deal with fair matching. Box bodies are compiled using $\mathcal{C}_R/\mathcal{C}_{R'}$ (Figure 3). These rules compile matches for the outer level patterns using $\mathcal{C}_P$, then compile inner pattern matches using $\mathcal{C}_A$, before introducing **Consume** instructions for non-* input positions. The RHS can now be compiled. If more than one result is to be produced, the tuple of outputs is unpacked onto the stack. A **Check-Outputs** is inserted to verify that the outputs can be written using appropriate **Write** instructions. Finally, a **Reorder** is inserted if needed to deal with fair matching, and a **Schedule** returns control to the scheduler. The compilation of function/handler bodies using $\mathcal{C}_F/\mathcal{C}_{F'}$ is similar, except that $\mathcal{C}_{P'}$ is used rather than $\mathcal{C}_P$, there is no need to deal with box inputs/outputs or fair matching, and a **Return** rather than **Schedule** is inserted at the end of each compiled rule. For simplicity, but without loss of generality, we ignore exception handlers.

Finally patterns are compiled using $\mathcal{C}_P/\mathcal{C}_{P'}$ (Figure 4), where $\mathcal{C}_P$ inserts the **MatchNone/ MatchAvailable** instructions that are needed at the box level, and $\mathcal{C}_{P'}$ compiles simple patterns. Constructed values are matched in two stages: firstly the constructor is matched, and then if the match is successful, the matched object is deconstructed on the stack to allow its inner components to

$$\mathcal{C}_R \; \rho \; f \; m \; \langle \; r_1, \ldots, r_n \; \rangle \qquad = \quad \mathcal{C}_{R'} \; \rho \; f \; m \; r_1 \; +\!\!+ \; \ldots \; +\!\!+ \; \mathcal{C}_{R'} \; \rho \; f \; m \; r_n$$

$$
\begin{aligned}
\mathcal{C}_{R'} \; \rho \; f \; m \; (\; \langle \; p_1, \ldots, p_n \rangle \; \rightarrow \; e \;) \quad = \quad & \textbf{let } \rho' \; = \; bindVars \; \langle \; p_1 \;, \ldots, p_n \; \rangle \rho \textbf{ in} \\
& \langle \; \text{Label } lr, \text{MatchRule} \; \rangle \; +\!\!+ \\
& \mathcal{C}_P \; p_1 \; +\!\!+ \; \ldots \; +\!\!+ \; \mathcal{C}_P \; p_n \; +\!\!+ \\
& \mathcal{C}_A \; p_1 \; +\!\!+ \; \ldots \; +\!\!+ \; \mathcal{C}_A \; p_n \; +\!\!+ \\
& \mathcal{C}_C \; 0 \; p_1 \; +\!\!+ \; \ldots \; +\!\!+ \; \mathcal{C}_C \; (n-1) \; p_n \; +\!\!+ \\
& \mathcal{C}_E \; \rho' \; e \; +\!\!+ \\
& (\textit{if } m \; > \; 1 \; \textit{then} \; \langle \; \text{Unpack} \; \rangle \; \textit{else} \; \langle \; \rangle) \; +\!\!+ \\
& \langle \; \text{CheckOutputs} \; \rangle \; +\!\!+ \\
& \langle \; \text{Write } (n-1) \; \ldots \; \text{Write } 0 \; \rangle \; +\!\!+ \\
& (\textit{if } f \; \textit{then} \; \langle \; \text{Reorder} \; \rangle \; \textit{else} \; \langle \; \rangle) \; +\!\!+ \\
& \langle \; \text{Schedule} \; \rangle
\end{aligned}
$$

$$
\begin{aligned}
\mathcal{C}_C \; n \; (\textbf{*}) \qquad & = \quad \langle \; \rangle \\
\mathcal{C}_C \; n \; (p) \qquad & = \quad \langle \; \text{Consume } n \; \rangle
\end{aligned}
$$

$$\mathcal{C}_F \; \rho \; \langle \; r_1, \ldots, r_n \; \rangle \qquad = \quad \mathcal{C}_{F'} \; \rho \; r_1 \; +\!\!+ \; \ldots \; +\!\!+ \; \mathcal{C}_{F'} \; \rho \; r_n$$

$$
\begin{aligned}
\mathcal{C}_{F'} \; \rho \; (\; \langle \; p_1, \ldots, p_n \; \rangle \; \rightarrow \; e \;) \quad = \quad & \textbf{let } \rho' \; = \; bindVars \; \langle \; p_1 \;, \ldots, p_n \; \rangle \rho \textbf{ in} \\
& \langle \; \text{Label } lf, \text{MatchRule} \; \rangle \; +\!\!+ \\
& \mathcal{C}_{P'} \; p_1 \; +\!\!+ \; \ldots \; +\!\!+ \; \mathcal{C}_{P'} \; p_n \; +\!\!+ \\
& \mathcal{C}_A \; p_1 \; +\!\!+ \; \ldots \; +\!\!+ \; \mathcal{C}_A \; p_n \; +\!\!+ \\
& \mathcal{C}_E \; \rho' \; e \; +\!\!+ \\
& \langle \; \text{Return} \; \rangle
\end{aligned}
$$

Fig. 3. Compilation Rules for Rule Matches and Functions

be matched against the inner patterns. These nested patterns are compiled using $\mathcal{C}_A$ and $\mathcal{C}_N$. $\mathcal{C}_A$ inserts **CopyArg** and **Unpack** instructions to decompose function/box arguments, where $\mathcal{C}_N$ deals with the general nested case using **Copy** instructions to replicate items that are in the local stack frame.

3 Static Analysis Using the aiT Tool

Motivated by the problems of measurement-based methods for WCET estimation, AbsInt GmbH has investigated an approach based on static program analysis [22,19,13]. The approach relies on the computation of abstract cache and pipeline states for every program point and execution context using *abstract interpretation*. These abstract states provide safe approximations for all possible concrete cache and pipeline states, and provide the basis for an accurate timing of hardware instructions, which leads to safe and precise WCET calculations that are valid for all executions of the application. The results of AbsInt GmbH's *aiT* tool [12] can be combined using Integer Linear Programming techniques to safely predict the worst-case execution time and a corresponding worst-case execution path. Whilst the analysis works at a level that is more abstract than

$$
\begin{aligned}
\mathcal{C}_P\ (*) &= \langle\ \text{MatchNone}\ \rangle \\
\mathcal{C}_P\ (\_\ *) &= \langle\ \text{MatchNone}\ \rangle \\
\mathcal{C}_P\ (\overline{p}) &= \langle\ \text{MatchAvailable}\ \rangle\ +\!\!+\ \mathcal{C}_{P'}\ p
\end{aligned}
$$

$$
\begin{aligned}
\mathcal{C}_{P'}\ (i) &= \langle\ \text{MatchInt32}\ i\ \rangle \\
&\cdots \\
\mathcal{C}_{P'}\ (c\ p_1\ \ldots\ p_n) &= \langle\ \text{MatchCon}\ c\ n\ \rangle \\
\mathcal{C}_{P'}\ (var) &= \langle\ \text{MatchVar}\ var\ \rangle \\
\mathcal{C}_{P'}\ \_ &= \langle\ \text{MatchAny}\ \rangle
\end{aligned}
$$

$$
\begin{aligned}
\mathcal{C}_A\ (c\ p_1\ \ldots\ p_n) &= \mathcal{C}_{A'}\ \langle\ p_1, \ldots,\ p_n\ \rangle \\
\mathcal{C}_A\ (\ p_1,\ \ldots,\ p_n\ ) &= \mathcal{C}_{A'}\ \langle\ p_1, \ldots,\ p_n\ \rangle \\
\mathcal{C}_A\ (x\ p) &= \mathcal{C}_{A'}\ \langle\ p\ \rangle \\
\mathcal{C}_A\ p &= \langle\ \rangle
\end{aligned}
$$

$$
\begin{aligned}
\mathcal{C}_{A'}\ \langle\ p_1, \ldots,\ p_n\ \rangle &= \langle\ \text{CopyArg}\ n\ ,\text{Unpack}\ \rangle\ +\!\!+ \\
&\quad \mathcal{C}_N\ p_1\ +\!\!+\ \ldots\ +\!\!+\ \mathcal{C}_N\ p_n\ +\!\!+ \\
&\quad \mathcal{C}_{P'}\ p_1\ +\!\!+\ \ldots\ +\!\!+\ \mathcal{C}_{P'}\ p_n
\end{aligned}
$$

$$
\begin{aligned}
\mathcal{C}_N\ \langle\ p_1, \ldots,\ p_n\ \rangle &= \langle\ \text{Copy}\ n\ ,\text{Unpack}\ \rangle\ +\!\!+ \\
&\quad \mathcal{C}_N\ p_1\ +\!\!+\ \ldots\ +\!\!+\ \mathcal{C}_N\ p_n\ +\!\!+ \\
&\quad \mathcal{C}_{P'}\ p_1\ +\!\!+\ \ldots\ +\!\!+\ \mathcal{C}_{P'}\ p_n
\end{aligned}
$$

Fig. 4. Compilation Rules for Patterns

simple basic blocks, it is not capable of managing the complex high-level constructs that we require. It can, however, provide useful and accurate worst-case time information about lower level constructs. We are thus motivated to link the two levels of analysis, combining information on recursion bounds and other high-level constructs that we will obtain from the Hume source analysis we are constructing, with the low-level worst-case execution time analysis that can be obtained from the AbsInt analysis. In order to achieve this, we will eventually require two-way information flow between the analyses. In the short-term, it is sufficient to provide one-way flow from the language-level analysis to the lower-level analysis.

The **aiT** tool is a robust commercial tool. It has previously been applied to several other architectures used in embedded systems with similarly good results. It has also proved sufficiently flexible to deal with a variety of application domains including real-time operating systems [26], an automotive communications system [5], construction vehicles [27], and avionics [28]. The use of an abstract machine as the analysis target represents a new challenge for the **aiT** tool, however, since the structure of instructions that need to be analysed can be significantly different from those that are hand-produced, and the associated technical problems in producing cost information can therefore be more complex.

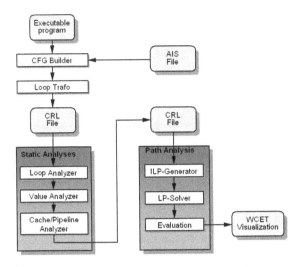

Fig. 5. Phases of WCET computation

3.1 Determining WCET Using the aiT Tool

The **aiT** tool determines the worst-case execution time of a program task in several phases, as shown in Figure 5. These phases are:

- **CFG Building** decodes, i.e. identifies instructions, and reconstructs the control-flow graph (CFG) from an executable binary program;
- **Value Analysis** computes address ranges for instructions accessing memory;
- **Cache Analysis** classifies memory references as cache misses or hits [11];
- **Pipeline Analysis** predicts the behavior of the program on the processor pipeline [22];
- **Path Analysis** determines a worst-case execution path of the program [30].

The cache analysis phase uses the results of the value analysis phase to predict the behavior of the (data) cache based on the range of values that can occur in the program. The results of the cache analysis are then used within the pipeline analysis to allow prediction of those pipeline stalls that may be due to cache misses. The combined results of the cache and pipeline analyses are used to compute the execution times of specific program paths. By separating the WCET determination into several phases, it becomes possible to use different analysis methods that are tailored to the specific subtasks. Value analysis, cache analysis, and pipeline analysis are all implemented using abstract interpretation [9], a semantics-based method for static program analysis. Integer linear programming is then used for the final path analysis phase.

Instruction	gcc	IAR	Ratio
Call	73	70	1.04
Copy	43		
CopyArg	40	35	1.14
CreateFrame	76	72	1.06
Goto	5	3	1.67
If (true)	41	32	1.28
If (false)	41	32	1.28
MakeVar	43	36	1.19
MatchExn	808		
MatchedRule	11	11	1.00
MatchInt	811	137	5.92
MatchRule	22	22	1.00
MatchVar	46	36	1.28
MkBool	136		

Instruction	gcc	IAR	Ratio
MkChar	136		
MkCon 2	348	242	1.44
MkFun 0	198	165	1.20
MkInt	136	91	1.49
MkNone	26	21	1.24
MkVector 3	392	205	1.91
Pop	13		
Push	12	11	1.09
PushVar	40	35	1.14
Return	1756		
Schedule	410	602	0.68
Slide	62	53	1.17
SlideVar	94		
TailCall	91	178	0.51

Fig. 6. aiT HAM analysis: gcc and IAR compiled code

3.2 Worst-Case Execution Time for HAM Instructions

Figure 6 lists guaranteed worst-case execution time results for a subset of Hume Abstract Machine instructions, ordered alphabetically, and reported in terms of clock cycles. These timings were obtained using the **aiT** tool from code generated using the **ham2c** Hume to C compiler, cross-compiling through either gcc Version 3.4 or the IAR C compiler [29] to the Renesas M32C. As expected from a commercial compiler targeting a few architectures, the IAR compiler generally produces more efficient code than gcc, with our results being 42% lower on average, and up to 5.92 times more efficient in the case of **MatchInt**. In a few cases, the **aiT** tool was unable to provide timing information directly, requiring additional information such as loop bounds to be provided in order to produce timing results. Missing entries in this table represent cases where this information could not be obtained. In the long term, we anticipate that we will be able to provide this information by analysis of Hume source constructs. In the short term, we have calculated the information by hand, where possible. For some instructions, however, we were unable to provide this information for the IAR-compiled code, and results for these instructions are therefore given only for gcc-produced code.

4   Experimental Timings

We have developed an approach based on repeated timing of code fragments. Each fragment to be timed is executed a certain (large) number of times. This ensures that we obtain a measurable time, even for times that are below the clock threshold. In order to ensure that computations can be repeated, it is necessary to save and restore the computation state between executions, thereby incurring some time overhead. So that this overhead does not affect our timing results, we must therefore first take a witness timing that simply incurs this overhead. This is subtracted from the measured time to give an average time for the code fragment of interest. Since the M32C/85 clock is cycle-accurate, it is also possible to obtain an exact execution time for a given code fragment. We have adapted the timing approach described above to give measured worst-case execution times, by recording the measured maximum time for the code fragment of interest. The same approach can also be used to give best-case timings.

4.1   Timing Results

Figure 7 shows average execution and worst-case execution times obtained using the timing approach described above, for HAM instructions compiled using the IAR compiler. Each average and worst-case entry has been obtained from 10000 individual timings. We can see from the table that the worst-case times and average-case times are very similar for most instructions, indicating that the instruction timings are highly consistent in practice. Since certain instructions are parameterised on some argument (for example, **MkVector** is parameterised on the vector size), in these cases, we have measured several points and applied linear interpolation to obtain a cost formula. It is interesting to note that in these case, the linear factor is identical for both WCET and average times and the constants are also very close. In each case, we have subtracted the least time obtained from timing the empty sequence of instructions (39 clock cycles), in order to give a conservative worst-case time. Since the worst-case time for the empty sequence was 42 cycles, this means that the worst-case may, in fact, be up to three cycles less than the numbers reported here. Since we must save and restore the abstract machine state (and this will, as a side effect, clear the cache and other processsor state), we needed to develop code that does this correctly. A few abstract machine instructions have therefore not been costed, mainly because they perform more complex state changes that may require additional intervention. It is worth noting that the values included in this table give a good timing predictor, but one that could only be used to provide absolute worst-case guarantees under some statistical probability.

4.2   Quality of the Static Analysis Using the aiT Tool

Figure 8 compares the upper bounds on worst-case execution timing obtained using the aiT tool from Figure 6 with the corresponding measured worst cases from Figure 7. We can see that in all cases apart from **MatchRule**, the static analyis gives an upper bound that is greater than or equal to the measured execution time. For **MatchRule**, the static analysis yields an upper bound that is one cycle smaller than our measured worst-case. Since our worst case timings are conservative, and may have an experimental error of up to three clock cycles, as described above, we conclude that the static analysis correctly yields upper bounds on execution costs for these HAM instructions. For the instructions we have compared, the bound given by the static analyis is at most 50%

Instructions	AVG	WCET	Ratio
Ap	760	761	1.00
Call	61	62	1.02
Callprim			
== Bool	246	251	1.02
* Float	240	242	1.01
+ Float	262	267	1.02
== Float	255	260	1.02
− Int	114	119	1.04
* Int	130	132	1.02
/ Int	168	177	1.05
+ Int	114	119	1.04
< Int	215	220	1.02
== Int	216	221	1.02
> Int	217	223	1.03
Consume	27	31	1.24
Copy	27	31	1.15
CopyArg	27	30	1.11
CreateFrame	51	57	1.12
Goto	1	2	2.00
If (true)	24	29	1.21
If (false)	24	26	1.08
MakeVar	26	31	1.19
MatchAny	6	10	1.67
MatchAvailable	7	10	1.43
MatchBool	24	29	1.21
MatchCon	22	26	1.18
MatchedRule	8	12	1.50
MatchExn	22	28	1.27
MatchFloat	24	29	1.21
MatchInt	23	29	1.26

Instructions	AVG	WCET	Ratio
MatchNone	6	10	1.67
MatchRule	18	23	1.28
MatchString n	$3 \times n + 45$	$3 \times n + 47$	
MatchTuple	6	10	1.67
MatchVar	26	31	1.19
MaybeConsume	20	28	1.40
MkBool	63	70	1.11
MkChar	63	70	1.11
MkCon n	$41 \times n + 84$	$41 \times n + 89$	
MkFun n	$42 \times n + 108$	$42 \times n + 113$	
MkInt	64	65	1.02
MkNone	15	21	1.40
MkString n	$13 \times n + 133$	$13 \times n + 140$	
MkTuple n	$41 \times n + 63$	$41 \times n + 66$	
MkVector n	$41 \times n + 63$	$41 \times n + 65$	
Pop	6	9	1.50
Push	6	9	1.50
PushVar	27	30	1.11
PushVarF	37	40	1.08
Raise	374	377	1.01
Return	112	116	1.04
Slide	41	44	1.07
SlideVar	58	63	1.09
Unpack	114	118	1.04

Fig. 7. Experimental average and worst-case timings for HAM instructions

greater than the measured worst-case (for **Goto**, representing a difference of only one clock cycle); the mean difference is 22%, with a standard deviation of 16%. We conclude that the static analysis provides an accurate upper bound on execution time.

5   Worst-Case Execution Time for Hume Expressions

In this section, we outline a cost model for deriving worst-case time based on the Hume operational semantics, and compare the results we obtain against measured execution times. Our cost model is defined in terms of a formal operational

Instructions	aiT bound	Measured WCET	Ratio	Instructions	aiT bound	Measured WCET	Ratio
Call	70	62	1.13	MatchVar	36	31	1.16
CopyArg	35	30	1.17	MkCon 2	242	170	1.42
CreateFrame	72	57	1.26	MkFun 0	165	113	1.46
Goto	3	2	1.50	MkInt	91	65	1.40
If (true)	32	29	1.10	MkNone	21	21	1.00
If (false)	32	26	1.23	Push	11	9	1.22
MakeVar	36	31	1.16	PushVar	35	30	1.17
MatchRule	**22**	**23**	**0.96**	Slide	53	44	1.20

Fig. 8. Quality of the Static Analysis

semantics for the Hume Abstract Machine that is related back to Hume source expressions. Our cost rules are given in a derivation form as follows:

$$\mathcal{V}, \eta \vdash^t_{t'} e \rightsquigarrow \ell, \eta'$$

where e represents an expression in our source language. t is an upper bound of the number of time units available to evaluate e, and t' is the number of time units available left after execution of e. The time required for evaluating e will then be $t - t'$. η/η' are the dynamic memory before/after execution of e, ℓ is the result value after execution, and $\mathcal{V}$ represents a mapping of variable names to values. In order to provide pattern matching costs, we add rules of the form:

$$\eta \vdash^t_{t'} \ell : \vec{\ell}, pat : \vec{pat}, \mathcal{V}, \mathcal{A} \rhd \vec{\ell}, \vec{pat}, \mathcal{V}', \mathcal{A}'$$

This means that a single step match of ℓ against pat succeeds (with ℓ interpreted within heap η). In order to complete the whole pattern match, the sublists $\vec{\ell}$ and $\vec{pat}$ must still be matched. Further, $\mathcal{V}'$ is the environment $\mathcal{V}$ extended with any bindings made in this, and $\mathcal{A}'$ extends $\mathcal{A}$ with the locations that have been matched successfully in this step. Finally, $t - t'$ is the time required to match the location ℓ against pat. We then write

$$\eta \vdash^t_{t'} \vec{\ell}, \vec{pat}, \mathcal{V}, \mathcal{A} \rhd^* \vec{\ell}', \vec{pat}', \mathcal{V}', \mathcal{A}'$$

to denote that the quadruple $\vec{\ell}, \vec{pat}, \mathcal{V}, \mathcal{A}$ reduces in several steps to the quadruple $\vec{\ell}', \vec{pat}', \mathcal{V}', \mathcal{A}'$, which is irreducible under $\rhd$.

In order to illustrate our approach we include only a few representative rules here. A complete set of rules, forming a complete cost model for Hume in terms of the costs incurred by the HAM, may be found at `http://www.embounded.org`. Each rule in the cost model is derived from the formal translation of Section 2, and this translation also allows us to derive formal properties including the soundness of the cost model against the formal operational semantics of the HAM which we have previously constructed. The first rule we consider (CONST INT) deals with contant integers. We first allocate a new location ℓ for the given constant n. The cost of the evaluation is given by the constant `Tmkint`, which is the time required by the `MkInt` instruction, as calculated above. Similar rules can be constructed for any other kind of constant.

$$\frac{n \in \mathbb{Z} \quad \text{NEW}(\eta) = \ell \quad w = (\text{int}, \text{n})}{\mathcal{V}, \eta \vdash_{t'}^{t' + \text{Tmkint}} n \rightsquigarrow \ell, \eta[\ell \mapsto w]} \qquad (\text{Const Int})$$

The VARIABLE rule looks up x in $\mathcal{V}$ to obtain the variable location. The time this takes is given by the cost of the underlying `PushVar` instruction, `Tpushvar`.

$$\frac{\mathcal{V}(x) = \ell}{\mathcal{V}, \eta \vdash_{t'}^{t' + \text{Tpushvar}} x \rightsquigarrow \ell, \eta} \qquad (\text{Variable})$$

The VECTOR rule deals with costs for literal arrays (vectors). It is an example of a typical rule that exposes costs for constructed expressions. Each component of the vector is evaluated to yield a heap location. Since memory must be allocated for each component and this will incur some time cost, the cost of constructing the vector therefore depends on the number of components `Tmkvec(k)` plus the time costs for evaluating each component. While this is not theoretically necessary, we use the convention of showing the `Tmkvec()` costs below the line to make it clear that they are incurred after evaluating each of the vector components in the HAM implementation.

$$\frac{\mathcal{V}, \eta_{(i-1)} \vdash_{t_i}^{t_{(i-1)}} e_i \rightsquigarrow \ell_i, \eta_i \quad (\text{for } i = 1, \ldots, k)}{k \geq 1 \quad \text{NEW}(\eta_k) = \ell \quad w = (\text{constr}_c, \ell_k, \ldots, \ell_1)}{\mathcal{V}, \eta_0 \vdash_{t_k - \text{Tmkvec(k)}}^{t_0} \langle\!\langle e_k \cdots e_1 \rangle\!\rangle \rightsquigarrow \ell, \eta_k[\ell \mapsto w]} \qquad (\text{Vector})$$

Finally, the APP rule is broken down into several steps. First, all the given arguments have to be matched against the patterns, where the first $j-1$ matches will fail. For each match, the cost of `Tmatchrule` is added to the cost of evaluating the match. The successful match incurs an additional cost of `Tmatchedrule`. Finally the function body is evaluated. Before and after evaluation, we incur costs of `Tcreateframe` and `Treturn` respectively, corresponding to the time costs of constructing a stack frame and returning from the function call.

$$\frac{\Sigma^{\mathcal{F}}(\mathit{fid}) = (k, [\vec{pat}_1 \rightarrow e_1, \cdots, \vec{pat}_h \rightarrow e_h]) \qquad 1 \leq k = b}{(\text{for } i = 1, \ldots, j-1)}$$

$$\left\{ \begin{array}{c} \eta \vdash_{t_i}^{t_{(i-1)} - \text{Tmatchrule}} [\ell_1, \ldots, \ell_b], \vec{pat}_i, \varnothing, \emptyset \rhd^* \vec{\ell}_i, \vec{pat}_i{}', \mathcal{V}_i, \mathcal{A}_i \\ \vec{\ell}_i \neq [] \qquad \vec{pat}_i{}' \neq [] \\ \eta \vdash_{t_j + \text{Tmatchedrule}}^{t_{(j-1)} - \text{Tmatchrule}} [\ell_1, \ldots, \ell_b], \vec{pat}_j, \varnothing, \emptyset \rhd^* [], [], \mathcal{V}_j, \mathcal{A}_j \end{array} \right.$$

$$\frac{\mathcal{V}_j, \eta \vdash_{t'_{e_j}}^{t_j} e_j \rightsquigarrow \ell, \eta'}{\mathcal{V}, \eta \vdash_{t'_{e_j} - \text{Treturn}}^{\text{Tcreateframe} + t_0} \text{APP}(\mathit{fid}, [\ell_1, \ldots, \ell_b]) \rightsquigarrow \ell, \eta'} \qquad (\text{App})$$

5.1   Example: findNewCentre

As an example, we have chosen to use findNewCentre, a key function from the *mean-shift* image tracking algorithm [6], which we have recoded in Hume [4]. The input to the algorithm is an image sequence, and the output is a track of the target in the image plane over the whole sequence. The idea is to *model* a region of an initial image by a probability density function that describes the first order statistics of that region. If the image sequence is in colour then the usual choice is to employ a colour histogram. Then, the task is to find a *candidate* position for the target in a subsequent image by finding the minimum distance between the model and candidate histograms using an iterative procedure. This findNewCentre function corresponds to the inner loop of the algorithm that determines the final candidate position, and can be defined as:

```
findNewCentre centre dx old_dx nloops frame Qu  =
  if dx==<<0,0>> || nloops>4 || addCoord dx old_dx == <<0,0>>
  then centre
  else findNewCentre (addCoord centre dx)
          (computeDisplacement
            (updateWeights (updateModel
                              frame
                              (addCoord centre dx)
                              theKern)
                Qu frame (addCoord centre dx)) theDeriv)
          dx (nloops+1) frame Qu;
```

The cost model gives us the following two formulae for calculating time costs:

$$T_{init} = \texttt{Tcall} + 5 \times \texttt{Tpushvar} + 3 \times \texttt{Tmkint} + \texttt{Tmkvec}(2) +$$
$$\texttt{Tcreateframe} + \texttt{Tmatchrule} + 6 \times \texttt{Tmatchvar} + \texttt{Tmatchedrule} +$$
$$T_c + \texttt{Tiftrue} + \texttt{Treturn} + \texttt{Tslide}$$
$$T_{loop} = \texttt{Tmatchrule} + 6 \times \texttt{Tmatchvar} + \texttt{Tmatchedrule} +$$
$$T_c + \texttt{Tiffalse} + T_{rec}$$

Where T_c is the time for the conditional computation, and T_{rec} for the recursive branch. The time consumption of k iterations of the function (depending on T_c and T_{rec}) is then $T_{global} = T_{init} + k \times T_{loop}$.

Figure 9 gives concrete values for these variables produced using either the aiT tool or by measurement. Experimental figures for *Tcall* etc are obtained from Figure 7, while those for **aiT** are obtained from Figure 6. Note that while there is, in principle, no technical problem with obtaining upper bounds on T_c and T_{rec} using the **aiT** tool, since we do not have figures for all HAM instructions, we have chosen to measure these values, giving worst-case execution times of $T_c = 1429$ and $T_{rec} = 539$. For similar reasons, we have also used the gcc figure for the **Return** instruction. This is a clear over-estimate of the worst-case time. We can see from the figure that the aiT tool gives a result that is within 24% or 19% of

Clock cycles	aiT (gcc)	aiT (IAR)	average (IAR)	WCET (IAR)	Measured
T_{init}	4704	4314	2390	2449	
T_{loop}	2317	2249	2173	2215	
T_{global}	16289	15559	13255	13524	13120
Ratio predicted/measured	1.24	1.19	1.01	1.03	

Fig. 9. Example: findNewCentre

the actual measured cost for T_{global}, and that the experimental result is within 1% for the average measurement and 3% for the WCET measurement. This shows both that good predictions can be obtained for code fragments using the **aiT** tool, and that the approach of summing abstract machine costs to provide an overall time predictor can be a valid one.

6   Related Work

This paper represents the first study of guaranteed worst-case execution times for functional languages of which we are aware, and the first to consider time predictions based on analysis of underlying abstract machine instructions. Our static analysis approach is unusual in being based on high-level analysis of source code, rather than being reconstructed from the more usual low-level control-flow or data-flow graphs (e.g. [2,5,8,27]), which are inevitably approximate in terms of representing programmer intent or high-level language constructs. A good survey of other recent work on WCET analysis can be found in [33].

The use of atomic timings to predict overall worst-case execution times has previously been addressed in the literature. For example, Wong [34] has considered the use of sequences of bytecodes, and Meyerhöfer and Lauterwald [24] have considered code blocks for the same purpose. Generally, however, authors have concluded that bytecodes (and even basic blocks) are at too small a granularity to form reliable timings. Where individual JVM bytecodes are measured, it can also be tedious and problematic to save/restore system state by hand [25]. There are also issues with garbage collection etc., and a real-time implementation is clearly required. By considering a simple architecture with a cycle-accurate clock we have, however, been able to obtain measured worst-case execution times for bytecode instructions. Because we have full access to the abstract machine implementation, we are able to systematically save/restore complete system states for many HAM instructions. We have also confirmed that, for at least one simple architecture, the Renesas M32C, composition of bytecode cost information is a good WCET predictor for sequences of such bytecodes. We are not aware of any previous work that gives similar results.

7   Conclusions and Further Work

By conducting a series of experiments and applying a low-level static analysis to a representative subset of the Hume Abstract Machine instructions, we have been able to demonstrate that our time cost model is capable of predicting good upper bounds on execution time of a given Hume program both on a bytecode-by-bytecode basis (Section 4) and overall for a simple function (Section 5). Our results are shown on a microcontroller hardware platform that is typical of those found in small embedded systems. We have shown that we can obtain guaranteed worst-case execution times for a number of HAM instructions that are within 50% of the measured worst-case. Although we need to conduct further experiments to verify our results, we have been able to show that we can derive guaranteed worst-case times that are within 24% of the measured worst-case. While we have given **aiT** timings for a sufficiently representative subset of HAM instructions to allow us to explore cost information for some simple examples, we have not yet been able to obtain information for all HAM instructions. We do not anticipate any technical problems in doing this, however. We also anticipate that the general approach we have described here will apply to similar abstract machine settings, such as the JVM.

The time cost model we have outlined here is formally derived from an underlying operational semantics of the HAM. We are in the process of constructing a static analysis to automatically obtain time information for Hume source programs. This analysis builds in an essential way both on the time cost model and on the concrete time information we have presented here. By demonstrating that the cost model is a good predictor of worst-case execution time, we have increased confidence that, provided our static analysis conforms to the cost model, it will also be a good predictor of worst-case execution times.

Acknowledgments

This work has been generously supported by the Systems Engineering for Autonomous Systems (SEAS) Defence Technology Centre established by the UK Ministry of Defence; by EU Framework VI grant IST-2004-510255 (EmBounded); by EPSRC Grant EPC/0001346; and by a personal Support Fellowship from the Royal Society of Edinburgh. We would like to thank Charlotte Bjuren, who assisted with obtaining detailed timing information; Robert Pointon, who assisted with the Renesas implementation and timing instructions; and Steffen Jost and Hans-Wolfgang Loidl, who assisted with the cost model.

References

1. Augustsson, L.: Compiling Lazy Functional Languages, Part II. PhD thesis, Dept. of Computer Science, Chalmers University of Technology, Göteborg, Sweden (1987)
2. Bernat, G., Burns, A., Wellings, A.: Portable Worst-Case Execution Time Analysis Using Java Byte Code. In: Proc. 12th Euromicro Intl. Conf. on Real-Time Systems (ECRTS 2000), Stockholm (June 2000)
3. Bernat, G., Colin, A., Petters, S.M.: WCET Analysis of Probabilistic Hard Real-Time Systems. In: Proc. 23rd IEEE Real-Time Systems Symposium (RTSS 2002) (December 2002)

4. Bonenfant, A., Chen, Z., Hammond, K., Michaelson, G.J., Wallace, A., Wallace, I.: Towards resource-certified software: A formal cost model for time and its application to an image-processing example. In: ACM Symposium on Applied Computing (SAC '07), Seoul, Korea, March 11-15 (2007)
5. Byhlin, S., Ermedahl, A., Gustafsson, J., Lisper, B.: Applying static WCET analysis to automotive communication software. In: 17th Euromicro Conference of Real-Time Systems, (ECRTS'05), Mallorca, Spain (July 2005)
6. Comaniciu, D., Ramesh, V., Meer, P.: Kernel-based object tracking. IEEE Transactions on Pattern Analysis and Machine Intelligence 25(5), 564–575 (2003)
7. Renesas Technology Corp. (2006) Home Page http://www.renesas.com.
8. Corti, M., Gross, T.: Approximation of the Worst-Case Execution Time Using Structural Analysis. In: Proc. ACM International Conference on Embedded Software (EMSOFT '04) (2004)
9. Cousot, P., Cousot, R.: Abstract interpretation: a unified lattice model for static analysis of programs by construction or approximation of fixpoints. In: 4th ACM Symposium on Principles of Programming Languages, pp. 238–252. ACM Press, New York (1977)
10. Crary, K., Weirich, S.: Resource Bound Certification. In: POPL'00 — Symposium on Principles of Prog. Langs. pp. 184–198, Boston, MA (January 2000)
11. Ferdinand, C.: Cache Behavior Prediction for Real-Time Systems, Saarland University, Saarbrücken, Germany. PhD thesis (1997)
12. Ferdinand, C., Heckmann, R., Langenbach, M., Martin, F., Schmidt, M., Theiling, H., Thesing, S., Wilhelm, R.: Reliable and precise WCET determination for a real-life processor. In: Henzinger, T.A., Kirsch, C.M. (eds.) EMSOFT 2001. LNCS, vol. 2211, pp. 469–485. Springer, Heidelberg (2001)
13. Ferdinand, C., Martin, F., Wilhelm, R., Alt, M.: Cache behavior prediction by abstract interpretation. Science of Computer Programming 35(2), 163–189 (1999)
14. Hammond, K.: Exploiting Purely Functional Programming to Obtain Bounded Resource Behaviour: the Hume Approach. In: Horváth, Z. (ed.) CEFP 2005. LNCS, vol. 4164, pp. 100–134. Springer, Heidelberg (2006)
15. Hammond, K., Ferdinand, C., Heckmann, R., Dyckhoff, R., Hofmann, M., Jost, S., Loidl, H.-W., Michaelson, G.J., Pointon, R., Scaife, N., Sérot, J., Wallace, A.: Towards Formally Verifiable WCET Analysis for a Functional Programming Language. In: Proc. Intl. Workshop on Worst-Case Execution Time (WCET) Analysis (April 2006)
16. Hammond, K., Michaelson, G.: Bounded Space Programming using Finite State Machines and Recursive Functions: the Hume Approach. ACM Transactions on Software Engineering and Methodology (TOSEM), in preparation. (2006)
17. Hammond, K., Michaelson, G.J.: Hume: a Domain-Specific Language for Real-Time Embedded Systems. In: Pfenning, F., Smaragdakis, Y. (eds.) GPCE 2003. LNCS, vol. 2830, pp. 37–56. Springer, Heidelberg (2003)
18. Hammond, K., Michaelson, G.J.: Predictable Space Behaviour in FSM-Hume. In: Peña, R., Arts, T. (eds.) IFL 2002. LNCS, vol. 2670, Springer, Heidelberg (2003)
19. Heckmann, R., Langenbach, M., Thesing, S., Wilhelm, R.: The influence of processor architecture on the design and the results of WCET tools. Proceedings of the IEEE 91(7), 1038–1054 (July 2003) Special Issue on Real-Time Systems.
20. Hofmann, M., Jost, S.: Static Prediction of Heap Space Usage for First-Order Functional Programs. In: POPL'03 — Symposium on Principles of Programming Languages, New Orleans, LA, USA, ACM Press, New York (January 2003)
21. Hughes, R.J.M.: The Design and Implementation of Programming Languages, DPhil Thesis, Programming Research Group, Oxford (July 1983)

22. Langenbach, M., Thesing, S., Heckmann, R.: Pipeline modeling for timing analysis. In: Hermenegildo, M.V., Puebla, G. (eds.) SAS 2002. LNCS, vol. 2477, pp. 294–309. Springer, Heidelberg (2002)
23. Li, Y.-T.S., Malik, S., Wolfe, A.: Efficient Microarchitecture Modeling and Path Analysis for Real-Time Software. In: Proc. RTSS '95: IEEE Real-Time Systems Symposium, pp. 298 (1995)
24. Meyerhöfer, M., Lauterwald, F.: Towards Platform-Independent Component Measurement. In: Proc. WCOP 2005 – Tenth International Workshop on Component-Oriented Programming, Glasgow (July 2005)
25. Puschner, P., Bernat, G.: WCET Analysis of Reusable Portable Code. In: Proc. 13th Euromicro Intl. Conf. on Real-Time Syst. (ECRTS 2001), pp. 45–52 (2001)
26. Sandell, D., Ermedahl, A., Gustafsson, J., Lisper, B.: Static timing analysis of real-time operating system code. In: Margaria, T., Steffen, B. (eds.) ISoLA 2004. LNCS, vol. 4313, Springer, Heidelberg (2006)
27. Sehlberg, D.: Static WCET analysis of task-oriented code for construction vehicles. Master's thesis, Mälardalen University, (October 2005)
28. Souyris, J., Le Pavec, E., Himbert, G., Jégu, V., Borios, G., Heckmann, R.: Computing the Worst Case Execution Time of an Avionics Program by Abstract Interpretation. In: Proc. 2005 Intl Workshop on Worst-Case Execution Time (WCET) Analysis, pp. 21–24 (2005)
29. IAR Systems. http://www.iar.com/. Home Page, (2006)
30. Theiling, H., Ferdinand, C.: Combining abstract interpretation and ILP for microarchitecture modelling and program path analysis. In: Proc. RTSS '98: IEEE Real-Time Systems Symposium, pp. 144–153, Madrid, Spain (December 1998)
31. Vasconcelos, P.B.: Cost Inference and Analysis for Recursive Functional Programs. PhD thesis, University of St Andrews, 2006, in preparation
32. Vasconcelos, P.B., Hammond, K.: Inferring Costs for Recursive, Polymorphic and Higher-Order Functional Programs. In: Trinder, P., Michaelson, G.J., Peña, R. (eds.) IFL 2003. LNCS, vol. 3145, pp. 86–101. Springer, Heidelberg (2004)
33. Wilhelm, R.: Determining bounds on execution times. In: Zurawski, R. (ed.) Handbook on Embedded Systems, CRC Press, Boca Raton pp. 14–1,14–23. (2005)
34. Wong, P.: Bytecode Monitoring of Java Programs, MSc thesis, University of Warwick (2003)

Automatic Partial Inversion of Inductively Sequential Functions*

Jesús M. Almendros-Jiménez[1] and Germán Vidal[2]

[1] University of Almería, Spain
jalmen@ual.es
[2] Technical University of Valencia, Spain
gvidal@dsic.upv.es

Abstract. We introduce a new partial inversion technique for first-order functional programs. Our technique is simple, fully automatic, and (when it succeeds) returns a program that belongs to the same class of the original program, namely the class of inductively sequential programs (i.e., typical functional programs). To ease the definition, our method proceeds in a stepwise manner: normalization (introduction of let expressions), proper inversion, and removal of let expressions. Furthermore, it can easily be implemented. Therefore, it forms an appropriate basis for developing a practically applicable transformation tool. Preliminary experiments with a prototype implementation of the partial inverter demonstrates the usefulness and viability of our approach.

1 Introduction

Program inversion is a fundamental transformation within the functional programming paradigm. Having a fully automatic inversion tool could be very useful for programmers because there are many functions that can be seen as the inverse of other, sometimes easier, functions (e.g., encoding and decoding, compression and decompression, etc). Moreover, having a function and its inverse can also be useful for defining *views* [19], where one needs to implement translation functions from a built-in data type to an algebraic data type and vice versa, so that both functions are inverses of each other.

Intuitively speaking, given a function f of arity n, the *total inversion* of function f is a new function f^{-1} such that

$$f^{-1}(t) = \langle t_1, \ldots, t_n \rangle \quad \text{if and only if} \quad f(t_1, \ldots, t_n) = t$$

for all terms $t_1, \ldots, t_n, t$. Computing the total inversion of a function is a difficult task and, in most cases, the inverse of a function does not exist (e.g., when the given function is not injective).

---

* This work has been partially supported by the EU (FEDER) and the Spanish MEC under grant TIN2005-09207-C03-02 and by the ICT for EU-India Cross-Cultural Dissemination Project ALA/95/23/2003/077-054.

Z. Horváth, V. Zsók, and A. Butterfield (Eds.): IFL 2006, LNCS 4449, pp. 253–270, 2007.

In this paper, and in contrast to most of the previous work on program inversion, we consider the computation of *partial inverses*. Roughly speaking, given a function f, the *partial inversion* of f w.r.t. the set of parameters $I = \{i_1, \ldots, i_m\} \subset \{1, \ldots, n\}$ is a new function $\overline{f}_I$ such that

$$\overline{f}_I(t, t_{i_1}, \ldots, t_{i_m}) = \langle t_{j_1}, \ldots, t_{j_k} \rangle \qquad \text{if and only if} \qquad f(t_1, \ldots, t_n) = t$$

for all terms $t_1, \ldots, t_n, t$, with $\{j_1, \ldots, j_k\} = \{1, \ldots, n\} \setminus I$. Clearly, partial inversion subsumes total inversion (when $I = \varnothing$). In contrast to total inversion, however, the considered function needs not be injective in order to be acceptable for partial inversion. Nevertheless, some form of injectivity w.r.t. the parameters I is required (see Sect. 3.1).

Consider, for instance, the usual definition of the addition on natural numbers (built from *zero* and *succ*):

$$
\begin{aligned}
add(zero, y) \quad &\rightarrow \quad y \\
add(succ(x), y) \quad &\rightarrow \quad succ(add(x, y))
\end{aligned}
$$

Here, there exist three possible partial inverses: $add_\varnothing$ (the total inversion), $add_{\{1\}}$ and $add_{\{2\}}$. The specifications of these partial inversions are as follows:

$$
\begin{aligned}
\overline{add}_\varnothing(t) = \langle t_1, t_2 \rangle \quad &\Leftrightarrow \quad add(t_1, t_2) = t \\
\overline{add}_{\{1\}}(t, t_1) = t_2 \quad &\Leftrightarrow \quad add(t_1, t_2) = t \\
\overline{add}_{\{2\}}(t, t_2) = t_1 \quad &\Leftrightarrow \quad add(t_1, t_2) = t
\end{aligned}
$$

Their definitions can be given, respectively, as follows:

$$
\begin{aligned}
\overline{add}_\varnothing(y) \quad &\rightarrow \quad \langle zero, y \rangle \\
\overline{add}_\varnothing(succ(w)) \quad &\rightarrow \quad \textbf{let } \langle x, y \rangle = \overline{add}_\varnothing(w) \textbf{ in } \langle succ(x), y \rangle
\end{aligned}
$$

$$
\begin{aligned}
\overline{add}_{\{1\}}(y, zero) \quad &\rightarrow \quad y \\
\overline{add}_{\{1\}}(succ(w), succ(x)) \quad &\rightarrow \quad \overline{add}_{\{1\}}(w, x)
\end{aligned}
$$

$$
\begin{aligned}
\overline{add}_{\{2\}}(y, y) \quad &\rightarrow \quad zero \\
\overline{add}_{\{2\}}(succ(w), y) \quad &\rightarrow \quad succ(\overline{add}_{\{2\}}(w, y))
\end{aligned}
$$

Observe that both $\overline{add}_{\{1\}}$ and $\overline{add}_{\{2\}}$ define the subtraction on natural numbers (though they are syntactically different).

The original definition of function *add* is *inductively sequential* [1]; roughly speaking, a function is inductively sequential when its definition is left-linear (i.e., there are no multiple occurrences of the same variable in the left-hand sides) and does not have overlapping left-hand sides (i.e., no left-hand sides unify). However, in the above partial inversions,

- the definition of the partial inverse $\overline{add}_\varnothing$ has overlapping left-hand sides, and
- the definition of the partial inverse $\overline{add}_{\{2\}}$ is not left-linear.

Therefore, program inversion can generally produce programs which do not belong to the same class of the original programs.

In this work, we consider that ensuring that partially inverted programs are inductively sequential (as the original ones) is mandatory, since otherwise the practical applicability of these partially inverted functions is unclear. For instance, although $\overline{add}_{\{1\}}$ and $\overline{add}_{\{2\}}$ are semantically equivalent (in the sense that both implement subtraction: $\overline{add}_{\{1\}}(t, t_1) = t_2$ iff $\overline{add}_{\{2\}}(t, t_2) = t_1$), the first function $\overline{add}_{\{1\}}$ can be used in any functional programming language or environment, while the second one $\overline{add}_{\{2\}}$ is often illegal (e.g., in Haskell) because it is not left-linear.

Furthermore, we consider *partial* inverses because they subsume the computation of *total* inverses and because functions need not be injective. Moreover, there are many practical cases where the computation of a partial inverse is more useful; e.g., while function $\overline{add}_{\{1\}}$ implements the subtraction on natural numbers, the practical use of the total inverse $\overline{add}_\varnothing$ is not so obvious.

The main features of the partial inversion method that we introduce in this paper can be summarized as follows:

- The method proceeds in a stepwise manner: normalization (introduction of let expressions), partial inversion, and removal of let expressions.
- The method is purely static, i.e., no (partial) computations are performed. As a consequence, it can be efficiently implemented.
- Finally, our method always terminates, either returning an inductively sequential program—defining the partial inversion of a function—or a failure.

2   Preliminaries

We follow the standard framework of *term rewriting* [2] since it suffices to model the first-order component of many functional programming languages.

Term Rewriting Systems. In term rewriting, a set of rewrite rules (or oriented equations) $l \to r$ such that l is a nonvariable term and r is a term is called a *term rewriting system* (TRS for short); terms l and r are called the left-hand side and the right-hand side of the rule, respectively. If there are variables in the right-hand side of a rule that do not appear in the corresponding left-hand side, we say that the TRS contains *extra variables*. In this work, we only consider TRSs without extra variables. Given a TRS $\mathcal{R}$ over a signature $\mathcal{F}$, the *defined* symbols $\mathcal{D}$ are the root symbols of the left-hand sides of the rules and the *constructors* are $\mathcal{C} = \mathcal{F} \backslash \mathcal{D}$. We often write f/n to denote that the arity of the function or constructor f is n. We restrict ourselves to finite signatures and TRSs. We denote the domain of terms and *constructor terms* by $\mathcal{T}(\mathcal{F}, \mathcal{V})$ and $\mathcal{T}(\mathcal{C}, \mathcal{V})$, respectively, where $\mathcal{V}$ is a set of variables with $\mathcal{F} \cap \mathcal{V} = \varnothing$.

A TRS $\mathcal{R}$ is *constructor-based* if the left-hand sides of its rules have the form $f(s_1, \dots, s_n)$ where s_i are constructor terms, i.e., $s_i \in \mathcal{T}(\mathcal{C}, \mathcal{V})$, for all $i = 1, \dots, n$. The set of variables appearing in a term t is denoted by $Var(t)$. A term t is *linear* if every variable of $\mathcal{V}$ occurs at most once in t. $\mathcal{R}$ is left-linear if l is linear for all rule $l \to r \in \mathcal{R}$. The *definition* of f in $\mathcal{R}$ is the set of rules in $\mathcal{R}$ whose root symbol in the left-hand side is f. A function $f \in \mathcal{D}$ is left-linear if the rules in its definition are left-linear.

The root symbol of a term t is denoted by $root(t)$. A term t is *operation-rooted* (resp. *constructor-rooted*) if $root(t) \in \mathcal{D}$ (resp. $root(t) \in \mathcal{C}$). As it is common practice, a *position* p in a term t is represented by a sequence of natural numbers, where ϵ denotes the root position. Positions are used to address the nodes of a term viewed as a tree: $t|_p$ denotes the *subterm* of t at position p and $t[s]_p$ denotes the result of *replacing the subterm* $t|_p$ by the term s. A term t is *ground* if $\mathcal{V}ar(t) = \varnothing$. A *substitution* σ is a mapping $\{x_1 \mapsto t_1, \ldots, x_n \mapsto t_n\}$ from variables to terms such that its domain $\mathcal{D}om(\sigma) = \{x \in \mathcal{V} \mid x \neq \sigma(x)\}$ is finite. The identity substitution is denoted by id. We write $\overline{o_n}$ for the *sequence of syntactic objects* $o_1, \ldots, o_n$.

The evaluation of terms w.r.t. a TRS is formalized with the notion of *rewriting*. A *rewrite step* is an application of a rewrite rule to a term, i.e., $t \to_{p,R} s$ if there exists a position p in t, a rewrite rule $R = (l \to r)$ and a substitution σ with $t|_p = \sigma(l)$ and $s = t[\sigma(r)]_p$ (p and R will often be omitted in the notation of a reduction step). A term t is called *irreducible* or in *normal form* if there is no term s with $t \to s$. We denote by $\to^+$ the transitive closure of $\to$ and by $\to^*$ its reflexive and transitive closure. Given a TRS $\mathcal{R}$ and a term t, we say that t *evaluates* to s iff $t \to^* s$ and s is in normal form.

Inductively Sequential Systems. Inductively sequential TRSs [1] are a subclass of constructor-based left-linear TRSs. The formal definition of this class of programs requires the notion of *definitional tree* [1]. Essentially, a TRS is *inductively sequential* [1] when all its operations are defined by rewrite rules that, recursively, make on their arguments a case distinction analogous to a data type (or structural) induction (i.e., a typical functional program).

Example 1. Consider the following definition of the less-or-equal relation:

$$
\begin{array}{rcl}
zero \leqslant y & \to & true \\
succ(x) \leqslant zero & \to & false \\
succ(x) \leqslant succ(y) & \to & x \leqslant y
\end{array}
$$

This function is inductively sequential because the left-hand sides can be inductively organized as follows:[1]

$$
\boxed{n} \leqslant m \Rightarrow
\begin{cases}
zero \leqslant m \to true & \text{(first rule)} \\
succ(x) \leqslant \boxed{m} \Rightarrow
\begin{cases}
succ(x) \leqslant zero \to false & \text{(second rule)} \\
succ(x) \leqslant succ(y) \to x \leqslant y & \text{(third rule)}
\end{cases}
\end{cases}
$$

Inductive sequentiality is not a limiting condition for programming. In fact, the first-order components of many functional and functional logic programs written in, e.g., Haskell, ML or Curry, are inductively sequential.

---

[1] Actually, this is the *definitional tree* of function "$\leqslant$".

3   A Method for Partial Inversion

In this section, we present our stepwise method for the partial inversion of inductively sequential TRSs.

In the following, we consider the partial inversion of a given function f/n w.r.t. a set $I \subset \{1,\ldots,n\}$ of input (or "known") parameters. Therefore, we want to obtain a new function, which we call $\overline{f}_I$, which takes the output of the original function and the input parameters (according to I), and returns the remaining parameters of the original function, which we denote by $\overline{I} = \{1,\ldots,n\}\backslash I$ (the "unknown" parameters).

Observe that $I = \{1,\ldots,n\}$ is not allowed because it would imply that, in the inverted function, all arguments, together with the output, would be known, which would be meaningless unless one wants to produce a sort of "Boolean test". Now, we formally introduce our notion of partial inversion:

Definition 1 (partial inversion). *Let $\mathcal{R}$ be an inductively sequential TRS that includes the definition of function f/n. Then, $\mathcal{R}'$ is a partial inversion of $\mathcal{R}$ w.r.t. f and $I = \{i_1,\ldots,i_m\} \subset \{1,\ldots,n\}$ iff the following conditions hold:*

1. *$\mathcal{R}'$ is inductively sequential and*
2. *it includes the definition of a function $\overline{f}_I$ such that $f(t_1,\ldots,t_n) \to^* t$ iff $\overline{f}_I(t, t_{i_1},\ldots,t_{i_m}) \to^* \langle t_{j_1},\ldots,t_{j_k}\rangle$ for all ground constructor terms $t_1,\ldots,t_n$, t, where $\overline{I} = \{j_1,\ldots,j_k\}$.*

In this case, we say that $\overline{f}_I$ is the partial inverse of f w.r.t. I.

As mentioned before, the first condition above is often ignored (e.g., [15]), but we require it in order to produce partially inverted programs which are useful in practice.

3.1   Preconditions

In this section, we present three preconditions for our partial inversion algorithm to be successful. These preconditions are *local*, i.e., should be checked for every function involved in the partial inversion process (see Sect. 3.3).

As mentioned in the introduction, functions need not be injective to be partially inverted. However, some form of injectivity is still necessary. Let us consider a function f/n that we want to partially invert w.r.t. $I = \{i_1,\ldots,i_m\} \subset \{1,\ldots,n\}$. Assume a relation $Rel(f)$, defined as follows:

$$Rel(f) = \{(t_1,\ldots,t_n,t) \mid f(t_1,\ldots,t_n) \to^* t\}$$

where $t_1,\ldots,t_n,t$ are ground constructor terms (i.e., *values*). Then, we say that the partial inversion of f w.r.t. I is *well-defined* if $(t_{j_1},\ldots,t_{j_k}) \neq (s_{j_1},\ldots,s_{j_k})$ implies $(t_{i_1},\ldots,t_{i_m},t) \neq (s_{i_1},\ldots,s_{i_m},s)$ for all tuples $(t_1,\ldots,t_n,t),(s_1,\ldots,s_n,t)$ in $Rel(f)$, where $\overline{I}frm[o]-- = \{j_1,\ldots,j_k\}$.

Trivially, a total inversion is well-defined when the considered function is injective. In general, however, the set of functions that can be partially inverted is greater than the set of functions that can be totally inverted.

For instance, the total inversion of the addition function *add* shown in Sect. 1 is not well-defined because *add* is not injective. On the other hand, the partial inversion of *add* w.r.t. $\{1\}$ is well-defined because, given the evaluations $add(t_1, t_2) \rightarrow^* t$ and $add(s_1, s_2) \rightarrow^* s$, whenever $t_2 \neq s_2$, we have $(t_1, t) \neq (s_1, s)$, where t_1, t_2, t, s_1, s_2, s are ground constructor terms.

Unfortunately, determining if a partial inversion is well-defined is generally undecidable. Therefore, we introduce three (decidable) preconditions for partial inversion. The first precondition, which regards extra variables, is very simple:

Precondition 1 (extra variables). Let f/n be a function to be partially inverted w.r.t. $I = \{i_1, \ldots, i_m\} \subset \{1, \ldots, n\}$. Then, function f/n must fulfill the following condition: $\mathcal{V}ar(\{t_{j_1}, \ldots, t_{j_k}\}) \subseteq \mathcal{V}ar(\{r, t_{i_1}, \ldots, t_{i_m}\})$ for every rule $f(t_1, \ldots, t_n) \rightarrow r$ in the definition of f, with $\bar{I} = \{j_1, \ldots, j_k\}$.

For instance, a function *fst* defined by a rule of the form $fst(x, y) \rightarrow x$ cannot be partially inverted w.r.t. $\{1\}$ since $\mathcal{V}ar(\{y\}) \not\subseteq \mathcal{V}ar(\{x, x\})$. Indeed, the definition of the partially inverted function $\overline{fst}_{\{1\}}$ would contain an extra variable: $\overline{fst}_{\{1\}}(x, x) \rightarrow y$.

In the following, we denote by $C[e_1, \ldots, e_n]$ a term with a constructor context C and *maximal* operation-rooted subterms $e_1, \ldots, e_n$. For instance, the term $c(f(a), s(g(b)))$, with $f, g \in \mathcal{D}$ defined functions and $a, b, c \in \mathcal{C}$ constructor symbols, can be represented by $C[f(a), g(b)]$, where the context C denotes the constructor term $c(\bullet, s(\bullet))$ with two "holes". A constructor term (or a variable) can thus be denoted by $C[]$, i.e., a term with no maximal operation-rooted subterms.

The second precondition regards left-linearity and is also rather simple:

Precondition 2 (left-linearity). Let f/n be a function to be partially inverted w.r.t. $I = \{i_1, \ldots, i_m\} \subset \{1, \ldots, n\}$. Then, C must be linear and must not share variables with $t_{i_1}, \ldots, t_{i_m}$ for every rule $f(t_1, \ldots, t_n) \rightarrow C[e_1, \ldots, e_l]$ in the definition of function f.

Consider, e.g., the following function *double*:

$$double([\,]) \rightarrow [\,]$$
$$double(x : xs) \rightarrow x : x : double(xs)$$

where lists are built from $[\,]$ and ":". This function does not fulfill the second precondition because the constructor part in the right-hand side of the second rule, $x : x : \bullet$, is not linear. Actually, the partial inversion of *double* w.r.t. $\varnothing$ would return the following rules:

$$\overline{double}_{\varnothing}([\,]) \rightarrow [\,]$$
$$\overline{double}_{\varnothing}(x : x : xs) \rightarrow x : \overline{double}_{\varnothing}(xs)$$

Also, the partial inversion of function *fst* w.r.t. $\{1\}$ above does not fulfill the second precondition because the right-hand side x is linear but also occur in the first input parameter x. On the other hand, the second precondition holds for function *fst* w.r.t. $\{2\}$ since x and y do not share variables.

We note that the second precondition could be removed by allowing the replacement of repeated occurrences of the same variable in the left-hand side of a rule by equality tests in the corresponding right-hand side. For example, the definition of $\overline{double}_\varnothing$ could be transformed as follows:

$$\overline{double}_\varnothing([\,]) \to [\,]$$
$$\overline{double}_\varnothing(x:y:xs) \to cond(eq(x,y), x : \overline{double}_\varnothing(xs))$$

where $cond(c,t)$ returns t if c evaluates to *true* and $eq(t_1, t_2)$ is a Boolean equality test. Such a transformation, however, would not be useful in a lazy context because eq should be regarded as a *strict* equality and, thus, the inverted function would be more strict than the original function. It could be useful in the context of a strict language though.

We now present our last precondition for ensuring the inductive sequentiality of the partially inverted function.

Precondition 3 (inductive sequentiality). Let f/n be a function to be partially inverted w.r.t. $I = \{i_1, \ldots, i_m\} \subset \{1, \ldots, n\}$. Then, there must be a definitional tree for a function $\overline{f}_I$ whose definition contains the following left-hand sides:

$$\{ \, \overline{f}_I(C[x_1, \ldots, x_l], t_{i_1}, \ldots, t_{i_m}) \mid f(t_1, \ldots, t_n) \to C[e_1, \ldots, e_l] \in \mathcal{R}_f$$
$$\text{and } x_1, \ldots, x_l \text{ are fresh variables} \, \}$$

where $\mathcal{R}_f$ contains the rules in the definition of function f.

Observe that the above precondition can be tested *before* partial inversion proceeds, since only the left-hand sides are relevant to determine the existence of a definitional tree associated to a function.

Consider, for instance, the following function *app*:

$$app([\,], y) \to y$$
$$app(x:xs, y) \to x : app(xs, y)$$

If we consider its partial inversion w.r.t. $\{2\}$, then the third precondition does not hold since there is no definitional tree for a function defined by a set of rules whose left-hand sides are $\{\overline{app}_{\{2\}}(y, y), \overline{app}_{\{2\}}(x : w, y)\}$ (roughly speaking, because the left-hand sides overlap).

Now, we present our stepwise process for partial inversion.

3.2 Normalization

The first stage of our transformation is used to *flatten* the right-hand sides of the rules so that no nested function calls occur. This transformation is not really necessary for partially inverting functions, but it greatly simplifies the definition of the inversion algorithm in Sect. 3.3.

Definition 2 (normalized TRS). *A normalized TRS contains either rules of the form*

$$l \to p_0 \quad or \quad l \to \textbf{let } p_1 = e_1, \dots, p_n = e_n \textbf{ in } p_0$$

where $p_0, p_1, \dots, p_n$ are constructor terms and $e_1, \dots, e_n$ are operation-rooted terms with constructor terms as arguments (i.e., nested defined function symbols are not allowed). Each equality, $p_i = e_i$, is called a pattern definition. *We further require that $Var(e_i) \subseteq Var(l) \cup Var(p_1) \cup \dots \cup Var(p_{i-1})$, for $i = 1, \dots, n$, and $Var(p_0) \subseteq Var(l) \cup Var(p_1) \cup \dots \cup Var(p_n)$.*[2]

Although let expressions may introduce extra variables, these are a kind of *local* variables that can easily be removed by either inlining or lambda lifting (see below). The following definition introduces our normalization process:

Definition 3 (normalization). *Given a TRS $\mathcal{R}$, the normalized TRS $\mathcal{N}(\mathcal{R})$ is obtained by replacing every rewrite rule $l \to r \in \mathcal{R}$ by $l \to r'$ in $\mathcal{N}(\mathcal{R})$, where r' is obtained from r by applying the following transformations as much as possible:*

$$
\begin{aligned}
C[\overline{e_k}] &\implies \textbf{let } x_1 = e_1, \dots, x_k = e_k \textbf{ in } C[\overline{x_k}] \\
f(\overline{e_k}) &\implies \textbf{let } x = f(\overline{e_k}) \textbf{ in } x \\
\textbf{let } p_1 = e_1, &\implies \textbf{let } \overline{x_{jm_j} = e_{jm_j}}, \ p_1 = e_1, \\
\dots, & \qquad \dots, \\
p_i = f(\dots, C[\overline{e_{jm_j}}], \dots) & \qquad p_i = f(\dots, C[\overline{x_{jm_j}}], \dots), \\
\dots, & \qquad \dots, \\
p_k = e_k \textbf{ in } p & \qquad p_k = e_k \textbf{ in } p
\end{aligned}
$$

where $x, x_1, \dots, x_k, x_{j1}, \dots, x_{jm_j}$ are fresh variables. The process stops when no rule is applicable—clearly a terminating process.

Roughly speaking, normalization proceeds as follows: if the right-hand side is a constructor term, then it is already normalized; otherwise,

- If it is an operation-rooted term, then it is completely replaced by a fresh variable and a new pattern definition in a let expression is returned.
- If it is a constructor-rooted term that contains some maximal operation-rooted subterms, normalization replaces those operation-rooted subterms by fresh variables and adds new pattern definitions by means of a let declaration.
- Once the right-hand side is transformed into a let expression, we continue by flattening the arguments of operation-rooted terms in the right-hand sides of pattern definitions so that all function arguments become constructor terms. We note that new pattern definitions are added to the left in order to fulfill the condition on the variables of Def. 2.

Observe that, if we take a TRS and normalize it using Def. 3, then it could be transformed back into an ordinary TRS by applying *inlining*, i.e., by applying the following rules to the right-hand sides of normalized TRSs as much as possible:

$$
\begin{aligned}
\textbf{let } p_1 = e_1 \textbf{ in } p &\Rightarrow \{p_1 \mapsto e_1\}(p) \\
\textbf{let } \overline{p_n = e_n} \textbf{ in } p &\Rightarrow \{p_n \mapsto e_n\}(\textbf{let } p_1 = e_1, \dots, p_{n-1} = e_{n-1} \textbf{ in } p) \quad n > 1
\end{aligned}
$$

---

[2] This is similar to the notion of *deterministic* conditional TRS.

Input: a normalized TRS $\mathcal{R}$, a function f/n, and a set $I \subset \{1, \ldots, n\}$;
Output: a normalized TRS $\mathcal{R}'$ (the partial inversion of $\mathcal{R}$ w.r.t. f and I) or a failure;
Initialization: $\mathcal{R}' := \{\,\}$, $Inv := \{\,\}$, $Pend := \{(f/n, I)\}$;
Repeat
    1. select a pair $(f/n, I) \in Pend$
    2. if $I = \{1, \ldots, n\}$
        then stop with failure; /* Boolean tests are not allowed */
        else update $Inv := Inv \cup \{(f, I)\}$ and $Pend := Pend \setminus \{(f, I)\}$
    3. if the Preconditions 1, 2 and 3 hold
        then proceed with step 4
        else stop with failure /* $\mathcal{R}'$ would not be inductively sequential */
    4. let $\mathcal{R}_f^I = pinv(\mathcal{R}, f, I)$; update $\mathcal{R}' := \mathcal{R}' \cup \mathcal{R}_f^I$
    5. $Pend := Pend \cup (pcalls(\mathcal{R}_f^I) \setminus Inv)$
Until $Pend = \{\,\}$
Return $\mathcal{R}'$

Fig. 1. Partial inversion algorithm

Note that these rules are well-defined in our case because patterns p_i are always variables in TRSs obtained by applying Def. 3. In general, however, some form of lambda-lifting [9] is required to remove let expressions (see Sect. 3.4).

Example 2. Consider the following inductively sequential TRS that defines the function *incL* for incrementing all the elements of a list by a given value:

$$incL([\,], i) \quad \to [\,] \qquad\qquad add(zero, y) \quad \to y$$
$$incL(x : xs, i) \to add(i, x) : incL(xs, i) \qquad add(succ(x), y) \to succ(add(x, y))$$

The normalization of this program returns

$$incL([\,], i) \quad \to [\,] \qquad\qquad\qquad add(zero, y) \quad \to y$$
$$incL(x : xs, i) \to \textbf{let } w_1 = add(i, x), \qquad add(succ(x), y) \to \textbf{let } w = add(x, y)$$
$$w_2 = incL(xs, i) \qquad\qquad\qquad\qquad \textbf{in } succ(w)$$
$$\textbf{in } w_1 : w_2$$

3.3 Partial Inversion Algorithm

Our algorithm for partial inversion is shown in Fig. 1. Roughly speaking, our iterative algorithm for computing the partial inversion of a function proceeds as follows:

- The algorithm takes a normalized program and returns either a failure or a normalized program (the desired partial inversion).
- In every iteration, the partial inversion of a function denoted by a pair $(f/n, I)$ is considered, where f is a function symbol of arity n and $I \subset \{1, \ldots, n\}$.
- Given such a pair $(f/n, I)$, we first check the preconditions of Sect. 3.1 in order to stop the inversion process if the partial inversion of f w.r.t. I would not be inductively sequential (with no extra variables).

$$((\mathbf{let} \ \ldots, p_l = e_l, \ldots \ \mathbf{in} \ p))_V^l = ((\mathbf{let} \ \ldots, p_l = e_l, \ldots \ \mathbf{in} \ p))_{V \cup \mathcal{V}ar(p_l)}^{l-1}$$
$$\text{if } \mathcal{V}ar(e_l) \subseteq V \text{ and } p_l \notin V$$

$$
\begin{aligned}
&((\mathbf{let} \ p_1 = e_1, && = ((\mathbf{let} \ p_1 = e_1, \\
&\quad \ldots, && \quad \ldots, \\
&\quad p_l = g(\overline{q_b}) && \quad \langle q_{j_1}, \ldots, q_{j_k} \rangle = \overline{g}_{\{i_1,\ldots,i_m\}}(p_l, q_{i_1}, \ldots, q_{i_m}) \\
&\quad \ldots, && \quad \ldots, \\
&\quad p_a = e_a \ \mathbf{in} \ p))_V^l && \quad p_a = e_a \ \mathbf{in} \ p))_{V \cup \mathcal{V}ar(q_{j_1}) \cup \ldots \cup \mathcal{V}ar(q_{j_k})}^{l-1} \\
& && \text{if } \mathcal{V}ar(q_w) \subseteq V \text{ for all } w = i_1, \ldots, i_m, \ m \geq 0, \\
& && \quad \mathcal{V}ar(q_u) \not\subseteq V \text{ for all } u = j_1, \ldots, j_k, \ k \geq 0, \text{and} \\
& && \quad \{i_1, \ldots, i_m\} \uplus \{j_1, \ldots, j_k\} = \{1, \ldots, b\} \\
&((\mathbf{let} \ \overline{p_a = e_a} \ \mathbf{in} \ p))_V^0 && = \mathbf{let} \ \overline{p_a = e_a} \ \mathbf{in} \ p
\end{aligned}
$$

Fig. 2. Auxiliary function $(\!(\ )\!)$

- If the preconditions hold, then we compute the partial inversion $\overline{f}_I$ of f w.r.t. I by means of function $pinv$ (see Def. 4).
- The iteration terminates by updating the set of pending partial inversions; this is done by using the auxiliary function $pcalls$, which simply traverses the right-hand sides of a function definition and then returns a set which includes a pair $(g/m, J)$ for each call $\overline{g}_J(t_1, \ldots, t_m)$ in these right-hand sides.

The following definition formalizes the main component of our partial inversion algorithm:

Definition 4 (function $pinv$**).** *Let $\mathcal{R}$ be a normalized TRS, f/n be a function, and $I \subset \{1, \ldots, n\}$ be a set. The partial inversion of f w.r.t. I, in symbols $pinv(\mathcal{R}, f, I)$, is obtained as the set*

$$\{ \ [\![l \to r]\!]_I \mid l \to r \ \text{belongs to the definition of } f \ \text{in } \mathcal{R} \ \}$$

Function $[\![\ ]\!]$ is defined as follows:

$$
\begin{aligned}
[\![f(\overline{p_n}) \to C[]]\!]_I &= \overline{f}_I(C[], p_{i_1}, \ldots, p_{i_m}) \to \langle p_{j_1}, \ldots, p_{j_k} \rangle \\
[\![f(\overline{p_n}) \to \mathbf{let} \ \overline{q_l = e_l} \ \mathbf{in} \ C[]]\!]_I &= \overline{f}_I(C[], p_{i_1}, \ldots, p_{i_m}) \to ((\mathbf{let} \ \overline{q_l = e_l} \\
& \qquad\qquad\qquad\qquad\qquad \mathbf{in} \ \langle p_{j_1}, \ldots, p_{j_k} \rangle))_V^l
\end{aligned}
$$

where $I = \{i_1, \ldots, i_m\}$, $\overline{I} = \{j_1, \ldots, j_k\}$, and $V = \mathcal{V}ar(\overline{f}_I(C[], p_{i_1}, \ldots, p_{i_m}))$. The auxiliary function $(\!(\ )\!)$ is defined inductively as shown in Fig. 2.

Essentially, function $pinv$ above considers sequentially[3] each pattern definition $p_l = g(q_1, \ldots, q_b)$ in the let declaration and transforms it into a new pattern definition according to the set V of "known" variables (which is initialized to the variables of the new left-hand side) as follows:

- If all variables in $q_1, \ldots, q_b$ are known (i.e., belong to V), then we do not modify this pattern definition (i.e., a call to a function of the original program is performed);

---

[3] It proceeds from right to left in order to transform outer function calls first.

– Otherwise, we divide the parameters of g into a set $\{i_1, \ldots, i_m\}$ of input parameters—i.e., associated to those arguments of g whose variables belong to the current set V of "known" variables—and output parameters $\{j_1, \ldots, j_k\}$, and replace the original pattern definition by $\langle q_{j_1}, \ldots, q_{j_k} \rangle = \overline{g}_{\{i_1, \ldots, i_m\}}(p_l, q_{i_1}, \ldots, q_{i_m})$.

Example 3. Consider the normalized TRS of Example 2. The stepwise computation of $pinv(\mathcal{R}, incL, \{2\})$ proceeds as follows:

$$[\![incL([\,], i) \to [\,]]\!]_{\{2\}} \quad = \quad \overline{incL}_{\{2\}}([\,], i) \to [\,]$$

$$[\![incL(x : xs, i) \to \mathbf{let}\ w_1 = add(i, x),\ w_2 = incL(xs, i)\ \mathbf{in}\ w_1 : w_2]\!]_{\{2\}}$$
$$= \overline{incL}_{\{2\}}(w_1 : w_2, i) \to (\!(\mathbf{let}\ w_1 = add(i, x),\ w_2 = incL(xs, i)\ \mathbf{in}\ x : xs)\!)^2_{\{w_1, w_2, i\}}$$

where

$$(\!(\mathbf{let}\ w_1 = add(i, x),\ w_2 = incL(xs, i)\ \mathbf{in}\ x : xs)\!)^2_{\{w_1, w_2, i\}}$$
$$= (\!(\mathbf{let}\ w_1 = add(i, x),\ xs = \overline{incL}_{\{2\}}(w_2, i)\ \mathbf{in}\ x : xs)\!)^1_{\{w_1, w_2, i, xs\}}$$
$$= (\!(\mathbf{let}\ x = \overline{add}_{\{1\}}(w_1, i),\ xs = \overline{incL}_{\{2\}}(w_2, i)\ \mathbf{in}\ x : xs)\!)^0_{\{w_1, w_2, i, xs, x\}}$$
$$= \mathbf{let}\ x = \overline{add}_{\{1\}}(w_1, i),\ xs = \overline{incL}_{\{2\}}(w_2, i)\ \mathbf{in}\ x : xs$$

Now, function *pcalls* would return the set $\{(add/2, \{1\}), (incL/2, \{2\})\}$, though only $(add/2, \{1\})$ is added to *Pend* since $(incL/2, \{2\})$ already belongs to *Inv*. Then, the computation of $pinv(\mathcal{R}, add, \{1\})$ begins so that the following partial inversion is computed:

$$\overline{add}_{\{1\}}(y, zero) \to y$$
$$\overline{add}_{\{1\}}(succ(w), succ(x)) \to \mathbf{let}\ y = \overline{add}_{\{1\}}(w, x)\ \mathbf{in}\ y$$

The final transformed program is thus as follows:

$$\overline{incL}_{\{2\}}([\,], i) \to [\,]$$
$$\overline{incL}_{\{2\}}(w_1 : w_2, i) \to \mathbf{let}\ x = \overline{add}_{\{1\}}(w_1, i),\ xs = \overline{incL}_{\{2\}}(w_2, i)\ \mathbf{in}\ x : xs$$
$$\overline{add}_{\{1\}}(y, zero) \to y$$
$$\overline{add}_{\{1\}}(succ(w), succ(x)) \to \mathbf{let}\ y = \overline{add}_{\{1\}}(w, x)\ \mathbf{in}\ y$$

which implements a function $\overline{incL}_{\{2\}}$ that decrements all the elements of the input list by a given value (using the auxiliary function $\overline{add}_{\{1\}}$ to perform subtraction on natural numbers).

3.4   Removal of Let Declarations

Let expressions in transformed programs can easily be removed by applying a simplified version of *lambda lifting* [9]. In particular, we follow the transformation presented in [4, Appendix D], where a rule of the form

$$l \to \mathbf{let}\ p_1 = e_1, \ldots, p_{i-1} = e_{i-1}, p_i = e_i, p_{i+1} = e_{i+1}, \ldots, p_m = e_m\ \mathbf{in}\ e$$

is transformed into the rules

$$
\begin{aligned}
l & \rightarrow g(\overline{x_k}, e_i) \\
g(\overline{x_k}, z) & \rightarrow g'(\overline{x_k}, g_1(z), \ldots, g_m(z)) \\
g'(\overline{x_k}, \overline{y_m}) & \rightarrow \mathbf{let}\ p_1 = e_1, \ldots, p_{i-1} = e_{i-1}, p_{i+1} = e_{i+1}, \ldots, p_m = e_m\ \mathbf{in}\ e \\
g_1(p_i) & \rightarrow y_1 \\
& \cdots \\
g_m(p_i) & \rightarrow y_m
\end{aligned}
$$

where $x_1, \ldots, x_k$ are the variables of l, $y_1, \ldots, y_m$ are the variables occurring in p_i, z is a fresh variable, and $g, g', g_1, \ldots, g_m$ are new function symbols. This step is repeated until all local patterns are eliminated.

Nevertheless, we allow the application of the simpler transformation of *inlining* (see Sect. 3.2) when the pattern definition has the form $x = e$.

Example 4. Consider the partially inverted TRS of Example 3. Here, inlining suffices to remove let expressions, so that the following inductively sequential system is obtained:

$$
\begin{aligned}
\overline{incL}_{\{2\}}([\,], i) & \rightarrow [\,] \\
\overline{incL}_{\{2\}}(w_1 : w_2, i) & \rightarrow \overline{add}_{\{1\}}(w_1, i) : \overline{incL}_{\{2\}}(w_2, i) \\[1ex]
\overline{add}_{\{1\}}(y, zero) & \rightarrow y \\
\overline{add}_{\{1\}}(succ(w), succ(x)) & \rightarrow \overline{add}_{\{1\}}(w, x)
\end{aligned}
$$

3.5   Correctness

Although there exist several approaches to function inversion in the literature (e.g., [6,8,10,17]), we only found a formal proof of correctness for the transformation in the work of Nishida et al. [15].

Basically, the correctness of our technique relies on [15, Theorem 9], regarding normalization and partial inversion, and the correctness of lambda lifting, regarding the removal of let expressions.

Let us first consider the work of Nishida et al. [15]. There are two kinds of differences between our method and that of [15]:

- *Restrictions.* In comparison with [15], we added several new restrictions in order to ensure that the result is "acceptable". For instance, [15] may produce non-deterministic functions containing extra-variables which require a logical extension of reduction—called *narrowing* [18]—in order to be able to evaluate inverse functions.
- *Simplifications.* Thanks to the new restrictions, the overall method can be presented in a simpler and more intuitive way.

Obviously, the addition of new restrictions do not affect to the correctness result of [15] and, thus, Theorem 9 is still applicable.

Regarding the simplifications, they are not difficult to prove. For instance, we could easily prove that partially inverted functions are indeed inductively sequential and do not contain extra-variables; this is an immediate consequence of the preconditions in Sect. 3.1. Also, we have replaced the (more complex) unraveling of [15] by a simpler form of lambda-lifting. This is not as immediate as the above property, but could easily be proved by showing that the partial inversion of each function returns a normalized TRS. In this case, since the partial inversion is a deterministic TRS (in the terminology of [15]), then standard inlining (in most of the cases) or lambda-lifting suffices to produce a program without extra variables.

On the other hand, the correctness of the removal of let expressions is derived from the correctness of either inlining or lambda lifting [9] (see also [3,13]), whose correctness is proved in [5]. We note that a similar transformation is considered in [15] by means of the definition of a so called *unraveling* [11].

4   Extensions of the Method

In this section, we describe how our method can be extended to cope with higher-order functions and lazy evaluation.

Higher-Order. Let us first consider a straightforward application of our method to a higher-order program. Consider, for instance, the well-known function map:

$$map(f, [\,]) \rightarrow [\,]$$
$$map(f, x : xs) \rightarrow f(x) : map(f, xs)$$

Then, in order to compute the partial inversion of map w.r.t. $\{1\}$, our method proceeds as follows. First, the normalized program is computed:

$$map(f, [\,]) \rightarrow [\,]$$
$$map(f, x : xs) \rightarrow \textbf{let } w = f(x), \ ws = map(f, xs) \textbf{ in } w : ws$$

Now, the partial inversion step returns the following program:

$$\overline{map}_{\{1\}}([\,], f) \rightarrow [\,]$$
$$\overline{map}_{\{1\}}(w : ws, f) \rightarrow \textbf{let } x = \overline{f}_{\{1\}}(w), \ xs = \overline{map}_{\{1\}}(ws, f) \textbf{ in } x : xs$$

Finally, by removing let expressions we get

$$\overline{map}_{\{1\}}([\,], f) \rightarrow [\,]$$
$$\overline{map}_{\{1\}}(w : ws, f) \rightarrow \overline{f}_{\{1\}}(w) : \overline{map}_{\{1\}}(ws, f)$$

so that $\overline{map}_{\{1\}}$ maps the inverse of a function to each element of a given list. Now, the problem of how the partial inverse $\overline{f}_{\{1\}}$ can be computed arises. Since function f is not known at compile time, the pair $(f, \{1\})$ cannot be considered in the next iteration of the partial inversion algorithm.

In order to deal with such a situation, we could produce a partial inversion of the form

$$\overline{map}_{\{1\}}([\,], f) \rightarrow [\,]$$
$$\overline{map}_{\{1\}}(w : ws, f) \rightarrow inv(f, \{1\})(w) : \overline{map}_{\{1\}}(ws, f)$$

where the auxiliary function inv is used to compute the name of the partially inverted function at run-time. In order to determine the possible values of variable f above, one could apply a standard closure analysis and/or ask the programmer. For instance, if we determine that function map is only called with functions foo and boh, then only $\overline{foo}_{\{1\}}$ and $\overline{boh}_{\{1\}}$ should be computed. Moreover, we should add the following definition of inv to the partially inverted program:

$$inv(foo, \{1\}) \rightarrow \overline{foo}_{\{1\}}$$
$$inv(boh, \{1\}) \rightarrow \overline{boh}_{\{1\}}$$

Laziness. Regarding non-strict functions, our method can already be applied to lazy programs. Consider the following program:

$$foo(n, m) \rightarrow take(n, repeat(m))$$
$$take(zero, xs) \rightarrow [\,]$$
$$take(succ(n), x : xs) \rightarrow x : take(n, xs)$$
$$repeat(m) \rightarrow m : repeat(m)$$

where $foo(n, m)$ returns a list of n elements, all of which are m. The normalization step returns the following program:

$$foo(n, m) \rightarrow \mathbf{let}\ x = repeat(m),\ xs = take(n, x)\ \mathbf{in}\ xs$$
$$take(zero, xs) \rightarrow [\,]$$
$$take(succ(n), x : xs) \rightarrow \mathbf{let}\ w = take(n, xs)\ \mathbf{in}\ x : w$$
$$repeat(m) \rightarrow \mathbf{let}\ w = repeat(m)\ \mathbf{in}\ m : w$$

Then, the partial inversion of foo w.r.t. $\{1\}$ returns

$$\overline{foo}_{\{1\}}(xs, n) \rightarrow \mathbf{let}\ m = \overline{repeat}_{\{\}}(w),\ w = \overline{take}_{\{1\}}(xs, n)\ \mathbf{in}\ m$$

Now, the next iteration computes the partial inversion of $take$ w.r.t. $\{1\}$:[4]

$$\overline{take}_{\{1\}}([\,], zero) \rightarrow xs$$
$$\overline{take}_{\{1\}}(x : w, succ(n)) \rightarrow \mathbf{let}\ xs = \overline{take}_{\{1\}}(w, n)\ \mathbf{in}\ x : xs$$

Therefore, the next iteration computes the partial inversion of $repeat$ w.r.t. $\{\}$, and the problem shows up:

$$\overline{repeat}_{\{\}}(m : w) \rightarrow \mathbf{let}\ () = \overline{repeat}_{\{1\}}(w, m)\ \mathbf{in}\ m$$

In our current method, the last step suspends the partial inversion process and returns a failure because "Boolean tests" (i.e., function calls where both the arguments and the result are known) are not allowed.

The method of [15] allows the partial inversion of functions even when the result includes Boolean tests. However, observe that if one would allow such

---

[4] Although the first rule violates the first precondition, we ignore this fact in this example since it is orthogonal to the kind of problem that we want to illustrate.

Boolean tests, we would have obtained a program like the following one (after removal of let expressions):

$$\overline{foo}_{\{1\}}(xs, n) \rightarrow \overline{repeat}_{\{\}}(\overline{take}_{\{1\}}(xs, n))$$
$$\overline{take}_{\{1\}}([\,], zero) \rightarrow xs$$
$$\overline{take}_{\{1\}}(x : w, succ(n)) \rightarrow x : \overline{take}_{\{1\}}(w, n)$$
$$\overline{repeat}_{\{\}}(m : w) \rightarrow m$$

Observe that the let expression in the right-hand side of $\overline{repeat}_{\{\}}$, i.e., the Boolean test, does not appear in the rule above because in a non-strict language its computation is not needed. Here, the meaning of function $\overline{repeat}_{\{\}}$ is as follows: given a call $\overline{repeat}_{\{\}}(xs)$, return the first element of list xs, which is clearly incorrect! (it should also check that all elements of xs are equal). This situation does not happen in our technique because the so called Boolean tests are forbidden.

5   An Inversion Tool

We have undertaken a prototype implementation of our partial inversion method in order to test its applicability and usefulness. It is implemented in Prolog (around 500 lines of code) and it is publicly available at

```
http://www.dsic.upv.es/~gvidal/german/finv/
```

Once the program is loaded into Prolog,[5] the user can load in a functional program from a file using the predicate `loadf/1`. The functional program should be written according to the following syntax for rules:

```
lhs := rhs.
```

Function and constructor symbols start with a lowercase letter and variables start with an uppercase letter (i.e., typical Prolog notation). Function definitions may also include type declarations. For instance, function *add* (see Sect. 1) can be defined as follows:

```
add :: nat -> nat -> nat.

add(0,X)    := X.
add(s(X),Y) := s(add(X,Y)).
```

Arbitrary data types (like **nat** above) can also be defined by the user. For instance, natural numbers and lists can be defined as follows

```
datatype nat     ::= 0   | s(nat).
datatype list(A) ::= nil | (A : list(A)).
```

Partial inversion is then started by executing a goal of the form

```
?- invert(function_name, input_parameters_list).
```

---

[5] Currently, it has only been tested on SWI Prolog.

For instance, if we type in the following goal

```
?- invert(add,[1]).
```

we get the partially inverted program:

```
add_[1](A,0)      := A.
add_[1](s(A),s(B)) := add_inv(A,B).
```

where the partial inversion of the given function is denoted by `add_[1]`.

Our preliminary results point out the viability and potential usefulness of the technique. We note, however, that one should be very careful with the election of the function and input set used for partial inversion, i.e., by choosing an arbitrary function and input set, the result is often a failure.

We also note that the current tool can only deal with first-order programs, but it could be extended to higher-order programs along the lines of the previous section. A web interface for the partial inverter can be accessed from the URL above so that the reader can easily test the system.

6 Related Work

The work by Glück and Kawabe [6] (further improved in [7]) presents an automatic program inversion algorithm for first-order functional programs. In contrast to ours, a *total* inversion algorithm is considered (a particular case of our partial inversion) and, thus, only *injective* functions produce useful results.

The closest approach is that of Nishida et al. [15], where the authors present a very general inversion algorithm for term rewriting systems which is able to perform both partial and total inversions. The main differences with our approach are the following:

- The method of [15] allows the partial inversion of functions even when the result includes "Boolean tests". As discussed in Sect. 4, such a situation is avoided in our method in order to have a method applicable to a lazy language.
- The (more general) inversion technique of [15] introduces some additional rules that are not needed in our approach. For instance, in order to preserve the correctness, [15] adds the following rule:

$$\overline{add}_{\{2\}}(add(x,y),y) \rightarrow \langle x \rangle$$

to the definition of $\overline{add}_{\{2\}}$. These rules are not needed in our restricted method.
- Furthermore, they require a form of *narrowing* [18] to perform computations in the inverted program due to extra variables, while functional reduction suffices in our case because extra variables in partially inverted functions are not allowed.

To summarize, our method is simpler than that of [15] and can be applied in fewer cases, but when it succeeds, the resulting program is inductively sequential.

Partial inversions were also considered in [16] but, in contrast to ours, their aim is not the definition of an automatic method. Function inversion is extensively considered by Mu [14], though the author considers a different, calculational approach.

Finally, Mogensen [12] has recently introduced a method for computing the *semi-inversion* of a functional program with guarded equations. Basically, semi-inversion means taking a program and producing a new program that as input takes *part* of the input and *part* of the output of the original program and as output produces the rest of the input and output of the original program. This work tackles a more general objective than ours but might produce functions that are non-deterministic, contain extra-variables, etc., and, thus, it is not appropriate in the context of the most common functional languages. Furthermore, in contrast to ours, the semi-inversion method is rather inefficient (due to a number of non-deterministic choices); therefore, it is unclear whether an efficient implementation would be possible.

7   Discussion and Future Work

We have presented a novel method for the partial inversion of inductively sequential rewrite systems. When the method succeeds, it returns an inductively sequential system without extra variables, which is essential to have a practically applicable method. In contrast to other related approaches, our method is easy to implement and works well in the context of lazy evaluation.

As future work, we plan to extend the partial inversion method to cope with higher-order functions along the lines of Sect. 4. This is an interesting challenge that will allow us to design a partial inversion tool for a realistic functional programming language like Haskell.

Acknowledgements

We gratefully acknowledge the participants of IFL 2006 and the anonymous reviewers for many useful comments and suggestions.

References

1. Antoy, S.: Definitional trees. In: Kirchner, H., Levi, G. (eds.) Algebraic and Logic Programming. LNCS, vol. 632, pp. 143–157. Springer, Heidelberg (1992)
2. Baader, F., Nipkow, T.: Term Rewriting and All That. Cambridge University Press, Cambridge (1998)
3. Danvy, O., Schultz, U.P.: Lambda-Lifting in Quadratic Time. Journal of Functional and Logic Programming, 2004 (2004)
4. Hanus, M. (ed.): Curry: An Integrated Functional Logic Language Available at: http://www.informatik.uni-kiel.de/~mh/curry/

5. Fischbach, A., Hannan, J.: Specification and correctness of lambda lifting. J. Funct. Program. 13(3), 509–543 (2003)
6. Glück, R., Kawabe, M.: A Program Inverter for a Functional Language with Equality and Constructors. In: Ohori, A. (ed.) APLAS 2003. LNCS, vol. 2895, pp. 246–264. Springer, Heidelberg (2003)
7. Glück, R., Kawabe, M.: Derivation of deterministic inverse programs based on LR parsing. In: Kameyama, Y., Stuckey, P.J. (eds.) FLOPS 2004. LNCS, vol. 2998, pp. 291–306. Springer, Heidelberg (2004)
8. Harrison, P.G.: Function Inversion. In: Proc. of Int'l Workshop on Partial Evaluation and Mixed Computation, pp. 153–166. North-Holland, Amsterdam (1988)
9. Johnsson, T.: Lambda Lifting: Transforming Programs to Recursive Equations. In: Jouannaud, J.-P. (ed.) Functional Programming Languages and Computer Architecture(Nancy,France). LNCS, vol. 201, pp. 190–203. Springer, Heidelberg (1985)
10. Khoshnevisan, H., Sephton, K.M.: InvX: An Automatic Function Inverter. In: Dershowitz, N. (ed.) Rewriting Techniques and Applications. LNCS, vol. 355, pp. 564–568. Springer, Heidelberg (1989)
11. Marchiori, M.: Unraveling and Ultraproperties. In: Hanus, M., Rodríguez-Artalejo, M. (eds.) ALP 1996. LNCS, vol. 1139, pp. 107–121. Springer, Heidelberg (1996)
12. Mogensen, T.Æ.: Semi-inversion of Guarded Equations. In: Glück, R., Lowry, M. (eds.), Proc. of the 4th Int'l Conf. on Generative Programming and Component Engineering (GPCE'05), LNCS 3676, pp. 189–204. Springer (2005)
13. Morazán, M.T., Mucha, B.: Improved Graph-Based Lambda Lifting. In: Proc. of the Int'l Conf. on Software Engineering Research and Practice (SERP'06), pp. 896–902. CSREA Press (2006)
14. Mu, S.-C.: A Calculational Approach to Program Inversion. PhD thesis, Oxford University Computing Laboratory (2003)
15. Nishida, N., Sakai, M., Sakabe, T.: Partial Inversion of Constructor Term Rewriting Systems. In: Giesl, J. (ed.) RTA 2005. LNCS, vol. 3467, pp. 264–278. Springer, Heidelberg (2005)
16. Pareja-Flores, C., Velázquez-Iturbide, J.A.: Synthesis of Functions by Transformations and Constraints. In: Proc. of the Int'l Conf. on Functional Programming (ICFP'97), pp. 317–317. ACM Press, New York Poster (1997)
17. Romanenko, A.: Inversion and metacomputation. In: Partial Evaluation and Semantics-Based Program Manipulation, Sigplan Notices, vol. 26(9), pp. 12–22. ACM, New York (1991)
18. Slagle, J.R.: Automated Theorem-Proving for Theories with Simplifiers, Commutativity and Associativity. Journal of the ACM 21(4), 622–642 (1974)
19. Wadler, P.: Views: A Way for Pattern Matching to Cohabit with Data Abstraction. In: Proc. of 14th ACM Symp. on Principles of Programming Languages (POPL'87), pp. 307–313. ACM Press, New York (1987)

Author Index

Lecture Notes in Computer Science

For information about Vols. 1–4543

please contact your bookseller or Springer